Date Due

The American College of Physicians, a national medical association representing internal medicine and its subspecialties, and the W. B. Saunders Company feel there is a need for the health sciences professions to provide timely information to the public about health and disease. This book, a product of the American College of Physicians and The Saunders Press, represents an effort to provide accurate and comprehensive information on a health-related subject to a non-medical audience. It is one in a series of books to be published under this joint imprint, each written by an expert in the field and designed to be accurate and easy to read.

The opinions expressed herein, although approved by a committee of the College, are those of the author and do not necessarily represent the official view of the American College of Physicians or the W. B. Saunders Company.

THE
MIDDLE
YEARS

Donald L. Donohugh, M.D., F.A.C.P., *1924*

An American College of Physicians Book

THE SAUNDERS PRESS

W. B. Saunders Company

Philadelphia • London • Toronto

The Saunders Press
W. B. Saunders Company
West Washington Square
Philadelphia, PA 19105

IN THE UNITED STATES
DISTRIBUTED TO THE TRADE BY
HOLT, RINEHART AND WINSTON
383 Madison Avenue
New York, New York 10017

IN CANADA
DISTRIBUTED BY
HOLT, RINEHART AND WINSTON
55 Horner Avenue
Toronto, Ontario
M8Z 4X6
Canada

Library of Congress Cataloging in Publication Data

Donohugh, Donald L 1924-
    The middle years.

    Includes bibliographical references.
    1. Middle age—Psychological aspects.   2. Middle age—Care and hygiene.   3. Middle age—Sexual behavior.
4. Middle age—Family relationships.   I. Title.
HQ799.95.D66   305.2'4   80-50719

Acknowledgment is gratefully extended to the following for permission to reprint from their works:

For the passage on page 341 from THE WORLD'S GREAT SCRIPTURES edited by Lewis Browne © 1946 by Lewis Browne, renewed 1974 by Rebecca Tarlow and Bessie Leton. Reprinted by permission of Macmillan Publishing Company, Inc.

For the characteristics of a self-actualizing person on pages 381-384 abridged and adapted from MOTIVATION AND PERSONALITY, Second Edition by Abraham H. Maslow. Copyright © 1954 by Harper & Row, Publishers, Inc. Copyright © 1970 by Abraham Maslow. Reprinted by permission of the Publishers.

For the passage on page 183 from "Intelligence—Why it Grows, Why it Declines" by John L. Horn. Published by permission of Transaction, Inc. from HUMAN INTELLIGENCE edited by J. McVicker Hunt. Copyright © 1972 by Transaction, Inc.

For the four excerpts from GIFT FROM THE SEA by Anne Morrow Lindbergh, Copyright 1955 by Anne Morrow Lindbergh. Reprinted by permission of Pantheon Books, a division of Random House, Inc.

For the passage on page 191 from THE PORTABLE JUNG edited by Joseph Campbell, Copyright © 1971 by The Viking Press, Inc. Reprinted by permission of the Publisher.

W.B. Saunders Company ISBN: 0-7216-3144-4

Holt, Rinehart and Winston ISBN: 0-03-057658-X

Print Number 9 8 7 6 5 4 3 2 1

First Edition

Contents

Preface

To each stage of existence has been allotted its appropriate quality . . . each bears some of nature's fruit
which must be garnered in its own season.

CICERO

    Several years ago, after a rather harrowing experience with a
middle-aged patient, I dropped by the local medical school
library, as I usually do when I have encountered a situation that I
could have handled better. This patient's problems had more to
do with his age—with relationships both at home and at work that
seem to be more difficult at this time of life—than anything
medical. So I thought I'd look to the experts for a little guidance.
But I found only one book there dealing with middle age, *The
Second Forty Years* by Edward Stieglitz. As I leafed through it, I
could see that the author was an outstanding physician, but he
was a geriatrician and had therefore concentrated on the medical
problems of those over sixty. And his comments were at least two
or three decades out of date, which was easily explained when I
looked to see when the book had been published. Then I went
through all of the professional journals—they proved equally
barren. In fact, nothing having to do with the middle years of life
had been published that entire year.

    This intrigued me. There I was, working with middle-aged
patients in all aspects of their lives every day, and when I wanted
to learn a little more from the experts, I learned only one
thing—there were no experts. I wondered then what the middle-
aged person himself might have available to *him*. So the next
chance I had, I went to the much larger general library of the
nearby branch of the University of California, which had about

750,000 volumes at that time. There I found literally shelves of works on childhood, adolescence, and old age, but only *seven* books having to do with middle age! Let me list some of the seven for you, and you will see why I became even more intrigued.

The earliest was that well-known classic, *Life Begins at Forty*, by Walter Pitkin, published in the 1930s. It was interesting just for the exhortative tone characteristic of its author and time—sort of a combination of the power of positive thinking and how to win friends—but not very helpful, then or now. Another book, by psychoanalyst Edmund Bergler, *The Revolt of the Middle-Aged Man*, was actually disturbing. His perspective had been distorted by the nature of his patients and practice, with a resulting view of middle age as some sort of war, with conflicts and casualties. A similar work by Barbara Fried, *The Middle-Age Crisis*, was saturated with the same psychoanalytic tradition. Neither had much to offer. From my practice and my life I have learned that most of us in middle age are not crippled by "crises." But we *are* aware of changes we are going through, and we do want to know more about them.

There were a couple of others too peripheral to the subject to mention, but then I found a truly monumental work, *Middle Age and Aging*, edited by Bernice Neugarten. If you can lift this book and understand the terminology, I heartily recommend it. It is a treasure, but a textbook for students in the social sciences, not a work written for the middle-aged person. It is also limited in scope to certain psychosocial aspects of middle age, and, as the author admitted in her foreword, she regretted that she could not touch upon any others.

The last book listed in the card catalog in the library at that time was by James Thurber—*The Middle-Aged Man on the Flying Trapeze*. That this fabulous, humorous book was included in the category of middle age must have been due to some error in the Dewey Decimal System, but I enjoyed reading it anyhow.

That was it, then. There wasn't one worthwhile book on middle age for the average reader, either. During my spare time in the next few years I continued to search via interlibrary loan systems, computerized retrieval at the National Library of Medicine or the Library of Congress, as well as visits to these and other libraries and plain old browsing at bookstores for whatever I could find on middle age. An article or two appeared each year in various journals, so I began to accumulate them. By the early

1970s I had gathered together enough to be reassured that a physician or other professional could extract enough from them to use as a guide in his practice. Yet even today there is no text on the subject. There could be and should be. But what concerned me more was that the general reader was still without a good book to help him or her through the middle years. A total of about thirty have appeared to date. A dozen or so do have something of value, each in its own way; these are given in the Bibliography at the end of this book.

One of them stands out from the rest: Anne Simon's *The New Years*. Although she left out many things that are important, she possessed two attributes that came through clearly. As a psychiatric social worker, she had extensive experience in dealing professionally with people of this age. She was also middle-aged herself and therefore understood these years in a personal way. When I read her book, it struck me how essential these two characteristics are for an author on the subject. I don't know if it is because they increase one's interest, introspection, or intuition in addition to one's knowledge, but it seems that one has to have both of these before beginning to understand this time of life well enough to write a book about it.

Through the early 1970s, the articles in the professional literature increased in both quantity and quality. In 1976 alone fifteen excellent papers on various aspects of middle age appeared. It was then that I first began to be encouraged and came to the conclusion that a definitive book written for the person in middle age was due.

Yet it seems that if a little knowledge is a dangerous thing, none of us is really out of danger. In that one year, six books for the general reader on middle age were published, but each seemed to be less helpful than the one before it. The last of the lot was Gail Sheehy's *Passages*, which demonstrated an agonizing lack of either personal or professional experience with this time of life. Although her work was the most popular of all, giving some indication of our growing hunger to know more, it could only be characterized as shallow and slick.

The books published in that one year truly discouraged me, but at least they made me reflect more on the sort of person who could best write on the subject. Obviously, professional writers who skim the surface with the sole intention to sell could not be considered. Too many had tried, and too many had failed. The author had to *know something* about middle age—both by being middle-aged and by having had years of professional experience with middle-agers. Beyond these two fundamental requirements, one must understand the physiology of aging in the human organism, so someone skilled in this area—a physician—appeared to be the best choice. But what sort of physician? Because the psychological changes are as important as the physiological, I concluded that a psychiatrist would be best qualified, being trained in both. His background would also enable him to penetrate related disciplines such as sociology and anthropology to extract what was worthwhile there.

My thoughts went on from there, however, to develop some reservations. The training a psychiatrist receives after leaving medical school is in the more severe psychopathologies found in mental institutions. Afterwards in practice, he or she sees only those who cannot cope without help—the walking wounded—and then only in crises, usually for a few weeks or months, rarely for the many years that would be necessary. No psychiatrist could hope to acquire experience with those who cope well with their middle years; this would be essential if the book were to be balanced.

Then I considered the family practitioner. But his training does not include an adequate background in psychology or psychiatry. He treats those of all ages, usually for only a few minutes at a time and only when his patients are ill. This sort of practice would not allow him to acquire the understanding of middle-agers that would be necessary for writing an authoritative book on the subject.

It was then that I began to wonder if an internist might be able to do it. Internists treat mostly the middle-aged and aged; spend considerable time with them when they are healthy and happy—and when they are not; and follow them in depth for years through all the changes in their lives. So far so good. But internists generally do not have enough interest, training, or experience in psychiatry—in fact the stress in their specialty training is upon the most complex and serious diseases in medicine, almost to the exclusion of the person who *has* the disease. It is only later in practice that most adopt a more humanistic approach—out of necessity, if nothing else.

The term *humanistic* has become somewhat slippery in our society, even in medicine, so what it connotes in this context should be explained. To me, it means that a physician considers his patient in terms of life goals, marriage, family, job, social situation, and emotions—i.e., in terms of all the factors in his or her life. Such a physician's concentration is consistently upon his patient as a human being, rather than upon the disease he or she might have—his patient is a *person*, not just a "case" of something or other. This inevitably implies a strong emphasis on disease prevention—early and minimal intervention, rather than too much treatment too late, as is characteristic of much medical care in our country.

It was at this point that I first began to think about writing such a book myself. My practice in internal medicine was humanistic. And I believe so strongly in preventive medicine that I had obtained a Master's degree in public health and taught preventive medicine on the faculties of two medical schools before entering private practice. Also, I had more training and experience in psychiatry than most internists, much of this with Eric Berne. So perhaps I was qualified, but I was absolutely appalled at the prospect. I had written many medical articles, but never a book. One difficulty especially was insurmountable then: lack of time. Although the other disciplines involved in a comp–rehensive approach to the mysteries of middle age and open to a physician with an inquiring mind use a vocabulary that can be deciphered, as well as a methodology and statistical presentation that are similar to those in medicine, the sheer impossibility of trying to stay in practice while thoroughly reviewing the litera-ture in all relevant fields and writing such a book was all too apparent.

So I procrastinated and continued to cope with my own middle age, but not too well. Physician, heal thyself. A menopausal wife. An affair. A marriage of twenty-one years ended by divorce. Problems with teen-aged children. Doubts about values. Goals achieved, some without satisfaction. Parents increasingly infirm and dying. Signs of my own aging—intimations of mortality.

But I gradually came to the conclusion that it might be possible, not only to "heal" myself but to help others if at least I tried. So I quit practice, called the time a sabbatical, and started to write this book. It turned out to be a long sabbatical, and in that time I learned a lot. Two things that I learned should be shared with you right here. The first is that our most essential task in middle age is to search for our own values—to pause and consider where we are and why, and where we are to go from here. In order to do so, we have to understand ourselves better than most of us do. So you will find that a long section at the end of the book is concerned with this. A second thing I learned is that in none of the relevant fields is the literature as extensive or as helpful as I had hoped it would be. We simply do not know as much yet about middle age as I thought we did. So I came to rely upon my own experience where knowledge from other sources was lacking or incomplete. This ranges over more than a quarter of a century with approximately five thousand middle-aged patients, and I felt much more secure here at times than with faulty theory or fallacious research. What I have tried to do in writing this book is to take what is worthwhile from all professional sources, blend it with my own experience, and present the combination under-standably to the intelligent reader. I give guidance where I can. Where I cannot, I present what is known and provide references so that the reader can go on from there.

This book does not have all the answers. As a matter of fact, it doesn't even have all the questions. It is offered for what it is, with the hope that it will help you in the reading as much as it has helped me in the writing. The most important thing I learned is that middle age can be the best part of life if it is lived as it can be, a time of challenge and change.

To my wife, Bea, for all that she means in my life, and to our children—Ruth, Laurel, Marilee, Carol, Leslie, Greg, and Andrea—who will be middle-aged themselves some day, though they do not suspect it now.

Acknowledgments

I wish to express my appreciation to all those who helped me at the University of California at Irvine Library, especially Sherry McGee, Mary Ritchey, Pamela LaZarr, and Sally Bomar; to Phyllis Bocian and Barbara Jasperson, who assisted in the editing; to my professional colleagues of the American College of Physicians who amended and approved the manuscript; to those who performed the interminable task of typing and retyping—Rosemary Carroll, Jeanne Brownell, and Sue Duley; to the copyeditor, Bob Oskam; and above all, to my editor, Howard E. Sandum. Any failing this book may have is not theirs, it is mine.

THE
MIDDLE
YEARS

I

Myths of Middle Age

Whatever advantages youth and age have are found combined in the mature; wherever either of the two shows excess or deficiency, the mature hold an even balance.

ARISTOTLE

My favorite definition of middle age is "that time of your life when you still haven't found out where you are going, but suddenly realize that you're already halfway there." Another one often heard is that it's "your age plus ten"—whatever your age. It has also been defined by someone as "halfway between adolescence and obsolescence." And by someone else as "when you begin to count calories instead of cost when dining out." A rather dour patient of mine thought it was "when you find you are doing fewer things for the first time and more things for the last time." An equally gloomy one told me it is "the age when you begin to pause at the obituaries between the headlines and the sports section." A friend said she first felt she was there when she was stopped for a traffic ticket and observed that the policeman was obviously too young for the job. A playboy acquaintance thinks it was when pretty girls first stopped looking back. Perhaps it was because the gleam in his eye came from his bifocals! And a somewhat vain lady confided to me that she knew she had arrived when she stepped out of the shower one morning and was *glad* the mirror had fogged over.

These definitions are fun and full of insights, but they're hardly satisfactory. So, this being a scientific age, let's see what the scientists have to say about when middle age occurs. Demographers define it as the years between forty-five and sixty-five, but then add that sixty-five is used only for convenience, since it's the standard retirement age. They'd really prefer to use sixty, but won't say why. And when asked why they pick forty-five as the beginning rather than, say, thirty-five or forty, they don't have a satisfactory answer. Demographers really don't help us much.

Sociologists have surveyed people of all ages to see what period of life is generally considered to be middle age. The majority of respondents chose the decade between ages forty and fifty. But these studies also showed that women tended to select the span thirty-five to forty-five, while men picked forty-five to fifty-five—a ten-year difference between the opinions of the sexes. And both men and women tended to extend by about ten years whatever span they had designated as middle age for *others* when they were asked to define it for *themselves*. A surprising number in the Geritol set picked their own ages. Sociologists long ago learned not to ask adolescents. To them, thirty is middle-aged, and those over forty are truly in their dotage. So much for sociology.

Biologists estimate potential human lifespan—with the elimination of all accidents and diseases—at one hundred to one hundred and twenty years. But life is hardly free of these, so we can't simply take the mathematical midpoint of that span and call it middle age. We might use biological expertise in another way, however. We could take the age at which the first physiological function begins to decline, call that old age, and work backwards. That sounds reasonable. All right, our thymus gland starts to atrophy after infancy; the ability of our eyes to accommodate to near vision lessens from age five; our ability to hear high frequencies begins its decline around age ten; and male sexual potency starts its downward trend at about the age of twenty. So we have to abandon the biological approach—it can't even define *old* age.

What about psychology? Studies have shown that middle-aged people consider their lives in terms of health, career, and family, rather than chronological age. Women most often look at their age in relation to events in the family cycle, and men do so more in relation to careers. Bernice Neugarten observed, ". . . chronological age is not a meaningful index by which to order the social and psychological data of adulthood. . . ."

Then perhaps the first *awareness of aging* is the clue—when we begin to notice the bulges, bags, and balding that gradually have been becoming part of us. Or the death of a friend or parent may shock us into the realization that we are not immortal, that time, wherever it is going, is taking us with it. Whatever the reason, there is a point in our lives when we somehow stop believing that our stay here on earth is infinite and realize for the first time that it is not. We pause and ponder. We look ahead and look back, like the Roman god Janus with his two faces. From then on, we are changed, subtly but significantly. Whether or not we understand life any better than we ever have, or whether we ever will, we at least begin to try from then on.

Middle age then is not an *age*, but a *stage* in our lives. It begins when we first face the fact, the finality of our own death; it ends when we begin to withdraw from life and its concerns.

We arrive at this point with precepts and prejudices about middle age that we've been accumulating throughout our lives, many of them negative. The process started early. Our parents may have seemed tired before their time when we were children. Our grandparents were old in our eyes then, and in fact, when they reached sixty or so, they *were*. But we have had the advantage of more modern medical care. Our own level of knowledge about health is so much better now that most of us can feel younger and accomplish more at forty, fifty, or even sixty than anyone at those ages could during the first part of this century. It has been estimated by those who should know that we are about ten to fifteen years younger—both psychologically and physically— than our parents were at our age.

In the first half of our lives we assimilated the attitudes of a culture that places a premium on youth, that tells us in ways both subtle and overt that our lives are worth living only while we are young. At one time, in hunter-gatherer societies and, to a lesser extent, in early agricultural and industrial ones, the strength and skill that are at their height in late youth and early adulthood were of crucial importance for the survival of the individual and the race. But in our highly technological society today, they are not nearly as important. So this is a hangover from the past. Nevertheless, because our society is so oriented toward productivity, we place much importance on the value of an individual in terms of his or her place in the scheme of production and consumption of goods and services. We tend to categorize people as "preproductive," "productive," and "postproductive." As a result, we shamelessly coddle the "preproductive" adolescent and dismiss or ignore the "postproductive" person who is tapering off from his work or has retired.

Many of us have been influenced either directly or indirectly by the literature we have read. But most of this, too, is from the past, reflecting the conditions of earlier times, not of our own. Cicero, in *De Senectute*, writes dismally of the years darkened by approaching death. Dante, in *The Divine Comedy*, talks of the "gloomy wood" midway in the journey of life. Milton, in *Paradise Lost*, writes: "And in the lowest deep, a lower deep. . . ." Setting forth the seven ages of man in *As You Like It*, Shakespeare is downright depressing. Disraeli speaks of the delusion of youth, the disappointment of manhood, and the despair of old age. And Byron penned the words "My days are in the yellow leaf" when he was only thirty-six! More recently, existentialist Simone de Beauvoir has dwelled on the desolation, defeat, and death that follow youth.

Even in modern fiction some characters reflect the complexity and challenge that aging entails, and they either face it or flounder. We find Sinclair Lewis's Babbit middle in every way, including age; Saul Bellow's Herzog, who, after a barrage of troubles in middle age, emerges with a grim willingness to take the rest of life on its own terms; Kurt Vonnegut's Pilgrim, suffering from a malaise of meaninglessness; and Arthur Miller's Willy Loman, facing life with a smile, a shoeshine, and little else. The plays of Chekov, Ibsen, and Hellman all treat middle age in a depressing way. And Eugene O'Neill tells us we are only waiting for the iceman who cometh for all. Hermann Hesse seems to be one of the few who provides a more inspiring version of what middle age can be. Harry Heller, the hero of *Steppenwolf*, reflects Hesse himself as he approached fifty. After some solitary years in a remote village in Switzerland where Hesse rejected the materialism and mediocrity of his world, in *Demian* he provides a sense that such unchanging values as are found in Mozart and Goethe make life worth living.

Some of our impressions were formed by exposure to the pathological orientation of psychoanalysis and those who wrote in this tradition that middle age consists of a series of "crises." I mentioned two such examples in the preface. But we should realize that many, if not most, of these psychoanalytic theories about middle age have been challenged by the more heartening ones of humanistic psychology. And we should always remember the tendency for fallacies to become self-fulfilling prophecies.

So when we arrive at middle age, we find we have been given a role without a script. If we could have learned more of the physical and psychological facts about this time in our lives, we would have acquired a more positive viewpoint. But they were not available. The scientific study of aging and of the aging themselves began only well into this century, and until the past two decades it dealt mostly with those in mental hospitals, nursing homes, and other such institutions. This then expanded into the study of the elderly generally and has solidified since into the respected discipline of gerontology. We have yet to develop such a discipline—presbyology or presbyatrics—for the middle years of life.

There are many reasons for this. As I've begun to indicate, the very concept of middle age is a new one. Fossil remains of prehistoric eras show that the average age at death then was about eighteen. In Greek and Roman times it was still in the twenties. Throughout the next millenium and more it hovered around thirty. At the start of this century, it was still just thirty-seven. Only in our own time is middle age becoming recognized as a definable portion of the life span. Another reason is that the middle-aged, who study these things, were too concerned with childhood earlier in this century, adolescence since the 1930s, and senescence since the 1940s to take the time to study *themselves*. Only in the last decade or so have we begun to study middle age. It is time we did. In the last century, the proportion of the population between the ages of forty-five and fifty-four was less than 10 percent in the United States. By 1960 it had become 20 percent, and today it is approaching 25 percent. As to the future, those born in the "baby boom" between 1949 and 1957 will begin to arrive at middle age in the 1980s and constitute the fastest-growing population group by far, resulting in about 48 million people between the ages of thirty-five and forty-four in 1990, and 78 million by the year 2000.

People who are now forty-five have already lived as long as the average person born in 1900 could expect to live. Now, at age forty, a white male can expect thirty-two more years of life, and a white female, thirty-eight. And this expectancy increases as we live, so that at fifty, a man has a probable twenty-three and a woman twenty-nine more years of life. We must remember that statisticians, in producing these data on life expectancy, can only presume that the same rates of mortality that have prevailed in the past will continue to apply in the future. They cannot even take into account medical advances of today that will increase our life expectancy. But as a physician, I can at least make an estimate. With what we now know about coping with the main causes of mortality, at least a dozen years of vigorous life could be added to the foregoing statistics. With what we *hope* to learn in our lifetime, perhaps another half-dozen, so that a person who is forty or even forty-five today can confidently look forward to an average of at least as many years of active and rewarding life ahead. Much of this book is devoted to just the sort of information you need to bring this about in your own life.

As we will see in the next chapter, the process of aging itself is beginning to be understood, holding out the hope that a much more dramatic lengthening of life may not be far off. Later in the book we will see what has been discovered about the changes in our ability to learn and to remember as we age—and about intelligence itself—all of it encouraging. What happens to our personality throughout the middle years is also clearer, so that the so-called "midlife crisis" can be avoided or considerably modified in favor of a more fulfilling life.

Marriage too has changed in many ways. Consider just one that affects us directly. In 1900, the average couple was separated by death before the last child left home. Increased longevity, earlier marriages, and smaller families have given modern Americans a substantial "postparental" phase of family life. We can now expect twenty-five years together with our mates after the last child leaves. It is during this time that reduced financial pressures and more free time provide each spouse more opportunity than they have ever had before to explore long deferred interests and to enrich their relationship in a way they never could before.

Even sex can be better during middle age. With children going about their own concerns or no longer living at home, privacy returns. We are more mature now, so sexual expression can be more meaningful. Women's interest in sex usually increases by middle age to match their mate's, and by then men's blind drive for orgasm has moderated. The slowing of the man's physiological responses blends with his increased appreciation of closeness and caressing. These factors and others can combine to make sex more satisfying for both than it has ever been.

Until recently most women looked forward to menopause with dread. We have finally gotten around to ask those who have passed through it to learn that it actually brings women a new sense of freedom. And we understand much more about it now. Medical management can prevent or ameliorate most of the problems women feared in the past. The "myth of the menopause," that it is something far worse than it really is, originated mainly because only those women who had difficulties consulted physicians or psychiatrists, and these are the ones who wrote the books that spread the myth.

At midlife, work, for both men and women, can be viewed in a new light and made more rewarding. Retirement can be anticipated as a time of greater fulfillment than ever before. The concept that education, work, and leisure should be reserved respectively for the young, the adult, and the elderly is changing. More and more we are realizing that a healthy mix of these three should continue throughout life.

Middle age is perhaps the last time we have to reconsider our values and goals in life. In adolescence we shook off the "shoulds" of our parents only to shoulder those of our peers—and later, those of others "out there." Middle age is the crucial time to avoid what Ogden Nash has called "hardening of the oughteries." We should now search for our *own* values, reassess our route, and make a midcourse correction in our lives. Our concerns can broaden from career or children to the community, to civilization, and to the meaning of life itself.

Too much attention has been paid in the past to what we lose by middle age—and not nearly enough to what we gain. Some recent sociological studies have been done on this point. One, for example, was by Paul Cameron, who found that those of all ages described the middle-aged with such phrases as "wealthiest," "greatest sense of competence," "most knowledgeable," "most autonomy," and "maximum capacity to handle life." Another by Angus Campbell reported that most men and many women in middle age were happier than they had ever been before in their lives. The most consistent theme in all such studies is that we have acquired more ability and authority than we've ever had or ever will have again. Bernice Neugarten commented on this: "The successful middle-aged person describes himself as no longer driven, but as now the driver, in short, in command." *Time* magazine followed up on this idea and devoted an issue to us, the middle-aged, calling us "the Command Generation." During the first part of life, our elders were in charge—now *we* are.

The most important thing that we have gained by middle age is experience. We have learned that the worst wounds heal, crises pass, and calm always follows the storm. We have learned about life by living, and there is no other way. We understand ourselves and others better and have come to know the meaning of love and friendship. We are also aware that what we have yet to do is inevitably easier than what we have done so far. Instead of competing and clashing with the outside world, our tasks now lie more within us—to explore ourselves and our lives. And we care for the moment more now than before and savor it more—or should—because we now know that our future is not forever.

Middle age is truly a phenomenon of our century, of our time. It is only during our generation, during the lives of those of us who are now in our forties, fifties, and sixties, that factors have coincided to make middle age potentially the best time of life. But first we must sort out the facts from fearful fictions. For not nearly enough is yet generally known about the trials and triumphs of this time by those who should know, the middle-aged themselves. After all, we are the architects of our own added years. In this book I'll present and try to interpret what we now know and dispel some of the myths that have grown around the topics I've mentioned, myths that we have too long accepted as truths.

Remember the Spanish adage "health, wealth, and love—and time to enjoy them." This should be the motto of middle age. For the first time, we have them all. Futurity or futility—it's up to us. As Robert Browning wrote:

Grow old along with me!
The best is yet to be.
The last of life, for which the first was made.

2

Man and Mortality

Time travels in divers paces with divers persons.

SHAKESPEARE

*T*he ultimate question is the nature of the aging process itself. Well, perhaps the penultimate question—life itself is the ultimate mystery. By middle age we want to understand more about what has been happening to us. We see the wrinkles, the gray hair, the widening waist. But what is *really* going on? What is actually known about this basic biological process? Why, in fact, do we age at all?

Everything that lives has a limit to its life on earth. This may sound obvious, but sometimes the modern world can make us forget this fact and our relationship in this respect to all living creatures. Each species appears to have its unique and particular life span. A mayfly lives for a day, a rat two or three years, a dog twelve or thirteen, a horse about twenty-five, and so on. No one has ever recorded even one instance of a member of any species under natural conditions outliving by a substantial margin the maximum mean life span of that species. So one thing we know is that this mysterious process of aging is remarkably species-specific.

The term *maximum mean life span* is quite different from *average life expectancy* and others we are used to. It is the average duration of life found in each species if all accidents and diseases were eliminated. It was once thought that aging did not occur in the wild because privation, predation, and parasitism take their toll, leaving the young and healthy. But if animals are protected from these, the process of aging continues relentlessly in all. Small laboratory animals of any one species thus protected tend to die within days of one another. So another thing we know is that the process is one characterized by precision. As the wide variety of causes of death of man in middle age and beyond are looked into more deeply, fewer mechanisms are found the deeper we probe. Underlying most of them seems to be one—aging itself. So there is precision in the aging process in humans, too.

The maximum mean life span of the human being can be arrived at several ways. One is to test each organ system over a span of years after adulthood is reached. From this, a point can be extrapolated beyond which any one organ system could no longer support the life of the whole body. Another is to average the ages of those who simply pass away with no clear-cut disease process, much like the "One-Hoss Shay" of Oliver Wendell Holmes. One can also average the longest-lived individuals throughout history whose age at death is known. All such methods give a cluster of ages ranging from 100 to 120.

This potential life span of man is much longer than that of any other mammal. One wonders how this has come about. Possibly it is linked to his most unique attribute—intelligence. As man's intellectual capacity increased through evolution, replacing tooth and claw, more years of childhood care were required for the development of a more complex central nervous system and the acquisition of the unique survival skills based upon this. Parental protection would be required during these years, and the wisdom of the older members of the social unit would enhance the survival of the members of that unit. So if one abandons the narrow view of Darwin, which stresses mutation in an individual "sport" giving rise to new species characteristics, to consider as well man in his general social setting, our longevity may also be due to natural selection.

The secret of aging has always fascinated man. One ancient Greek myth recited by the poet Pindar tells of the Hyperboreans, who lived beyond the north winds without ailments or aging. Another describes how the dawn goddess, Aurora, pled with Zeus to grant immortality to her lover, Tithonus. Zeus finally relented. But then as the years went by, Tithonus became aged and withered. Aurora realized she had failed to request eternal youth for him as well. So she turned him into a grasshopper and forgot him. The moral of this myth is, if the aging process were to be understood and controlled, we would like to have our extra years somewhere in the middle and not just add them on to the end as more old age. (The Gerontological Society has adopted a motto reflecting this: "To add life to years, not just years to life.") This fascination with aging continued with Ovid, Seneca, and the legend of Fata Morgana's ring. Medieval alchemists sought the elusive *elixir vitae*, and Ponce de Leon his fountain of youth.

The earliest speculations on the cause of aging were necessarily vague. With a dying person's last breath, life seemed to leave him with that breath. This is actually where the word *expire* comes from. Ever wonder why we say "God bless you" when a person sneezes? In effect, we are praying that his breath will return and his life continue. So the earliest theory of aging had to do with a person's "vapor" slowly leaving him as he aged. Such speculations continued through the centuries—they are interesting, but there is no need to review them here. Each theory reflected the theorist and his time. During the Industrial Revolution, for example, man was regarded as a machine, and aging was believed to be due to simple "wear and tear." This concept was even supported by crude epidemiological work which showed that manual laborers had a shorter life span than members of the upper classes—without considering such factors as nutrition, exposure to disease, or work environment. It also did not take into account the fact that living organisms have many effective means to repair "wear and tear."

It has only been in this century that serious attempts have been made to study aging. The first two publications on the subject in the literature were both in 1908—Charles Minot wrote on some of the psychological aspects of aging, and Elie Metchnikoff produced his work, composed of approximately equal parts of biology and speculation.

A little later, the Abkhasians of the Caucasus, the Hunzas of Himalaya, and the Vilcabambas of Ecuador, all of whom were widely reputed to live up to 150 years were studied, but such claims were found to be without foundation. They have a somewhat longer *average* life span, approaching man's maximum potential closer than some of the rest of us do, but this was explained by factors we already understood, such as genetic predisposition, healthy diet, avoidance of obesity, and continued exercise.

When hormones were first discovered, there was some thought that these, or perhaps the master endocrine gland, the pituitary, held the answer. Among the earliest seekers of a hormonal "cure" for aging was Charles Brown-Sequard, who reported enthusiastically on the rejuvenating effect of self-administered injections of an extract from the testicles of young dogs. It is particularly poignant to note on reading his publication that he used an aqueous extract that could not have contained the testosterone to which he attributed the benefit. It was all in his mind. Sex hormones do decline with age; this will be discussed elsewhere. Except for these, there is little or no change in hormone production with aging, nor have hormones been found to be implicated in any way as a cause of the aging process.

The search for magic elixirs took some strange forms before and after the First World War. Serge Voronoff transplanted testicles of animals (he would have preferred human, but could find no volunteer donors) to older men, without benefit. Injections of cells such as those from fetal lambs was practiced for a time by Paul Niehans in Switzerland and others. This, too, failed to alter aging, so "CT" or cell therapy has all but vanished, even in Europe. The only magic elixir whose popularity has persisted to our time is a slightly altered version of procaine called Gerovital or GH3, which first gained popularity many years ago when one investigator reported that procaine prolonged the life of a small worm. Subsequent work with animals and humans failed to demonstrate any effect. This concept has since been held in disrepute, and the substance is available now only in certain clinics in other countries, such as those of Ana Aslan in Bucharest. However, the Nevada legislature recently made it available in Reno and Las Vegas, cities that have always welcomed those who gamble and lose.

Next, two human diseases resembling aging came under study, progeria and Werner's syndrome. The study of progeria provided little insight, because children with this disease, who die of what appears to be senility in their teens, do not show many of the signs of senescence and thus are not true examples of the aging process. Werner's syndrome is probably a delayed manifestation of the same disease. It has its detectable onset between ages fifteen and twenty; its victims die in their fifties or sixties. As with progeria, all we learned is that some internally programmed deterioration is going on that somewhat resembles aging.

The stress theory was proposed in the 1930s by Hans Selye. He held that each of us is born with a given amount of "adaptation energy," which is used up by stress. This theory was then tested experimentally in the laboratory, where animals were subjected to various forms of stress. The average life span of the stressed animals was identical to that of the controls, unless stress was increased to the point of continuous exhaustion. Even then, none of the characteristics of senescence were observed. In fact, it was found in these experiments that an optimum amount of stress *enhanced* longevity! Erdman Palmore found the same to be true in humans in his studies at Duke University, as have several other eminent investigators elsewhere. So this theory was abandoned.

When scientists began to use the microscope on aging tissues, they found many observable changes—facts, but still no answers. For example, a pigment called lipofuscin was observed to accumulate in cells with age and was therefore thought to play a role in aging. Then it was found not to correlate with decreasing cellular function—and was even detected in liver cells of the *newborn*. What it is, we still do not know—perhaps it is some sort of by-product of metabolism. We *do* know that it is not a cause of aging.

The first laboratory experiment bearing on longevity was reported in 1935 by Clive McCay. He gave calorically restricted diets to newly weaned rats and increased their life span significantly. The difficulty in interpreting this experiment is that rodents, unlike man, are characterized by lifelong growth. The diet given them was so restricted that they were unable to grow. Other investigators have since confirmed McCay's findings with other rodents (but could not with any higher orders) and noted that even in rodents the restriction can only be caloric; the diet must otherwise be nutritious. Attempts to find human populations that have received caloric restriction but otherwise nutritionally adequate diets have not been possible, and therefore this work has not been substantiated in human beings. It is probably not even applicable, because of the fundamental physiological differences between rodents and humans.

This brings us to the currently held theories of aging. There are half a dozen of these, and the first we should discuss is the autoimmune theory. It is well known that as we grow older, some of the antibodies we produce as defense against foreign substances act less specifically. When they become unable to discriminate between our own tissues and foreign substances, they attack and destroy the former. But because these autoantibodies increase linearly with time, there is no way that this theory can explain why organ function deteriorates rapidly after a certain age. Furthermore, no cause-and-effect relationship has been demonstrated, even with careful study. For example, investigators have bred and raised several species of laboratory animals in a germ-free environment, seeing to avoid all stimulation of the immunological system, but the animals mean life span was not extended. Immunosuppressive chemicals have also been used to eliminate nearly all antibody production. The animals were then protected against their increased susceptibility to infection by various means, but little or no effect has been observed on life spans. And there is the inescapable fact that many lower forms of life do not even have an immune system such as ours, yet they, too, age and die. So there does not appear to be enough evidence for this theory to be a tenable one. Few adhere to this theory today.

The next we should consider is the cross-linkage theory. The term *cross-linkage* was first used to describe the chemical bond formed between large protein molecules that normally are separate from each other. Collagen, a type of tissue that is widespread in the body, is especially prone to this process in a gradual way as we age. This is responsible for the decreasing elasticity of our skin, among other things. An extreme example of cross-linkage of collagen is the chemical tanning of leather. Johan Bjorksten is foremost among those who posit that this change causes aging as it interferes with the vital functions of certain organs. There was very little to support this theory until cross-linkage was also found to occur between structures within the cell itself. This would be particularly important with DNA because a nonbreakable cross-linkage between the two strands (helices) would make it impossible for one to act as a template to repair the other. But then several investigators tested the theory in laboratory animals with substances such as penicillamine and lathyrogens that prevent the formation of such cross-links within the cell. They found that the life span of animals studied was not increased. In addition, certain specific enzymes have recently been discovered that prevent cross-linkage from occurring in DNA. So although cross-linkage does occur in our skin and other tissues with aging, it appears to be a result rather than a cause of the process.

Because some understanding of molecular biology of the cell is required for the theories to follow, a brief review at this point cannot be avoided. A cell can be thought of (in two dimensions) as a circle with a large dot in the center. The circle is the plasma membrane through which molecules move in and out in a controlled manner. Within the plasma membrane is the cytoplasm. This is a gelatinlike substance in which there are mitochondria, ribosomes, and many other structures. (Ribosomes will be mentioned again later—they are tiny particles in the cytoplasm that can only be seen with an electron microscope, which is about one thousand times more powerful than the light microscope.) The nucleus is the large central dot in the circle. Within the nucleus is the nucleolus, which is the factory for producing ribosomes. The nucleus also contains the chromosomes. In man there are forty-six of these in all cells except for sperm and ova—the germ cells. Each chromosome is made up of a series of genes, usually several hundred, and the chromosomes are tightly coiled except when the cell is dividing.

Every single cell in an individual contains an identical set of genes, but in any given type of cell only a small fraction of the total genes is functioning, and it is this fraction that determines the particular kind of cell and what it does. The remainder of the genes is kept inactive by a process that is not yet fully understood. What we do know will be mentioned later. The genes are essentially blueprints for the cell to use in the reproduction of other identical cells or specific protein substances. Each gene contains several thousand deoxyribonucleic acid (DNA) molecules, each of which is made up of four building blocks (amino acids), arranged according to a specific code in a double helix structure. The discovery of the structure of DNA in 1952 by James Watson and Francis Crick was one of the most important discoveries of all time, and this structure has been called the "language of life."

DNA is found only in the nucleus. Another type of nucleic acid contains ribose sugar, so it is called ribonucleic acid or RNA, which is single-stranded, and this type is found mostly in the cytoplasm. There are three kinds of RNA: messenger RNA, ribosomal RNA, and transfer RNA. The precise function of ribosomal RNA is not yet known, but it appears to be a sort of workbench on which proteins are made. The messenger RNA is made on the DNA template of a gene in the nucleus. This RNA molecule then separates from the DNA and goes into the cytoplasm, where it directs the ribosome as it builds a protein molecule. Each gene, therefore, using its RNA messenger, gives a definite amino acid sequence to the protein that is synthesized and thereby the specific properties of the protein. Transfer RNA is charged with the task of bringing the amino acids to the ribosomes where the particular protein is constructed. With this much knowledge of molecular biology, we can now discuss the other currently held theories of aging.

Though long known, the fact that total body irradiation shortened the mean life span of many species received renewed attention after the atomic bomb blasts of World War II. But such radiation results in few symptoms similar to those of aging. It has been calculated that the radiation an average person receives from all sources in a normal life span is about 200 rads. It requires at least 3600 rads in the laboratory to begin to affect animal life span. The survivors of Nagasaki and Hiroshima (except for those who succumbed to cancerous diseases), and individuals who have been given intensive radiation for certain diseases and survived those diseases, were observed to age normally. Moreover, the most radioresistant tissues in man are those most intimately involved in the aging process. For these and other reasons, the theory of radiation as a cause of aging is not supported by many investigators today.

However, this research led to other hypotheses, among which is the free radical theory. Free radicals are highly reactive molecules produced by low levels of radiation. They are also products of the normal metabolism of fats in our bodies and can result from exposure to chemical toxins as well. Free radicals are highly damaging to tissues, because each contains an unpaired electron. They can and do attach to other molecules, damaging DNA, cell membranes, and other cell structures. Denham Harman in 1961 proposed the theory that free radicals are the cause of aging. He reported that the addition of protective chemicals (antioxidants such as Vitamin E) to the diet of rats increased the mean life span of some (but not others) by 15 to 30 percent. But he and his associates have been unable to reproduce these results in subsequent experiments and are at a loss to explain their first findings. Other investigators, too, have used antioxidants without significant effect on the longevity of many animals, and even in cell cultures they have produced mixed results. The only positive finding emerging from these experiments was that, above a low dosage, antioxidants in the diet actually *shorten* life.

There are several theoretical objections to the free radical theory as the cause of aging, but I will mention only a practical one. It is now known that, when damaged by free radicals, DNA is immediately repaired, and the lipids damaged in the membranes are rapidly replaced. Only in these two sites are antioxidants protective. They offer no protection against damage to other vital structures within the cell. So even if the free radicals were even partially responsible for aging, there is no antioxidant known that would have any effect. Research limited to antioxidants is therefore stymied and from this point should concentrate on radical scavengers, of which several are known. Such scavengers can seek out and neutralize free radicals before any damage is done. Until we have some reliable results from such experiments, the free radical theory must be regarded as interesting but without sufficient scientific support.

Those who take Vitamin E in the hope of prolonging their lives because they heard of the early research should be aware of the subsequent studies. They should also know that an adequate diet contains all the Vitamin E we need to cope with the free radicals that our bodies produce. And we consume many other substances that act as antioxidants—ascorbic acid, selenium, glutathione, cysteine, and sulfhydryl proteins, as well as butylated hydroxytoluene (BHT), a common food additive and preservative. I have found it strange that those who take Vitamin E are often the same ones who avoid foods that contain BHT.

Besides the free radical theory, experiments in the effects of radiation also led to the concept of somatic mutation as the cause of aging. Most people are familiar with the general notion of mutations—spontaneous errors—that occur occasionally in the germ cell line. Most of these occur as these cells divide. This, along with natural selection, forms the basis for the Darwinian theory of evolution.

Throughout our lives, many cells in the body divide in the same way; some do so continually, such as the cells lining the gastrointestinal tract and the blood cells. Others do so intermittently in order to repair damage—in the liver, kidneys, and bones. Others, nerve and muscle cells, for instance, never divide. Whenever such division takes place, there is an increased chance of an error, or mutation. Mutations in body cells are called somatic to distinguish them from germ cell mutations. The rate of somatic mutations was first observed to increase with radiation, then found to occur at a regular rate over time as well. This latter observation resulted in the somatic mutation theory of aging, which holds that those cells that are so altered will no longer function properly, that they in fact will harm the host or produce substances that do and, by accumulation, cause aging.

Several authorities adhere to this theory, so I'd like to set out some of the arguments against it, even though they are somewhat technical. If these arguments do not interest you, just skip this paragraph. Calculations of observed mutation rates yield a possible maximum number of altered cells for man at age one hundred that is too small to have any adverse effect at all. Further, there is no proportionality between the number of observed mutations and the manifestations of aging. The altered cell would have to be normal enough to survive the body's immune defense mechanism and then reproduce. It is hard to conceive of a cell line so nearly normal causing aging. In actual fact, there has never been a demonstration of a line or clone of such cells in any human or animal, nor even the effects of such a cell line. In Down's syndrome and Klinefelter's syndrome there are extra chromosomes in every cell that would at least partially compensate for such errors. But individuals with these syndromes actually age more rapidly than would be expected. Also, when chromosomal changes have been determined in cell cultures, there is no relationship between their number and the longevity of the cell line. Many cells in the body, as we have noted, do not divide at all; therefore, somatic mutation could not take place at an appreciable rate in these cells, and thus, according to this theory, they should be ageless or nearly so. In laboratory experiments, substances that cause mutations (noncytotoxic monofunctional alkylating agents) were found neither to accelerate aging nor to shorten life span in a variety of experimental animals. Peter Alexander and Dorothea Connell noted no relationship between mutation caused by radiation and life spans. Howard Curtis irradiated mice when they were young to produce the number of chromosomal abnormalities seen in old mice, but their lives were not shortened either. Such observations as I made above and experiments such as these lead me to conclude that this theory cannot explain the aging process.

A variation of this theory suggests that random errors short of actual chromosome changes or mutations occur in certain processes within the cells with the passage of time and cause aging. Leo Szilard calls these "aging hits." He believes that aging is caused by errors in the system of protein synthesis we discussed previously. Leslie Orgel is another prominent investigator who advocates this as the explanation for the aging process. Most proponents of this theory have concentrated on the transcription part of the process whereby messenger RNA picks up its instructions from DNA.

Because this is the theory that is most widely held at present, I have to go into some detail on the arguments against it, even though they are even more technical than those against the somatic mutation theory. (Again, you may wish to skip the next paragraph.)

To be compatible with this theory, the life span of a species should be proportionate to the DNA content of the chromosomes in its germ cells, but the opposite is the case in all species, as well as in certain genetic syndromes in man. If a "hit" or error occurs, there are other identical portions of the DNA and corresponding transcription and translation systems that can be utilized. We are discovering more such "back-up" DNA sequences and enzyme systems all the time, and it appears that there are more than enough to compensate. The "hit" theory implies a constant rate of errors occuring over time, which could not explain how these errors can occur and be uncorrectable in rodents who survive for only one year, but somehow be postponed for seventy times as long or more in man. Nor can it account for the rapid decline in cellular function after a certain age. If one goes to nonmammalian species, the problem is multiplied a hundredfold or more. Most importantly, we have learned just in this past decade how the double-stranded DNA helix repairs itself using the normal strand as a template. Therefore the "hits" would have to knock out the same sites on both strands simultaneously, because repair is rapid, or somehow knock out one site and its specific repair enzyme simultaneously. Also, if this theory were true, the DNA repair mechanism activity should be proportional to the life span of the species, but it is not. For example, man has a repair activity five times that of a rat, but lives twenty-five times longer. Very recently, the error accumulation theory has been tested by the use of viral probes. Viral replication uses the host cell synthesis machinery; therefore, an increased potential for errors in an old cell can be detected easily in the viral progeny. Leonard Hayflick and others have found that the older cells are just as capable of producing normal virus particles as the younger cells.

So until more is known, this theory remains an interesting one, currently providing the basis for most of the research now being done on aging. However, in my opinion, such observations as those above make it an unlikely explanation for the aging process.

Let's return to one fact mentioned at the start of this chapter—each living species appears to have a finite life span. The maximum mean life span in mammals, unless accident or disease interferes, ranges from one year in the smoky shrew, through seventy years in the elephant, to approximately 110 years in man. As I implied earlier, there must be some sort of control mechanism operating in each species that is specific for that species. And it is a precise one. Furthermore, within any one species, long-lived strains have been created in the laboratory by inbreeding that have a mean life span more than twice as long as inbred short-lived strains. These facts could only mean that the control mechanism resides in the genes.

As for humans, life insurance data show that individual longevity is determined to a great degree by that of one's parents and grandparents. Longevity is also more nearly the same for identical than for nonidentical twins. One study with a large population of U.S. men and women placed them in seven classes in accordance with the summed longevity of their parents and grandparents. The mortality of the population studied was directly proportional in all seven groups with their ancestral longevity. This type of evidence also suggests that the determining mechanism in humans is genetic.

Sex makes a difference. In all mammals, the female lives longer than the male with two exceptions, the horse and the Syrian hamster. In the human, some of the difference may be due to cultural causes—the male's usual experience of more stress than the female—as well as to other differences in life styles. But even the male fetus has a 10 percent higher mortality, and studies done in religious orders where life styles of men and women are similar still show a significant difference in life span between the sexes. And sex is determined genetically. Again, we are brought to the conclusion that there is a genetic program in the aging process.

Let's look at one research methodology that could shed further light on this—the technique of growing human tissue cells in the laboratory. When first developed some thirty years ago, it was used only for viral research, but within the last decade or two it has also been used to study aging. The earliest reports were confusing—it seemed that certain lines of vertebrate cells cultured in the laboratory would live indefinitely. Then it became apparent that the techniques used for supplying nutrients to the culture also included young cells of the same line, so that the population was constantly being renewed. Then investigators who avoided this error but still seemed to have cell cultures of indefinite life span found that the cells had become transformed into cancerous cells. It is true that cancer cells appear to be capable of indefinite life. They go right on doubling forever, as long as adequate nutrients are provided. It is this characteristic that makes cancer in the body so lethal, and it reflects a disturbance in the genetic control system. No normal cells, however, have been found to do so in culture or the body. They all have a limited life span.

Leonard Hayflick found that the age of cultured cells was not measured as much by chronological time, but by the number of reproductions the cells were capable of undergoing. Cells taken from human embryos underwent roughly fifty divisions in culture before stopping their duplication, then dying. Cells taken from a man of twenty underwent about thirty divisions before stopping, and those from an old man only about twenty. This work has since been confirmed in other laboratories. Hayflick went one step further by arresting the duplication of his cells by freezing them with liquid nitrogen. For many years now he has thawed some periodically, and the cells retain their finite doubling capacity no matter how long they have been frozen. Recently he has removed the nuclei from young cells, replaced them with nuclei from older cells, and vice versa, demonstrating that this finite doubling capacity is controlled by the nucleus, where the genetic material is located.

Other investigators have shown a direct proportion between the life span of several species of animals and the number of doublings their cells are capable of undergoing in culture. And the transplantation of tissue to animals has shown that the aging of the transplanted tissue corresponds with the donor, not the recipient, so the control mechanism carried in the cells is a phenomenon found in living animals, not just in cultured cells. Therefore observations on cells in culture appear to be directly applicable to living organisms.

Cultured cells which stop doubling are not dead, but death follows after varying periods of time depending upon the cell type. No difference can be demonstrated by means of either electron or light microscopy between cells that have ceased reproducing and cells which continue to reproduce. However, studies using a radioactive precursor showed that DNA synthesis had ceased in the nonreproducing cells even though all of the necessary ingredients were present for such synthesis. Something had simply shut down the process. This finite doubling capacity is not *responsible* for aging, of course—a fact that becomes obvious when one remembers that many cell types in the human body do not duplicate once growth is completed. However, if this finite capacity is regarded as a manifestation that is *representative* of aging, then it has profound significance.

In the last few years many observations have been made on other genetically controlled decremental changes that occur in cultured cells with age. There are now over one thousand publications showing the decremental changes of more than one hundred biochemical activities during the life spans of many tissues from many different species.

Morris Rockstein, for example, found that there is a predictable stepwise series of such biochemical changes with age in the muscle cells in, of all things, the housefly. He then went on to find that there are similar age-related changes in the heart muscle of the white rat. Therefore, aging research on insects is not as ridiculous as one might first think. The flight muscle of the housefly is strikingly similar to muscles of higher vertebrates, including man. This opens up a method for the study of aging using species that are numerous, cheap, easily maintained, and above all, short-lived.

One other important link in the evidence that aging is controlled genetically comes from the work of Phil Gold. As mentioned previously, this control is lost when a cell becomes cancerous. He was able, not to change a cancerous cell culture back to normal cells, but to restore some normal functions and a finite life span to the cells and show that this was brought about by changes in the genes. This is a fascinating area for further research. Over a thousand genes have now been located and identified in normal cells. As this work progresses, we might find from the study of near-normal transformed cells that only a few genes control aging, then be able to locate and identify them. Recombinant DNA research could also pursue this problem. The technology presently available in the field is adequate to do so.

There are more than 100,000 genes in the nucleus of each human cell. As I mentioned earlier, these are identical in every cell in the body. What causes the cells themselves to differentiate and have different functions is apparently a shutting down of a pattern of genes in each particular cell line, allowing residual patterns to continue to function and govern the destiny of that cell line. Francois Jacob and Jacques Monod won the Nobel Prize in medicine for showing that cells contain not only structural genes but *control genes* as well. These control genes have the power to start and stop the activity of the structural genes.

In view of all the evidence for a "genetic clock" as the cause of aging, my contribution is to suggest that we try to abandon our idea that development and death are two distinct processes. We have long recognized genetic control of development, but we have overlooked the fact that development itself involves involution and cell death. Even in the uterus, much fetal tissue dies as new is formed—in the molding of the limbs and organs especially. In fact, *more cells die during fetal development in the uterus than are present in our bodies and die when we do as adults.* We seem somehow blind to the fact that cell *death* is an integral part of the development that is known to be controlled genetically.

It may become clearer to us if we consider a few examples that occur in the human *after* birth. During the first few months of life, the cell line that produced the specialized hemoglobin necessary for intrauterine life dies as the production of adult hemoglobin is taken over by another cell line. In later childhood, when its role in defense against the many infectious diseases of childhood is no longer so crucial, the thymus begins to involute. Ultimately its cells die. After the menopause, the ovaries wither away. Their cells die. All of these events are genetically controlled. So death of any cell line—indeed of our whole body—can be considered as a point on the continuum of development and probably under the control of relatively few genes. These "aging genes" are almost certainly identical or very similar in every cell in the body.

The implications of this thought are almost overwhelming. If the theory with the most support at present, the random error or "hit" hypothesis, is true, then our prospect of altering the aging process is so distant as to be entirely over the horizon and out of sight. If, however, a genetic program controlled by a few genes closes down certain cell functions causing aging and death, then we are already at the point where we may be able to alter this within the next decade or two. Researchers even now are discovering substances—enzymes, hormones, histones, and certain nonhistone nucleoproteins—that repress and "de-repress" certain genes. They have been successful with such techniques in correcting certain genetic abnormalities in cell cultures and, to some extent, in animals. *We need only to locate those genes responsible for aging and discover which substances control their repression, and we will have arrived on the threshold of immortality.* And this could happen in our lifetime!

It is possible that researchers in the area of random errors may come around to this genetic program concept, because it actually may be behind the random error hypothesis itself. Consider the following line of reasoning: It is well known that aging is accompanied by a higher incidence of most malignant tumors, and epidemiology has suggested that a large portion is caused by chemicals. The obvious assumption would be that such chemicals, accumulating with the years, would be the cause of cancers. This is not necessarily so. A truly exquisite experiment conducted by P. Ebbesen controlled all variables involved except tissue age. He transplanted old and young skin to young mice, exposed them to known cancer-causing chemicals, and found more than a three-fold increase in the incidence of cancer in the old transplants versus the young ones. Therefore, for the first time we are in the position to say that older cells are more susceptible to carcinogenic influence by virtue of their age alone. Thus the random error theory may be compatible with the genetic program theory if the genetic program acts by simply shutting down repair mechanisms.

Though we do not have to have the whole process of aging solved to affect our own life span, the obsolescence of senscence may be near. One small advance could extend our lives long enough to allow time for another advance, and so on. But as exciting as this progress and prospect in aging research may be, right now we have no choice but to come down out of the clouds and deal with earthier things, those we face every day as we find ourselves aging. In the next several chapters I'll talk about what each of us can do with the resources now at our disposal to make our lives not only longer, but healthier and happier.

3

The Body

The aim of medicine is to let our patients die young—as late as possible.

HIPPOCRATES

YOUR HEALTH

*I*n the last chapter, the general process of aging was discussed, but its specific effects upon us by and through middle age were not. In this chapter, "The Body," and in later chapters, "The Mind" and "The Person," we will deal with these effects in greater detail.

The bodily changes fall fairly easily into two categories— those directly due to the aging process itself, which present evidence leads us to conclude is internally programmed, and those over which we have much more control, which in fact reflect our life styles for the most part.

Literally hundreds of papers have been published on the first category, ranging from endocrine function through lung capacity to muscle strength and dexterity. I have reviewed most of these. Rather than presenting you with a bewildering barrage of statistics, let me point to a rough rule of thumb that seems to emerge. That is this: With some allowance made for genetic differences, the physical and physiological systems in the body decrease in their efficiency approximately ½ percent a year from age twenty until about age fifty to sixty, when the rate of decline appears to increase slightly to approximately 1 percent per year. Around age seventy for most, this process begins to accelerate until death eventually supervenes.

In the second category, those over which we have much more control, we are actually considering the wide array of all the causes of morbidity and mortality in middle age and beyond. Ideally, I'd like to discuss each one, but this would be another book, a medical encyclopedia. There are several of these already available, but even the best falls far short of what a fine physician can do for you. So this introductory section to "The Body" will just present information that will help you select your own physician wisely. Following this will be a few sections covering some of the most important areas in which you have more responsibility for your health than he does.

Selecting a good physician becomes much more important as we grow older. When we were young, our parents took care of this for us, and until age thirty or thirty-five nearly all of our medical needs were rather simple and could be handled by almost any physician we picked from the telephone book. Not so in middle age. Let me give you a little background on this.

Before this century, most physicians knew about all there was to know about medicine, which wasn't very much. They took on all cases and gave their patients what they had most of—time and compassion. They really couldn't do much else. Since then, knowledge in medicine has increased to the point where any physician who hopes to care for you competently now *must* narrow and deepen his skill in one specialty. And he is aided in practicing his specialty by other specialists and an ever-increasing variety of sophisticated technology and highly trained paramedical assistants.

For the first three or four decades of this century, the general practitioner had the dual role of primary physician and coordinator of any care you might require from specialists, and he did very well. If the "G.P." had concentrated on this role but limited his treatment to simple conditions, he could have continued to do well indefinitely. Unfortunately, most kept trying to be all things to all people, despite the impossible amount of knowledge and skill this began to require, so the more sophisticated patients began bypassing them and going directly to specialists or prestigious medical centers. This had obvious disadvantages, so during the past quarter of a century the pediatrician came to take over the primary care and coordination for children, as did the internist for adults. This system worked satisfactorily until the last few years, when it too has shown signs of breaking down. We really need a radical revision in the way primary medical care is delivered today. I'll talk more about this later.

The evolution of generalists during the past two decades should be sketched briefly, because many middle-agers started with them for all-around care earlier in their lives and still go to them, believing they are receiving the best medical care. Prior to the 1940s, the postgraduate training of the G.P. consisted of only a year of internship after medical school. When this was seen to be inadequate, general-practice residency programs of one or two years following internship were set up in the hope that one physician would still be competent to render quality care in all areas. I myself wanted to be a general practioner early in my career and took a year of such residency before I realized how impossible this goal was. Since 1970, the general practitioners themselves have tried to make some changes in recognition of this. They have changed their name to "family practitioners" to create a new image; formalized their residency at three years (including internship); and follow this with an examination and certification, as specialists have done. Best of all, they have set up a program of periodic re-examination and re-certification every six years.

Personally, I believe this sort of physician—the "F. P."—is ideal for areas where specialists are scarce. For that reason I have taught in their residency programs and supported them in other ways. But many of the family practitioners stay in urban and suburban areas where they simply cannot compete with the specialists there, who offer care of higher quality. Some have said that the good old family doctor went out with the good old family. That isn't true. There are still some of each.

But in areas where they are available, a certified internist should now serve as your primary-care physician and entry point into the medical care system. Although since 1970 the system of training internists has been changed in favor of producing subspecialists, with less time spent learning general internal medicine, most certified internists active today have this background: one year of internship, followed by three or four years of residency training in all aspects of internal medicine. They have subsequently been subjected to a rigorous written examination, to two or more years of approved practice experience, and then to an oral examination at the bedside of patients before receiving certification by the American Board of Internal Medicine. Because of the recent emphasis on subspecialization, with less training in all aspects of internal medicine and the abandonment of the bedside examinations, you may wish to select an internist who finished his residency before 1970. The training program in internal medicine includes all branches of medicine except pediatrics, obstetrics, and the various types of surgery, but it exposes the young physician to enough in these fields to make him able to coordinate your care under these specialists. Because of the immense amount of knowledge he must absorb and the difficulty of both the residency and the examinations, a certified internist usually has come from the upper 10 percent of his class in a major medical school, and usually he has been trained in a university teaching hospital. There is no need now to inquire, as one might have in the past, about his medical school or where he took his residency. If he is *certified*, that certification speaks for all the rest. His personality or some other characteristic may not be exactly what you want, but his competence can't be questioned. This prolonged selection and training results, too, in the sort of physician who keeps abreast of rapidly advancing medical knowledge.

One word of caution: Many general practitioners are refused surgical privileges at the local hospitals, or are cutting back their practices as they get older, or do not care to deliver babies at night, or whatever, and so call themselves internists. This is legal at the present time. Other physicians may have finished one or two years of internal medicine residency training, but for some reason did not continue. They, too, can call themselves internists. And there are those who have completed the full course of training but for one reason or another have failed the examinations—or have elected not to take them. This usually means they have had inferior training in a nonuniversity hospital. These physicians also can call themselves internists. But none of them have board certification, the hallmark of competence. To check on this, either ask to see the certificate in the internist's office or consult the *Directory of Medical Specialists* at any large library. If you cannot find out if an internist is certified in either of these ways, write to the American Board of Internal Medicine, 3930 Chestnut Street, Philadelphia, Pennsylvania 19104, or call them at (215) 386–7551 and ask.

The first step in selecting your physician is to get the names of a half dozen certified internists who have offices near you from the closest medical school teaching hospital. The best of them volunteer their time to teach at these hospitals. If there is not such a teaching hospital near you, get some names of certified internists from your local medical society. Then call the finest hospital in your vicinity—the one you would wish to use—and find out which ones are on the staff. The hospitals themselves monitor the quality of care physicians on their staff render. You might even get the opinions of nurses who work in the hospital or, better yet, of other physicians on the staff who work closely with the internists you are interested in. Then call the two or three left on your list, and go in and talk to each one. Many do not charge for such a visit, but if they do, it's worth the cost of the office call. While you are there, pay attention to the internist's personality and how it meshes with yours. Is he thorough? Is he sensitive? Does he listen? Does he care? Does he explain things clearly? Ask him about such things as to whom he refers patients for complications outside of his field and how his practice is covered when he takes time off. From these interviews you should be able to select the best one for you. Then set up an appointment for a complete physical examination with him. One caution: Do not rely upon recommendations from friends or neighbors. Studies have shown that medicine is too complex today for a patient to judge with any degree of accuracy the quality of care he or she is receiving from his physician. No one should make recommendations unless his or her own choice was along the lines suggested above.

I won't attempt to describe in detail the initial physical examination that a person of middle age needs, but I will list some of the most important elements so that you will be able to judge its quality to some extent yourself. Not all these elements need be included, but if they are not, you should ask why not and be satisfied with the reason given.

1. The internist should send for all of your previous medical records well before the examination so he can go over them with you when he sees you.
2. A careful medical history is extremely important. Half an hour or more should be spent on this. It is usually based on a form that you fill out at home so you can take your time, consult records or family members, and complete it more accurately. If no such form is used, an hour or more may be required in the office.
3. When he or his nurse determines your height and weight, he or she should also pinch your skin with special calipers at

three or more places, not just weigh and measure your height with your clothing on. The double-fold skin thickness measurements are the only accurate way to determine in the office where you are in relation to your ideal weight.

4. When your blood pressure is taken the first time, it should be done on *both* arms. There are certain abnormalities that are detectable by doing it this way the first time. Thereafter it can be done on the *right* army only, usually while you are seated and have been sitting quietly for several minutes.

5. During the physical examination, the internist should examine your skin carefully all over. Some physicians hesitate to do so for fear they might embarrass you. Many a tiny mole that later turns malignant or an early clue to a serious disease has been overlooked because of this hesitation.

6. Your eyes should be tested for both near and far vision as well as color vision. You should also be examined with a device that detects glaucoma and one with which he can see inside your eyes, *while the room is dark.*

7. Hearing should always be tested with an audiometer—never by watch tick or the whispered voice.

8. The internist should use a little mirror like that the dentist uses, along with one of those large round mirrors with a hole in it strapped to his head when he examines your mouth, throat, and vocal chords. And he should feel anything suspicious with a gloved finger. A flashlight and tongue depressor just do not do the job.

9. He should listen to your heart with his stethoscope when you are in at least two different positions and also listen to each side of your neck and the areas over your kidneys.

10. Not only is a chest X-ray with both front and side views essential, but your lung function must be evaluated by breathing in and out of a special machine. Listening with a stethoscope alone is no longer adequate.

11. An electrocardiogram of course must be done while are you lying down, but most importantly, also *while you are on a treadmill exercising.* A rough way to put it is that the resting EKG shows only what has already happened—the exercise EKG shows what *will* happen. The "two-step" test is totally inadequate. This was the first exercise EKG ever developed, by Dr. Masters in 1929. The only reason it is still used by some physicians is that the steps cost about $20, whereas the

modern equipment for a treadmill test may cost up to $10,000.

12. Women require an adequate visual and manual pelvic examination—not just a pap smear, although that is essential if the uterus is still present. The physician should not only examine both breasts carefully—while you are sitting *and* lying down—but show you how to do this monthly at home.*

13. Men must have their prostate palpated carefully via rectal examination.

14. A proctosigmoidoscopic examination (a tube in your rectum) must be done for both males and females. If the internist or his assistant hasn't asked you to bring in three daily stool samples to check for traces of blood chemically or given you a kit so you can do this at home, he should take a sample with a long "Q-Tip" at the time of the sigmoidoscopy for such a test. This is important to detect cancer and other abnormalities beyond the limit of the sigmoidoscope.

15. As to laboratory tests on blood and urine, these are mostly done now on a sequential multiple analyzer and other sophisticated equipment, often controlled by computers, and are fairly standardized. Most physicians order an adequate battery of laboratory tests, but two give an indication of the quality of the examination you are receiving:

   a. A two-hour postprandial blood sugar, that is, a blood sugar drawn two hours after eating a large meal or after drinking a special sugar preparation. A blood sugar determination while you are fasting is not enough. If there is a history of diabetes in your family or suspicion of hypoglycemia, a glucose tolerance test over several hours should be done instead.

   b. Cholesterol and triglyceride levels (or a more sophisticated lipid panel) must be determined on blood drawn while you have been fasting at least twelve hours after your last meal.

   Notice that in a careful physical examination blood is drawn on *two* specified occasions, even if you don't remember the names of the tests.

---

*I was greatly embarrassed once when I was examining a lady with rather small breasts. When I usually say "Do you regularly check your breasts for lumps?", I said instead, "Do you regularly check your lumps for breasts?" I never saw her again.

16. Then a week or two later, your internist should spend at least half an hour discussing the results with you. At this time he will give you several recommendations for improving your health. A written report for your later reference should be given you then or mailed to you later. You really can't remember everything he says in his office.

The so-called "annual examination" should be modified in terms of your internist's findings at the initial examination. That is, he might want just to talk with you a time or two, then do some sort of minor checkup every few months. Or he may see you briefly each year, with a thorough examination only every two or three years. He will suggest whatever he thinks best. There is no rationale for a rigid annual examination. I have heard and read a lot of controversy over checkups and periodic physical examinations that misses the main point. The primary purpose of every visit to your physician is so that he can *counsel* you—to use all he knows about you in a meaningful way to guide you to live the healthiest and happiest life possible. The visits are not just for detection of disease, although he could not counsel you without paying close attention to possible disease conditions or precursors. Passing out pills runs a poor third. Multiphasic screenings and other such attempts to "systematize" physical examinations all miss this point. Stop and think a moment. Other than with immunizations, how many diseases can a physician acting alone actually *prevent?* Very few. Most prevention is up to you. So is most treatment, in the long run. The best the physician can do is detect early signs, diagnose, and work with you on both prevention and treatment. Remember, the principal diseases of middle age are not "acts of God," but *acts of man*.

Please don't ask your physician to make house calls. High quality modern medicine cannot be practiced in the home. Your emergency needs will be handled in his office during hours or in the emergency room of a nearby hospital after hours. Many people think the reluctance of physicians to make house calls today is due to laziness or whatever, but it is just good practice of medicine. I made it a point in my practice never to refuse a house call if one was requested despite this explanation, but on arrival at the home I always tried again to convince the patient to go with me to a hospital where modern medicine could be practiced. In all those years, only one patient refused. He said he had a "stomach ache." Although I warned him that he might have sustained a heart attack that could not be either diagnosed or cared for in his house, he chose to stay at home and died later that night—of his heart attack. He was only forty-nine and left a beautiful family. It was a terrible and unnecessary loss.

For the future, a new profession, that of "health counselor," would seem to be an ideal entry point into the medical care system. Trained for about two years after graduating from college with a degree in the biological sciences, such a person would act as a coordinator of medical services—he could take a medical history, do an adequate screening examination, obtain appropriate laboratory and other studies, and then refer the patient with this information to one or more specialists for appropriate care without himself undertaking any treatment whatsoever. Here is where the computerized medical questionnaire and the multiphasic screening examination could fit in. Health education with emphasis on prevention would be an important function of the counselor, as would continued coordination of care. Once again, under this kind of supervision, the patient would receive the time, warmth, and overall personal understanding essential to good health care which are so often missing today. The quality of care would be better, time taken would be little more, and the overall expense would ultimately be much less. Such a health counselor is not to be confused with a nurse practitioner or physician's assistant, both of whom are essentially extenders of physicians' services. Either one could be converted to excellent health counselors, however, as could health educators.

The counselor could still refer simple cases to family practitioners for care. With this screening, the latter would not tend to treat complicated cases beyond their competence, because they would never even see them. For this sytem to function, patients would have to return to the counselor after the purpose of each referral had been achieved for continued counseling and coordination of care. And for it to work best, the counselor would be part of the team at large clinics. With assistance such as this, family practitioners could improve the extent and quality of their care in areas where physicians are scarce. In areas where specialists are plentiful, the lack of patients referred to F.P.s would cause many of them to move to under-doctored areas, further improving medical care there.

For some time I had been reading reports from health

maintenance organizations (HMOs) and others offering prepaid medical care plans that contained superb statistics on the results of their focus on the prevention of disease rather than "crisis care" —lowered hospitalization rates with shorter stays, less surgery and lower costs all around, with maintenance of high quality medical care. Intrigued by these statistics and knowing that the patients of such organizations seemed to be reasonably satisfied, I hoped to recommend some to you. So I toured the country posing as an applicant for a position and visited several of the best-known ones. I couldn't believe things could be as bad as they seemed to be from this inside vantage point, so I actually went to work for several weeks at two that were supposedly the best in California. Sad to say, things were that bad in these, too. I found physicians and personnel of the lowest quality employed, simply because they were the cheapest; their attitudes were poor, their standards low. At the HMOs I visited and where I worked, high quality specialist care outside their own staff, as well as expensive tests and procedures, are actively discouraged if not impossible to obtain. The most minimal quantity and quality of x-ray, physiotherapy, and other ancillary services are provided, and laboratory tests are generally the cheapest available, without sufficient regard for accuracy. The hospitals with which these HMOs are affiliated (and which the patients must use) follow the same trend—the cheapest and lowest quality. Even so, hospitalization is actively discouraged even when clearly indicated, as are surgical procedures. These organizations' cheaper costs come from these practices and because the majority of their patients are selected—they are mostly groups of employees whose age and health permit them to be actively employed. The poor, the elderly, and the chronically ill are rarely cared for by HMOs. Worst of all, preventive medicine is almost nonexistent. For example, health educators *are* sometimes employed, enable the HMO to qualify for federal financial assistance, but then are assigned other tasks. Reports to Federal agencies are falsified— crisis care prevails and there is little or no "health maintenance" despite the deceptive name. From what I found, the bottom line with most HMOs is the dollar, not the patient. So unless you can obtain reliable and accurate information on one that interests you *from an inside source*, don't believe their publicity. I am sure there are exceptions in the country, but I did not find any that I could recommend to you. Frankly, this shocked me. It is sad that our tax dollars under federal legislation passed in 1973 are actually encouraging these organizations without more being done to ensure quality of care in those that are receiving such funds.

Locating a competent physician, having a good examination, and getting settled in as his patient is much more important now during the middle years than it has ever been before in your life. Many organs and systems in your body are just beginning to show first signs of future illness that can be detected by a careful examination. And future catastrophic complications can only be avoided by competent care and counseling. *Don't wait for symptoms to develop.*

At the start of this chapter, I stated that I could not cover all the causes of morbidity and mortality in middle age. But you should at least know what the leading causes of death are during these years. First, a bit of background. Prior to about 1930, the developed nations of the world experienced a steadily declining mortality rate for all ages in which medical care played only a minor role. Much more significant were such factors as improved education and economic conditions, as well as more adequate nutrition. Since that time, most of the decline in mortality has been due to a lowering of infant mortality, where the two most potent arms of medicine, vaccines and antibiotics, have had profound effects. Infant mortality continues to decline today due to other medical advances, more liberal abortion laws, and more efficient contraception, but is reaching a limit largely determined by maternal education and motivation, *not* the quality of available medical care, as you so often hear. The death rate for the elderly declined also over the last forty to fifty years and is still falling, for reasons that are mostly medical. But the life expectancy of the middle-aged has not followed these favorable trends. In the United States, a male infant born today can expect 21.7 more years of life than he could have at the turn of the century; a female 26.1 more years. As to the elderly, a woman sixty-five today has an increased life expectancy over her counterpart in 1900 of nearly six years; a man has two years more. Yet over the same span in this century, a middle-aged person's life expectancy increased only a little more than that of the elderly and has actually tended to plateau over the last two decades.

The reasons are to be found in the life styles most of us in middle age pursue—and have pursued. Availability and quality of medical care are much less important. For example, New York

State, which has more physicians per capita than any other state
in our country, ranks thirty-first from the top in health! Sweden
has medical care comparable to ours in most respects, yet we have
twice that nation's incidence of the diseases that are major causes
of death in the middle-aged. And it is illustrative to contrast the
two states Utah and Nevada, which are at opposite poles in terms
of the health of the middle-agers living there, as measured by
most criteria. The two states are adjacent geographically and are
alike in income, schooling, urbanization, climate, and most other
variables. Even the number of physicians and hospital beds per
capita are similar. The differences in all these areas are due to life
styles. And Seventh-Day Adventists live seven years longer than
the average American, with far fewer illnesses. Life styles again.

The next several sections will describe in more detail some of
the elements of life style that are the most significant for our
health. But to give you an idea, one succinct summary is based on
data from the Human Population Laboratory of the California
State Department of Health in Berkeley, where seven thousand
adults in Alameda County were followed for over ten years.
Seven simple health habits emerged as promoting longevity for
them: (1) meals at regular times; (2) regular breakfast; (3) exercise;
(4) adequate sleep; (5) no cigarette smoking; (6) normal weight;
and (7) alcohol in moderation. Their data show that a forty-five-
year-old man who practices six of these habits can live eleven
years longer than a man the same age who follows fewer than
three. The gain is seven years for a woman the same age.

Dean Lester Breslow of the School of Public Health at the
University of California, Los Angeles, summed it up by stating,
"Medicine is becoming increasingly effective in conquering
specific health menaces. But I firmly believe the American people
are depending far too much on their doctors to stay healthy. All of
us must take more responsibility for our own health—the choices
we make in our daily lives with regard to certain habits." Dr. John
Knowles, former president of the Rockefeller Foundation, commented, "The next major advance in the health of the American
people will result only from what the individual is willing to do
for himself."

To see how true this is, let's look at the five leading causes of
death during the last decade in the United States for those aged
forty-five to sixty-four, listed as percentage of the total causes:

	Males	Females
Heart disease	46.3%	30.4%
Cancer	19.7%	33.5%
Stroke	5.4%	8.6%
Accidents	5.4%	3.8%
Cirrhosis of the liver	3.0%	2.7%

The role of life styles in these statistics is obvious. Heart disease and stroke are almost entirely due to life styles. Even a third of the cancer is. Most accidents and essentially all of the cirrhosis is, too. It is interesting that the same leading causes of death prevail for the most part from age sixty-five on. The exceptions are diabetes in the female and pneumonia in the male, which join the first five as cirrhosis leaves the list for both sexes, having taken its toll. This list contrasts dramatically with the leading causes of death in 1900, which were mostly infectious diseases. *If just this list of the five leading causes of death were eliminated at age fifty, a male could expect 15.7 years added to his life and a female 19.2!*

Although it's impossible to discuss even this limited list in a general book on middle age, perhaps I can comment upon the factors that contribute to two of them—heart attack and stroke—because for the most part they are the same; and this will reinforce what I've said about the importance of the way we lead our lives.

Remember the words of John Dryden—they are still applicable today, although perhaps not exactly in the way he intended:

Better to hunt in fields for health unbought
Than fee the doctor for a nauseous draught.

HEART ATTACK AND STROKE

The Captain of Death in the middle years and beyond in our country is atherosclerosis, the artery disease responsible for almost all heart attacks and strokes. It accounts for about half of all deaths during middle age, and over three-fourths of those after age sixty-five. If only heart attack and stroke were eliminated—and they could be—the average life span in the United States would be extended by more than seven years.

What is this killer, atherosclerosis? It is one of the three kinds of hardening of the arteries—the three together are sometimes referred to as arteriosclerosis. The first type is a thickening of the inner lining of the smaller arteries, arterioles, and is found in patients with high blood pressure. In the second type, the artery wall undergoes hardening and even calcium deposition in its middle layer. This appears to be an accompaniment of the aging process and is not responsible for any disease by itself.

The third and most deadly type of hardening of the arteries is atherosclerosis. Several theories exist that speculate on how this disease first develops in an artery. All of them, however, agree that at certain places the inner layer of the artery wall absorbs fat particles containing cholesterol from the bloodstream. Fibrous tissue forms in these spots, other changes take place, and they are then called plaques. From this point on, the serious consequences occur in one of two ways. The plaque can cause a hemorrhage within the wall of the artery so that the inner lining swells into the artery channel and blocks it. More often, the size of the plaque itself gradually encroaches upon the channel. This slows the stream of blood, and when it is sufficiently slowed, a clot forms within the channel and closes it completely. Either way, the blood supply to a portion of the heart or brain is cut off, that portion dies, and the result, respectively, is a heart attack or stroke.

Atherosclerosis is a phenomenon of this century and is caused by the way we live. The first heart attack ever reported in the medical literature was in 1912. Over the next fifty years, the incidence of heart attacks and strokes increased dramatically until over one million people were dying every year in this country from these causes. However, it was not until the late 1950s that the several causes of atherosclerosis, called "risk factors," became clarified. There are about a dozen of these factors, three of which we can do little or nothing about:

1. *Age*. Although autopsies of troops killed in the Korean and Vietnam wars and even of children show the beginnings of the process at an early age, it is usually only by middle age or later that it becomes advanced enough to cause serious manifestations. For example, the peak age period for heart attacks in men is fifty to fifty-nine.
2. *Sex*. Men are far more susceptible than women to atherosclerosis, but the reasons for this are not clearly under-

stood. Female hormones may very well be protective, as may
also the different levels and kinds of stress men and women
experience in our society. One typical study implicating both
factors found that female executives have five times as much
coronary artery disease as other women of the same age, and
the ratio rose to eight times as high after the menopause.

3. *Family history*. This in itself is not an isolated risk factor like the
others, but abundant evidence shows that many predisposing
mechanisms, some still unknown, are inherited. A most
important one is the ability to metabolize fats and cholesterol
efficiently; another is diabetes, which is often considered a risk
factor in itself. Although all these inherited mechanisms are
not yet known, their presence is suggested by the occurence of
heart attack or stroke in close relatives.

These three unalterable risk factors might tend to cause a
fatalistic and complacent attitude. But they should actually be a
stimulus to work harder to change the others which *can* be
changed. All the risk factors relate in a synergistic way—that is,
in combination. They aren't just *additive* in increasing the chances
of atherosclerosis; they tend to *multiply* the chances.

Fats in the Blood

The most important of the risk factors that can be changed is
the level of cholesterol and certain fats in your blood. This factor
used to consist only of total serum cholesterol, but now different
fractions of cholesterol and several types of fat are known to be
involved. One such fat, triglyceride, is discussed in more detail in
the chapter on nutrition. It tends to be too high in the overweight
and those who consume excess alcohol, saturated fats, starches,
sugar—in fact, calories in any form—and who do not exercise
enough. Rarely are high levels due to an inherited metabolic
abnormality.

High-density lipoprotein, another fat in the blood, is actually
somewhat protective, because it carries cholesterol to the liver,
where it is eliminated, preventing its deposition in the arteries.
Women prior to the menopause, nonsmokers, those who exercise, and those with a diet high in vegetables and low in saturated
fats have been found to have higher levels of protective HDL.
Low-density lipoprotein, on the other hand, is a dangerous fat.
LDL carries most of the cholesterol in the blood and has a greater

tendency to deposit on the artery walls. Its levels correlate closely with the occurrence of atherosclerotic disease. Most of this is dietary in origin.

Cholesterol itself is usually discussed with the fats, although it is actually a sterol, a waxy member of the alcohol family. Total serum cholesterol is measured as milligrams per 100 milliliters (deciliters). This is the oldest and simplest test, yet still has considerable predictive value. For example, if a fifty-year-old man has a total serum cholesterol level between 245 and 260, his chances of dying of coronary artery disease within six years are *tripled* over what those chances would be at a level below 200. If the level is over 260, his chances are multiplied six-fold!

How high levels of cholesterol occur in the serum is the result of a very complex process. People absorb, excrete, and manufacture cholesterol in the body at different rates. I'm often asked why some people with high serum cholesterol levels do not have a heart attack or stroke. There is more than one answer to this. But most important is the interrelationship of the other risk factors. High blood pressure is the most important in affecting this process, but others are too. A thin person, exercising regularly and not smoking, would more than compensate for a high serum cholesterol level and might never develop a complication of atherosclerosis.

Diet is the most important cause of high serum cholesterol, and I'll talk about this in detail in the next section. Other factors such as stress, obesity, the amount of saturated fat in the diet, and exercise also affect serum cholesterol levels. In rare cases, inherited metabolic abnormalities do, too. But don't look to pills for a solution. In the massive Coronary Drug Project, eight thousand people were given various medicines to lower their cholesterol levels without discernible benefit in preventing the complications of atherosclerosis. The medications just could not lower their cholesterol levels enough to help, and caused problems of their own.

The "normal" levels of serum cholesterol as determined by the laboratory need some comment and clarification. These have been determined by averaging values of samples taken from large numbers of Americans. Determined in this way, the upper limit of "normal" for a man aged fifty may be as high as 350. The lower "normal" limit is usually around 150. Tables of such "normal" values not only vary with age, but also with sex.

However, the cholesterol level in newborn infants is around 80, and that found in populations in which atherosclerosis is almost unknown is between 100 and 150. And we have already seen that whenever the serum cholesterol level rises over 200, the incidence of coronary heart disease increases sharply. Most of the heart attacks in the Framingham study occurred in persons who were at the middle of the "normal" range! In fact, if your cholesterol level is below the American "normal" values, your chance of getting a heart attack is approximately *one-tenth* that of a person with a "normal" level. So what is average is not always best. The best range is from 100 to 200 for either sex at any age, as evidenced by a large amount of clinical and epidemiological data from our country and others.

High Blood Pressure

High blood pressure is the second of the three most important causes of atherosclerosis that can be changed. It operates in two ways. The stress and strain over a long period damages the inner linings of the arteries, and then the high blood pressure seems to "pound" fat droplets into these sites. The importance of blood pressure can be illustrated by one dramatic example: atherosclerosis is almost never found in the artieries of the lung, a separate system in which the pressure is about one-fourth that in the rest of the body *no matter what other risk factors may be present*.

High blood pressure—*hypertension* in medical terminology—is often called the "silent killer" because approximately 30 million Americans have it, yet less than half of them know that they do. Another reason it is called this is because symptoms generally do not occur until many years after high blood pressure first develops. Yet damage to vessels such as those in the heart, brain, eyes, and kidneys continues silently all through this time. When the first manifestation occurs, it is usually serious, and the damage resulting then is largely irreversible.

Blood pressure is developed entirely by the pumping action of the heart against the resistance of the arteries, primarily the small arteries. When the heart squeezes, its outlet valve closes at the end of the beat, and this pressure then, the maximum, is called the systolic blood pressure. The lowest blood pressure between beats, maintained by the squeezing of the large elastic arteries, is known as the diastolic blood pressure. So blood pressure is always given as two figures, the systolic over the diastolic.

"Normal" blood pressure is difficult to define. There are immense amounts of data showing that the *average* blood pressure in samples of apparently healthy adults in this country is 120 systolic over 80 diastolic, measured in millimeters of mercury. These samples inevitably include some of the thirty million with hypertension, however. So we should look further. There are some sound data from large studies indicating that blood pressure below this—perhaps in the vicinity of 100 to 110 over 60 to 70—is associated with the lowest morbidity and mortality from cardiovascular disease. Athletes in top condition have blood pressures in this range. That of a healthy adult immediately upon awakening is about 90 over 60, and this is similar to the blood pressures found throughout the day in primitive populations who do not have any of the complications of hypertension. So the *best* blood pressure is not known, but it is certainly closer to 100/60 than the traditional 120/80. Whether an increase with age should be considered normal is debatable. The systolic pressure obviously rises as the larger arteries lose their elasticity. So perhaps some increase in this could be regarded as normal. But an increase in the diastolic pressure with age should never be considered normal. Of the two blood pressures, the systolic is the more variable, rising with smoking, coffee, stress, and exercise, and returning to base levels rapidly in all of us. The diastolic blood pressure, however, is more reliably indicative of true hypertension and subsequent complications when it is elevated.

As I implied above, blood pressure varies considerably throughout the day, and blood pressure readings themselves are not absolutely accurate—they may vary by several millimeters on serial determinations at the same time and under identical conditions at different times of the day. Therefore, before a diagnosis of high blood pressure is established, three or more readings are usually taken, preferably one day or more apart.

Aside from obesity and arthritis, hypertension is our most common disease in middle age, and its incidence rises linearly throughout the middle years. In the United States, it is found in about 20 percent of men in early middle age and about 30 percent by late middle age. Women have a somewhat lower incidence until the menopause, after which it rises strikingly, passing that of men, until at age sixty almost 40 percent have high blood pressure.

As common as high blood pressure is, it should never be ignored. With all other conditions being equal, a fifty-year-old man with a blood pressure of 160/90 has triple the risk of a heart attack, and with 180/100, *seven times* the risk of a man with a "normal" blood pressure of 120/80. And it is even more serious for those in later middle age. One large study showed that of men aged fifty to fifty-nine with high blood pressure, 10 percent had a stroke within five years, 2 percent congestive heart failure, and 8 percent a heart attack or chest pain due to heart disease. A total of 27 percent developed one or more complications of hypertension during the five-year period of the study.

It is believed that approximately 90 percent of hypertension has its basis in inherited predisposing factors, so it is called "essential" hypertension. A better term would be primary, because the remaining 10 percent is secondary to kidney disease or other well-defined causes. These rather rare types will not be discussed here. If one of your parents or siblings has essential hypertension, you have about a 28 percent chance of having it too; if two close relatives are effected, your chance is about 50 percent.

But along with this inherited predisposition, one or more other factors are required to precipitate hypertension, the most important of these being excess salt in the diet. The average American consumes from 10 to 15 grams of salt a day, but *less than 0.2 gram* is all that is needed for proper body functioning. The second most important precipitating factor is obesity; stress, smoking, caffeine intake, and a sedentary life style are also significant.

So while one can do nothing about genetic predisposition, the most important precipitating factors in hypertension *are* under your control: salt ingestion, obesity, stress, cigarette smoking, excess coffee drinking, and lack of exercise. There is good evidence to indicate that those who keep these under good control from an early age will *never* develop hyptertension, even if they are predisposed to do so by heredity. And if you already have hypertension, these form the foundation of your treatment. If medication is necessary, that is between you and your physician. I have only three comments about medical treatment. Many studies have shown that early and adequate therapy can reduce or eliminate the complications of high blood pressure so that an individual who has it can enjoy normal or nearly normal health and life expectancy. Secondly, some medications may make you feel worse, when you felt perfectly all right before taking them. Most of these side effects pass with time, and your physician can almost always work out a regimen that will be satisfactory for you. My last point is that the medications usually have to be taken for life, unless or until enough of the precipitating factors can be changed. Think *control*, not *cure*, when you take antihypertensive medication.

If you wish to learn more about high blood pressure, two readable and reasonably accurate books are: Norman Kaplan, *Your Blood Pressure: The Most Deadly High* and Lawrence Galton, *The Silent Disease: Hypertension*. More technical sources are listed in the Bibliography. Ask your local chapter of the American Heart Association also—they have excellent pamphlets on all aspects of hypertension.

Cigarette Smoking

Cigarette smoking is the third of the three most important alterable risk factors. It acts in several ways, the most important of which are: constriction of small arteries everywhere in the body, increasing the rate and work of the heart while interfering with its metabolism, reducing the oxygen availability in the blood, increasing blood pressure, and enhancing clot formation. Smoking two packs a day increases the chance of heart attack in middle age by three times, and the chance of having a stroke by more than twice. The risk is directly proportional to the number of cigarettes smoked, but is not as related to the duration of smoking, as lung cancer is. And when one quits, the risk begins to drop immediately, so that in two or three years it is not much greater than in one who has never smoked at all.

We hear a lot about smoking as a cause of cancer of the mouth, esophagus, stomach and lungs, but far less about its role in atherosclerosis. Let me leave one thought with you. The greatest risk of dying from these cancers is fifteen to twenty years later than that of a heart attack. Those are a lot of lost years, and some of the best in our lives. A death may be just a death to a statistician. To us and to our families, it is also important *when* it occurs.

There is an abundance of information available on smoking and its dangers, as everyone knows. In addition to the annual reports of the U.S. surgeon general available in most libraries, you can write the American Cancer Society, 777 Third Avenue, New York, New York 10017; the American Lung Association, 1740 Broadway, New York, New York 10019; and the American Heart Association, 44 East 23rd Street, New York, New York 10010, or The National Clearinghouse for Smoking and Health, Bureau of Health Education, Center for Disease Control, Atlanta, Georgia, 30333.

Further Risk Factors

Stress is the next risk factor, but it is a complicated subject, and the methods of coping with it are many. Since it is so important and affects us in many other ways in middle age, I'll devote a separate section to stress alone.

Lack of exercise. Researchers first began to study the relationship between exercise and atherosclerosis in the late 1950s. Although the role of exercise was uncertain in these early studies, they have gradually discovered more about the types, amounts, and frequency required to slow or prevent the development of the disease. Exercise, too, deserves a separate section.

Obesity has been known to be a risk factor in atherosclerosis for more than twenty years. Most of the original data came from life insurance statistics, which found that those who were overweight had roughly a 50 percent greater chance of developing coronary heart disease than those who were of average weight. Later studies indicated that as subjects' weight increased, the levels of their serum fats and cholesterol also increased. A decrease in weight brought a lowering of these levels. Obesity also tends to precipitate hypertension and diabetes and is indicative of a sedentary life style. There will be a separate discussion of obesity, since it affects most of us in middle age and in more ways than those mentioned.

Other minor risk factors are known to exist, such as uric acid level in the blood, type of body build, and an abnormal resting pulse rate or electrocardiogram, but I won't expand upon them here. The relative importance of each is now known, so that your physician can calculate your own individual risk profile. Don't just assume you are free of any of these risk factors because you *feel* all right. *See your physician.* In the American Pooling Project involving 6,427 apparently healthy men age thirty through fifty-nine, 83 percent were found to have one or more.

Once these risk factors became known to physicians, several studies were done attempting to control them. Unfortunately most of the results were equivocal at best, simply because the goals of optimum body weight, physical fitness, a proper diet, and so forth were not achieved by the majority of the subjects studied.

Yet during this time the public was quietly conducting a "study" on its own. When *they* learned about the risk factors in the mid-1960s, many were motivated to give up smoking, take up regular exercise, reduce their body weight, and decrease their intake of saturated fats and cholesterol. Mortality from heart attack, which had been rising rapidly since the early years of this century, began to level off and, by 1968, actually began to decrease. Since then the decline has been more than 20 percent. A conference held at the National Heart, Lung and Blood Institute in 1978 attributed most of this drop to risk factor reduction and very little to such innovations as widespread cardiopulmonary resuscitation courses, paramedic programs, and cardiac care units in hospitals.

Because most, if not all, of us in middle age have some atherosclerosis, it would be especially important to us if we knew the process could not only be *arrested* but actually *reversed*. It was long doubted that it could. Autopsies done during World War I and World War II first suggested that it might be. Then laboratory studies using several species of animals, including primates such as Rhesus monkeys, demonstrated that reversal *was* possible. These studies, sacrificing the animals and examining their arteries under the microscope, showed that up to three-fourths of atherosclerosis would regress under proper treatment. Similar studies on humans were not done, for the understandable reason that very few people would volunteer to have their coronary and other arteries biopsied before and after a treatment regimen. So, for some thirty years after World War II, the only evidence supporting reversibility in humans came from autopsies of those dying from chronic wasting diseases.

But in the last few years, sophisticated techniques using x-ray angiography with computerized image resolution have been developed and brought to bear on this question. The first report appeared in 1976—and there are still only a few so far in the literature. In one of these, the arteries of a forty-nine-year-old woman cleared remarkably of atherosclerosis when the high levels of blood fats had been well controlled. In another, twenty-five patients with an average age of forty-eight were studied. They were asked to adhere to a diet of low saturated fat and low cholesterol. After thirteen months, the angiograms revealed that nine patients' atherosclerosis had regressed. There was no change in three, and progression continued in thirteen. The goal of reduced serum cholesterol and triglycerides was attained in the group which improved but not attained in the group that showed continued progression. There are several such encouraging studies now in progress or recently completed and not yet reported that indicate atherosclerosis *can* be reversed in the human being if the serum cholesterol is reduced below 160, cigarette smoking is stopped, and high blood pressure controlled.

In 1974, the National Heart, Lung and Blood Institute started the Multiple Risk Factor Intervention Trial, the largest and best-controlled study so far designed to evaluate the effect of reducing the three major risk factors: serum cholesterol, high blood pressure, and cigarette smoking. The study is now being conducted at twenty centers throughout the United States on over thirteen thousand subjects. Although the goals of this study in reducing these risk factors are unfortunately low, it will still be interesting to watch, because the number being studied is so large. There should be enough enthusiastic individuals who voluntarily go beyond the specified goals to form a statistically significant group. These may approach zero risk. The first results will not be available until the early 1980s.

In the meantime, there is enough evidence at hand for you with your physician's guidance to take vigorous action against atherosclerosis. Despite technical advances, surgery after the fact is not the answer. We all know the long-term results of heart transplants, and coronary bypass surgery has been shown to be less effective than good medical management over the long run. It does not affect the subsequent incidence of heart attacks or survival at all. The best it can do is provide relief from pain so that a vigorous exercise program can be incorporated into an effective preventive regimen. This is why I have gone into detail in the following sections on what you can do for yourself, starting now.

NUTRITION

This should be one of our primary health concerns in middle age, because in our country most of us at this time in our lives are actually malnourished—not *under*nourished, but *mal*nourished. Such a statement may stun you, but please hear me out.

Nutrition began to be a science scarcely a hundred years ago, and only in this century have surveys been done to determine the nutritional status of different groups within our population. Such studies began as small and rather informal surveys by local public health and other physicians, often assisted by dieticians. Forty or fifty years ago, these surveys became more systematized as they began to be sponsored by state departments of health, major universities and medical schools, HEW, and the Department of Agriculture. And in the last twenty to thirty years they have become more sophisticated as well. A variety of experts and instruments now supplement the physician's examination; the simple diet interview has been extended to an exact diary over several days, with spot checks in the home to see how much and what kind of food is actually consumed. Samples of food from the table are analyzed in the laboratory, and various biochemical tests determine the precise levels of nutrients present in subjects' bodies.

From the vast literature produced by these more modern studies, the most important findings can be condensed into one paragraph. In infants and growing children, deficiencies of iron, calcium, and protein have been found and, occasionally, of certain B-complex and other vitamins. Adolescent girls who have begun to menstruate and young women in the child-bearing years often have iron deficiencies, and pregnant women also sometimes have calcium deficiencies. Among the elderly, nutritional deficiencies are variably present, depending upon individual circumstances. But *nutritional deficiency in the middle-aged is almost absent*, unless there is some accompanying serious disease or alcoholism.

These surveys found most of the deficiencies in so-called "poverty pockets" and very little among those of average or greater affluence, so at first income was believed to be the determining factor. Then it was noted that providing more food and money did not alter the situation. A variety of factors— physical disability, ignorance, low intelligence, and lack of motivation—emerged as the reasons. A very nutritious and palatable diet can, in fact, be prepared on an income at the poverty level.

So nutritional deficiencies are not difficult to avoid. As a middle-ager, if you could afford to buy this book, understand it, and are sufficiently motivated to read it, then you are virtually certain to have no nutritional deficiencies. Then why are you along with most middle-agers almost certainly malnourished— that is, *poorly* nourished? Two reasons: excesses for most, faddism for a few. To understand these terms, you'll have to endure a short course in nutrition; these two concepts can then be delineated against this background as we go along. But before we start, let me give you two quotes as clues. The U.S. Surgeon General states, "Americans are eating too much sugar, salt, red meat, fat and cholesterol." And Dr. John Knowles adds, "We were simply not made to each so much fat, so much salt, so much refined sugar, and so little fiber."

Biochemists divide foods into the following categories: protein, fat, carbohydrate, vitamins, and minerals—and, of course, water and indigestible fiber. I'll talk about them in this order.

Protein

The word *protein* comes from a Greek word meaning "to take the first place." This is an appropriate term, because protein is the most important ingredient in our diet. It occurs in both plant and animal tissues, and its molecules are made up of various combinations of the twenty amino acids that are its building blocks. Only eight amino acids cannot be manufactured by the adult human body, so these eight are termed essential amino acids—it is *essential* they be provided in our diet.

Proteins can be categorized as complete, partially complete, or incomplete, depending upon whether they have enough of the essential amino acids in proper proportion, along with a good supply of the others, to maintain the body in a healthy state. The complete proteins are mostly of animal origin—eggs, milk, meat, poultry, and fish. Wheat germ and dried yeast approach the animal sources in terms of quality. Partially complete proteins are those such as beans and peas that will allow life to continue, but not the body to grow, heal well, or respond to stress effectively. The incomplete proteins are those which will not even sustain life.

Digestion breaks down the proteins we consume into their constituent amino acid building blocks. These are then absorbed and carried to cells in the body, where they are used to be made into other proteins or burned for energy. If protein is used as a source of energy, each gram produces 4 calories. Some special cells in the body make proteins that are required to sustain not just themselves, but the body as a whole. When any proteins are constructed, all of the necessary amino acids must be present together at the same time. Therefore, a complete protein or a complementary combination of partially complete proteins should be eaten at least every day, if not at every meal. It has always seemed to me that a simple numerical or color code on packages would help greatly in the selection and serving of complementary proteins, but this is yet to be.

The recommended daily protein allowance is 56 grams for the average 154-pound adult male and 44 grams for a 120-pound adult female, but you do not need to remember these numbers, because the average American diet easily exceeds them. If you have four servings per day of protein, half from an animal source and half from legumes such as beans or peas, you will have more than this recommended amount, and in proper balance.

With one major exception, the only problems arising with protein for adults in the United States outside the "poverty pockets" are from excessive consumption. This excess is mostly found in bodybuilders and some other athletes and in those on high-protein reducing diets. In middle age we aren't concerned with bodybuilding—or shouldn't be—and the various high-protein fad reducing diets are discussed in the next chapter. As to possible deficiencies, we are not likely to be lured by the few deficient diets such as the Zen macrobiotic diet either. The exception mentioned is vegetarianism, where there is a dangerous risk of deficiency. So a word on these diets would be appropriate. They *can* be carried out successfully, but careful calculation is necessary for every meal every day, and correct proportions of animal products other than meat *must* be included. A vegetarian diet that is adequate in protein and other nutrient essentials is just not possible otherwise.

One of the reasons given by vegetarians for following their diets is that they feel heavy or bloated after eating a meal with meat. This is actually true, because the fat content of meat slows stomach and intestinal activity. Another reason given is that eating meat is not "natural," which is not true. Man and his ancestors have been omnivorous for at least two million years. According to studies of the teeth of very ancient skulls, man has always been primarily a carnivore, but capable of adapting to a vegetarian diet temporarily if necessary when prey was scarce. Only in our century, because of our lengthening life span, have we had to give some thought to the long-term effects of the animal fats present in meat and other animal products while continuing to benefit from their nutritious qualities. Other reasons given for vegetarian diets are moral or religious in nature and beyond our scope here.

Finally, two comments on protein fads. Some "health food" promoters claim we need more enzymes in our diets for digestion and would sell them to you. Don't buy either the idea or the product. In fact, the activity of such enzymes is destroyed by gastric acid, and their only value is in their protein content. Partially predigested liquid or powdered protein is also pushed by the same individuals; it can cause serious calcium and copper deficiencies as well as other electrolyte disturbances, occasionally resulting in cardiac arrest and death. Avoid these products too.

Fat

The fatty acid is the basic building block of fats. When three of these long molecules are joined to glycerol, the result can be thought of as looking like a capital *E*. The glycerol is the vertical bar, and the horizontal bars are the fatty acids. This is a triglyceride, or neutral fat. Although this is the most common type of fat in our diets, in our blood, and in our bodies, there are many others, and they are carried in our bloodstream in various combinations with proteins.

Fats contribute substantially to the smoothness of food and to the feeling of satiety after a meal. This is our downfall. In our country today, fat supplies approximately 43 percent of our caloric intake, and a typical study on middle-aged men found it to be over 50 percent. This is in strong contrast to statistics from countries where obesity, heart attack, and stroke are practically unknown. There fat provides only about 10 percent of the daily calories. Evidence is accumulating from many sources suggesting that this percentage would in fact be ideal. Most recently, the statistical association of a high fat consumption with cancer of the colon and of the breast, and possibly with other cancers, was demonstrated. So we see that the primary problem we face with fat in our diet is also excess.

In 1974, the recommended daily intake of dietary fat was lowered in the RDA to 35 percent of total daily caloric intake, certainly a step in the right direction. In 1977, the Select Committee on Nutrition of the United States Senate recommended a further reduction to 30 percent, with no more than a third of this from animal sources. Their first report, before the meat and milk lobbies went to work, was even lower than this. The 1980 RDA urged that 35 percent not be exceeded and that the proportion that is saturated be reduced as much as possible. So official recommendations are slowly approaching the 10 percent ideal. Theoretically, *one drop* a day of fat containing the requisite fat-soluble vitamins and enough of the one essential fatty acid, linoleic acid, is all we need nutritionally.

We make fat easily in our bodies from protein and carbohydrates in our diets. Actually, its efficiency—9 calories per gram—as a form of stored energy is the main reason for the presence of fat in both animals and human beings. But it doesn't make much sense to consume the storage form of energy of an animal when most of us already have too much stored in our own bodies. But because of the smoothness and satiety fat provides, it is unlikely that we'll ever manage to reach the 10 percent ideal, much less the theoretical one drop. We can at least try to avoid those fats that are the most detrimental to our health—the saturated ones.

The term *saturated* deserves some explanation. If every carbon atom of the fatty acid has two hydrogen atoms attached, it is called "*saturated*" because no more hydrogen atoms can be attached. If one of the hydrogen atoms is missing, it is "monounsaturated"; if two or more, it is "polyunsaturated." Two things— the length of the carbon chains of the fatty acids and the degree of saturation—are shown by the relative solidity of the fat at room termperature. Therefore, a rough but useful guide is not only to reduce *all* the fats you eat as much as possible, but to consume only those that are liquid, not solid, at room temperature.

Most animal fats are about half saturated and half monounsaturated; most plant oils are unsaturated to some degree. So the source—animal or plant—can also serve as a useful guide, with only a few exceptions. In general, meat from land animals has more fat and more of it is saturated than that from cold-blooded aquatic animals, although fowl without the skin is about equal to fish. Your diet should stress the latter two, with veal (the least saturated red meat) occasionally. If you want other red meat now and then as a treat, at least trim off all the visible fat, and broil it so that some of the rest can drip off during cooking. Or if you use it in a stew or soup, prepare it a day ahead, chill it in the refrigerator overnight, and skim off the congealed fat on the surface before reheating and serving.

The least saturated of plant oils is safflower oil, but sunflower, corn, soybean, and cottonseed oils are almost as unsaturated. Coconut and other palm oils are the major exceptions among plant sources—they are more saturated than most animal fats. Use "nonstick" pans without any oil or grease for frying, and substitute unsaturated oils whenever you can in recipes calling for butter or shortening. One thing can fool you—manufacturers change unsaturated oils to saturated solids by a process called hydrogenation. The package often states in large print that the products within are made from plant oils and contain no cholesterol. But in reality hydrogenation makes them just as harmful as fats from animal sources, if not more so, because such fats interfere with the body's regulation of cholesterol synthesis, raising serum cholesterol levels.

Dairy products are a basic essential food group, but they're also a major source of saturated fat. So some cautions are necessary. Avoid cream and all products made from it, and use only skim milk (nonfat) for drinking and cooking, never whole or homogenized. It usually takes a few days for your taste buds to adjust to the thin quality of skim milk, but after that, you'll probably prefer it to the sticky feeling left in your mouth by whole milk. By the way, "low fat" milk is just an advertising gimmick used to prey on those who've been given such sound advice as this. Whole milk varies in its fat content from state to state, but the average standard is around 3.25 percent. This is reduced to just 2 percent and labeled in large letters, "low fat." The difference is insignificant as far as your health is concerned. The same sort of labeling is beginning to be used in cheeses, which are usually made half of cream and half whole milk. Don't tumble to this either. Some delicious cheeses are made from whole milk without added cream, and a few such as cottage cheese, from skim milk alone. The same "low fat" labelling is often used on yogurt, which is normally made of whole milk. Buy a kit and make your own from skim milk. Beware also of imitation milk. In it, coconut oil (one of the most highly saturated oils) or a hydrogenated vegetable oil, sugar, and other products are put together in a form resembling milk. Most nondairy creamers are made in the same way. Use only skim milk, liquid or powdered, in coffee or tea. Try to cut out butter completely. If you must use a substitute, select the softest margarines, ones that come in tubs or squeeze bottles, and use them sparingly. Better yet, use small-curd cottage cheese or non-fat yogurt as spreads.

These suggestions may seem stringent to you, but that is because only about two-fifths of the fat we consume is visible, as in butter, cream, fat on meat, and so on. The rest is invisible. For example, if all the visible fat is trimmed off a choice cut of meat, still as much as half of the steak is fat. So we have to be stringent with what we can see.

Some years ago there were those who advised adding polyunsaturated fats to diets already too high in fat in the hope somehow they might be protective against the saturated fats one could then go right on eating. This is simply not true. The rule is simple: Lower all fats as much as possible, and have the proportion of those you do consume as low in saturation as possible.

Although mentioned in the previous chapter (along with the damage it does) and not strictly a fat, cholesterol has a place in this discussion. Some of it is necessary for our bodies to function properly, but our livers and intestines make more than enough every day. Consequently, we need none in our diets and should avoid it whenever possible. Only products from animals contain cholesterol. Those with the highest amounts of cholesterol are liver, egg yolks, kidneys, brains, sweetbreads, and fish roe. Smaller amounts are present in milk, cream, butter, cheese, and meat. Shellfish, especially lobster and shrimp, are quite high. But the most important source for Americans is egg yolk, each one containing about 250 milligrams of cholesterol.

One of the confusing aspects about cholesterol was pointed out earlier—the fact that the serum level may not have a direct relationship with the incidence of heart attack and stroke. This was explained by the interaction of all the risk factors in causing such events. The other confusing aspect is that there is not always a predictable relationship between dietary intake and serum levels either. The most important reason for this is that the fat content of the diet—especially saturated fat—enhances cholesterol absorption and raises serum levels in other ways. There are also metabolic differences among people, and the effects of other factors such as obesity, stress, and exercise upon the serum levels. This unpredictability is not great, and except for those with rare metabolic disorders, most of it occurs between daily intakes of 200 to 400 milligrams. The average American diet each day contains about 600 milligrams, so a reduction does have a direct effect upon the serum level in everyone down to an intake of about 400 milligrams a day. The relationship is then less direct because of the other influences mentioned as the daily intake is further reduced, but when it gets below 200 milligrams a day, *as it should be*, all but metabolic abnormalities (present in one person in 500) are overcome, and the relationship once again becomes direct. Those who are frustrated in trying to reduce their serum levels by dietary restriction simply have not reduced their intake enough.

If you are successful in eliminating butter, cream, high fat cheeses, and eggs from your diet, you must give some thought to getting enough vitamin A in some other way, since they are the best sources of it. A glass or two a day of nonfat milk enriched with vitamin A will take care of this. If you don't like the taste of it, use it or the powdered form in cooking or some other way.

Everything I've just said about fats and cholesterol has been intended to point a direction for you, not to insist on absolutely scrupulous adherence. If we did so, we could never even go out for dinner! However, for those who prefer an even more spartan approach, the Pritikin diet is available in any bookstore. A compromise most people can adhere to easily is the Prudent

Diet developed by Norman Joliffe, which can be obtained from your local library or the American Heart Association. The AHA also publishes a guide to use in dining out.

So much for fat excesses. Now faddism. "Health food" stores advertise exotic oils high in linoleic acid, emphasizing that it is essential. It is, but a deficiency of this fatty acid has *never* been demonstrated in the adult human being other than in those who have been completely deprived of it in experimental laboratories. Any reasonable diet contains more than an adequate amount. And it is found in the highest concentrations in the various plant oils I have already recommended. Lecithin is a substance required in many ways by the body, but it is manufactured in adequate amounts by the liver. Its sale is also promoted by the same faddists. My advice on both is the same—and obvious.

Carbohydrate

Carbohydrates are called that because they contain a carbon atom combined with hydrogen and oxygen in the same ratio as water, hence *hydrate*. Carbohydrates come only from plants and are found inside the plant cells. Cellulose, the strong outside part of a plant cell, is simply a good source of fiber and bulk, helping us to avoid constipation and other problems. We cannot digest cellulose, unlike cattle and other ruminants, which have a series of stomachs containing bacteria capable of breaking it down.

Carbohydrates are usually grouped according to structure. The simplest is a single sugar or monosaccharide. There are many, among them glucose, galactose, and fructose. Glucose, also known as dextrose, is the most well-known. It is our main source of energy and is, in fact, the only source of energy utilized by the brain and central nervous system. It is easily extracted from any vegetable and can be manufactured in our bodies as well. In nature, it is found in sweet fruits, and it makes up half the sugar content in honey. The double sugars or disaccharides consist of two single sugars linked together. The most common, sucrose, we know as table sugar. The third type of carbohydrate is starch, which is made up of many sugars linked in chains. These vary in their length and complexity. Refined starches are shorter and resemble simple sugars in their action in the body. We store carbohydrate in a form similar to starch in our liver and muscles. This form is called glycogen.

Cereals and other grain products contain about 80 percent carbohydrate and 5 to 10 percent protein, with the rest consisting of fiber and other products. Tubers such as potatoes and legumes such as beans are somewhat higher in protein, averaging about 20 percent, with the remainder carbohydrate. These, the products consumed *as grown*, are our principle sources of complex carbohydrates.

Each gram of carbohydrate, when burned for energy, gives 4 calories. Depending upon one's size and amount of activity, about 100 grams of carbohydrate per day are recommended, but most Americans consume two to three times this much, so again we don't have to worry about deficiencies—only excesses. Just this excess is detrimental to our health, as we will see later in reference to obesity, but the type of carbohydrate we eat is much more so. Three-fourths of what we eat is refined, and most of this is sugar. In fact, sugar forms about one-fourth of our total daily caloric intake! So here is where we have to start in reducing our carbohydrate excess.

No one really knows why we have this desire for sweets. Man seems to regard meat and fruits as the tastiest of natural foods, and they actually are somewhat complementary nutritionally. At one time in our distant past, this desire may have helped us to survive, but now we are able to put just the sugar, not the whole fruit, into almost everything to increase palatability and saleability. This adds only "empty" calories, with no nutritional value.

Sugar in this isolated form has become widely used just in the last two hundred years or so. In 1850, for example, the total world production of sugar was 1.5 million tons, but by 1950 it was 70 million tons. Today the average American consumes about 125 pounds of sugar in a year, more than half of it in processed foods and beverages. This consumption continues to increase alarmingly.

The harmful effects of excess sugar on the body are many. It decays the teeth, precipitates diabetes, contributes greatly to obesity, and increases the blood level of triglycerides, one cause of atherosclerosis, among many other deleterious effects. Even if sugar in its visible form is avoided as much as possible, we will still be consuming it in excess, because it is in so many prepared products. Our bodies can derive all the energy we need from the complex carbohydrates in our diet and other sources. We simply don't need *any* sugar in our diet. One authority, Professor John

Yudkin, states, "If only a small fraction of what is already known about the effects of sugar were to be revealed in relation to any other material used as a food additive, the material would promptly be banned."

So the essential point has been made in regard to sugar: Excess is the problem again. The only faddism regarding it is the advocacy of brown sugar, raw sugar, or honey by some food faddists as a substitute, but the simplest knowledge of high school chemistry reveals that this makes no difference whatsoever.

Before leaving the subject of sugars, I should touch upon hypoglycemia. The role and regulation of glucose levels in our bodies is intricate and fascinating. When we eat complex carbohydrates, sensitive internal mechanisms maintain our blood glucose at a constant level for our energy requirements. But when we eat sugar or refined carbohydrates in large amounts the mechanisms can be overwhelmed. For example, if your breakfast consists of a danish, coffee, and a cigarette, your body is abnormally stimulated to produce insulin by all three. The excess insulin then lowers the blood glucose level shortly afterwards to below normal and may keep it there for an hour or two. Any nevous stress over that period of time just adds to the effect. Then another high-sugar snack at coffee break will raise blood glucose temporarily, but the problem is only compounded as the process repeats itself. And every time, the amount of sugar not burned immediately as energy is stored as fat. The long-term result of this pattern may be obesity, diabetes, and worse. The periods of low blood sugar sometimes cause symptoms such as weakness, trembling, and sluggish thinking, and this is hypoglycemia as most of us know it. A few rare forms are caused by certain endocrine abnormalities. They result in symptoms lasting longer—three or four hours—or cause fainting. If you have symptoms this severe, you should consult your physician. Otherwise, to avoid the usual type of hypoglycemia, have regular meals, *including breakfast*, as low as possible in sugar and high in good sources of protein and complex carbohydrate.

A word on coffee, because it is pertinent here, as one cause of hypoglycemia—and more. Most of us drink too much of it, along with other sources of caffeine, which is what does the harm. The average brewed cup of coffee contains about 80 milligrams of caffeine, a cup of instant about 60 milligrams, and decaffeinated about 3 milligrams. Some people are unaware that tea and cocoa have about 30 milligrams per cup, and cola drinks about the same per can. And chocolate in all forms is high in caffeine. As few as two or three cups a day of coffee (or an equivalent amount of caffeine) have been linked by some rather poor studies to heart attack, stroke, ulcers, and other diseases. But better studies have shown a clear-cut correlation of higher amounts with elevation of fat levels in the blood and other deleterious effects such as abnormal rhythms of the heart, some of which can cause sudden death. And we all know that the "lift" we expect from a cup of coffee begins to vanish if we drink more than two or three cups a day. Our central nervous system adjusts, so we then run the risks of high caffeine intake without even the benefit we seek from it.

But let's return to hypoglycemia itself. Many of us have this condition in a mild form at one time or another, and we represent a large market for the unscrupulous, some of whom have seized upon this for their own fame and fortune. Their peculiar point of view contends that those who are under stress and are there-fore tense or anxious are this way *because* of hypoglycemia. Then they offer to cure the anxiety by one nostrum or other—at a price, of course. But as we've seen, the truth is the reverse. Stress *causes* both the hypoglycemia and anxiety. Some even go further by victimizing those suffering from serious diseases who are under both physical and psychological stress and as a result may have hypoglycemia. They claim the disease itself is caused by the low blood sugar, then offer to "cure" the cancer or whatever with such nostrums. These people should be run out on a rail.

Besides sugar, the other major carbohydrate excess is refined starch in the form of white flour and products made from it. When whole grain is ground between stones in the old-fashioned way, the result is graham or whole wheat flour. All the original contents of the grain are still there. If it is milled in the modern way between steel rollers, the bran (outside husk) and the wheat germ (little kernel inside) are sorted out, and that yields un-bleached flour. This is then bleached to produce the white flour you find in the market. This was originally done because white flour could be kept longer without spoiling. Historically, there was also a certain status consciousness involved, because in the Old World it was more expensive—only peasants ate dark bread. We have far more effective and harmless methods today to keep bread fresh, and there is certainly no "status" in eating white bread. In fact it connotes ignorance, considering what is now known. Above all, we need the roughage that is lost in this modern process. And "enrichment" doesn't begin to replace the original vitamin content of whole grain flour. Of the twenty or so nutrients originally present in the grain, only some of the B-complex vitamins, Vitamin D, calcium, and iron salts are added. And even these "enrichment" standards exist in only thirty-five states, so use only whole grains and products made from them.

Though not strictly speaking a carbohydrate, alcohol is closely related and is something many of us in middle age tend to consume in excess also. Moderate consumption—up to two or three glasses of table wine *or* cans of beer *or* one-jigger drinks (all are roughly equivalent)—does no demonstrable harm. More than this has been shown to damage to our health in many ways. It is also a little known cause of hypoglycemia. Much more could be said on the subject, but space does not permit, and sources of information are readily available everywhere.

Vitamins

Excesses and faddism are one and the same with vitamins. So I should be able to list the vitamins, their functions, sources, the recommended daily allowances according to the RDA and conclude the discussion. But some believe that if a little is necessary, a whole lot must be just that much better. As a result, controversy, confusion, and even outright conflict reign in this area, and I have to go into greater detail.

A vitamin is an organic trace substance necessary to all animals for health and reproduction. The word *organic* is properly used to describe a chemical compound that contains carbon and usually comes from a living source, although many can now be synthesized. The term *inorganic* refers to all other chemical compounds. The usual function of a vitamin is as an enzyme or part of an enzyme, a complicated chemical that works as a tool or catalyst inside a cell without being completely consumed in the process. Vitamins were first designated by letter in order of their discovery, but later as their chemical natures became known and they were able to be synthesized in the laboratory, chemically descriptive names have become more correct, though not widely used by the average person. In some cases a vitamin has been found to be a group of chemicals, so retains its letter designation even in scientific circles.

The fat-soluble vitamins are A, D, E, and K, and it is in these that we find most of the harm from excesses.

Vitamin A occurs in several forms. Plants contain precursors such as carotenoids, while animal products have a mixture of both precursors and Vitamin A itself that has been manufactured by the animal. All of the functions of Vitamin A are not yet fully known, but they are widespread. This vitamin is best known for its function in maintaining normal vision in dim light. In this role, it is vital to the formation of a photosensitive chemical called rhodopsin (visual purple) in the retina of the eye. But it has nothing to do with visual acuity nor accommodation to near and far vision.

The recommended daily allowance of this vitamin for our fifty-year-old reference adult male whose weight is 154 pounds is 5,000 international units (or 1000 retinol equivalents), and for a female weighing 128 pounds, 4,000 international units (or 800 retinol equivalents). The average American diet will provide about twice this recommended allowance, which in itself is generous. But still some may wish to take supplements, for whatever reason. If this applies to you, bear in mind that toxicity results if 100,000 units a day or more are consumed by an adult over short periods, and with less than half that if taken over longer periods, so daily intake of over 25,000 IU or 7500 retinol equivalents from all sources should be avoided. If just carotenoids of plant origin are taken instead of Vitamin A, they are not toxic, but they will turn the skin orange. One of the most popular reasons for taking Vitamin A supplements now that enthusiasm for curing all eye problems has faded, is as a protectant against air pollution. Neither belief has any basis in fact.

Vitamin D consists of a group of ten chemically related sterol compounds, but it is customary to speak of the group as if it were one vitamin. Of the ten, only two are of nutritional interest. Vitamin D_2 is the chief precursor in plants, and Vitamin D_3 is the form occuring in animal cells, developing in the skin upon exposure to sunlight. The most important roles of Vitamin D are in regulating the absorption and excretion of calcium and phosphorous and in the calcification of bones and teeth.

Because adults are no longer growing, their need is nil in the diet. In fact, the average exposure to sunlight anywhere in this country usually supplies all the Vitamin D required, even to heal broken bones and maintain an adequate surplus in storage. But if you wish to take supplements, be cautious. This vitamin can be toxic in doses as low as 3,000 units (75 micrograms) per day in children, although usually 100,000 units (2500 micrograms) a day are required to produce serious toxicity in adults. Over long periods, because the vitamin is stored in the body, less than half this intake can produce toxic effects.

Vitamin E first came to fame when it was noted to be necessary for large litters in rats and was found to be related to premature graying of a strain of guinea pigs. These two facts, that the vitamin had something to do with manifestations of both sex and aging in animals, were the original reasons for the leap to assumptions about its role in humans and the excessive enthusiasm about this vitamin that has been seen ever since on the part of food faddists.

There are several compounds with Vitamin E activity. Alphatocopherol possesses the greatest, so the others are often measured in terms of this and expressed as milligrams of alphatocopherol. The older measurement still widely used is in international units (IUs).

As I noted in the chapter on aging, the only known function of Vitamin E is as an antioxidant, and it is not even required by the adult human body for that function. Nonetheless, the RDA suggests that adults have about 10 international units per day in the diet. But since Vitamin E is found in many oils and dark green leafy vegetables in the average diet, the usual adult intake easily exceeds this. Dr. L. Jean Bogert says, "The recommended level is very generous and should cover all contingencies. . . ." and adds, "The allowance may be set too high. . . ." As she is a world-wide recognized authority, perhaps I should add one more comment of hers: "There is no convincing evidence that Vitamin E deficiency in man causes reduced athletic performance, heart disease, weakened sex drive . . . or reduced longevity as is often claimed."

So there is more than enough Vitamin E in the average diet of the middle-aged adult, and again the only potential problem is that of excess. Because vitamins A and D are stored and gradually accumulated in the tissues, toxicity did not begin to be widely reported in the literature until some years after the period of their excessively enthusiastic use. This was when we were children. (Remember cod liver oil? Ugh.) We have been into the Vitamin E fad for only a little over ten years now, and so far only scattered reports have appeared in the literature on its toxicity. These have had to do mostly with impairing the utilization of estrogen in women and raising the level of serum cholesterol in both sexes. There have not been many well-documented studies yet, so we really don't know *enough* about its potential toxicity when taken in excess. We must wait until there is better information over the next few years before coming to definite conclusions. In the meantime, if you wish to take a supplement for some reason, it should not be over 100 international units daily for safety.

Among the many promoters of Vitamin E, perhaps the most famous—or infamous—is Dr. W. E. Shute. He claims to be a cardiologist and nutritionist when, in fact, he is neither. In his book, *Vitamin E for Ailing and Healthy Hearts,* he encouraged self-diagnosis of a wide range of ailments and recommended Vitamin E as a cure-all for them. You should know that studies have been carried out on Vitamin E at several prestigious medical centers throughout the world, and not one of his claims has ever been substantiated. In fact, studies that have deprived humans of Vitamin E have not even resulted in the symptomatology that can be demonstrated in laboratory animals! It is an established fact that no symptom attributable to Vitamin E deficiency has ever been demonstrated in the adult human being.

In 1935, Vitamin K was named by its Danish discoverer after its only known function in the human body. It is an ingredient in the formation of a vital blood coagulation factor and the Danish word for coagulation is spelled with a *k.* It is widely distributed in the foods we eat, and we also manufacture it in our bodies, so there is no recommended dietary allowance. Nor is there any known adverse reaction from excess. When the Vitamin E fad has faded, a Vitamin K fad might well take its place. By then more should be known about the effects of excess Vitamin K, so that the less prudent among us won't be guinea pigs as in the past with the other vitamins.

B-complex and C are the water-soluble vitamins. Because their functions are so extensive, I'll omit them here, but you can easily learn more about them from any book on nutrition. Excesses of the B-complex vitamins are not known to cause any harm, because they are rapidly eliminated in the urine. Deficiencies do not occur in the average American diet; they have been found only in those with extremely poor diets, in people with alcoholism or a few other diseases, and in those taking certain medications that interfere with B-complex utilization. Those who take supplements should realize that they must be balanced—taking one B vitamin alone will interfere with the functions of the others. Vegetarians, of course, should receive supplemental B-12 injections regularly. Avoid those substances wrongly labelled as B-complex vitamins by "health food" sources, such as "B-15" and "B-17." They can be hazardous to your health.

Of all vitamins, C is the most easily destroyed in food handling and preparation. It is easily oxidized if exposed to air, and this process is accelerated in the presence of light, heat, and baking soda. The recommended daily allowance (60 milligrams) is generous because 10 milligrams per day for the average adult is all that is necessary to prevent scurvy.

Some food faddists have made much of the fact that Vitamin C in milk is destroyed by pasteurization, but they have overlooked the simple fact that milk does not contain significant amounts of Vitamin C in the first place. Yet for this reason they urge consumption of unpasteurized milk. Some add the arguments that pasteurization lowers the B-complex vitamin content by about 10 percent and alters the taste slightly. These are both true. But in all of this promotion they have somehow lost sight of the fact that pasteurization protects against tuberculosis, undulant fever, staphylococcal and streptococcal infections, enteric fevers due to salmonella, and Q fever. One wonders at their motives. And these are just the diseases you can get from the cows—many more can be introduced by the equipment and handlers. And only these—not the cows—are regulated by the commissions "certifying" raw milk or allowing the designation "Grade A." The modern HTST method of pasteurization involves holding milk at 161°Fahrenheit for three to five seconds and protects you from all of these diseases. So don't risk drinking raw milk for an insignificant loss of Vitamin C and a 10 percent loss in B-complex. Just take another sip of pasteurized skim milk. This will more than make up the difference.

The highly promoted "health food" sources of Vitamin C are the West Indian cherry Acerola, the Peruvian jungle fruit Camu-Camu, and rose hips. If one were to take the daily requirement of Vitamin C as a supplement from such exotic sources as these, the size of the pill would range from that of a large marble to a golf ball, depending upon the origin and method of refinement. So most of the Vitamin C contained in supplements labeled in large letters with such exotic sources is synthetic out of necessity. One wonders why such supplements are so highly touted until one realizes that a day's supply in this form costs about fifty cents or more, pocketed by the promoters, while more than enough Vitamin C for a day is contained in a few cents' worth of citrus or other fruits. Similarly, the related bioflavinoid products are just another lucrative deception. The bioflavinoids have been thoroughly studied; there is no requirement for them in the body, nor have any of the beneficial effects claimed for them by "health food" faddists been substantiated. So save your money.

A simple rule to remember is that a large glass of orange juice contains almost twice the daily amount recommended. Huge dosages, as espoused by Linus Pauling to prevent or cure the common cold and cancer, have been shown in sound scientific studies to have no benefit on these or anything else. In fact, because the body has difficulty excreting more than a tenth of a gram per day, taking amounts in excess of this can produce all sorts of adverse effects. It upsets the stomach, causes diarrhea, leaches minerals from the body, counteracts the actions of the B vitamins, disrupts growing bone, produces a false positive urine test for sugar and blood in the stool, irritates the bladder, and causes kidney stones. Even rebound scurvy can occur when such high dosages are stopped. And claims of psychiatric and other benefits from megadoses of various vitamins by "orthomolecular" and other such faddists have absolutely no scientific support.

One last misconception about vitamins should be mentioned. That is the notion that natural vitamins and synthetic ones are somehow different. Rather than belabor the point, I'll quote Robert Shank, chairman of the Council on Foods and Nutrition: "It can be stated unequivocally that there is no difference, chemically or biologically, between the natural and synthetic vitamins."

Minerals

Minerals, inorganic substances necessary for our health and reproduction, can be grouped in two categories: those, like sodium, chloride, potassium, calcium, phosphorous and magnesium, that we need every day in amounts greater than 100 milligrams, and those we require in smaller or "trace" amounts. The first are often referred to as macrominerals, the second as microminerals.

Sodium and chloride occur together in nature as salt, which is made up of 40 percent sodium and 60 percent chloride. So we can discuss them together, although it is only the sodium we are concerned about, as we will see. Eons ago, our wiggly ancestors emerged from the ocean carrying their salt water environment inside their skins as they made their way on dry land. As salt was lost by several routes, its replacement was essential for survival. Some sort of instinct has carried over from that, because man ever since has been driven by the urge to search for and consume salt. In the past, when it was difficult to find, this strong instinct probably prevented us from perishing. Even in historical times, salt was so valued it was used as a medium of exchange and payment for labor. The word *salary* comes from the Latin word for salt. A person was either "worth his salt" or was not. Yet today this instinct to consume salt is working against us simply because it has become so cheap and easily available. The average American consumes fifty to seventy times more salt than the body needs. The solution is not as easy as avoiding the addition of it in cooking and at the table and shunning obviously salty foods. This much must be done, of course. But we will still be consuming an excess of twenty to thirty times what we need. Sodium is hidden in many substances, such as baking soda and monosodium glutamate. All convenience foods—frozen, canned, and baked—and restaurant meals have a large amount, because they sell better. If you have a water softener, the sodium content in your tap water is too high. Disodium phosphate is added to shorten the cooking time of cereals; sodium citrate is added to enhance the flavor of gelatin desserts and beverages; sodium propionate is widely used in cheeses, breads, and cakes to retard mold growth; sodium alginate is used to provide a smooth texture in chocolate milk and ice cream; and sodium sulfite is also in common use to prevent discoloration of dried foods. Even salt substitutes don't help. Those without sodium are too bitter to sell well, so most of those in the market contain as much as *half* table salt.

This sodium overload plays a major role in hypertension and thus in heart attack, stroke, and other cardiovascular disorders.

Many studies among people such as the Cuna Indians of Panama, the aborigines of Australia, and certain tribes in the mountains of China, who naturally have a low salt intake have found hypertension to be virtually nonexistent there. In contrast, countries where salt intake is very high, such as Japan and our own, have an alarming prevalence of hypertension. Authorities have recently produced evidence that if daily salt intake from birth is kept below 2 grams per day, high blood pressure will never develop even in those predisposed to it by hereditary factors. Of all the additives in our food, salt is clearly the most dangerous. So, as difficult as it is, we have to avoid it as much as we can in all the above sources—and we will still have more than enough for our needs. Remember, your food needn't taste blah—herbs and spices can work wonders.

Potassium is the principal mineral found within the body's cells. Because it is present in many foods, the potassium in a normal diet far exceeds what the body needs. Deficiencies occur only with certain diseases and medications. Toxic effects from excesses in the body are essentially unknown, unless supplements are taken for some reason or kidney disease is present, because normal kidneys excrete potassium easily.

Calcium is present throughout the body, with most of it concentrated in bones and teeth. Deficiencies do occur but can be easily documented by your physician—don't guess. Excess calcium intake can upset the sensitive and complicated mechanism controlling body levels of this mineral, so you should take supplements only on your physican's advice. A balanced diet, with one glass of skim milk and one serving of some other milk product per day, supplies plenty of calcium for the average adult.

Phosphorous combines with calcium to make the hard structure of the bones and teeth and plays other roles in the body as well. The recommended daily intake is the same as that for calcium, and the sources are similar. The same caution regarding excesses also applies.

Magnesium deficiencies do not occur in normal diets, but they are common in alcoholics and vegetarians. An excess in the body is nearly impossible because of limited absorption from the intestine, but can occur if large amounts are taken as supplements or in laxatives.

Of the microminerals, iron is by far the most important.

About 20 percent of the iron in our bodies is held in storage in such places as the liver, spleen, and bone marrow; the rest functions elsewhere. Most of this active portion is found in the hemoglobin or red pigment in the red blood cells, and the rest in myoglobin, a similar substance in the muscles. A small fraction is found in certain enzymes. Hemoglobin, of course, is the carrier of oxygen from the lungs to the tissues, and myoglobin stores oxygen for immediate use in the muscles.

We absorb iron from our intestines according to our bodies' needs by means of an intricate and delicate system. As men and postmenopausal women lose about 1 milligram per day in various ways, this same amount is normally absorbed from the intestine no matter how much is contained in the food. The average diet has about six times this. But women who are menstruating and child-bearing need all of this and may have to give some thought to iron sources in their diet. Vegetarians—not because of losses, but because of poor iron sources in such diet—will find it difficult to avoid iron deficiency. For them, and sometimes for young women, supplements may be prescribed. But iron supplements and "tonics" taken without medical advice can easily overwhelm the delicate system regulating the absorption of iron and cause serious—even fatal—complications. Here again, your physician can determine if you are iron-deficient easily and accurately. Don't guess.

Iodine is an essential ingredient in thyroid hormone. It is not found in adequate amounts in the soil and water of certain parts of the country, such as the Northwest and Great Lakes region. Prior to this century, when diets were limited to local crops and local water, thyroid deficiency and goiter (enlargement of the thyroid gland) were problems in those areas. But now that we consume foods and beverages from all parts of the country, iodine deficiency does not occur. Iodized salt played no role in this. Of course, such "health food" supplements as seaweed are completely unnecessary.

Fluoride is found in the drinking water in many parts of the country in the ideal proportion of one part per million, a concentration that not only reduces the development of dental caries by over 50 percent, but that also helps bone formation and the function of other tissues. Efforts to raise the amount in areas where it is deficient have encountered a puzzling opposition. As a result, only about half the water in the United States has the proper amount of fluoride. But it has been added to many toothpastes, and from these one can absorb enough to protect the teeth and for other essential functions in the body. In certain areas it is found in excess—well-known by the inhabitants, who solve the problem by using bottled water.

Other trace minerals required by the body are copper, manganese, zinc, molybdenum, selenium, chromium, cobalt, vanadium, nickel, tin, eadmium, and silicone. Current research is discovering about one new trace mineral every year or two. Each has had, or will have, its period of popularity as a supplement among food faddists. Selenium is the one that is now at its peak. Deficiencies of these minerals have never been demonstrated, because they are so widespread and abundant in food. Zinc is the one exception. It cannot be assimilated by the body from many plant sources, so a supplement should be taken by vegetarians. Toxicity from excesses is found only in those exposed in their occupation or otherwise to large amounts of some of these substances or in those who take "health food" supplements containing them.

Well, this has been a long discussion, but it was necessary in order to make my points on excesses and faddism. We have touched upon every excess in our diets except one, that of calories, and that deserves a section all its own, which follows this. In summary, we can easily get all the nutrients we need by eating a balanced diet from the four classic food groups. Everyone knows these and the proper proportions of each or can find out from many available sources. Reliable references are given in the Bibliography if you want to learn more about any details of a properly balanced diet or pursue any particular point that interests you.

Fads and Facts

We really should go into a few of the major dietary fads, because we in middle age are especially prone to pay attention to any panacea promoted to lessen the effects of the years upon us. They are offered to us from all sides, and it is often difficult to know what to believe.

First, some guidance on where you can obtain reliable information. Your physician is trained to focus his knowledge of nutrition along with other sciences on the improvement of your health. We are taught the basics about nutrition in medical school in courses on the subject and as part of other courses, acquire a little more in our internship, but the major knowledge that we have is acquired during our specialty residency as related to that specialty. For example, pediatricians are extremely knowledgable about formulas, vitamins, and other nutritional requirements during growth; orthopedists are competent concerning requirements for bone healing; and so on. But physicians who have not had specialty training usually are not well-grounded enough in nutrition to be considered authorities or write books on the subject. Internists have the broadest and deepest knowledge of any medical specialists, but the most we should attempt is a chapter such as this. Registered dieticians are trained to supervise the preparation of specialized diets in hospitals and other medical institutions under the direction of physicians and counsel patients in these diets. But as a rule, they shouldn't write books either. The most authoritative knowledge about nutrition comes from those with a Ph.D. degree who hold respected positions as professors of nutrition at major universities or medical schools doing research and teaching in this discipline. These are the authors you should search for and rely upon.

You will find it strangely difficult to obtain reliable literature. Only in larger libraries and bookstores are any good books to be found. Rarely will a reliable source be found in a small public library or bookstore and never in a "health food" store. So, anticipating the difficulties you may encounter, I have listed several in the Bibliography. You may have to order them through your library or bookstore, because the mass market seems to prefer easy fads to sound nutritional guidance. Always bear in mind that anyone can—and many who are completely incompetent do—call themselves "nutritionists."

Excellent pamphlets and brochures can be obtained from: Superintendent of Documents, The Government Printing Office, Washington D.C. 20402; The Committee on Nutrition, American Medical Association, 535 North Dearborn Avenue, Chicago, Illinois 60610; The American Dietetic Association, 430 North Michigan Avenue, Chicago, Illinois 60611; and The Nutrition Foundation, 888 17th Street, N.W., Washington,

D.C. 20006. This Foundation publishes an index available for $5.00 that contains over one thousand reliable references.

The best guide as to our nutritional needs is promulgated by the National Research Council, National Academy of Sciences. This is the booklet "recommended dietary allowances" (RDA) which is revised every few years. I have referred to the RDA for every nutrient discussed in this chapter. The most recent edition appeared in 1980, and is summarized in any good book on nutrition or can be obtained directly from the National Research Council at 2101 Constitution Avenue, Washington, D.C. 20418. In general, the allowances in the RDA are designed to offer a substantial margin of about one-fourth to one-third above average needs in order to allow for all conceivable variations in individuals and conditions.

For the purpose of labeling foods, the Food and Drug Administration has set up a different table of "minimum daily requirements" (MDR). Unfortunately, the levels of nutrients in this table differ from the RDA. The clue to the difference is to be found in the words *recommended* and *minimum*. The MDR is presently being phased out in favor of the RDA, which will eliminate confusion.

Now to a few of the fads we hear so much about. First, "organic" foods. There are no standards or definitions for the term *organic* as used by faddists, but there are three rather vague usages.

The first is to describe food which is grown with natural fertilizer instead of synthetic fertilizer. The position here is that because fertilizers are synthetic, they may not contain all the elements necessary to grow products with proper nutrition; therefore animal or human feces, as in ages past, should be added to the soil instead, with their attendant risk of parasitic and other diseases. This concept was introduced by Jerome Rodale, who, when asked why "organic" fertilizing was superior to chemical fertilizing, stated; "We feel that in organically grown food you have things you don't even know exist." That's the closest he ever came to clarifying his position. Rodale is another one of those "nutritionists" who had no training in nutrition. In fact, his only formal education consisted of accounting at night school. As you might expect, he had many other strange ideas, such as that people do not get enough electricity from the atmosphere and so should sit under a short-wave radio transmitter every day and that prostate problems could be prevented by eating pumpkin seeds.

Let's think this concept through together. First of all, we know that soils do vary in their content of minerals and other substances. Because of this, the crops that can be grown in any one type of soil will vary just as they will vary with other conditions required for their growth, such as sunlight, temperature, and water. This much is obvious. What is not as obvious to some is that the nutritional requirements of any one plant species are set down in a chemical code in its genes. For this reason, in any given soil, a particular plant either will grow well or will not. If it grows, is harvested, and appears in the market, then it has to contain all the nutrients that were required by its genetic code. If it does not grow, the farmer has two choices: Either he can add the required nutrients to the soil to make it grow or change his crop to one that will grow. *Either way, the plant product that reaches your market has all the nutrients that it should have.*

The origin of Rodale's idea might have come from confusion with a fact long known in agriculture and veterinary medicine. There are many, many types of grass, and almost always one or more can be found that will grow on soil that lacks certain substances. An animal grazing upon any one type of grass has *its* requirements laid down in its own genes. If the grass does not contain sufficient nutrients for that animal, it will not thrive. The farmer either has to add the missing substances to the soil and change the type of grass to one that supplies the required nutrients to the animal, or have the veterinarian prescribe the necessary nutrients as direct supplements to the animal. In either case again, the animal product in the market contains all the nutrients that it must have as laid down in its genetic code. We, of course, are not grazing animals relying upon one food source grown in one place for our diet. This is probably where the confusion came from—by analogy comparing us to grazing animals.

There is no need to rely upon the above reasoning, because the actual nutritional value of "organic" foods has been investigated by many experts. An editorial by L. A. Maynard in the *Journal of the American Medical Association* summarizes these many studies in one phrase: ". . . there is no basis for claiming significant nutritional superiority of such foods."

A second way the word *organic* is used is for those plant products that have not had any pesticides applied. This use does not stem from inaccurate analogy, as does the first—it is just deliberate deception. "Health food" stores often purchase products on the open market, then claim they were grown without pesticides. Some of their suppliers claim they have not used pesticides when in fact they have. The "health food" stores, of course, do not test for their presence on the food. Most "organic" food suppliers simply take advantage of the wide use of pesticides by farmers on either side of them and are able to grow a crop without the direct application of pesticides because of the surrounding protection against insects plus the carry-over onto their product by aerial spraying and drainage of irrigation. Whatever the method of deception employed, you can be sure you are *not* buying foods free of pesticides. When such products that sell in "health food" stores at much more than the price of the same product elsewhere are tested by reliable agencies and universities, they find that they almost always contain pesticides. The only way to be sure that plant products are grown free of pesticides is to *grow them yourself*, wipe off mold, trim leaves, and pick off pests by hand. This is obviously not possible commercially.

There seems to be almost a paranoia about the presence of pesticides on plant products, when it is so simple to be free of any worry by just washing them off. Of course, there should be restrictive regulation on the use of pesticides, and there is, by not only the Environmental Protection Agency and the Department of Agriculture, but by equivalent state agencies as well. We, as citizens and consumers, should continue to insist that we be protected. But we should have a balanced and reasonable attitude about pesticides. Careful use of these substances allows us to have much greater food production to keep us healthy at lower cost and to feed our own poor as well as the hungry of the world.

I can't leave the subject without mentioning one of the many ways we are protected—none of which you hear about—from those who promote and would sell you "organically grown" foods. The Food and Drug Administration does regular Market Basket studies in eighteen regions of the nation. Several times a year two weeks supply of food for an average family is bought, prepared for eating, and then analyzed for the fifty most commonly used pesticides. Levels usually run from a high of one-twentieth of the "allowable daily intake" (ADI) to a low of one-two hundredth. Whenever possible harmful levels are found, the appropriate corrective action is taken through the agencies mentioned in the preceding paragraph.

The third way that the term *organic* is used—or more frequently the term *natural*—is for food that has not had preservatives or other additives included during processing. Additives other than salt were first put into processed foods starting nearly a century ago in order to preserve them so that they could reach the market and the table unspoiled. Manufacturers over the years then began adding substances that enhanced the appearance, smoothness, taste, and color of their products. They often did this with more concern for profit than for those who consumed their products.

By the 1950s this practice was getting out of hand, so legislation was passed in 1958 to ensure the safety of food additives. A list of 674 substances was prepared, which has come to be called the GRAS list, for "generally regarded as safe." These were substances that had been used as additives for many years and that in the opinion of the scientific community were safe. Only these additives were then allowed. After the 1969 White House Conference on Food, Nutrition and Health, President Nixon ordered a complete testing and review of the GRAS list. Most of us are familiar with the few additives brought into question by this review: red No. 2 dye, the cyclamates, saccharin, and diethylstilbestrol. This testing is still going on, and any additives posing even a *theoretical* threat are removed from the GRAS list. Subsequent amendments to this legislation require that new additives be proven safe by extensive testing before a manufacturer may apply for permission to use them in a food product. So anyone preying on your concerns to sell you their "no additives" product now should be reminded that they are more than a decade out of date.

I'll conclude with the official position of the National Research Council: "The preponderance of data concerning food additives confirms that they have been used safely, effectively, and to the benefit of consumers. The occasional action taken to remove previously used additives, in light of new data that limit their margin of safety, confirmed the general effectiveness and stringency of the regulatory system. There is no evidence that consumption of foods in which those substances and regulated additives were properly used has endangered human health."

One important last point. As Professor E. H. Rynearson has stated, we now know more about the safety of food additives than we do about the more than 250 *naturally* occurring toxic substances in our food. And we know next to nothing about the effects of chemical pollutants in our irrigation and drinking water. The continuing concern of some of the more vocal elements of our society about food additives is only distracting research and regulation from areas in which it should be concentrated.

Some of those whom I've asked to read this section and offer their comments and criticism suggested that I discuss some of the leading figures in nutrition misinformation. This is a large order, as there are so many. It would take another book to do justice to this request—but it would be an interesting task.

The two asked about the most were Adelle Davis and Carlton Fredericks, so perhaps we could discuss just these two.

Adelle Davis's background consisted of a Master's degree in biochemistry with some training in dietetics. As I read her books, I became convinced of her sincerity, and her enthusiasm is certainly contagious. One can easily see why she was so popular—and still is. Perhaps something like 50 to 60 percent of what she advocates has been verified by research, another 20 to 30 percent is controversial, and only about 10 percent is frankly contrary to all scientific evidence.

In this latter small percentage are statements that range from the harmless to the dangerous. Some of the harmless are humorous, such as that fertile eggs are superior to infertile eggs or that a stool from a healthy person is odorless. Among the dangerous are her opposition to pasteurization, stating that drinking a quart of milk a day prevents cancer, and claiming that crib deaths can be prevented by breast feeding. This last statement could cause terrible guilt on the part of parents whose bottle-fed infants had died. There is absolutely no evidence to support this. Evidence indicates instead that an inherited defect in respiratory regulation by the central nervous system is the cause. The most dangerous statement I found is that patients with nephrosis should take potassium chloride, which could be fatal.

So overall, not much harm was done by her books—in fact, probably a great deal more good than harm. For this reason I was somewhat puzzled by the consistently adverse reaction reputable authorities have towards her. Therefore, I went once again into her books, conferred with some of those authorities, and may have found the answer. It's that her superficially scientific manner of presentation disturbs the truly scientific. In other words, she pretends to be what she is not—one of them. And this upsets them. A typical example can be found in *Let's Get Well*, in which she lists 2,402 references and claims that 95 percent of the references are articles by professors in medical schools, which is simply not true. The proportion is less than 10 percent.

There are many such minor examples I could give, but by far the most important one is her pattern of developing a particular topic. She starts her presentations with rather broad noncontroversial statements, for which she cites reputable authorities accurately. Then, as she develops her points, the references cited decrease in both quantity and quality. And as she approaches her conclusions, the references are either misquoted, completely irrelevant, contradictory, or she gives none. You realize at the end that these are just her personal opinions expressed in a way that superficially seems scientific. There would have been much less sound and fury if she had simply stated her beliefs without making any such attempt.

Carlton Fredericks is something else altogether. I first read his *Food Facts and Fallacies* and found the facts and fallacies to be so intertwined as to be indistinguishable. The "facts" themselves come from research that subsequently has been refuted, distortions of the conclusions of perfectly valid research, quotations from those who have done no research or those whose research findings never could be confirmed or accepted by reputable scientists, and findings lifted out of context from a report that came to a different conclusion. He then closes the gaps between these with his own opinions or by frequent attribution to such vague authorities as "other investigators" or "personal communications." So again we have a superficially scientific style that is, if anything, presented even more persuasively. The difference is that every one of his conclusions I read was wrong, and many were downright dangerous. I made an honest effort to read all of his other books but must confess that I could not finish any, because the same sort of thing was in all of them.

In reading these two authors, I was struck by the contrast between him and Adelle Davis. She sincerely had good health in mind, was enthusiastic about proposing her preconceived ideas, and her good intentions were clearly evident. With Carlton Fredericks, it seems to be quite the contrary. The theme throughout his writing is apparently an attempt to destroy all reputable authorities in the field of nutrition in order to exalt himself and thereby establish his own conclusions as the correct ones. He appears to be unconcerned as to what might happen to the reader as a result of this.

About this time I was made aware that he had a daily program on a Los Angeles radio station, KFAC, for a "health food" chain called Lindberg Nutrition Service. I listened carefully to thirty broadcasts at random, took notes, and went to the literature to either verify or refute his statements. I was stunned to find that not one of his statements of substance in any of the broadcasts was correct! And again, many were dangerous. This moved me to do a little investigation on him, after which I felt I should write a letter about my investigation to the director of programming of the station. The latter acknowledged my letter, but no action was taken and the broadcasts are still going on at this writing.

Some excerpts from the letter are:
- "Is it true that Carlton Fredericks graduated from the University of Alabama in 1931 under the name of Harold Fredericks Caplan, with a major in English and a minor in Political Science, without taking a single course on nutrition?"
- "Is it true that he received his M.A. degree in 1949 and Ph.D. degree in 1955, both in education, from the New York University School of Education, still without taking a single course in nutrition? Has he *ever* taken a course in nutrition anywhere? I could find no record of one. How, then, does he justify calling himself a nutritionist?"
- "Please explain his use of the title "Doctor" in giving health care advice without clarifying his background further. In my opinion, this is misleading—many people would assume him to be a Doctor of Medicine."
- "Why does he claim to hold a faculty position at Fairleigh Dickinson University when, in fact, he does not?"
- "What affiliation, if any, does he have with an institution of higher learning? I could find no evidence of any."
- "Please send a bibliography listing his published research in the field of nutrition. I am unable to find any with a computerized search."
- "Please look in to the action by the state of New York in April

1945, when he was found guilty of practicing medicine without a license. My information shows that he was sentenced to a $500 fine or three months in jail and chose to pay the fine. With this a matter of public record, why do you allow his broadcasts? He appears to be doing essentially the same thing on your station now."

- "Please also look into the several actions taken against him by the Federal Communications Commission and the Food and Drug Administration. These should concern you—they appear to be directly applicable to his present program on your station."

- "Please obtain comments from authorities in the field of nutrition in regard to any of his statements on your broadcasts. I think you should if your station is to have any integrity or credibility in its programming."

- "I would like to know what evidence he has to justify his statements that vitamin therapy and diet can prevent or cure such diseases as cancer, multiple sclerosis, leukoplakia, club foot, epilepsy, stroke, arthritis, rheumatic fever, and polio."

There was much more to my letter, but this should give you an idea.

This one example emphasizes that you should be cautious when you see the word *doctor* on the cover of food fad books or hear it on the air. As the public has become more sophisticated and skeptical, publishers now want the books to be written by some sort of doctor so that the word can be used in the title and the rest of it go something like *Doctor So-and-so's Magic New Umpty Diddle Diet*. When the "doctor" title is looked into, he is most often a chiropractor or osteopath, never a qualified nutritionist and only rarely a Doctor of Medicine. If he *is* a physician, he is most likely to be a general practitioner. As I mentioned before, an M.D. without specialty training including nutrition as related to that specialty should not be writing such books. There is one such who once told us all we wanted to know about sex, claiming to be a psychiatrist, and was ridiculed by authorities on the subject. He is now writing books on nutrition only to be ridiculed by authorities on *that* subject. He is not listed in the *Directory of Medical Specialists* or any other reference I consulted as either a psychiatrist *or* nutritionist. Avoid this sort of author.

Although I could go on about food fads, I must stop here. With reliable information available to all for the searching, the only way to explain the existence of such fads is to take into account the one element they all have in common: Those who promulgate them are attempting to sell something, whether a pill, powder, book, or even ordinary food products at higher prices, by misleading the public. Even if we don't have the time or inclination to look up the facts, we now know one rule of thumb: What is wrong with our diets is that we eat too much of certain things, and we even know what they are. If our diet is adequate according to authoritative standards, there is no evidence that taking more of anything, unless our physician advises us to, will benefit us. We should just eat less of the things that harm our health. Note one theme: No food faddists recommend reductions, or if they do, it is only because they are selling a substitute.

Those of us who have reached middle age are naturally concerned about our health and may be more vulnerable to such manipulations of the truth for profit than others. We have the right to be informed so we can make intelligent decisions of our own. I hope the discussion in this section has helped toward that end.

WATCHING YOUR WEIGHT

The standard statistic that over 60 percent of American adults are overweight has been substantiated by many studies. We may not like to admit it, but among middle-agers, the figure is even higher—approaching 90 percent! Younger adults have had less time to become overweight, and the heavier have already started to die off before they reach their later years.

Given this astonishingly high figure, our first thought is that there must be something wrong with the definition used—or with the studies themselves. Strictly speaking, the term *obesity* means more than 20 percent over one's desirable weight. The gentler term, *overweight*, is used for those who are over their desirable weight by 10 to 20 percent. These definitions both rest on the word *desirable*, so this word is the key, and how it came to be used is an interesting story.

The first height-weight tables were prepared during the early part of this century. These were simply averages of those who had been examined for life insurance by many companies. The Metropolitan Life Insurance Company was the first to realize by the 1940s that any increase in weight once an individual had reached his adult height adversely affected his survival. As a result, the earlier height-weight tables, which implied that such a gain with age was normal, were discarded and new tables made up. Age did not even appear in the new tables. Frame size (small, medium, and large) was introduced, but strangely, no clear-cut definition of frame size was decided upon or described.

In 1959, the tables were improved further when the Society of Actuaries, using data obtained from twenty-six U.S. and Canadian life insurance companies on several million policy holders, analyzed mortality in this population over a twenty-year period in relationship to body build, height, and weight. There are the tables you will usually find in your doctor's office. The major improvement made then was that instead of just providing averages, with most of the population being overweight, they state your desirable weight *in terms of your survival*. This is the origin of the term. It does not mean you will be more desirable yourself. In fact a person at his or her desirable weight will look a little too thin to most of us.

Unfortunately, the vague concept of frame size was still retained. Most overweight people, when they discover this, suddenly develop "large bones." This problem wouldn't be difficult to solve, actually. Radiologists, forensic pathologists, and others have assembled data allowing an accurate estimation of frame size from any one of a number of bone measurements, so accurate grouping into small, medium, and large would be both possible and useful. In my practice, I used calipers at the widest point of the wrist, and from this could get a fairly accurate idea of the frame size of my patients.

The worst aspect of these tables is that muscle mass is not dealt with at all. So a muscular football tackle with very little actual body fat would automatically be labeled obese. There are some other bothersome features—heights are given with shoes on, assuming a standard 1-inch heel height for men and 2 inches for women, and weights are in "indoor clothing." This makes little sense in view of changes in clothing styles. Tables *are* available giving desirable nude heights and weights, but they are not used much except in the privacy of one's own home.

So the best method for your physician to use is the measurement of doublefold skin thicknesses at certain specified places on your body, using specially designed calipers. When this is done, prepared tables give the percent of body fat with remarkable accuracy. For men, the proportion of body weight that is fat should not exceed 15 percent; for women, 18 percent. These are outside limits—the most desirable percentages have not been worked out, but are probably about half of these.

Many other methods are used, but mostly in research. These involve calculations based on radioactive potassium, soft tissue X-rays, and densimetry, in which a person is completely submerged in water. Formulas or computers are used to arrive at the percentage of body fat with all these methods.

There are two simple ways you can get a rough idea if you are overweight without any equipment at all. The first is to recall your weight when you reached your present height and frame size, usually about sixteen to eighteen years of age. If you were satisfied with your appearance then, and are not over that weight now, then you are probably about right. Fat slowly replaces muscle tissue as the years go on, so that you should be about 5 pounds below that at age forty, and about 10 pounds below that at age sixty. Another simple way is the pinch test. Pinch a skinfold at the side of your chest toward the bottom of your rib cage. One-fourth inch thickness means approximately 5 to 10 pounds of excess fat; one-half inch, 10 to 20 pounds, and so on. If you try these two methods right now, you might be surprised to find you are overweight. The most *desirable* weights in terms of survival are much lower than most people think. An even simpler way is to look at yourself nude in the mirror—it seldom lies.

Through most of recorded history, it was actually "desirable" to be overweight. In those days little was known about the various diseases that ravaged the people, only that emaciation often preceded death. It seemed logical to assume that if one stayed fat, one would also stay healthy. There was also a certain class consciousness involved—only the upper class could afford enough food to be fat. We have come a long way and learned a great deal since then. On the latter point, current studies show that obesity is six times more common among those of *low* social status, and it is twice as frequent in those who are downwardly mobile as in those who are upwardly mobile.

Let's rapidly review what else we have learned. Psychological studies have found that the person who is overweight tends to have a poor self-image and that this affects every aspect of his life adversely. The obese truly ricochet from gloom to gluttony and back again.

Sociological studies have documented what everyone already knows—the opinion of others is usually negative. The obese are unattractive to the opposite sex, and employment and promotion discrimination against the obese is an established fact.

There are some other things we know without being told. For example, the difficulty that the overweight person has in exertion, the fatigue he feels from carrying his excess weight around, and the impossibility of wearing attractive clothing. And what about embarrassment in everyday situations such as walking through crowded corridors, getting to theater seats, and sitting with others in a car? A layer of fat is better insulation than a wool blanket or a quilt, so in warm weather those who are overweight are troubled by increased discomfort and embarrassing perspiration.

But most important of all is health. We have learned a lot in this area. The diseases associated with excess weight are many: angina, hypertension, congestive heart failure, heart attacks, strokes, intermittent claudication, thromboembolic phenomena, rupture of intervertebral discs, osteoarthritis, varicose veins, gallstones, cirrhosis of the liver, diabetes, and various back, hip, knee, and foot disorders. Those who are overweight also have an increased susceptibility to all sorts of accidents and a sharply increased risk of complications and fatality in surgical operations.

More grim statistics show obesity linked closely with various causes of death. The data of the Metropolitan Life Insurance Company are instructive in this regard. They show that cardiovascular-renal diseases are increased by 49 percent in men and 77 percent in women; death due to accidents, 131 percent and 193 percent respectively; diabetes 383 percent and 372 percent; cirrhosis of the liver, 249 percent and 147 percent; and the list goes on. *In fact there is an increased association of obesity with all causes of death except tuberculosis and suicide.* What about the bottom line, the effect of excess weight on overall mortality? Data from the same source give a figure that is easy to remember. For a person aged forty-five who is 10 pounds over his or her desirable weight, danger of death is increased by 8 percent; if 20 pounds over, it is increased 18 percent; 30 pounds overweight, 28 percent; and at 50 pounds, 56 percent. It comes out to about 1 percent per pound.

To sum it up, obesity is the single most common preventable factor associated with excess mortality and morbidity in middle age. To put it even more briefly, the longer the belt line, the shorter the life line.

The two points have been made, I think, that excess weight is mostly a problem of the middle-aged and that it is bad for us. Then how do we get that way?

We become overweight for several reasons. Our basal metabolic rate (that is, the rate at which we burn energy while we are at rest) declines with age about 2 percent per decade after age twenty. Our random activity also becomes less and our movements more purposive with the years, thereby using fewer calories. We are also more able to afford not only a greater quantity but also more appealing and more fattening food. And by this time in life, many of us are more comfortable with our environment—we have learned to cope better with stress—and therefore have less muscle tension, resulting in less energy burned. But the most important factor of all is that we exercise less.

What can we do about it? We can control the calories we consume and those we expend as energy. That sounds so simple and yet can be so difficult. We have all heard dismal statistics on successful reducing and maintaining desirable body weight. There is no need to review them here. Don't they indicate the task is almost impossible? Not at all. Let's take a closer look at them.

Most of the published statistics come from medical centers or clinics that specialize in the treatment of obesity. Patients have been referred there by their own physicians because they have already failed to lose weight under *his* care. And which ones went to their physicians in the first place? The ones who failed to reduce on their own. So these statistics really deal with those who are at the end of the line. In my own practice, approximately 90 percent of my middle-aged patients were successful in achieving and maintaining their desirable weight. There was no magic about this. I merely stressed two elements that I'm going to describe in detail and combined these with continuing concern.

First of all, we must know something about the factors that control our appetite. We have long known that there were such natural factors by observing animals. With unlimited available food, wild animals match their intake closely to their energy expenditure and do not become fat. Long ago, however, the farmer found that if he penned in animals, the natural mechanisms seemed to go awry, and he could then fatten them for market.

There are three main physiological mechanisms that control appetite. The primary one is the appestat or "satiety center." This is located in the ventromedial area of the hypothalamus in the brain and limits our desire for food. Another area near it increases our appetite and is called the "feeding center." Connections between the satiety and feeding centers have been demonstrated and a delicate balance exists between them. They both respond to the level of glucose in the blood in the presence of insulin. So this mechanism acts to keep our blood glucose within a narrow range.

A second mechanism has been shown to operate independently of blood glucose and insulin levels. Animals allowed to be active reduce their weight over a period of several days to normal when they have been made overweight artifically, and increase their weight to normal over a similar period of time when they have been starved. There is no clear answer yet as to how this works, but a possible answer has been found in recent work suggesting that each fat cell may produce a hormone or similar substance when it is low in fat and stop producing the "signal" substance when it is full. The actual *number* of fat cells in obese animals and humans is often much greater than in those of normal weight. This number is determined early in life—especially during infancy and the years just preceding puberty—depending upon whether the animal or person was overfed or underfed in those years. The number thereafter remains constant throughout life, but the cells vary in fat content as the person becomes fatter or thinner. In humans, those who are obese from childhood have up to 100 billion fat cells, while the normal number is about one-fourth of this. So if there is such a substance, it would be especially significant to those who have been overweight since early life—but almost as important for all of us.

It should be possible to determine whether such a substance exists by using parabiotic rats in the laboratory, but I could find nothing in the literature indicating this method had been tried. Such rats are surgically connected to have a common blood supply—like Siamese twins. One rat, overfed in its early life and thus with a large number of fat cells, could be connected to another rat that was underfed during his early life, having a smaller number. If there *is* a "signal" substance liberated from fat cells, more would be produced by the obese animal on reduced rations and would pass into the bloodstream of the thin animal. If the appetite of the latter should increase, this would at least establish the existence of such a substance. Then it could be isolated, identified, and its mode of action delineated. Then perhaps some way could be developed to counteract it. Research should be intensified in this area. For now, the possible existence of such a substance only means that those who have been overweight since childhood will have a more difficult time controlling their weight.

The third physiological mechanism of appetite control is the "full-stomach" one. It was first discovered by blowing up balloons in the stomach of animals, decreasing their appetite somewhat. Then the same device was found to work in humans. Two interesting observations emerged from this work. First, inert bulk itself worked to a limited degree, but appetite was more effectively suppressed when food was used. It was discovered that hormones are released from the stomach and intestinal wall by the presence of food but not by bulk; these then inhibit the appetite by means that have not been completely clarified, although some reasonable theories have been brought forth.

The second observation is of much more interest to us. Albert Stunkard in 1964 discovered that when balloons were inserted in obese individuals, contractions of the stomach characteristic of hunger or satiety *showed little correspondence with the individual's sensation of hunger or lack of it*. There was, however, fairly accurate correspondence of the stomach contractions with subjective hunger or satiety in subjects of normal weight. This was the first clue that obese persons are less sensitive to their inner environment than normal persons. This work has been extended to include other internal cues, such as blood glucose and fat levels, gastric acid, amount of food in the stomach, and so forth, and the same insensitivity to some of these has been reported. More recent research has demonstrated that *the obese are in turn much more responsive to external cues to eat* than persons of normal weight. This insight has opened up a whole new avenue to appetite and weight control.

The three basic physiological mechanisms were first found in animals, then shown to exist in humans as well. But it has long been known that in man the psychological factors could over-power the physiological mechanisms, yet classic psychotherapy has failed to help. The psychological factors are simply not well enough understood to make any of the usual treatment methods effective. Yet here, by a simple observation on internal versus external cues, the most effective way known at present to control appetite in man was found. I'll tell you more about it in a moment. It resembles the behavioral approach in psychology—changes in behavior can be brought about even though all the underlying psychological mechanisms are not understood. Let me review a few of the experiments on this for you. I think you'll find them interesting.

One investigator gave what was called a "taste test" to obese and normal humans just after they had consumed a large meal. In this test, subjects were just asked to list their preferences among various crackers. But during the test, those who were obese consumed many more crackers than did those of normal weight. Here the cue—the *presence* of food—was visual and external and led to excess eating by the obese, despite internal satiety in both groups.

Another study offered a dull diet, unlimited in quantity, to both obese and normal subjects confined in a laboratory. The obese invariably reduced their intake and lost weight, but those of normal weight maintained their intake and their weight with remarkable accuracy in tune with their internal cues. When returned to a more interesting diet, the obese promptly regained their lost weight and more, but the normals did not. The cue was again external, the *attractiveness* of the food.

To test the effect of another external cue, threat, Stanley Schachter strapped obese and normal subjects to a horrendous-looking machine and told the subjects that they would receive painful electric shocks at unexpected times. They were left alone with food, but no shocks were actually forthcoming. The obese devoured three times as much food as did the normal controls.

Schachter also devised an ingenious experiment to test the effect of still another external cue. He adjusted a clock so it could run either too slow or too fast. Obese and normal subjects were called into the laboratory an hour or two before their regular meal time and left with a nondescript task to do and food immediately at hand. When the speeded-up clock showed that it was the obese subjects' usual meal time, even though it was not, they began to eat. The normal controls tended to ignore the clock and began to eat at approximately their regular time. But when the clock was adjusted to run slow, the obese tended to wait until the clock showed their usual meal time. The normal controls, again responding more accurately to their internal cues, invariably began to eat closer to their customary meal time.

In another study, subjects were asked to do a task with a bowl of nuts close at hand. When these nuts were brightly lit, the obese consumed much more than the normals, but when they were dimly lit they ate even less than did those of normal weight. There are now many studies such as these in the literature, and you can even do some of your own. For example, watch the dietary habits of the obese struggling to control their weight. They will eat fewer meals, but far more once they do eat, and therefore a greater daily total amount. They cannot resist the cue of the food set before them. Another is to follow those who go to "fat farms," where they are surrounded by positive cues of all kinds. Most lose weight while there, but regain it soon after they return to their usual environment.

In addition to experiments showing the greater effect of external cues on the obese, others have consistently shown that the obese are less willing to put forth effort to obtain food than persons of normal weight. A simple one showed that the obese tended to devour shelled nuts but hardly touched those that were unshelled. One of the most unusual consisted of observing patrons in a Chinese restaurant. There only 4.7 percent of the obese ate with chopsticks, while 22.4 percent of the normal-weight individuals did so. Most of these studies had to do with more ordinary obstacles, such as distance to food, difficulty in opening containers, and trouble in preparing it.

Such experiments as these have led to the most promising method yet for weight reduction and maintenance—behavior modification. The first reports using this method appeared in the literature during the 1960s, but such reports have begun to gain wide recognition only in the last few years. If you want to find out more about it, some good references are listed in the Bibliography. One of the best is *Habits, Not Diets* by Dr. James Ferguson.

There are three approaches under the heading of behavior modification in weight reduction. The first uses aversion. Here, food thoughts or food stimuli are paired with aversive odors or thoughts or other unpleasant stimuli. This works well for some individuals with certain specific foods, such as chocolate in "chocoholics." It results in a small weight loss for them, but it is ineffective for most people.

The second approach consists of operant reinforcement-punishment methods. Here positive reinforcement through rewards or negative reinforcement through deprivations or punishments have been tried, but the results again have been disappointing, being transient at best.

The third is an eclectic group of techniques that teach people how to achieve control of their eating by understanding and manipulating the antecedent and consequent conditions of their eating. This approach is by far the most successful, but it must be tailored precisely to each person. And it takes some time with strong support until the new habits are formed.

Let's see how this method works. I can at least sketch the general outlines for you. First, for two or three weeks, you keep an absolutely meticulous diary of all that you eat or drink, and look up the caloric value of each. This is standard in any good weight reduction program. Behavior modification therapy requires that you also write down the time, place, circumstances, and your emotional state whenever you eat, *before* you actually eat.

The first effect of keeping your diary is the gradual acquisition of calorie consciousness, which is absolutely essential. A calorie is, after all, just a unit of energy. In the physics laboratory, it is the amount of heat required to raise 1 milliliter of water 1 degree Centigrade (Celsius). The calories we are concerned with are 1,000 of these, more correctly called "kilocalories" or abbreviated "K-cals" or even capitalized as *Calories*.

Based upon your diary, the usual dietary advice will first be given you by your physician, with the total calorie content per day that is appropriate in your case. It will be calculated so that you will lose about 2 pounds a week. For carbohydrates, vegetables high in fiber content and water will be stressed; for protein, sources low in fat will be emphasized. You will remember that fat contains more than twice the calories of carbohydrate and protein, so fat will be discouraged as much as possible. Your physician will ensure that your diet is nutritionally adequate. Vitamins or other supplements are not usually necessary, but may be prescribed at his discretion. Alcohol has to be eliminated entirely, for three reasons. It provides 10 to 20 percent of the daily calories of the average affluent American, and it has two other effects besides its calorie content of 7 calories per gram. Taken before dinner, it increases appetite substantially by increasing gastric acid secretion and contractions, and during the meal it renders your judgment and self-control less effective just at the time you need it most. Emphasis will be placed upon dividing your total caloric intake among several small meals throughout the day, *starting with breakfast*. In fact, the best results in weight reduction are obtained when *seven* small meals are consumed. The worst time to eat is within two or three hours of going to bed. Then much less is burned for energy and more is deposited as fat.

After your physician gives you this routine advice, behavior modification comes in. Continue your diary. Together you will search for the external cues that prompt you to eat. If you snack while watching TV, then turn it off and substitute something else you like to do. In fact, try *never* to eat while you are doing something else. If bedtime is a cue for a snack, have a luxurious bath instead. If you tend to eat when tense or upset, then go for a brisk walk and enjoy the fresh air and sunshine. Learn to recognize the cues that give you the urge to eat and indulge yourself in some other enjoyable activity instead. This is the basis of the whole program.

One of the most important external cues is the sight or odor of food. Keep food out of sight and smell as much as possible. Don't even have high calorie snack foods in the house. Use opaque containers or aluminum foil for leftovers. Store the most fattening foods at the back of the refrigerator. Keep all containers that even suggest food to you, such as cookie jars, completely out of sight—or fill them with notes suggesting things you could do instead of eating cookies!

Establish your own cues for eating. Have a regular ritual for meals and try to select foods that require some effort to prepare. Have a definite time and place, with a full place setting, and always sit down. Above all, *never skip meals*—you will tend to eat more than you should at the next one. Your plate should be small, such as a salad plate, to give the illusion of a more bountiful meal, and the servings should be sliced thin and spread out so as to cover the plate as completely as possible. Enjoy each bite and make the entire meal last as long as you can. Always leave something on your plate. This cancels a very old cue that most of us in middle age have from the depression years of our childhood, "the clean plate" your mother insisted upon. If you don't want to waste food, save part of it for a snack. There is much more to the behavior modification method, but this will give you some idea. Notice that it is added to the usual dietary advice—it does not take the place of other sound principles. But it must be tailored precisely for you by your physician. General guidelines such as the Weight Watchers "Personal Action Plan" have not proved to be nearly as effective. Such groups, incidentally, do offer support at the start, which may be helpful for some in attaining short-range goals. But there is no evidence that they are beneficial in the long run. Eventually, the job of watching your weight is yours alone.

Earlier in this chapter I said that there are two essential parts of a successful weight maintenance program. So far we have just discussed one, the diet, with emphasis upon behavior modification in helping you with this.

The second element is exercise. When we were younger, we could control our weight rather easily by diet alone, but most of us in middle age cannot unless our diet is so restricted as to be almost unbearable.

The importance of exercise in weight reduction and maintenance cannot be overemphasized. One eminent authority, Dr. L. Jean Bogert, states unequivocally, "Of the two factors—food and exercise—exercise is the more important." Another, Dr. Jean Mayer, comments, "I am convinced that inactivity is the most important factor explaining the frequency of 'creeping' overweight in modern society. Our body's regulation of food intake was just not designed for the highly mechanized sedentary conditions of life."

For your interest, here are a few of the studies proving this. One researcher attached pedometers to housewives to measure the number of miles they walked during their usual activities. The results were astounding. The thin ones walked 35 miles in a week and the obese only 14. That's a difference of over a pound every week! In another, motion pictures were made of children at camp without their knowledge and later analyzed. The overweight children were shown to be in motion only a fraction of the time that those of normal weight were. One investigator invented a device that measured the time a person was on his feet during the day. He observed that those who were obese spent substantially less time out of bed, and while out of bed, 17 percent less time on their feet. And probably the most important of all, these studies found that the overweight invariably overestimated the amount of their physical activity, whether in daily tasks or an exercise program.

Such studies as these abound in the literature and are the major explanation for statements such as "Everything I eat turns to fat" or "I don't see how he gets away with it—he eats like a horse." There is no witchcraft here. It is simply the first law of thermodynamics. Every calorie consumed must be expended as energy or stored as fat.

But you often hear that exercise increases your appetite. It does, but it must consist of an hour or more of vigorous activity to begin to do so. From that point on, the body matches an increase in appetite with amazing precision to the energy expended during the exercise. It is the first hour that is interesting. As one goes from being completely sedentary, vigorous exercise for the first 15 minutes has little effect, but *exercise for more than 15 minutes will actually depress the appetite.* This effect is most pronounced when one exercises from 30 to 45 minutes then begins to lessen, and has no discernible effect upon appetite up to about one hour. Only vigorous exercise of *more* than an hour increases the appetite. Most of us in this modern world live somewhere in the first 15-minute zone and are so sedentary that this natural effect of exercise just does not operate. It is in this same sedentary zone that the farmer keeps his geese and cattle when he wants to fatten them. So the first benefit of any exercise program is achieved if you plan it to be vigorous and last 30 to 45 minutes each session. Its appetite-depressing effect is the greatest for about two hours after the exercise, then slowly tapers, so you might want to arrange your exercise just before the time you are most likely to nibble or have your largest meal.

Now, as to the calories actually burned by exercise, you have all heard discouraging stories. It *does* take a lot of exercise—3,500 calories worth—to lose a pound of fat. But many factors other than its appetite-depressing effect are overlooked in discouraging exercise for weight loss. One of them is that physical activity tends to decrease transit time in your intestines, so slightly less of the food you have eaten is absorbed by the body. Another point usually ignored is the reduction of tension you experience after exercising. You are more calm, less anxious and depressed, and therefore less likely to nibble. Still another is that the actual time required to exercise means less time that you can be tempted to go to the refrigerator. One other fact is that your metabolic rate is elevated by exercise and this elevation persists *up to six hours* after the exercise, burning up extra calories all this time. The most important factor you rarely hear about is the following. Whenever you reduce on any of the standard diets but continue your usual activity, the weight you lose is approximately half fat and half protein—mostly muscle, but some is from internal organs. If you diet *and* exercise, eighty to ninety percent of the weight you lose is fat. Little if any muscle is lost. Since this is the main tissue that burns calories, diet alone deprives you of just what you need to maintain your new lower weight. This is one reason, and often the major one, why you almost inevitably begin to gain weight again after being on a diet without exercising.

If you are still skeptical about the effect of exercise, look at any table of dietary allowances. They state that a completely sedentary man should eat about 1,200 calories a day; a normally active man about 2,400 calories; a very active man, 4,500 calories; and athletes up to perhaps 6,000 calories a day. To what are these astounding differences due? Exercise alone.

Your physician should prescribe a program for you much along the lines indicated in the section on exercise in this book. That is, the exercise has to be aerobic in nature. Calisthenics are almost useless for this purpose. When you "huff and puff," the amount of air going in and out of your lungs is directly proportional to the fat you are burning up as fuel, allowing for some variation in your physical condition. If you aren't breathing hard, you really aren't doing much good as far as weight control is concerned.

When you are tempted to try something easier, like one of those "wiggle machines," recall a quote from Morton Glen, former president of the American College of Nutrition: "These machines have no value whatsoever in weight loss . . . what they do basically is jiggle fat, and jiggling fat does not take off weight." I couldn't put it better. And remember, a sauna or Jacuzzi may make you feel wonderful, but the only weight you have lost is water. It comes right back in the next twenty-four hours or so.

Outside of your regular exercise program, you should have some idea in mind of caloric expenditures at various activities you do through the day. Rather than present a long and complicated list, I can group them simply:

- *Sedentary Activities:* These consist of seated activities involving writing, reading, watching television, etc., and average about 100 calories per hour.
- *Light Activities:* These involve slow walking and such household activities as dusting, washing dishes, and average office work. These burn about 150 calories per hour.
- *Moderate Activities:* Here you will be walking at a more brisk pace, scrubbing, sweeping, playing golf, bowling, or gardening, and these activities consume approximately 200 calories per hour.
- *Vigorous Activities:* These are rare both around the home and at work and usually involve the various athletic activities in your exercise program. Walking rapidly can be worth 300 calories per hour, and the most strenuous activities can go up in brief spurts to as high as 1,000 calories per hour.

The foregoing is all you have to know to get started on your own weight control program. If you'll pardon the pun, why weight?

A brief mention should be made of the "glandular conditions" reputed to cause obesity. This idea first arose from an article in 1901 describing a tumor of the pituitary gland in a patient who was grossly obese. Actually, the tumor had invaded and destroyed his satiety center. There was nothing "glandular" about it. The idea continued on the strength of the findings of low basal metabolic rates in the obese, implying a low thyroid gland function. The problem is that fat is not metabolically active to any appreciable degree, yet the method of calculating the BMR then was based upon skin surface, which was greater in the obese, hence the error. Thyroid deficiency does cause a slight weight gain by the accumulation of a substance called myxedema, not fat. It also causes a lowered basal metabolic rate, so that fewer calories are consumed while the person is at rest. But each calorie eaten must be burned or stored with those who have thyroid deficiency, just as with the rest of us. An association between diabetes and obesity kept the "glandular" myth alive for a bit longer. But the obesity was found to precipitate the diabetes, not the reverse. Another endocrine condition, Cushing's syndrome, was blamed for a while until it was learned that the fat from the hips and thighs was merely redistributed around the face and shoulders where it was more obvious. The total amount was not increased at all, unless more food was eaten because of the increased stomach acidity often found in this syndrome.

There is no "glandular" condition that causes obesity, period.

Fads and Facts

As in the chapter on nutrition, I cannot leave the subject of weight control without a caution against the misinformation that we encounter everywhere. Here, too, it is curious that reputable sources of information are so scarce. A selection of the best I could find is given in the Bibliography.

I suppose we should begin with the most popular fad weight loss book of the 1960s, *Calories Don't Count*. This has been refuted by all reputable authorities as nutrition nonsense. It has also been found in the courts to be "false and misleading," and the FDA has had it banned from the bookstores, so we do not need to concern ourselves with this. Calories *do* count.

Later in the 1960s, the canned liquid diet enjoyed popularity, mostly because of its convenience. There was no calorie counting —one just opened a can or added a powder to skim milk and that was it. But there were several problems with these diets. First, they lacked satiety value. About an hour or two afterward, one was hungry again. The second problem was that there was no increase in a person's knowledge of nutrition nor consequent change in his basic eating patterns, so the weight lost was always regained. Third, the diet was monotonous, and consequently people rarely lasted more than a few days on it. Fourth, because of the lack of bulk, such a diet was constipating. Still, these are not serious problems, so there can be no objection to the occasional use of such a formula to replace a single meal.

The prolonged total fast was investigated in several medical centers at about the same time. It was limited to grossly obese individuals who were hospitalized, observed meticulously, and given certain necessary supplements and medications as required. Unfortunately, it was learned that with total fasting the body broke down protein in preference to fat for energy, so that up to three-fourths of the weight loss was in terms of protein tissue and water, not fat. Some was from internal organs, including the heart, with serious consequences. Electrolyte disturbances, ketosis, and dehydration were constant problems, and psychological disturbances were frequent during the regimen. The most discouraging fact of all was that after the fasting almost all of the patients promptly regained the weight they had lost. It is now used in reputable medical centers only for unusual cases in the first few days of a comprehensive weight reduction program, mostly for morale. Fortunately, it never caught on with the public as a self-prescribed method of weight loss except for short and relatively harmless periods of fasting.

Recently an osteopath promulgated a total fast with the addition of liquid protein supplement, claiming to prevent the protein loss. Protein supplements had already been tried by reputable researchers with limited success when administered under carefully controlled conditions. But even a mild exercise program was found to work better—it at least reduced the loss of muscle mass. Research is still going on with various protein preparations, some with glucose added, but so far the loss of protein from internal organs—including the heart—has not been prevented. This osteopath advocated a partially predigested protein without adequate investigation or monitoring of the effects of this preparation. The year after his book was published, nearly 100 deaths were reported due to his diet, and *half* of those on it were found to have serious rhythm disturbances of the heart! The title of his book, *The Last Chance Diet*, should be "The Chancy Diet" and that of a similar book by another author, *The Ultimate Diet*, can be taken two ways, one of them being the last diet you will ever have on this earth.

The "bypass" procedure, in which a portion of the intestine that normally absorbs food is bypassed surgically, was done fairly frequently until a few years ago. This procedure incurred high surgical risk (about 6 percent mortality) and several serious postoperative complications. For these reasons the procedure is done only rarely today for those in whom the expected mortality from their obesity exceeds the risk of the surgery. Some surgeons are now making the stomach smaller by stitching or stapling techniques, but the results of this procedure are not yet in. It would be anticipated that they will be similar to those observed in the days when part of the stomach was removed for ulcers. Weight was lost by these patients only when the opening from the stomach to the intestine was left so large that food passed through before digestion could begin. Otherwise little or no weight loss occurred. The newer procedure doesn't affect the opening, and as the stomach can easily dilate, I can see no rationale for it.

Injections of human chorionic gonadotropin (HCG) are given by many so-called "fat doctors." Well-conducted studies by reputable authorities in which neither the person administering the injection nor the recipients knew whether they were receiving HCG or distilled water have demonstrated this to be without any merit whatsoever.

The amphetamines and related anorexic agents act by stimulating the satiety centers about which we talked before. They do have an effect of lessening appetite for about four to six weeks, but most of this is in the first week or two. The body becomes accustomed to them in this short time, and they are no longer effective unless the dosage is increased. They should not be used for this reason and several others: lack of any development of nutritional knowledge or self-reliance in weight reduction; the risk of addiction; side effects that can be serious, such as cardiac arrhythmias causing death; and an inevitable rebound in weight gain when they are discontinued. Various chemical configurations of these substances have been prepared to try to avoid some of these complications, and a few are now available without a prescription. But they all turned out to be correspondingly less effective in appetite control than the amphetamines themselves. My advice is not to use any of them.

Taking "water pills" or diuretics is also unwise. Electrolyte disturbance, gout, and other problems often result. The body does have some excess water if a person is obese, especially in the legs, because fat around the legs acts much like a garter. But the best way to lose this water is to lose the fat.

Thyroid hormone, when given to a person whose thyroid gland is normal, will increase his metabolic rate artificially for a time, and some weight loss will ensue. But the body has a very intricate balance system and soon produces less thyroid hormone, so within two or three weeks the basal metabolism has returned to normal. Many of the objections mentioned above to amphetamines also apply here, and the temptation to increase the dosage to obtain another transient effect is also similar. It should never be used for weight reduction in the normal person.

Some "fat doctors" use digitalis in those mysterious pills they pass out in unmarked envelopes. Digitalis is a well-known heart medication, but there is a narrow range between its therapeutic effect and its toxicity. One of the first toxic manifestations is a loss of appetite, followed by nausea and vomiting. It may be effective because of this, but the danger is that the other toxic side effects follow closely and can be serious—there is a high risk of death, and many have been reported.

The use of bulk agents to fill the stomach prior to a meal has also been disappointing. When this was first tested on experimental animals, adding 10 percent bulk to the meal resulted in their eating 10 percent more food, and so on. Approximately *half the dietary intake* has to be supplied in terms of indigestible bulk in animals and humans before voluntary intake begins to be reduced.

The use of caramel candies half an hour or so before meals is also advertised. But studies have shown that there is rarely a reduction in caloric intake during the meal, and if there is, the calories consumed in the candy are invariably in excess of this reduction.

There are too many other fad reducing diets in popular publications to cover here. The list is long. But probably the most popular and durable of all has been the high protein one, so let's end our discussion with this.

Around the turn of the century, biochemists believed that energy could only be derived from fat or carbohydrate, and that all protein eaten was either stored as such or eliminated as its breakdown products in the urine—none was stored as fat. This brought out the earliest diets emphasizing high protein without specifically altering the fat or carbohydrate content. It was soon discovered that protein was, after all, convertible to carbohydrate through a process called gluconeogenesis and thence to fat, so could be used for energy. Those on this diet actually *gained* weight. We heard very little more about high protein diets after this for several years. Then a concept known as "specific dynamic action" (SDA) was discovered. This has to do with the calories that are consumed in the metabolism of each type of food before the remainder of it is available for energy, other uses, or storage as fat. Protein was found to require much more energy for its metabolism than either fat or carbohydrate. In fact, about 30 percent of protein is required for this before the rest can be utilized, compared to about 5 percent for carbohydrates and fat.

There was then a new rush of enthusiasm for diets as high in protein as possible, letting the fat and carbohydrate content be what it may. This rush started with the Stillman diet.

Overlooked in this enthusiasm was another item the biochemists had pointed out at the same time. That is, if even a slight amount of carbohydrate or fat is consumed with the protein, this unique property of protein is largely lost. The mixture in the highest possible protein diet has a specific dynamic action of about 8 percent, which invalidates the whole concept.

Yet such diets have persisted and are popular. There are three reasons for this. One is that they are easy—most protein is delicious, and there is a high satiety or satisfaction value after such a meal because of its high fat content. Secondly, a diet consisting of even the most delicious high protein food that you can imagine, such as your favorite steak done to your taste, will become boring after a period of time so your total intake of calories actually declines somewhat. Thirdly, the diet is a dehydrating one, and some weight loss does occur with the loss of water, usually about 4 to 6 pounds.

The disadvantages outweigh these by far. A high intake of animal fat cannot be avoided even if sincere efforts are made to do so. About 75 grams per day of invisible saturated fat will still be in such a diet. We have already seen in our discussion of nutrition why this is unwise. The dehydration due to the solute overload on the kidneys can cause other problems. The cholesterol in such a diet averages about 1200 milligrams a day, and the health hazard of this has already been described. Furthermore, nutrients are not present in the proper balance in quantity or quality, and, to top it off, the diet lacks bulk and is constipating.

A more recent fad diet, hailed as *Dr. Atkins' Diet Revolution*, is just a variation of this. It certainly was not a revolution, because the same sort of diet has been known since the time of Harvey more than one hundred years ago. In a previous incarnation it was called the Mayo Diet (but had nothing to do with the prestigious Mayo Clinic). With alcohol added, it was known as the *Drinking Man's Diet*. Since then, the Dr. Atkins' version has (fortunately) begun to fade; a similar one now sweeping suburbia is called the *Scarsdale Diet*.

All of these diets are essentially the same and are easier to discuss now that we know about the high protein diet, because there is only one major difference: carbohydrate is specifically and sharply reduced. This restriction results in incomplete metabolism of fat. There is an old saying in biochemistry: "Fat burns in the flame of carbohydrate," which means that the processes whereby fat can be burned for energy require the presence of carbohydrate. Thus, the effect of the carbohydrate reduction is an accumulation in the body of the products of incomplete fat metabolism, called ketones. These ketones do have two weight-losing effects: When eliminated in the breath and urine, they represent a loss of about 100 calories per day; and they cause a loss of appetite, nausea, and even vomiting, which tends to lower total caloric intake.

Beyond these two effects, these diets work much like the high protein diet—they are palatable with high satiety that later becomes boring, and thus the total caloric intake tends to fall. The attendant dehydration also causes a loss of 4 to 6 pounds of water, as it does in the high protein diet.

But the disadvantages are the same—with four more. First, the low blood glucose levels cause lack of energy and fatigue. Second, the brain and central nervous system *require* glucose for energy—they cannot utilize ketones—so mental impairment in many forms is evident. Third, the ketones are acidic and so tend to put the body into acidosis. (This is the process that diabetics go into when they are out of control: in them it results in coma. The disturbance in a normal person is not as serious, because his metabolic resources prevent it, but the acid-base imbalance is still present with many undesirable consequences.) The fourth disadvantage is that the ketones interfere with the excretion of uric acid by the kidneys and thus can cause gout. For these reasons and more, this type of diet has been denounced by the National Institutes of Health, the National Academy of Science, and other reputable authorities.

If I were to hazard a guess as to the next fad in reducing diets, it would probably be a high bulk diet. Some are already trying to develop a tasteless fiber product out of wood to be added to flour and other foods. Others are working with such substances as sucrose polyester to be substituted for fat in recipes. But adding more bulk than is contained in a standard nutritious diet inter-feres with the absorption of minerals such as iron, zinc, copper, magnesium, and calcium, as well as causing other disturbances in digestion and absorption. And we have no idea of what the long-term adverse effects of some of these substances now under development might be. So until some sound scientific evidence supporting such diets is in hand, we should remember what we *do* know; that more than half our diet has to be bulk before the actual caloric intake begins to drop.

Let me leave one last word with you in weight reduction and weight maintenance: As in any area of nutrition, when you hear a quack, it's best to *duck*.

STRESS

The common thread running through the last two sections, this one, and the next, is prevention of heart attack and stroke. The topics discussed are risk factors resulting in atherosclerosis, but they are important enough beyond that role to us in midlife to be treated at more length.

This is especially true with stress. It enhances some of the other risk factors such as high blood pressure, obesity, and smoking and is a risk factor in its own right. In this latter role it operates through several mechanisms, resulting in: direct damage to the tissues of the heart and blood vessels; elevation of blood levels of glucose, free fatty acids, cholesterol, triglycerides, and beta-lipoproteins causing atherosclerosis; increased demand upon the heart, at the same time interfering with its metabolism and utilization of oxygen; and provocation of rhythm disturbances of the heart that can even cause sudden death. As we are becoming more successful in contending with some of the other risk factors that are both more definable and amenable to control, stress may in the future emerge as the *leading* risk factor.

But beyond this, stress is important to us in other ways. At this time in our lives, we are probably subject to more stresses than ever before—and certainly more than we will ever encounter later on. So we must know something about stress—what it is, what its other effects upon us are, and how to cope with it. But it is a subject much too complex to treat adequately in a short chapter such as this, and I hope you will go on to the many references in the Bibliography.

There is so much confusion and conflict in the terminology and methodology in the study of stress—reflected in vast quantities of misinformation in the popular literature—that the only way to introduce it to you is with a brief history of its development.

The term *stress* was first taken from physics, where it was used to describe a force acting upon a structure causing a strain in that structure. Walter Cannon, the father of the stress concept, brought the term from physics to physiology in 1914, and used it in the sense of an alteration, physical or psychological, in our environment that affects us. In his classic works he described the "fight or flight" way in which we respond to emergencies just as our primitive ancestors did. He noted that this "alarm" reaction causes glucose to enter our blood for quick energy, our breathing to be more rapid, perspiration to occur, the number of red blood cells in the blood to increase, more blood to be shunted to the muscles and brain and less to the intestines and skin, digestion to slow or stop, the blood clotting mechanisms to be enhanced, the heart rate to speed up, blood pressure to rise, the pupils to dilate, and even waste products to be eliminated involuntarily.

Then Helen Dunbar published her outstanding *Psychosomatic Diagnosis* in 1943, (revised in 1968) and Harold Wolff in 1953 combined much of the new knowledge of physiology and psychology in his superb work, *Stress and Disease* (revised in 1968 by Stewart Wolf and Helen Goodell).

Hans Selye is undoubtedly the most widely known figure in this field to laymen, so I must comment on his contributions in some detail. As a young medical student he observed quite correctly that the body has a limited range of reactions to an unlimited number of insults. But he went from this observation to seek a "unified theory of disease." In his research he used inbred rodents and restricted his stimuli for the most part to the physiological and his observations to physical, grossly demonstrable tissue alterations. This methodology virtually *guaranteed* he would find what he sought—a single "nonspecific" response to all stimuli.

Then he decided to redefine stress as "the nonspecific response of the body to any demand made upon it." Notice how such a definition of stress as a *response* actually rests upon his nonspecific response theory. This caused the confusion about the meaning of the term *stress* which continues in some quarters to this day. Most authorities still use it for the stimulus, some, as does

Selye, for the response, and a few even for the *interaction* between stimulus and response, as Selye did in some of his earlier writings.

Selye coined the term *stressor* for the external stimulus. He went on to postulate "pro-inflammatory hormones," which do not even exist; emphasized the pituitary-adrenal cortex axis almost to the exclusion of the sympathetic-adrenal medulla system, which is much more important; and made other questionable assumptions in order to round out his "general adaptation syndrome." Briefly, this consists of the alarm reaction, the resistance stage, and the exhaustion stage. In forming this concept, he not only ignored humans and any consideration of psychology, but failed to include many other manifestations of the stress response that are known to occur even in the animals he studied, such as changes in insulin, prolactin, growth hormone, TSH and thyroid hormone, prostaglandins, antidiuretic hormone, gonadotropins, and sex hormones. The opinion of many on Selye's contributions is summarized well in the words of George Vaillant, who reported as a result of the longest prospective study ever done on adults, "Hans Selye is wrong; it is not stress that kills us. It is the effective adaptation to stress that permits us to live." In other words, it is the individual human being's coping capability that affects his life and its length, *not* some theoretical "unified response."

One must be cautious in extrapolating the results of any animal research to man, especially in areas that have to do with mental and emotional functions. When subject to stress, animals tend to have species-specific responses—some attack, some snarl and threaten; some flee, others remain motionless; squirrels hoard, and opossums feign death. In the field of stress, animal research can only give us clues that then must be separately pursued in human research.

Selye not only applied the results of his rat research to man without studying man, he has most recently offered us a *philosophy of life* based upon it! Although many of those eminent in the field concur with John Mason, who states that Selye only caused a "prolonged period of stalemate and confusion" in stress theory and research, we must recall that his professional publications constitute considerably less than 1 percent of those in the field and can be more charitable. We can at least say that he stimulated interest in the subject and certainly did much to popularize it through his many articles and books written for the lay reader.

During the Second World War several field studies were done on the effects of stress upon combat troops, pilots, prisoners of war, and populations of occupied countries. Similar studies have since been carried out during civil disasters. These were valuable, despite weaknesses in the epidemiological design and methods used in many of them.

Richard Lazarus in the early 1960s was the first to emphasize the importance of psychological factors in the human. He pointed out that *most* of man's stress is psychological and that there is little relationship between this and the physiological stresses Selye and others following him used working with laboratory animals. He demonstrated that there is first an anticipation of stress that may be even more stressful than the event itself, then an awareness of the stressful situation at various levels, followed by an appraisal of the situation versus the resources the person possesses that enable him to cope. These resources are made up of many factors, among which are intelligence, motivation, past experience, and personality traits.

Other investigators since have noted the role of recall of similar stressful situations, the response patterns seen in pleasant stresses such as sexual excitement, physical exercise, and even in total deprivation of sensory input. They have shown that stresses within a certain range are actually beneficial to an individual— only when they are above or below this range do they cause harm.

Sociologists have investigated several aspects of stress from their point of view to conclude that "status incongruity," "cultural discontinuities," and the like cause stress, and some work has also been done on occupational stresses, but for the most part their findings have not been particularly helpful.

Neurophysiologists have described areas in the human brain that correspond with those of lower orders, such as the limbic-striatal portion concerned with social and self-preservational functions, and areas in the brain stem from which originate such drives as sex, hunger, and thirst. The human brain has unique areas in the cortex, called "cross-modal association areas," where these and other functions are coordinated. These findings have clarified many of our concepts regarding human response to stress. Endocrinologists have contributed much to our understanding of how the many hormones mentioned previously are involved in reactions to stress, and neuroendocrinologists are presently discovering centrally active neurotransmitters such as endorphin. More than a hundred of these have been discovered just in the last few years. This is a very active area of research that holds great promise for the future.

Psychologists have devised a variety of tests to try to solve the riddle of why one person's stress is another person's stimulus. The Minnesota Multiphasic Personality Inventory (MMPI) only showed that those who reacted most adversely to stress scored high in three scales called the "neurotic triad." Raymond Cattell developed his Personality Factor Inventory, which showed anxiety and depression to be higher in such individuals. Other personality tests, such as the Cornell Medical Index and the Eysenck Personality Inventory, similarly yielded meager results. So far, psychology seems to be at a stalemate, but hopefully this will not last for long.

The leading authority in the field at the present time is Lennart Levi, whose laboratory is at the Karolinska Institute in Stockholm. Recognizing the futility of studying animal models, as well as the weaknesses in the methodology of epidemiological studies, he has concentrated on creating simulated stressful situations using human subjects. In his studies he evaluates perception, appraisal of the threat in reference to the individual's resources, the effect of prior experience, and all of the adaptation techniques that are uniquely human. These are measured in three ways: by physiological responses, biochemical indices, and psychological testing. Among many other things, he has found that in the human, differences in individual attitude and preparation, as well as perception of the stimulus weighed against resources are actually more important than the stimulus itself.

Although he has published many valuable technical papers that are beyond our scope here, three of his most recent books are listed in the Bibliography. They are understandable and are highly recommended to the reader.

This, all too briefly, is where research on stress is today.

Although I am not an investigator in the field, it is impossible to resist making a few suggestions to those who are, because some seem so obvious. There seem to be three broad determinants in a person's response to stress. One is genetic—while still in the uterus a fetus can be shown to have characteristic responses to such stimuli as loud noises. The second has to do with "learned" responses to stress, especially in early life experiences. The third comprises all factors involved in the stressful event or situation itself. These three have to be unraveled backwards. Certainly animals can be studied to provide direction, but the definitive studies have to be upon humans. And either truly stressful situations or credible simulations should be used. As we study reactions to stress, there is only one element over which we have control, and that is the stressful situation. This should not be varied in quantity or quality at first because of the uncertainty introduced thereby. It should only be held constant while testing a large number of individuals under identical conditions.

All responses of any one individual under study should then be measured, and these responses fall into three categories. The physiological consist of pulse rate, blood pressure, respiratory rate, muscle tension, gastric acid secretion, pupil size, skin conductance, gastro-intestinal motility, etc. The biochemical are just coming into their own, and many of these, such as the catecholamines—chief of which are adrenalin and noradrenalin—can now be determined accurately. The third category would have to do with psychological responses, both those claimed by the subject and those observed by the investigator.

The factor of time will have to be discarded for the present, since there should be only one stressful event of any type given to any one subject. This would rule out any but general anticipation. The measurements must be made as instantaneously or as soon after the stress as possible in order to rule out the effects of recall.

From this it should be possible to learn more about the wide varieties of response people can have to each particular stress. We already know that there is poor correlation among the various responses in any one category, for example the physiological, let alone any correlation with the biochemical and psychological categories. Nonetheless, if enough subjects were studied, multivariate analysis could be applied and clusters of responses separated statistically. Current personality tests are admittedly inadequate to predict stress response, but they could be used in an attempt to correlate their various factors with the clusters derived from the mathematical analysis of the responses in the three categories described. With this approach, predictive personality tests possibly could be developed. Once this basic work is accomplished, it could be extended to include twins, both identical and fraternal, as well as other relatives, to determine the genetic contribution to certain patterns of response to stress, as opposed to those that are learned. Then the effects of learning could be separated and studied. So we might finally then be in a position to assay the most effective means whereby each person could "unlearn" certain harmful responses to stress and learn more favorable ones. But now we are far from this, so let's return to what we do know.

Adverse reactions to stress can be grouped into four categories:

1. *Hypochondriacal:* There are always sensations which are perfectly normal coming to our brain from all parts of our body. We are usually unaware of these sensations because they remain below our conscious level. Under stressful conditions a person may experience an enhanced awareness of these sensations—even search for them—and they may emerge into consciousness. One then becomes aware of such sensations as a pounding heartbeat, creaking of joints, or a twinge from the passage of gas in our intestines. The hypochondriac regards these as symptoms of disease.

2. *Functional:* Here there is no structural change in an organ or organ system, but stress produces a demonstrable abnormality in function. Examples of this are excess gastric acid, air swallowing, irritable or spastic colon, fatigue, insomnia, hyperventilation, excessive sweating, sexual difficulties, tension headaches, and accident-proneness, to name a few. In this category may also be included some of the less severe psychological entities such as anxiety, conversion reaction, and hysteria.

3. *Psychosomatic:* In this category, organ damage occurs. Most of these conditions grow out of functional disorders over a period of time. Usually the stress response is merely one of many factors operating. Examples are hypertension, colitis, duodenal ulcer, heart disease, asthma, and some allergies.

4. *Organic:* Here the disease is caused by a definable entity such as a bacterium, carcinogen, or trauma, but the psychological overlay is a significant part of the picture.

Philosophical speculation is fascinating when one considers the various diseases that result from stress. As mentioned, hypertension is one of these, and it is due to constriction of the small blood vessels located peripherally in the body. One effect of this constriction is to reduce blood loss when a cutting or crushing injury is sustained. Perhaps this had a protective purpose in our past. Another, duodenal ulcer, results from increased gastric acidity. This enhances digestion, and one wonders if this is not some sort of throwback to the time when our ancestors ate the raw meat of their prey after killing it, or, after combat that of their erstwhile enemies. Coronary artery disease, as we have seen, results from many factors, but a significant one is the elevation of fats in the blood produced by stress as well as by diet and other factors. These fats can be used for fuel by the body in stressful situations when sustained activity is required and the more immediately available glucose sources are exhausted. Most of the stress responses can be considered this way—they were probably of value to man in his ancient past but are not today. Under modern conditions they are not only inappropriate but, in excess, cause disease and even death.

So we must learn how to cope with stress effectively. With our present knowledge, the best methods of coping can be grouped most simply in four categories:

1. The stressful situation often may be avoided or overt action taken to alter it so that it is less damaging to us. This is merely a civilized version of the primitive "fight or flight" response. In our own lives we find it difficult to run from many stressful situations as our primitive ancestors did with their "flight" part of this response. This may be successful with some stresses, such as noise, crowds, or a particularly bothersome person. But with most, because of their very complexity and pervasiveness, avoidance may be impossible or, for various reasons, self-defeating in the long run. Nonetheless, we should consider this first. Similarly, the "fight" portion of the primitive response would not be particularly productive with a nagging spouse or a bothersome boss. It's even against the law! But a more acceptable version— taking action to solve and resolve the situation would not be. Even vigorous physical activity in some sport would be a harmless and healthy substitute. Most of the time, we are forced for the sake of society to live in conflict with our bodies' primitive demands. But appropriate action to avoid or alter the situation as a civilized version of the "fight or flight" response should first be tried.

2. A more effective way is to try to change how we perceive the stress in relation to our inner resources. It is well known that

one man's crisis can be another man's challenge. In Chinese calligraphy, crisis is depicted by two characters, one meaning danger and the other opportunity. There is a lesson for us here. Often, thinking through and clarifying a confused situation will reveal it not to be as threatening as it had at first seemed. Sometimes denial or distractions temporarily ameliorate the effect of a stressful situation, but this is rarely a permanent solution. Discussion with a friend—letting out our feelings and accepting his or her counsel—may help. There are many other *conscious* devices we can use, but unfortunately most of our perception of a stressful situation lies in our *unconscious*. Because of this, professional help in the form of a psychologist, psychiatrist, or other professional may be necessary. Group encounters and movements such as Arica and est have helped some persons to alter their perception of stressful situations temporarily, but the long-term value of these movements has not been demonstrated. Throughout the history of man, religion has worked this way, as well as offering comfort and consolation. For some, firm philosophical beliefs have formed frameworks in which stresses are seen in less threatening perspective. Medication may play a temporary role in the form of the psychoactive drugs only until one learns to cope with the stress in better ways.

3. Transmission of the stressful stimulus, once it has been perceived and interrelated at the level of the cerebral cortex, then switches to the hypothalamus and the autonomic nervous system and endocrine system. This process can also be modified and there are many means whereby this may done. Throughout history, among the Yogi in India, Taoists in China, Zen Buddhists in Japan, Sufi of the Middle East, and in many representatives of our own Judaeo-Christian religions, meditation has been one. Because of its recent popularity, we now find ourselves torn between meditation and the martini.

The scientific investigation of meditation was begun by Jacobsen in 1938 and has been continued by others, most notably, Herbert Benson of Harvard Medical School, who succeeded in separating meditation from both the mysticism and commercialism that had clouded it since its recent reintroduction from India. "Transcendental meditation" from the Advaita school of yoga, with a Vedic origin, as promulgated by Maharishi Mahesh Yogi and others, is being replaced now by the wiser among us with Benson's simple technique, explained in his book, *The Relaxation Reponse*.

Biological feedback is an electronic variation of meditation. It uses devices to make one more aware of autonomic alterations in the body. Transient changes in pulse rate, oxygen consumption, blood pressure, skin temperature, as well as improvement in migraine headaches have been demonstrated. Unfortunately, in most individuals these effects do not continue, so repeated and expensive sessions are necessary for sustained benefit. Modification of brain waves, producing general relaxation, has also been demonstrated. *Beta* waves are usually dominant when we perform tasks, *alpha* waves when we are in a contemplative mood, *theta* waves during creative activity, and *delta* waves during sleep. Some subjects have learned to convert to predominantly alpha waves after training, and occasionally to theta. Biofeedback is easier for some than meditation, but so far its claims exceed its results. The same is true for other related techniques so popular now, such as self-hypnosis, guided imagery, Rolfing, acupressure, and others.

Lastly, psychoactive drugs also may have a temporary role in this phase of the stress response.

4. The fourth effective coping method is to affect the target organ or organ system itself, that is, the way in which the tissue responds to the transmissions of the autonomic nervous system or to the hormonal influence. One simple example is heat or massage for tense muscles. Usually, however, one must resort to medication specifically designed for such conditions as peptic ulcers and high blood pressure. Occasionally, if the organ or organ system has sustained severe damage, surgery may be required.

The simplest, most natural and effective everyday method of coping, because it recognizes that the common denominator of either fight *or* flight is *vigorous physical activity*, is just such activity itself. As noted in the discussion following, exercise effectively neutralizes for a time most of the ill effects of stress upon the body. Because it supplements so well all of the other methods and is so effective itself, it is the one most highly recommended for most people under most circumstances as part of their everyday life. Any other methods can be added as one wishes.

In the final analysis, the reaction of a person to a stressful situation is as unique as that person himself. For this reason, if the stresses in your life cause symptoms you cannot counteract by yourself, you and your physician together should work out the best way for you to handle them.

I would like to end this section here, but there are two other approaches in the field of stress I must discuss, if only to discard. This is necessary because of the wide publicity given them in the lay literature. In 1949, Thomas Holmes adopted Adolph Meyer's method of keeping "life charts" on individuals' stressful events and illnesses, and he conducted a retrospective study based upon this. He concluded that these events appeared to occur before major illnesses. From this he developed what he called "The Social Readjustment Rating Scale," containing a list of forty-three stressful life events. He arranged these events in terms of arbitrary "Life Change Units." Richard Rahe, who had worked with him, then carried out a similarly designed retrospective study in the United States Navy on 2,500 men. This scale must have appeared in every Sunday supplement and woman's magazine in the country.

The effects of these "events" were considered to be independent of individual resources—such as financial when a mortgage of a certain amount was given, or background when social change was the event. No attention was paid to individual age, sex, or personality differences, nor to how events were perceived by the subjects. The authors also ignored individual health and psychological status of the subjects at the time of the stressful events, their individual intellectual capacity, in fact, *any* coping capability, even prior experience with similar phenomena! No attempt was made to qualify or gradate the events themselves, such as "change of health in a family member." Which family member, how close to the subject, what sort of change, how serious, what were the implications for the subject?

Such a scale gives an unwarranted illusion of precision and quantification to each event, implies that cultural changes do not affect responses over time, and that somehow a mysterious mathematical accuracy exists when the events are combined for predicting illnesses. There were other serious problems with these studies. Being retrospective, they depended entirely on the subjects' ability to recall past events, and their simple addition of units did not consider the sequence of the events in either order or the time separating them.

More carefully designed prospective studies, such as those of

Barbara Betz and Caroline Thomas at Johns Hopkins, Lawrence
Hinkle and Norman Plummer at Cornell, and George Vaillant at
Harvard, have come closer to the truth. These clearly show *that
those who do not deal effectively with their stresses* are the one who
subsequently tend to have physical illnesses. In other words, the
focus must be more upon the person and his coping capability and
not just upon the stress alone.

The second approach I'd like to discuss and discard is that of
Ray Rosenman and Meyer Friedman, who have attempted to
define a "coronary-prone" behavior pattern. Since the early years
of this century, when the famous physician Sir William Osler
described his typical heart attack patient as "a keen and ambitious
man, the indicator of whose engine is always set at full speed
ahead," clinicians have known that there was an element of truth
in this. So this is not the problem. It is the way these investigators
have gone about trying to find that truth and their denigration of
other well-documented risk factors in doing so. They described
their "Type A" behavior as characterized by competitiveness,
aggression, easily aroused hostility, a constant sense of time
pressure, restlessness, and similar characteristics. Their "Type
B" is defined simply as the absence of such traits. They first began
their study by asking patients, friends, and colleagues to send
them subjects who, in these varied opinions, fit either of these
criteria, and then looked into the heart attack history of those who
were so referred.

When this was soundly criticized for obvious reasons, they
had their subjects wired for motor movements and listen to a
record. This, too, was abandoned under fire, as was still another
method relying upon voice analysis.

Then they settled on an interview with a list of questions, but
soon reliance came to be placed upon the interviewers' subjective
evaluation of the subjects' manner of response to the questions,
not the answers themselves. Along the way these investigators
admitted that only about 10 percent of those they studied were
either "Type A" or "Type B", which seriously undercuts the
value of their thesis. Interviewers trained by them are able to
place the same individuals in the same category at a later date
only about two-thirds of the time. With different interviewers—
again, trained by them—evaluating the same subjects at the same
time, the reproducibility of results is even lower. And one last
criticism, which to me is crucial: These are only *behavior patterns*.

No attempt is made to go beyond these to the underlying personality mechanisms responsible, nor to consider any other manifestations of the patterns than coronary heart disease. So we really haven't learned anything about stress or coping with it from this approach—and won't until research in this area is improved beyond its present methodology.

The best way to predict heart attack is to assay the standard risk factors. These have been weighted, even computer-programmed, and a remarkably reliable risk profile can be given a patient today. Clinicians encounter patients who could be called "Type A" every day. Thse patients have a heightened response to stress, which tends to raise both blood pressure and serum cholesterol; usually eat, smoke, and drink too much; are often overweight; and they rarely exercise—or if they do, go at it grimly. So we come right back to the risk factors even if we start with the "Type A" behavior pattern! I'll confine my criticisms just to these, and refer the reader to more sophisticated critiques by Robert Keith, Kay Rowland, and other authorities.

For those who wish to learn more than this brief discussion can cover on the subject of stress, I would again suggest starting with the references in the Bibliography; they themselves have extensive bibliographies.

EXERCISE

Every day we become more aware of the surge of enthusiasm over exercise; we may wonder why this wave hasn't broken over us yet. The reason is simple. When we who are now middle-aged were young, exercise was just for athletes and a few fanatics. It certainly wasn't generally accepted then that exercise could have beneficial effects for the rest of us—on our bodies, minds, and emotions.

As a nation, we were even unaware that children, who should have been in excellent physical condition, were not. This was first pointed out to us in the mid-1950s when more than half of American school children were found to be unable to meet minimum standards of fitness. This prompted President Eisenhower to call the first President's Conference on Youth Fitness in June 1956 at Annapolis. Out of that conference grew the Council on Youth Fitness, which first met at West Point in

1957. By 1963, it had evolved into the President's Council on Physical Fitness and Sports, which has come to concern itself as much with adults as with children.

This was the series of events that spurred both popular and professional interest in exercise. The emphasis placed on youth fitness since the 1950s profoundly affected students in school programs but had little direct effect on the rest of us. If you look around again, you'll notice that most of those you see jogging are in their teens, twenties, and early thirties—they were school-children then. The few you see with gray hair have had to learn about exercise and its benefits on their own and motivate themselves. We have to do the same. That's what this chapter is for.

Actually, regular exercise, especially for the middle-ager, is the closest real thing to the "fountain of youth" I mentioned at the beginning of this book that so many of us persist in seeking in one way or another. Exercise, properly practiced and, above all, enjoyed, can literally transform a flaccid, lethargic, mildly depressed, flabby human being into one who looks and feels simply great. More of us are coming to understand this and to apply that understanding. But you can't just pick up any popular book on exercise, read it, and start in, nor join a friend without knowing more about exercise itself and about your own body. If you are going to begin to change your physical habits dramatically, you need to consult your physician and then work with him or with an exercise physiologist he recommends to determine the activities that will be right for you.

Frankly, even most physicians in practice didn't know much about exercise until this last decade or so. There were some good laboratory studies being done all along, but they were published in obscure Scandinavian journals where the information was hard for the practicing physician to find. About the only knowledge on specific exercise programs readily available to us for years after World War II was that the most popular one, the Canadian Air Force exercise program, was not scientifically sound in several respects. But we knew of nothing else to take its place, so many physicians hid behind such generalities as "get a little more exercise" and "don't overdo it"—or, as I did, dug the data out of those obscure journals and managed to calculate exercise programs for our patients.

Until the mid-1960s all we could glean from such sources was this: The psychological and physiological benefits began when a minimum of 400 calories of energy were burned in about half an hour to 45 minutes 3 or 4 days a week—and that there was not much greater benefit (except for athletes) when more than twice the calories were burned in twice the time more than 5 days a week. Knowing this range, the person's age, weight, and condition, we could lay out a satisfactory program in terms of specific activities. Then we learned that all of our complicated calculations could come down to one simple index. The pulse rate alone served as a fairly accurate indicator of the amount of energy being expended, and it even made a reasonable allowance for the person's condition. So we taught our patients to take their own pulses before, during, and after exercising, and with an exercise electrocardiogram and other information, we were able to prescribe programs somewhat more simply. More about this pulse rate method later.

Then in 1968 Kenneth Cooper published *Aerobics*. In it, he brought together much that was then known on the benefits of exercise and established specific levels of fitness for each age and sex that could be measured scientifically in the laboratory or estimated by field testing. So the definitions of fitness were no longer fuzzy. In this he also presented his now famous point system, based upon both the intensity and duration of exercise, along with tables for various activities using this system. For the first time, there existed a truly simple way to prescribe exercise programs without complicated calculations or counting pulse rates.

But Cooper had based his book on research with young air force personnel. The dangers of unsupervised exercise and exercising without adjusting for the changing physical condition of the middle-aged and those older became evident as people of all ages read and applied the information in his book by themselves. He had just not anticipated this. So he rushed *The New Aerobics* into print. In it, he urged those over thirty-five to have a thorough physical examination, including an exercise electrocardiogram, introduced a starter program for those in poor condition, and specified progressive programs for various ages. Still, he hadn't sufficiently considered women's needs, so with his wife, Millie, a convert to exercise from assisting him by typing the first two books, he published *Aerobics for Women*. Even taken together, these three books were incomplete in some respects.

Finally, in *The Aerobics Way*, Cooper has put all we need to know in one comprehensive work. I urge everyone in middle age to buy, beg, or borrow this book, because it is the only simple, scientifically sound system available. In this book, Cooper has applied his point system to twenty-eight different activities for those of all ages and either sex. He has added "endurance points," special tables for the obese and for those with heart disease—even for those who've had coronary bypass surgery. So, in less than twenty years, exercise has evolved from a program for unfit children to a way of life we can all adopt.

What should our goals in terms of exercise be? In scientific terms, it can best be measured by our maximal oxygen uptake. That is, if you are able to breathe in and your body utilize 42 milliliters of oxygen per minute per kilogram of body weight, you are right in the middle of the fitness range, with some allowance on either side of that for variables such as sex and age. But this doesn't mean much to us. Here is where the aerobics point system helps us. Based upon the oxygen consumption required, Cooper has calculated tables of points for each activity, starting with only a few points per week. The tables incorporate intensity, frequency, and duration. At the end of each table you arrive at 30 to 34 points a week for men, and 24 to 28 for women. You merely follow the tables to arrive at that level, and you are in the "good" to "excellent" range of fitness as defined scientifically above. The points given are for the average middle-ager—you should consult Cooper's book for details.

Such a scientifically based system is necessary if we are to achieve all the benefits that are possible from exercise; it is needed, too, to counteract those TV "exercise" programs and the nonsense in such books as *Total Fitness in 30 Minutes a Week*. It also dispels the notion that esthetic or spiritual disciplines such as yoga and t'ai chi, or recreations like softball, bowling, or golf are really beneficial as exercise. It is true that even such minimal exercise as a brisk 15-minute walk has *some* benefits. In fact, this level of exercise is just about equivalent in effect to one mild tranquilizer in coping with nervous stress. But the fitness levels specified by Cooper as "good" or "excellent" must be achieved to benefit from all that exercise has to offer. Let's see what these benefits are.

Psychological studies at several respected research institutions have shown that your self-image is improved, and ability to cope with psychological stress is much greater. You live life with more enthusiasm; you aren't as weighed down by fatigue at the end of a day; and even your mental ability is sharper.

As I pointed out when talking about obesity, vigorous exercise is absolutely necessary in middle age if you want to maintain a desirable weight, and it can eliminate many other problems that often start cropping up when you're over thirty-five or forty—backache, "pot belly," constipation, and muscle injuries, for example. You're able to respond better to physical stress and even to recuperate more easily from illness. Such exercise will also delay or prevent the onset of arthritis, as I'll describe further on. It also acts in many ways to reduce the risk of heart attack and stroke. It lowers blood pressure appreciably, lowers triglycerides in the blood, and reduces the level of harmful low-density-lipoprotein cholesterol while increasing the protective HDL form. It also shows the resting pulse rate, increases the capacity of coronary arteries and collateral circulation, and improves heart muscle tone and its metabolic efficiency. It elminates many of the effects of stress as pointed out in the last section, and even reduces the desire to smoke!

Sleep is sounder and more refreshing, so less is needed. There is a lower incidence of varicose veins and hernias, postponement or amelioration of diabetes, and fewer peptic ulcers. But most important in middle age is that *it can make your physiological age up to fifteen years less than your chronological age.* In other words, by all measurements, your body can perform as if you were fifteen years younger than you actually are. And you may even look that much younger. It is probable that your life expectancy will be extended by almost as many years, but this has not been proven yet because longitudinal studies to show this will require decades. Cross-sectional studies so far suggest that this may in fact be so. Should we wait for the lifelong studies to be completed before we take any action? We won't be around then!

You may hear the acronym MET used occasionally in relation to exercise. This is an abbreviation for "the metabolic cost of activity." One MET is the energy one expends at rest—roughly equivalent to 1 calorie per minute. So various exercises can be expressed as multiples of this. But duration is not included in this term, so it is not often used.

You've also probably heard the words *isotonic* and *isometric.* They refer to two ways that muscles work. In isotonic exercise, the muscles move through their natural range with constant tension; in isometric, they contract without motion of the limbs. Although isometrics do build muscles, they do not increase circulation of the blood to the muscles, and they result in poor flexibility and dexterity. They also raise the blood pressure dangerously while they are being done, requiring surging performance of the heart while at the same time interfering with its blood supply. For all these reasons, they are definitely *not* recommended for those in middle age. The same comments apply to "pumping iron"—weight lifting and strenuous use of those shiny exercise machines. Isotonic exercise is the type performed in calisthenics. They do improve muscle tone, which you may want for a specific reason, such as firming up a protruding abdomen. And they also improve flexibility. If you wish to do calisthenics for either reason, be sure to follow a good guide, because injuries may result and the benefits be minimal if they are not done properly. The best is the A.M.A. booklet *Basic Body-work*. Write to the Committee on Exercise and Physical Fitness, Department of Health Education, American Medical Association, 535 North Dearborn Street, Chicago, Illinois 60610, for a copy. The YMCA also puts out a good one. But be forewarned of one thing: Besides being of limited benefit, for most people calisthenics are frankly boring and are usually abandoned after a few days or weeks.

More important are the words we use in talking about exercise in terms of the entire body, not just in terms of the muscles. Anaerobic (literally "without air") exercise is performed in a sudden spurt. The muscles utilize the glycogen they have stored and glucose in the blood for energy, but because of the lack of time, oxygen cannot be used to metabolize such energy sources completely. Aerobic exercise, as the term implies, is of sufficient duration to utilize oxygen for complete metabolism. When a person starts to exercise suddenly, he relies upon anaerobic metabolism and first builds up an oxygen debt. Within a few seconds he is breathing heavily to make up this debt. After a few minutes, he reaches a steady state where aerobic metabolism takes over—this is the so-called "second wind." Little or no benefit has been demonstrated from anaerobic exercise, but aerobic brings with it all I've mentioned and more. It is for this reason that the type of exercise recommended today is almost always aerobic. Most aerobic exercises maintain general muscle tone and flexibility adequately; some do not. The best solution is to vary the aerobic exercises you do so that these are maintained well throughout the body, or add stretching and firming calisthenics to your basic aerobic program.

Now let's talk about an exercise prescription for you. I use the word *prescription*, because exercise is like medicine. If you don't have enough, it won't do you any good, and an overdose can do harm, especially in middle age. Like any prescription, it should be given to you by a qualified physician. Don't attempt to start an exercise program yourself, especially if you've been sedentary for a long time. Per-Olof Astrand adds rather wryly that the hazards of inactivity are so much greater than those that may be encountered in an exercise program, that a thorough checkup and a prescription *not* to exercise are even more important for those who wish to remain sedentary!

The exercise prescription consists of four parts. Your physician's role is to prescribe your program in terms of the first three —frequency, intensity, and duration. If you call the latter "time," you have an easily remembered acronym—FIT. Your physician will take into account your condition and such factors as body build, obesity, and other health problems. He will also advise you about proper stretching and warm-ups; the effects of heat, humidity, and altitude; ways of cooling down after exercise; and any specific precautions you should observe. The last part of the prescription is up to you: It is the selection of the type of exercise you want to do. I'll have more to say about this later.

The usual basis for an exercise prescription consists of the results of a treadmill stress test, your medical history, and a good physical examination. From this, your physician has three choices. He may either specify certain activities in a detailed and precise way, use Cooper's point system, or base his prescription on the pulse rate method. If he uses the latter, the intensity of exercise will be designed to achieve and maintain your pulse rate at 70 to 85 percent of your maximum heart rate. This maximum rate is the highest at which your heart can beat efficiently and healthily. For most people, it is about 220 minus their age. Benefit from exercise begins at about 70 percent of this, and 85 percent is usually not exceeded—for safety and because little more good is achieved beyond that except for athletes. This is often called the training range. For example, if you are fifty and healthy, your maximum rate is 170, so your exercise should be at a pulse rate of between 119 and 144, approximately.

Duration should be increased gradually over several weeks until it reaches at least 30 minutes to an hour, depending upon the intensity prescribed. The rate of increase should be determined by your physician. Frequency usually starts at one time daily three days per week, and the upper limit—possibly twice a day six days a week if either the intensity or duration is low— should be reached gradually as outlined by your physician. With such a program, even the most sedentary middle-ager can attain "good" or "excellent" fitness levels in four to six months.

When you begin your program, you should notice a good stretchy feeling in your muscles the mornings after you exercise. Aches and soreness then are a sign to slow down—they are due to stretching of the muscle tissue and microscopic injury to the muscle fibers. Muscle pain during and immediately after exercise, however, is caused by the accumulation of lactic acid and is to be expected. If you are fatigued the morning after, or if your pulse rate doesn't return to normal within ten minutes after exercise, you should report this to your physician. These are also signs to slow down.

The following list of various types of exercise should help you decide which is most appropriate for you, using either the pulse rate or point system. Different muscle groups are used so different degrees of muscle tone and flexibility are achieved, but as far as aerobic benefits go, they can be the same from any of the exercises that follow. This is the fun part of the prescription—and it's all yours.

- Walking briskly is probably the best way to start, but it's impossible for most middle-agers to condition themselves adequately doing this alone, even with very long walks. The elderly can get by this way, though. The rest of us would have to learn the odd race-walking they do in the Olympics.
- The best exercise, if you are an efficiency expert, is jogging or running. Well, there is cross-country skiing or rowing for the few who live where these can be done. You burn up to 800 calories an hour doing any of these. You can consider yourself a runner rather than a jogger when you cover a mile in less than 10 minutes. There is a real enthusiasm for both now, with more

than twenty million people participating in the United States today. But they are not wise for everyone, so check with your physician before you start. Studies have shown that more than half of middle-aged people who choose to run or jog develop difficulties in various weight-bearing areas such as the knees, ankles, Achilles tendon, arch, and even the muscles and tendons associated with these joints. If your physician clears you to run or jog, then be sure you get good shoes. Consult a podiatrist, or write to *Runner's World Magazine* (Box 366, Mountain View, California 94042) for their current guide.

- With the new types of wheels developed from skateboards, roller skating is just starting to become popular for children of *all* ages. It's a lot of fun, can be as good an exercise as jogging, and it's a lot less jolting on your leg muscles and joints.

- Swimming is also excellent, and doesn't carry the risks of injury that running does. Although lanky people do better with running, swimming is an exercise the more rotund will find easier for them. However, it may be hard to find a convenient, uncrowded pool, and boredom can sneak in doing laps in a small pool. There isn't much to look at either. One hidden advantage is that you'll burn up a few extra calories in maintaining you body temperature if the water is cool.

- Bicycling has the advantage of greater recreation on a beautiful day. You cover more ground and see more scenery than if you run. Weather can limit this as a regular activity—as it can running and roller skating—and there is certainly a challenge in confronting automobiles on the road. But car carriers are cheap, and you can drive to the area of your choice.

- Schoolyards have basketball courts you can use after school hours. Get friends or family members to join you, or in bad weather go to a Y or health club where there are groups that play regularly. Use the full court and be sure to keep moving to keep your pulse rate up.

- Tennis is enjoying immense popularity now, but there are a few cautions. You *must* play singles, not doubles, and you have to be a reasonably good player so that the ball is hit back and forth near the line or in the corners three or four times for each point before the amount of exercise is adequate. *Run* after loose balls, too. Keep the tempo of the game up constantly, or you'll spend two or three hours on the court without getting sufficient exercise. But tennis *is* fun and you can play it for the rest of your life and enjoy the sociability that goes with it.

- Handball is superb for conditioning. The equipment is inexpensive, and handball courts are available in cities at clubs and the Y, but there are two problems. First, it takes a while to toughen up your hands so you can endure hitting the hard ball. Second, most of us are not used to using both hands equally, and it may require time, patience, and practice to be able to play it well enough to get the exercise we need.

- Squash is played with a racket resembling a reinforced badminton racket and a ball similar to a handball. Imported from England in the 1880s, this first gained popularity in east coast prep schools and Ivy League Colleges, and it still carries a certain upper class aura. Until the last decade or so, squash was played almost exclusively in universities and private clubs, but the number of commercial courts is increasing and the number of players in this country has doubled in the last five years. Because of the long handle, it is difficult to play with facility at first, but the court is enclosed and you can hit all four walls, so it is easier to learn than tennis. Less time is spent picking up balls, and you can get a better workout in a shorter amount of time.

- Paddle tennis is not a very good exercise, but it has evolved into platform tennis in areas of the country where snow in the winter interferes with other outdoor sports. It is played with a wooden perforated paddle and a soft sponge rubber ball. The platform is raised to allow snow to be shoveled off and chicken wire keeps the ball within the court. This is the advantage. You can hit the ball off the wire, so the ball is kept in play longer, And it's also easy to learn. There are about seven thousand platform tennis courts now in this country.

- In the late 1940s, in Connecticut, handball players began using sawed-off tennis rackets, presumably because their hands hurt. Racquetball was born. A regular handball court is used, an advantage because there are so many of these already all over the country, even in cities. The rules permit bouncing the ball off the ceiling as well as all four walls, and the ball itself has more zip than in squash or handball, so it keeps you hustling. The main appeal of this sport is that anyone who can hit the broad side of a barn *from the inside* can play the sport in the first 5 minutes. The short handle of the racket makes the stroke a natural flick of the wrist, much like the motion used in throwing a ball. There are nearly ten million racquetball players in the United States today, and its popularity is zooming. Women are also taking it up, and now account for almost 40 percent of the players.

- If you are one of those with long busy days or live where the weather is often bad so you can't get out to exercise, you may have to resort to something you can do in your home. Running in place is one—boring, but efficient—but you can get it over with in a hurry. Skipping rope is another. In both of these, some of the same risks as with running and jogging exist, so use a small trampoline or a small rubber pad. A stationary bicycle or a treadmill can give you a good workout, and you can even relieve boredom using these while reading, or listening to the radio or Books On Tape (P. O. Box 7900, Newport Beach, California 92660). Headphone radios and the new small portable cassette players are coming into greater use in many types of exercise for this reason. One advantage of bicycle ergometers is that the better ones can be adjusted to a precise amount of energy expended even if the speed is varied. So you can just set the dial and not bother counting your pulse or anything else—the clock in front of you tells you when to quit.

There are other forms of exercise you might consider for variety—ice skating at a local rink, badminton in your yard without a court or net, folk or square dancing, or running in a park at a circuit training course. (On these you run from station to station, performing a specified exercise at each before continuing.) Aerobic dancing can be fun and is especially popular among women. But most instructors are untrained, and the dance routines aren't usually aerobic, except perhaps for the least conditioned in the group.

The most important thing about the exercise you choose is that it be *fun*. Pick a sport involving someone else if you can, so you have built-in motivation on the days you feel lazy. Be sure you avoid the use of salt pills and such drinks as E.R.G. and Gatorade unless they are prescribed for unusual conditions—also those air-tight sweatsuits. Remember, if you get out of breath or your muscles become uncomfortable while you're working out, you can stop for a few seconds and then resume without losing much benefit. With these few tips and all the above to choose from, you really don't have to suffer or be bored. The dread some people have of exercise is totally unrealistic. The first month is the hardest. The second is less so. After that, exercise will become such an enjoyable part of your life that you will miss it on the days you can't do it.

The average middle-aged person may be better off joining a good health club with ample facilities for aerobic exercises. Then you can keep up your regular routine after dark and in bad weather. If it has pleasant surroundings, if you're greeted by the personnel, have your own locker, and friends to talk with, you'll have good associations with your exercise program even before you begin. Most have a comfortable lounge for after-exercise socializing and a cold soft drink. But avoid advice of the people who work in the club, because they're not familiar with your problems and are often ignorant of even the basics of the physiology of exercise. For example, when I was a consultant for a chain of exercise facilities across the United States, I encountered one such instructor who was an enthusiast for "spot reducing." I referred him to reports of research in several professional articles disproving the concept. He still was not convinced that "spot reducing" did not exist. Another called fat "cellulite." I think I convinced him that there was no such thing, but he went on using the word because he thought it spared the feelings of those who were overweight. *Fat is fat, by any name.*

The saunas and whirlpools you find at such clubs add pleasure after your workout, but they don't provide any exercise benefit. Be sure to check with your physician before using either. The massage that's offered at many clubs does benefit muscles, though—those of the masseur.

Exercise is just as essential to the health of the human body as eating or sleeping, but sometimes we think we don't have time for it. Actually, when you exercise on a regular basis you'll find you have *more* free time because you'll need less sleep. You'll work more efficiently than you did before, and, if you care to look that far ahead, you'll probably live longer than you would without it.

If the references in the Bibliography don't have the answer to a particular question about exercise you might have, ask your physician, who has access to far more literature than could be listed there. Or write to the President's Council on Physical Fitness and Sports, Washington, D.C. 20202. You might even be interested in getting on their mailing list for the *Newsletter* or *Research Digest.*

Remember, the exercise you did when you were young, no matter how many letters it won for you, does not carry over into middle age. In fact, you're almost totally deconditioned in about a month if you stop exercising completely. Your program must be a part of your life and carried on for as long as you live. Intermittent exercise is one of the most dangerous things you can do. When a weekend athlete asks me when he might die, the answer is easy: on a weekend.

I'd like to conclude with the couplet of John Dryden that follows the one I quoted earlier:

> The wise, for cure, on exercise depend;
> God never made His work for man to mend.

ARTHRITIS

The several discussions that have preceded this dealt with the factors responsible for two of the leading causes of death in middle age, heart attack and stroke. These last three sections in this chapter are a departure from that theme. Although the scope of this book does not permit more, we should not conclude this section on the body at midlife without discussing three of our most common health concerns: arthritis, the menopause, and care of our skin and hair.

There are over 100 different types of arthritis, but the one that affects us all as we grow older is osteoarthritis. Because the ending *itis* actually means inflammation, which is only variably present, osteoarthritis is more correctly called osteoarthrosis or, more simply, degenerative joint disease (abbreviated DJD).

About half of middle-aged people have x-ray signs of DJD, and by age sixty-five nearly all do. The interesting thing is that these x-ray signs do not correlate well at all with symptoms. Less than half of those with such x-ray changes have *any* symptoms, and even when they are present, their severity does not correlate with the degree of x-ray changes. And in this type of arthritis laboratory tests are of little or no value. So the diagnosis is essentially a clinical one, by the objective examination of the joints and the subjective evaluation of the symptoms.

To understand DJD, you must know something about the structure of a joint. The two bones that come together have a springy, slippery pad of cartilage on the end of each. The joint is enclosed in a capsule, and the capsule is filled with lubricating fluid. Around this capsule are the ligaments, tendons, and muscles—the structures that lend support to the joint.

What happens first in DJD is deterioration of the cartilage pads. People appear to inherit the degree of toughness their cartilage possesses. If both your parents were troubled by this form of arthritis at an early age, you might have your first symptom as early as age thirty or forty. If not, you might not have a problem until you are much older—or never. The process starts with a roughening and fraying of the surface of the cartilage. The cartilage is then stimulated to repair itself, but the type of cartilage that is formed is not as tough as the original. Adjacent bone then is stimulated to grow spurs, or overgrowths, around the joint. Eventually, the cartilage can be worn away completely in places so that the bone ends themselves grate against each other. It is because the cartilage, which cannot be distinguished on X-ray, is the most important element involved that the radiological changes do not correlate well with symptoms.

These symptoms usually consist of a stiffness in the joints for the first few minutes after you have been sleeping or resting for some time; occasionally a grating noise can be heard coming from the joint when it is moved. Some moderate discomfort may be noted while the joint is being used; its range of motion may become limited; and after excessive use or injury there may be pain, swelling, and tenderness of the joint due to inflammation. The symptoms tend to progress slowly over the years, but the process is *not* usually crippling or deforming, and only rarely are the symptoms worse than this.

Osteoarthritis or DJD can best be divided into three types according to its location: first, that in the fingers, especially the last two joints. There is a stronger hereditary tendency in this type than in the others, and it is much more common in women than in men. The symptoms are mild, noticed mostly early in the morning and during cold or rainy weather. No medical treatment is needed or recommended for this type in most cases.

Secondly, that in the spine. It occurs mostly in the neck and lower back, rarely in the middle of the spine. This does not usually cause symptoms, except for a crackling noise sometimes when you bend your neck or, rarely, a limitation in its mobility. The aching in the back of the neck that is so frequently experienced by all of us is usually due to muscle tension, a result of sustained anxiety, and often moves upward to cause a typical tension headache. Pain in the lower back is most commonly due to strained muscles and ligaments when muscle tone or posture is poor. Infrequently, the spurs which can be seen by X-ray in almost everyone by late middle age pinch a nerve. In this case, or if a disc ruptures, medical or surgical care is necessary. Otherwise, no treatment is usually needed for this type, either.

The third category of DJD is that in the weight-bearing joints—especially the hips, knees, inside of the kneecap, and at the base of the big toes. In these joints, the wearing out of the cartilage is speeded up if one is overweight, and the symptoms are made worse also. This is because the shock to your joints as you walk is increased in a way that is *multiplied* by the excess pounds, not just added to a little bit by being overweight. You may remember the formula from high school physics: Force equals mass times acceleration. This is the type of osteoarthritis that usually requires treatment.

The basic treatment consists of four parts. Far and away the most important factor is your mental attitude. If you are enthusiastic about life and have a number of interests, you may not even be aware of the deterioration of the cartilage in your joints even if it is severe. Studies have shown that those who are unhappy for one or more reasons have a tendency to dwell on their symptoms and suffer far more.

The next most important is exercise. The cartilage itself is nourished by the squeezing action the joint movement has upon it. This is the only way waste products are removed and oxygen can be received by the cartilage from the joint fluid. With regular, moderate exercise, the cartilage will be healthier and its surface smoother, and even exposed bone becomes "eburnated" (polished). All of these results of exercise diminish symptoms considerably. The supporting ligaments and muscles are strengthened also, stabilizing the joint and the bones themselves will become stronger. And the mobility—the range of motion of the joint—usually will be maintained. The exercise should not be jolting or traumatic, however. Walking, bicycling, and swimming are three of the best. Pain is your guide. Push against this barrier gently but frequently. Your exercise should be as much as you can tolerate without pronounced discomfort during, immediately afterwards, or the next morning.

The third most important part of the treatment is to reduce to your ideal weight. This has no effect, of course, in DJD of the hands. There is some effect on that in the lower spine, but it is extremely important for the weight-bearing joints. Being over-weight may even obviate the benefit you should derive from exercise, because the trauma to the joints will simply be too great.

The fourth most important part of the basic treatment is aspirin. Because it is an acid, and for other reasons, aspirin upsets almost everyone's stomach. But because it is the single most effective medicine for DJD, it is necessary to understand how to use it and what it does. Incidentally, it has a few other side effects when used at high doses, such as ringing in the ears and slower blood clotting. The latter, with irritation of the stomach, may even cause bleeding from that site. These are common side effects—others are rare. But the main one is an upset stomach, occurring in almost everyone at any dosage. The best way to avoid this is to take the aspirin with meals. Next best is to take it with an ounce of antacid such as Mylanta or Maalox. The next best is to use a buffered form, such as Ecotrin, Cama, or Ascriptin. The least desirable is the coated type, because the absorption with these preparations is so unpredictable you may not get the benefit you deserve. As to brands, stick to plain aspirin, USP. Avoid brand names—they are no better and cost more.

Now, what does aspirin do? Well, it has *two* effects. The first everyone knows: As an analgesic (anti-pain) medicine, two tablets every four hours relieves about half—sometimes more—of any moderate discomfort such as a headache or that from DJD in the average adult. Taking more than this will *not* take away more discomfort. That's usually all the relief you need—the remainder can be borne easily by most people most of the time.

The second way aspirin works is not well understood by many. It is a very effective anti-inflammatory agent if used correctly for this purpose. If 12 to 24 tables are taken by the average adult every twenty-four hours, in dosages spaced out every four hours or so, inflammation begins to be reduced over the first few hours. The effect is maximal about four to six days after starting. Everyone eliminates aspirin through his/her kidneys at different rates—and even body weight is important in determining the correct dosage to obtain the anti-inflammatory effect. So whether you should take it 12, 24, or some dosage between has to be worked out especially for you. Blood levels can be determined, and the ideal level is 25 milligrams per deciliter of blood. But side effects such as ringing in the ears and prolonged blood clotting begin at about 30, so we are talking about a narrow therapeutic range for this anti-inflammatory effect. If blood levels are not determined, a simple way to achieve this effect is to increase the dosage gradually until ringing in the ears occurs, then back down slightly until the ringing goes away and stay at that dosage.

Most people with osteoarthritis do satisfactorily with the analgesic function of aspirin, using two every once in a while and that's all. In some, because the frayed cartilage and rough bone surfaces rubbing together cause inflammation after excessive use or traumatic injury, the anti-inflammatory action will be needed occasionally. When inflammation does occur, rest becomes more important than exercise—emphasize the former and minimize the latter until the joint is no longer swollen, hot, and red. So aspirin, in either the analgesic or anti-inflammatory dosage, is the principal medicine used in DJD, and the only one that needs to be in most cases.

Other drugs are not generally useful in this form of arthritis. The anti-inflammatory action of indomethacin (Indocin) and some cortisone preparations may be useful for a short time under your doctor's supervision. But they are not often used, due to their side effects versus the benefits obtained. There are several other anti-inflammatory drugs now on the market that have fewer side effects than these two medicines, and one of these may be prescribed for inflammation at your physician's discretion. About one new one is coming out every year or two with great publicity, and they sell well simply because many people have not learned how to take aspirin properly. Motrin, Nalfon, Naprosyn, and Tolectin have been around the longest; Clinoril is the newest. These all have roughly the same anti-inflammatory action as aspirin when it is used properly, but *much less analgesic action*. And the manufacturers of these drugs caution against their simultaneous use with aspirin because of excretion interference. That is, aspirin increases the excretion of these drugs through the kidney to the point where their blood levels are too low to be effective. So if you take them, you are denied the analgesic benefit of aspirin. The treatment of DJD is mostly analgesic, because inflammation is only occasionally present. Therefore these drugs rarely have a place in its treatment. They were actually developed for other types of arthritis that are primarily inflammatory. And they are up to ten times more expensive, with a wider range of side effects than aspirin.

Acetaminophen (Tylenol) is sometimes advertised for osteoarthritis. It does not upset the stomach, but I have found it to have less analgesic action than aspirin. It has *no* anti-inflammatory action, and it is much more expensive. Liver damage has been reported as dosage is increased by patients seeking the relief that aspirin could give.

Stronger pain-deadening agents such as Darvon and Talwin are not appropriate, nor are narcotics. Their effects are transient and the dangers are too great.

Other modes of treatment are sometimes added to the basic four. Although local heat helps, it should not be used for longer than a half-hour or so at a time, or it will actually make the discomfort worse by causing swelling and congestion of the tissue. Incidentally, the liniments purported to penetrate with "deep heat" do not. They only benefit by distracting your nerves (much like when you grab your thumb after hitting it with a hammer) through their irritating action on the skin.

If physiotherapy is advisable in your physician's opinion—for example, to improve range of motion in a joint or to improve muscle strength—this may be prescribed. Most of the techniques can be taught easily so that you can do them at home, saving considerable time, money, and trouble. Splints, crutches, or braces are rarely used, and only for specific purposes over a short period of time. Sometimes a podiatrist can help arthritis in the feet or even the knees with inserts and other orthotic devices.

If a joint becomes severely deformed or limited in its motion, surgery may be necessary. It is not done on hand joints in this type of arthritis, or on the spine unless nerve roots are being pinched. It is most successful in the hip. Here both the end of the thigh bone and hip socket are replaced—a total hip replacement—and a joint of nearly normal function and almost free of pain is the usual result. These artificial joints last ten to fifteen years. This type of surgery is less successful in the knee and is still in the experimental stage for toe joints. All these procedures are serious surgery, so second and even third orthopedic opinions are advisable before such surgery is done. And the surgeon selected should be an expert in the field.

Above all, avoid quacks. There is no diet or nutritional supplement that benefits this type of arthritis. Copper bracelets are pure witchcraft, and acupuncture is equivalent to hypnosis—if you are susceptible to this sort of thing, it might help for a time, but not permanently. Acupressure is a worthless spin-off, as almost everyone knows. Bee-sting venom and other such nostrums have no value. And those Mexican border clinics use some of the dangerous medicines I mentioned, so avoid them.

In the last analysis, your doctor can help you in two ways: making the diagnosis by ruling out other kinds of arthritis and getting you started on the four means of treatment that are effective. But for the long run you must learn to care for the condition yourself. If you would like to have more information, contact your local chapter of the Arthritis Foundation or write to their Public Information Department, 3400 Peachtree Road, N.E., Atlanta, Georgia 30326.

With the proper care, osteoarthritis symptoms can be controlled well enough in most of us so that we can continue to be active and enjoy life with little or no limitation.

MENOPAUSE

The one inevitable aspect of middle age for women is the menopause. This term derives from two Greek words meaning "month" and "cessation." It literally means cessation of menstruation. Sometime in the early forties, ovarian production of estrogen and progesterone begins to decline. The ovaries are the only glands that produce these two hormones in the female, and they cause the menstrual periods by their effects upon the inner lining of the uterus. By age forty-five to fifty, this decline usually reaches a point at which the periods become irregular, and in the next year or two they stop altogether. The ovaries, as they atrophy, also cease to produce ova (eggs). Because of this and the declining hormonal effects on the uterine lining, loss of reproductive capacity occurs at about the same age as the periods stop. But this process is not perfectly synchronized, so birth control precautions should be taken for about a year after the menopause. Ovarian hormone production ceases completely by about age fifty-five, and in the next few years, the ovaries wither away to strands of fibrous tissue. They are gone forever. How this whole series of events occurs is not yet completely understood, but several lines of evidence are converging to indicate that controller genes in the ovarian cells themselves are responsible.

Although we are beginning to understand *how* this occurs, we do not know *why* it does. Of all the animal species on earth, only the human and a few other mammals have a menopause. And in these other mammals it is very near the end of life—not near the middle, as it is in the human. It is interesting, if not too instructive, to speculate on this. The most obvious result is that women have a number of years to live after childbearing has ceased, so it is probably linked to this. It may have been an evolutionary adaptation to allow her more time for the increased duration of child care and sociocultural education required as the human being developed his greater intelligence. In all known societies, childrearing has traditionally belonged to women and the role of protector-provider has gone to men. Of course, not all women survived past this point—or even to it—but some would, and could have cared for the children collectively.

If this is so, women might well ask why such a loss of hormones and reproductive capacity shouldn't occur in men instead to produce the same result. The obvious answer is that an older woman could still be impregnated by a younger male, and she would be unable to care for these late children through the years they require. Or women might ask in fairness why the same process shouldn't occur at about the same age in both sexes. There is no clear answer here, but in addition to the above, the loss of testosterone by the male would reduce his muscle strength, bone mass, territoriality, deep voice, aggressiveness, and other characteristics which enhance his protector-provider role. So perhaps there is some reason in the great scheme of things for women to lose their reproductive capacity when they do.

But even if we accept this reason for a woman's midlife loss of reproductive capacity, it is still not clear why it could not come about in some other way, without the loss of her hormonal production. Because the loss of the male hormone would be so disadvantageous to men, this naturally raises the question of what happens to women when they lose their hormones. Several things. None of them affect survival of the species at all, but they do affect the woman herself throughout her later years. This is especially true of estrogen (a name which actually refers to three similar hormones: estradiol, estrone, and estriol). It would have been far better if only her reproductive capacity were to cease, because the effects of the hormone loss are all adverse for her. One wonders if nature's "scheme of things" isn't designed to benefit the species rather than the individual.

Many women think of the main menopausal symptom as unpredictable sweating and hot flashes, but many other changes due to declining hormone production begin at this time. Some are so gradual as to escape notice until years have gone by. A few of the more serious ones will be discussed in detail, but many of the minor though upsetting ones can just be listed. In addition to changes attributable to aging alone, the voice loses some of its soft quality and becomes more harsh; there is increased thinning and atrophy of the skin; the breasts lose some of their fullness, and there is a subtle redistribution of fat that alters feminine body contours; the vagina loses length and elasticity, and its lining becomes thinner; the vagina's lubricating Bartholin glands atrophy; there is also a decrease in the vaginal wall secretions, which at the same time become more alkaline, making the woman more susceptible to infections; the larger vaginal lips lose their fat pads and become thinner and wrinkled—this exposes the urethral and vaginal openings and the sensitive clitoris to irritation from undergarments; the uterus shrinks substantially; the walls of the bladder and the lining of the tube leading out from it become thinner, making urinary tract infections more likely; and the supporting tissues of the pelvic organs lose strength—this allows the bladder, urethra, and rectum to sag down, sometimes to the point where incontinence is experienced on coughing, laughing, or sneezing. More serious sagging of these internal organs is usually due to the trauma of previous childbirth. There are also adverse alterations of the cholesterol and lipid levels in the blood, which are believed to be the major factor in the increased mortality rate after the menopause of approximately four times over what would be expected from aging alone. As depressing as this list might seem, every one of these changes can be prevented by early estrogen replacement. And, despite what you might hear from food faddists and others, no nutritional supplement or other substance can compensate in any way for this hormone loss.

There are four changes other than those on this list that deserve more explanation. Sweating and hot flashes are known as vasomotor symptoms and are the result of unpredictable dilatation of blood vessels in the skin. The more proper term *hot flushes* has largely been replaced by the more popular *hot flashes*. They are caused by a disturbance in the autonomic nervous system, originating in the hypothalamus, a part of the brain, due to the drop in estrogen. Physicians, mainly in the past, have tried to give sedatives to ease hot flashes, but they are relatively ineffective during the day—and do not work at all during the night for the simple reason that the hypothalamus is not affected by sedation while one is asleep. Nor is any other medication helpful, except for its placebo effect. Only estrogen replacement therapy is successful in eliminating hot flashes, but they do gradually taper off over the years without it.

Hair on the head thins somewhat with aging, but the loss of estrogen aggravates this thinning and changes the hair pattern itself over the years. Production of male hormones by the adrenal glands continues after the menopause, so now without the opposing effect of estrogen, a masculine type of hair distribution on the head gradually becomes apparent in those who have inherited balding genes—about 60 percent of women. This is characterized by a "widow's peak"—recession on either side of the head and a tendency to bald in the center. In all women, the same unopposed male hormones cause an increased hair growth on the chest, upper lip, chin, and other areas where hair usually grows in the male but not in the female. Estrogen replacement prevents and halts the progression, but cannot reverse any of these hair changes once they have occurred.

Osteoporosis (thinning of the bones) is the most serious physical result of hormone loss. The density and strength of the bones decrease about 2 percent a year after the menopause in women; this is four or five times the decrease in men that age. Physicians for centuries have noted that postmenopausal women tend to have fractures of the lower forearm that have no counterpart in men, and develop a "dowager's hump," the exaggerated forward curvature of the back, due to the anterior collapse of the vertebral bodies of the spine. But the major reason osteoporosis is so serious is that more than 200,000 hip fractures a year occur in women over sixty-five in the United States, with a mortality of 25 to 40 percent depending mostly on the age at which the fracture occurs. Only a fraction as many occur in men.

The cause of osteoporosis is obviously complex and not completely understood. The leading theory is that without estrogen, bone is more sensitive to the dissolving effect of parathyroid hormone. As shown by Lila Nachtigall and others, if estrogen replacement is started sometime in the first three postmenopausal years, it will reverse the osteoporosis that has occurred. But if started later it cannot reverse—only retard the process as long as the therapy is continued. The best treatment regimen now known includes estrogen replacement with adequate protein and calcium in the diet. Exercise increases bone strength, so is also encouraged. Vitamin D supplementation is controversial, as is the role of fluoride. Calcium supplements are ineffective when taken alone, because the primary process is the deterioration of the protein matrix, not the crystalline structure, of the bone.

The fourth of the more serious results of estrogen loss has to do with the as yet poorly understood effects upon the brain and central nevous system. What is known so far is that most of the psychological problems that occur during and after the menopause were previously brewing just under the surface—the loss of estrogen merely precipitates them. Generally, women who were well-adjusted before menopause continue on through their lives without difficulty. So although estrogen replacement is the only effective way in which the other difficulties mentioned can be counteracted, if psychological problems arise its use should be in conjunction with the usually accepted psycho-therapeutic modalities. The psychological stresses that occur at this time of life certainly compound the problem, but are not usually considered. For example, menopause signals the undeniable loss of a woman's reproductive capacity, part of her previous reason for being. This and the subsequent changes in her feminine appearance are two direct blows at her feminine self-image. She is also made acutely aware of her own aging by the event itself. The loss of her role as a mother as her children are now more independent and leaving home further threatens her sense of self. Her husband may be having difficulties with his own middle age, and this can cause marital strain. She also may be increasingly concerned about his health at this age. All of these and more need to be evaluated in each particular person, and reliance upon estrogen to put them all right should be avoided.

I said all the effects of the loss of female hormones at menopause were bad. Not quite true. The androgen secretion from the adrenal glands continues—and with fewer restraints, fear of pregnancy gone, and no more messy menses, sex drive usually increases. In the few cases where it appears to drop off, the woman has only been putting up with sex and is looking for any excuse to stop. However, the genital changes mentioned may make intercourse uncomfortable without estrogen replacement, leaving the woman with increased desire and decreased ability to satisfy this desire, a frustrating situation.

Estrogen replacement therapy, as indicated above, prevents or ameliorates every one of this seemingly overwhelming array of disruptions brought about by its loss at the menopause. Estrogen for brief spans of time—weeks or months—was first used in the United States starting in the 1930s purely for the relief of hot flashes, but its use increased from about 1960 on as physicians and patients alike learned more of its other, long-term benefits. Approximately twenty million menopausal and postmenopausal women were receiving estrogen replacement in this country in 1975, but there has since been a decrease of about one-fourth, which I'll go into shortly. Most authorities seem to be in agreement that, ideally, estrogen replacement should be started in all women as ovarian production begins to fall, and continue for life *if there were no risk*. But as with anything else, advantages must be weighed against disadvantages. Let's look at some of the latter.

Years ago, high blood pressure was noted to develop in some women who were taking estrogen postmenopausally and to disappear when the estrogen was stopped. But further studies showed that hypertension usually occurred in these same women later on without their taking estrogen. It was then found that these women produced more of a hypertension-inducing substance in their livers or were predisposed to develop hypertension by other hereditary factors. Estrogen reduces salt elimination by the kidneys, and this is believed to be the principle way in which hypertension is precipitated at an earlier date. So we now know that the development of high blood pressure need not be a contraindication for estrogen, because the problem will tend to arise later anyhow. Rather, it should serve as a signal for reduction of salt intake and taking other appropriate measures as would be indicated for anyone so predisposed. The same is true with other conditions that may be adversely affected by salt retention and fluid accumulation, such as asthma, epilepsy, serious heart disease, and migraine. If you have any of these conditions, your physician's advice should be followed.

Vaginal infections are sometimes noted upon beginning

estrogen therapy, but careful study has shown that the organisms causing the infection were already present in the vagina before the estrogen was begun. That they were there at all was due to the loss of the protective effect of estrogen after the menopause. The increased secretions caused by estrogen merely formed a more favorable medium in which the organisms once there could multiply. The usual treatment to eliminate the infection should be instituted, and then estrogen replacement will maintain the natural balance of conditions that prevent the entry and establishment of such organisms in the first place.

About half of women in the postmenopausal years have benign fibroid tumors of the uterus. In most, the tumors are small and asymptomatic. However, estrogen may cause some of these to grow, so low dosage is usually prescribed to avoid this.

Some discomfort in the breasts may be noticed if estrogen therapy is begun several years after the menopause. This is due to enlargement from glandular stimulation, fat redistribution, and some fluid accumulation. If this is the case, the physician should begin the use of estrogens gradually, and again, the final dosage should be low. The same is true with nausea of other gastrointestinal symptoms that sometimes occur.

The increased tendency of blood to clot during pregnancy (when estrogen levels are very high) has been known for many years. This is regarded as a protective device on the part of nature to prevent excessive blood loss during pregnancy and child-birth from such complications as detached placenta and a tear of the cervix or vagina. The same increased tendency was then noted in those who were given estrogen in high doses. In any person who has varicose veins, severe atherosclerosis, or other vascular disorder in which the blood flow is slowed, clots may form with or without the enhancing effect of estrogen. Because such clots forming in veins may go to the lungs, or those in the arteries can cause heart attacks and strokes, this is a serious consideration. When such vascular abnormalities are known to be present, they are often regarded as a contraindication to the administration of estrogen. However, there is no evidence that estrogens cause clot formation in healthy women *without* such predisposing vascular factors. And although all forms of estrogen can be shown to have this clot-enhancing effect in the laboratory, most studies show that it is only the synthetic estrogens such as those in birth control pills (ethinyl estradiol and mestranol) that have this effect in clinical use. It is for this reason that birth control pills are not advised for women over forty, some of whom may have developed severe atherosclerosis. *But clot formation even in the woman with the above vascular disorders has not been shown to occur with conjugated natural estrogens at the lower dosage levels.* However, if you have had problems in the past due to clot formation (such as heart attack, stroke, thrombophlebitis), or have *any* vascular abnormality, be sure to discuss this with your physician.

An increased incidence of gallstones has been found in some women taking estrogens. This is because the solubility of cholesterol products in bile is lowered slightly by estrogen. Again, on closer look, it occurred mostly in women whose cholesterol levels were too high in the first place. I have already discussed why cholesterol levels in the blood can and should be kept low and how this can be done.

A few rare conditions may contraindicate estrogen replacement therapy, such as some types of porphyria and liver disease, severe kidney disease, and familial hypercholesterolemia. But to this point, we have found only advantages with estrogen therapy for normal, healthy menopausal and postmenopausal women, and no disadvantages.

Let's move on to the two areas of greatest concern: cancer of the breast and of the uterine lining. That estrogen might have some influence on the incidence of breast cancer has been suspected since 1896, and from then on there have been conflicting reports. Some have shown an increased incidence, some no effect, and some have shown protection against such cancer. The best review of the literature—by Robert Hoover of the National Cancer Institute—concluded that there may be a slight increase in the risk of breast cancer in those women who are so predisposed if they take estrogens. I would suggest that your physician carefully review the known factors that predispose to breast cancer with you before placing you on estrogen replacement therapy. For any woman these are: a strong family history of breast cancer, previous such cancer in the patient herself, age over thirty-five, lumps or thickenings in the breast, a late menopause, no childbirths, first childbirth at an age later than thirty, and an early onset of menstruation. Some of these have far greater weight than others, and their predictive value when more than one is present is also variable, so individual evaluation of each person should be made by the physician. Few women will be denied the benefits of estrogen replacement because of these factors. Most will merely be examined more frequently and urged to examine themselves regularly as well.

The most serious controversy over estrogen replacement concerns its possible role in causing cancer of the uterine lining (endometrial adenocarcinoma). Let's approach this problem with some of the background. Several facts relating to this are clear-cut and have been established for some time. In premenopausal women who produce constant high levels of estrogen over a long time—fifteen or twenty years—because of a certain type of tumor of their ovaries, or who are given high constant dosages by their physicians as treatment for surgical or congenital absence of ovaries or for cancer of the breast (some of these cancers regress on this therapy) over a similar length of time, the incidence of endometrial cancer is definitely increased. And the incidence increases the longer such high constant levels of estrogen are present. The lining of the uterus (endometrium) is known to be sensitive to all three estrogens, especially estrone, which stimulate cell growth in this tissue. Whenever this type of stimulation occurs in any tissue in the body, the probability of an error in duplication of the cells producing an abnormal or cancerous cell is increased. And the growth rate of hormone-sensitive cancers which occur at random is also increased by such stimulation. So there is a sound basis for concern about the effect of estrogen in this type of cancer.

But let's not leave out what we know about the role of progesterone. In the natural cycle prior to the menopause, estrogen is first produced each month by the ovaries and thickens the lining of the uterus. Progesterone is then produced by the ovary in the last half of the month as estrogen production tapers off. Progesterone makes the endometrial cells less sensitive to estrogen and after its peak, when estrogen production is at its lowest point, the decline of progesterone causes sloughing of the entire lining of the uterus, resulting in the menstrual period. Two other pertinent facts regarding progesterone should be pointed out. In premenopausal women with anovulatory cycles (no egg is released from the ovary) or dysfunctional bleeding due to progesterone deficiency, the risk of endometrial cancer is definitely increased. So progesterone is presumably protective. As long as the natural cyclic process continues, cancer of the endometrium is almost unknown. The second fact is that with the use of some of the earlier sequential birth-control pills, the incidence of this type of cancer was also increased. It was found that such an increase occurred only with those pills that had a low or ineffective progesterone effect, so these preparations were taken off the market. Those with a high progesterone effect were found to be protective against this type of cancer. All that I have said so far has been known for a long time and provides enough background to consider the problem.

But before I do so, let me present a perplexity. We have long known that estrogen at high levels over a long period of time increases the incidence of endometrial cancer. But why, when estrogen production by the ovaries is high from puberty to the menopause, and especially during pregnancies, does endometrial cancer almost never occur; and why, when estrogen production by the ovaries ceases, does most of it then occur? There is little such cancer in the thirties, a low incidence in the forties, and it rises after the menopause through the fifties to reach a peak in the sixties. The answer to the first part of the problem is easy: Progesterone is not only protective against such cancer formation, but any abnormal cells that might result despite this protection are sloughed off with the uterine lining each month before they can get established as cancer. The answer to the second part is a bit more difficult. I have already said that there is a long time lag in the effect of estrogen on this type of cancer. Constant high estrogen levels or dosages result in an increased incidence about fifteen to twenty years later. So let's look back that same length of time from the age span when this cancer typically occurs—we arrive at the menopause itself. *Something must start here* that increases the incidence later. But, as I have mentioned, both estrogen and progesterone production taper off, then cease after the menopause. I did not mention another fact, however—that a male hormone from the adrenal glands, androstenedione, is partially converted after the menopause to estrone by tissues throughout the body. Estrone is the most potent estrogen in its effect upon the cells of the endometrium, so although it is at a low level in the blood after the menopause, *it is constant and no longer counteracted by progesterone.* Incidentally, this conversion to estrone is more efficient in fatty tissue. So here we have the probable explanation for the occurrence of endometrial cancer in women who are fifteen to twenty years postmenopausal, as well as a reason for its being three to nine times more common in obese postmenopausal women than in those of normal weight.

With all of the foregoing, we are now in a position to review the studies that have appeared in the literature since December 1975 and that have caused so much concern. It is because of them that estrogen replacement therapy has decreased by about one-fourth. All of them contain flaws; oddly enough the one that created the most furor was the first and most flawed of all. As an epidemiologist (a physician trained to design and analyze such studies) myself, I have been appalled by most of them. They are all retrospective and therefore the methods used to determine the details of estrogen use gave results that were not only unreliable but sparse in details. There was no way of knowing if a cancer was present *before* estrogen replacement was started. Some 80 percent of the cancer found was stage 0 and I—and these are difficult to distinguish from benign hyperplasia, simple over-growth of the lining. Race wasn't even considered—this type of cancer is more than twice as frequent among whites as blacks, and the former are far more likely to take estrogens than the latter. The most important flaw has to do with the fact that most such cancer is known to be dormant or grow slowly over the years and thus is never detected during life. Estrogen administration increases the occurrence of post-menopausal bleeding, and it is in the investigation of this bleeding that most of the cancer has been found. This detection bias has not been corrected in these studies. It is similar to the dramatic increase that was noted in the incidence of cancer of the cervix when the Pap smear first became widely used. I could go on with criticisms of these studies—for example, the role of obesity was not considered by any of them. But, taken together (there are eight such reports as of this writing), the errors of one study are often cancelled out by another, so let's accept one fact that emerges from them: a statistical association between estrogen use (its dosage and duration) and the incidence of endometrial cancer is established. *This is no more than we already knew!* One wonders then why the widespread publicity in the media, causing so much concern in women. I am simply at a loss to explain it.

Three crucial points still have not been clarified by these (or any) studies:

1. It is well accepted that dosage is of the greatest importance,

yet to date *low dosage has not been adequately evaluated*. To quote one of the recent retrospective studies, "The risk in women taking the lowest dose (.3 milligram) remains uncertain." Most of these studies ignore dosage, refer to it merely as "high" or "low," or "above 1 milligram" and "below 1 milligram."

2. Although cyclic administration (twenty-one of twenty-eight days or twenty-five days a month) was shown in some of these retrospective studies not to decrease the risk significantly in comparison to constant dosage, the *combination of low dose and cyclic administration (as estrogen should be given) was not investigated by any of them.* The one that did separate out women on such a regimen showed that they had *less* risk than those who received no estrogen, but unfortunately the numbers in this group were too small to be significant statistically.

3. *The use of progesterone and estrogen together in a manner approximating their natural cycles was not dealt with at all in any of these studies.* We may come to realize that this is the way hormone replacement should have been handled all along. Several authorities have found in smaller studies of better design that such combination therapy resulted in little or no increased risk. The best such study in the literature was not even designed to answer this problem. It was done to determine the effect of estrogen on osteoporosis. Lila F. Nachtigall and her associates at New York University Medical Center in 1965 commenced a meticulously designed prospective double-blind study with eighty-four women receiving such a progesterone-estrogen regimen and eighty-four matched controls receiving placebos—pills without any activity whatever. *None of those receiving hormones has developed uterine cancer to this date, but two in the control group which did not receive hormones did!* The estrogen was in high dosage (2.5 milligrams), yet the progesterone provided complete protection.

Strangely, none of the retrospective studies that have aroused the furor by stating the incidence of endometrial cancer to be increased five to fifteen times by estrogen replacement therapy has mentioned what the low incidence is that is to be multiplied by those figures. Nor have they put the problem in relation to the fact that only 10 percent of women who develop this type of cancer ever took estrogen at all—or pointed out that over one-fourth of postmenopausal women have had a hysterectomy, so that the problem does not even exist for them. They also fail to mention that endometrial cancer accounts for just 1 percent of all cancer deaths in women and that the cure rate of this type of cancer is high—approximately 90 percent with early detection. Some perspective is sorely needed.

Even though the authors of some of these retrospective studies themselves urged caution in drawing conclusions, the FDA in 1976 issued a bulletin based on the first few urging restrictions in the use of estrogens after the menopause. There can be no quarrel with this—some of the restrictions suggested were sensible; the physician and patient could still use their own judgments. But in 1977 the FDA mandated that inserts be placed in all estrogens dispensed, describing the findings of these retrospective studies along with all of the possible side effects of estrogen therapy without a balanced explanation of the benefits. This may be the legislative mandate of the FDA—to protect us while not adequately advising us—but it is simply unfair to the women receiving estrogen. Caution in use is commendable, but ordering that such a one-sided view be given the patient is intolerable. Understandably, those organizations most responsible directly to the patient (the American Society of Internal Medicine, the American College of Obstetrics and Gynecology, etc.) have taken legal action, which is still pending, against the FDA to cancel this governmental edict.

So, until more is known, risk should be recognized, just as it is in any other action in our lives—even that of crossing the street. Everything we have reviewed here regarding possible adverse effects of estrogen therapy should be weighed by you with your physician against its advantages, and an individual decision made for you. His decision, if you are healthy, most probably will be low dosage (.3 to .6 milligram) of conjugated estrogen such as Premarin or Menest, administered cyclically. If your uterus is present, a progestogen such as Provera may be prescribed for the last seven to ten days of the cycle—or perhaps only every few months—as a precaution. This may cause periods to continue for a few years, but the protection is well worth it. He might elect to do an endometrial biopsy before starting estrogen and thereafter will examine you at regular intervals and if you have any bleeding. This examination should consist of both a Pap smear and an aspiration curettage or one of the newer techniques specifically designed to detect endometrial cancer in its earliest stages, such as the "jet washer." These are simple procedures and are done in the office without anesthesia. Also, your physician undoubtedly will use a blood test to ensure that the combination of your natural ovarian production and/or oral administration of estrogen is correct, because the older methods of using cervical mucous or a scraping of the vagina are known to be far too inaccurate. And he will not use injections nor make the mistake of prescribing only vaginal creams or ointments "to avoid the risk" of endometrial cancer, because he knows the absorption from these produces the same blood levels as oral estrogen. With these precautions, almost all menopausal and postmenopausal women can have the benefits of estrogen replacement therapy in safety, and grow older with beauty and grace.

The myth of a "male menopause" is mentioned again and again in the lay literature, and the time is long overdue to put it to rest forever. Since the word *menopause* means cessation of menstrual periods, it is not even applicable to men. The term *climacteric* could be used—it is more general, deriving from the Greek word *klimakterikos*, which means peak or climax. Even if it is used, the question is still whether any precipitous change occurs in males comparable to that in females. There is no doubt that there are physical, physiological, and psychological changes in men throughout the middle years. There is no sudden change, however, and for a true climacteric as in the female to occur would require a sudden cessation of testosterone and sperm production analogous to the loss of ovarian estrogen and ovum production in the female. In extremely rare cases this does occur—a male who once produced testosterone and sperm suddenly ceases to do so. But this can happen at any time in life—youth, middle age, or old age—and the term *climacteric* could be used then, but there are better terms. Otherwise, both testosterone and sperm production remain active until a man's death whatever his age, although they do decline gradually throughout his life. Except for these rare cases, there is no event that can be called either a climacteric or a menopause in men. One authority, Elmer Hess, who reviewed all the pertinent literature, has stated, "There is no such entity . . . we can only conclude that an unfortunate and misleading term has been coined. . . ." I agree.

SKIN AND HAIR CARE

It may have been a change in your skin or hair that first made you realize you might be approaching middle age. The skin is actually the largest organ in the body and certainly the most evident, but most of us do not pay much serious attention to it or our hair until some change that signifies aging is noticed. From that point on, both are of increasing concern to us. We can no longer be careless about them, even if we have been before. These are what we present first of ourselves to the world, whether we are men or women, so this discussion will omit topics such as makeup and hair styles—it is for both sexes.

Obviously one brief section cannot cover the whole range of medical conditions of the skin and hair at midlife. To do that would require a textbook on dermatology. I have listed one of the best in the Bibliography and will leave it at that. Nor, as I have said, will I talk about "cosmetology," for that is a world all of its own. When I did delve into it, I felt as if I had been transported back hundreds of years to the days of alchemy and witches' potions. I was amazed that so many could be so gullible at such incredible expense. Women who are interested in finding out some facts on this should consult a good guide, for example, *The AMA Book of Skin and Hair Care*, before consulting *any* cosmetician or "cosmetologist," as some like to call themselves.

Let's see how aging affects the skin by first discussing the structures just beneath it.

The facial contour is upheld by three broad muscles. One encircles the eyes; the second encircles the mouth, with a supporting branch from the corner of the mouth to the cheekbone. The third is the chewing muscle most easily felt at the side of your jaw when you bite hard. These muscles slowly lose some volume with age, producing a subtle change that is not noticeable until later middle age. Below the face, starting at the chin and extending down the neck, there is a wide but thin sheet of muscle that loses more tone than mass with the years. This may be noted somewhat earlier. Facial exercises, I'm sorry to say, do nothing to preserve the volume or tone of any of these muscles. They only make you look funny while you are doing them.

The pattern of fat distribution around the face is inherited to start with, but it is also affected by age and, in women, by the loss of estrogen after menopause. Both of these cause a gradual loss of volume in the fat pads, eventually altering facial contours. Even so, the fat pads just above and below the eyes may appear to be more prominent—this is due to loss of tone in the membranous tissue enveloping them. Estrogen replacement therapy helps maintain the facial fat pads in women after the menopause, but some loss continues due to aging itself.

The teeth lose a portion of their vertical dimension and the jawbone also undergoes some diminution. These latter two changes are not usually apparent until after the age of sixty or sixty-five, however. Artists have long known that the face of a young person can be divided into three equal vertical spaces consisting of the forehead, the nose, and the mouth and chin. You might recall the sketches of Leonardo da Vinci, which show this loss in the third dimension dramatically in his older figures. By that time in life, the nose has elongated slightly and widened a bit at the tip, tending to emphasize the loss of this lower dimension. But in middle age, we don't have to worry yet about these changes—most of our concern is with the skin itself.

Several changes take place in the skin during the middle years. The outer layer, the epidermis, has flat, dead cells on the surface, and these accumulate, tending to give the skin a coarser, duller appearance. This change also makes the pores seem larger. As the sweat glands gradually become less efficient, they moisturize the skin less. The oil glands also become less productive with age, and as this oil normally retards evaporation of natural moisture, this adds to the increasing dryness of the skin.

More skin growths and blemishes begin to appear, and some of these may be serious. You should visit your dermatologist as soon as you notice any new growth or change in pigmentation just to be sure, no matter how unimportant it might seem. The most common are the brown spots often called "age spots" or "liver spots." The medical term for them is *lentigines*. As pigment production in the skin lessens about 1 percent per year, some areas undergo a spontaneous increase in production, the exact cause of which is not known. These spots are not important, except cosmetically. Despite advertising to the contrary, they are not significantly lightened by the bleaching creams on the market which contain hydroquinone. In fact, allergies and other reactions often occur with the use of these preparations, so don't bother with them. However, the spots do fade considerably with less exposure to the sun, and I will have some tips on this later. Those that are the most distressing to you can be burned off without scarring if they are small, and dermabrasion, which I will also discuss later, can help with larger ones. Tiny red lines and "spiders" sometimes appear as one ages—these are dilated blood vessels. They are caused by heredity, heavy drinking, excessive warmth, and facial treatments that damage the skin. These vessels can be sealed off with an electric needle and made to disappear almost entirely.

Although the epidermis thickens, the inner layer of the skin, the dermis, actually becomes thinner as we age. Within this layer is the elastic meshwork of fibers, composed mostly of a substance called collagen, that provides the supportive structure for the skin. With age, this meshwork gradually becomes less elastic and slowly stretches. This is the process that is responsible for the larger wrinkles—"frown" lines, corrugations on the forehead, and the deep grooves running from sides of the nose to the corners of the mouth. The ground substance, which is the matrix for the supporting meshwork, also slowly degenerates. This is the cause of the smaller, shallow wrinkles. These are often referred to as "crepe paper" wrinkles, and occur mostly above and below the lips. Sometimes both processes work together—for example, in causing the wrinkles around the eyes.

These are the general facts behind wrinkle formation for everyone. When you yourself get wrinkles is affected by three major factors: heredity, exposure to sunlight, and habitual facial expressions. Some other factors such as vigorous scrubbing, facial massages and masques, certain cosmetics, heavy drinking, estrogen loss at the menopause, cigarette smoking, atmospheric pollutants, and exposure to wind play more minor roles. Contrary to advertising, dry skin is *not* a cause of wrinkles. Moreover, no magic formula will remove them once they are formed, so prevention is all-important. Cosmetic surgery is the only cure, and it is limited in what it can do.

The care of your skin at this or any age comes down to three basic procedures: protection, cleansing, and moisturization.

Protection

This means protection from the sun and ultraviolet tanning lamps. Frequent exposure to sun over many years can make your skin look up to twenty years older than you are, and most skin cancers are caused this way, too. The best way to appreciate the effect sunlight has on your skin is to compare an area at the lower part of your neck that is often exposed to the sun with any area that is not, such as the side of your buttocks. Most everyone is aware that many dermatologists, who are concerned only with the skin, caution against *any* exposure to the sun. If this advice were followed rigidly, it would restrict many activities that add a great deal of satisfaction and health in life. So seek a balance. Reduce unnecessary exposure and take suitable precautions when such exposure goes along with thoroughly enjoyable and healthful activities.

There are two or three things to keep in mind on this. One is that the closer you are to the equator, the greater the effects of the sun's rays. Another is the time. The worst is between 11 A.M. and 3 P.M., no matter where you are. Then, before you go out, give some thought to your clothing. Wear light colors that reflect the sun and cover as much of your body as possible. This leaves the face as the major remaining problem. Women are more fortunate than men because they can wear floppy hats with wide brims for outdoor activities and manage to look attractive in them. Men's hats haven't been an "in" thing for years. However, because wearing a hat is the easiest way to protect the face, a man should try this with a bit of imagination. He can wear a Mexican peasant straw hat or perhaps one of those grometted and stitched hats made out of sail canvas—something with a bit of dash—and set his own style. For additional protection, both men and women have to rely upon suntan lotions.

Only a small part of the ultraviolet spectrum of sunlight toward the shorter end is harmful to the skin. For this reason, the best suntan lotions over the last decade or two have come to contain chemicals that screen out this portion. The most efficient are para-aminobenzoic acid (PABA), PABA derivatives, and the benzophenones. There are others, such as the salicylate compounds, but they do not work as well. Whether a preparation is called a screen or a block depends upon both the chemical used and its concentration. Most people rely too much upon what the preparation is called and do not stop to think that no matter which they use, its efficiency also depends on how thickly and how often it is applied. Some preparations are in an alcoholic solution that dries conveniently. But the disadvantage of this type is that it drips off with perspiration and is removed completely by swimming and showering. These also tend to be irritating when perspiration runs into the eyes. So those in an oil base are better—a little messier, but they will stay on the skin longer and also help retain moisture in the skin. However, even these should be reapplied every two or three hours to ensure adequate protection, and after every swim or shower.

Both the nose and the lower lip usually catch the sun's rays more directly, and the skin of the lips is also thinner, so these require greater protection. Put a little more of whatever preparation you use on your nose. Women are fortunate again because lipstick protects their lips almost perfectly. Men and those women who do not wear lipstick should use a lip pomade containing a PABA derivative (such as Sea and Ski, Chap Stick, or Kristi). The best protection for both the lips and nose is afforded by ointments containing either zinc or titanium oxide. These are a little unsightly but provide a barrier that the sun cannot penetrate.

I have used three terms—*screen*, *block*, and *barrier*—because this is the best way to group protective sun preparations. It's about time I defined them—or tried to. There is some overlap. The barriers physically prevent all the sun's rays from reaching your skin; the blocks offer good protection but prevent tanning; the screens offer less protection and allow tanning to take place. Starting in the summer of 1980 all such products will be labeled with a numerical sun protection factor (SPF) which will be more precise than these terms are now. These range from 2 affording the least protection to 15 with the greatest. Examples of commercial barriers are A-Fil and Nos-Kote; of the blocks, Maxafil, Eclipse, Sea and Ski lotion, Pre Sun, Block Out and Uval; of the screens, Swedish Tanning Secret, Coppertone, Sea and Ski Dark Tanning Oil, and Sundare.

A few last cautions about exposure to the sun. At higher altitudes there is much more ultraviolet light because the atmosphere there is thinner and does not screen out as much as at lower altitudes. The problem is that you can't *feel* the harmful ultraviolet rays, only those toward the infrared end of the spectrum, so it is difficult to judge your exposure. There is a similar hazard on hazy days at any altitude. The high clouds stop much of the infrared and let ultraviolet through, so be careful. And a cool breeze or swimming in cool water can also make you think you're getting much less ultraviolet exposure than you actually are.

Several substances on the market produce an artificial tan by staining the outer layer of the skin. Remember when we added iodine to baby oil or mineral oil to do the same thing? The newer ones contain dihydroxyacetone (DHA). These preparations are perfectly safe if you keep in mind that they don't block out harmful rays, and you can get a serious sunburn underneath them. The stain wears off after a week or so, and you have to "tan" yourself again. Preparations advertised as "bronzers" or color gels are different—they do not stain and can be washed off easily.

Sunburn is just that—a burn from the sun. Once your skin has been burned, there is little you can do except make yourself as comfortable as you can until your skin heals. Using sprays and preparations that contain deadening chemicals such as the "caines" is not advisable. Used over such a wide area of damaged skin, they often lead to sensitivity; then the local anesthetics injected for surgery and dental procedures cannot be used for the rest of your life without the possibility of a dangerous reaction. The simplest way to get relief is by applying cool wet compresses or by taking a cool bath. Adding Aveeno, one cup per tub, helps. Lotions containing aloe are also soothing, but if your sunburn is severe, you should see your physician for more specific treatment.

A tan occurs with more gradual exposure. First, the lower layer of skin containing the pigment-producing cells is stimulated to produce more pigment. Dark-skinned sunbathers acquire some tan in just a few hours this way. Then over the next few days of exposure these pigment-containing cells hasten their migration through the outer layers to the skin surface. It is the depth of the layers containing these cells that causes the darker tan. A third result of sun exposure over several days is one you really don't want, the thickening of the outermost cornified layer of the skin. This gives the skin a coarse appearance. All three are nature's mechanisms to limit the harmful penetration of sunlight. People with light complexions, because they have fewer pigment-producing cells, will not tan as well, but do tend to freckle more in the sun.

One advantage of being middle-aged is that the outer layers have become somewhat thicker by then; this itself offers some protection. Another is that if you have not had too much sun exposure so far, you can be comforted by the fact that there is a ten to twenty year lag before the harmful effects of the sun begin to be evident, so you can be a little less compulsive with your protective measures.

Cleansing

This is the second basic precaution to take in caring for your skin in middle age. The most important rule to observe is that any cleanser must rinse off completely with water. Soaps and detergents are the best when used properly. Many cleansing lotions and creams are on the market, ranging from cold creams to the truly exotic. Most are a combination of detergent, wetting agent, beeswax, alcohol, water, oil, and borax. They may be used for preliminary removal of makeup, if a woman wishes to, but are inadequate for cleansing. Any preparation that must be *wiped off* cannot clean the skin. If you doubt this, try applying corkblack or dark makeup all over your face; then keep your eyes closed as you go through your usual cleansing cream routine. Then open your eyes. This *will* open your eyes! The so-called washing creams at least can be rinsed off, but they offer no advantage over simple soap or detergent and are much more expensive.

Soaps are made from alkali and fats. Those that contain a great deal of alkali are more efficient as cleansers and are designed to be used for the kitchen floor or woodwork, not your skin. The milder soaps, such as Ivory, Camay, and Lux, contain less than 1 percent free alkali and are the ones you should use. Detergents, of course, work better than soaps in hard water. Any of these that are packaged and labelled for personal use are satisfactory for the skin. Some soaps contain organic acids with the claimed advantage that the acidity of normal skin (the "acid mantle" maintained by skin bacteria) is not interfered with, but these soaps do not suds or clean as well as the others. And the organic acid is rinsed off anyway. No harm has ever been shown from temporarily altering this "acid mantle," and it is replaced within three or four hours by bacterial action. Save your money. Some soaps are manufactured with less animal tallow and more glycerin or castor oil than ordinary soaps and therefore are transparent. No advantage of such soaps has ever been shown, despite the advertising. There are also heavily fatted soaps on the market, such as Basis and Tone, or super-fatted detergents, such as Dove, that are advertised for dry skin. Most of the "moisturizer" goes down the drain, as does the extra money you paid, so don't be misled. Three tips that cost you nothing if you tend to have dry skin: You can reduce the amount of natural oil you remove by using warm water rather than hot, by not using a washcloth, or by not scrubbing quite so vigorously.

When you wash your face, suds the soap or detergent in thoroughly without undue rubbing. If you use a washcloth, use it gently or this, too, will enhance wrinkle formation. Rinse at least three times. Then, if you wish, splash on an astringent, but there is none better than plain cold water. Pat your face dry; never rub it vigorously with a towel. In general, the best time to wash most carefully is at night, because then you remove all the dirt and contaminants acquired throughout the day and can follow this with a moisturizer that will stay on most of the night.

Moisturizing

This is the third step in skin care. Cleansing removes most of the natural oil from your skin. This is replaced more slowly as the years pass by, so beginning at middle age, moisturizing the face should follow cleansing for both men and women. There is nothing magic about moisturizers, despite the wide variety of types, brands, and claims. They all just have an oil base, and their action is similar to that of natural oil in reducing the rate of evaporation of the moisture from the surface of your skin. By themselves, they don't moisturize at all—only *moisture* moisturizes.

Moisturized skin has a clearer look and wrinkles are less apparent. The simplest and cheapest moisturizer is light—not heavy—mineral oil, and you don't have to change oils for the winter, either! The slippery feeling of this may be objectionable, but that can be taken care of by removing the excess with toilet tissue. Most moisturizers are oils emulsified in water to avoid this problem—when the water evaporates, the amount of oil remaining is not slippery. They do *not* "rub in." If you prefer a commercial moisturizer, just get the simplest and least expensive, such as Vaseline Intensive Care, Lubriderm, Keri Lotion or Cream, and avoid all of the public relations nonsense about magical contents such as "Queen Bee Jelly," "Natural Moisturizing Factors," "Mink Oil," "Turtle Oil," herbs, lanolin,

Vitamin E, and so on. None of these has any advantage at all. And, as I have said, no moisturizer penetrates your skin. It just stays on the surface and retards evaporation of moisture, no matter what it says on the label or how high the price. So stay with the simplest and least expensive.

A word here about female hormones in skin preparations for women. These have a beneficial effect on the skin and underlying fat because they *are* absorbed. However, the FDA has restricted the hormone content of over-the-counter preparations to an ineffective level. Don't waste your money just because "with estrogen" appears on the label. If your physician thinks you should use a hormone cream, then he will give you one on prescription. But even the benefit of these is not magical—they must be used for weeks or months before the effects can be seen. If estrogen is taken orally, the use of such a skin preparation is unnecessary.

Most men do not have much interest in moisturizing more than their face. But many women want to moisturize their hands, and this can be done in the same way as the face. Some women also like to moisturize the skin of their entire body. The best way to do this is with a bath oil. Those that form a layer on the surface of the water are not very effective, however. The better ones are combined with an emulsifier or dispersant so the oil forms tiny globules which are evenly dispersed throughout the water. But after the bath, blot, don't rub, with your towel, or you will remove most of it. Among the best are Alpha Keri and Lubath.

Many people have misconceptions about our natural moisturizer, perspiration. Let's try to clear these up. There are two kinds of sweat glands. A few, in the armpits and the pubic area, are of a special type. These are called apocrene glands. Each one is attached to a hair and produces a type of perspiration that has a faintly musky odor. This is not unpleasant. Long ago, it may have played a role in sexual attraction, but no one knows. The vast majority of the glands distributed all over the body are of another type, called eccrine. These produce perspiration that is merely a diluted salt solution, having no odor whatsoever. So perspiration itself has little or no odor. The unpleasant smell of someone who has not bathed for a while actually comes from bacterial action upon the *oily* secretions of the skin. This oil turns rancid after a time, just as butter or any other natural oil does. The trick is to remove it before it can. Cleansing daily, or more often if necessary, with a soft wash cloth and adequate suds removes most of the bacteria and oil before any unpleasant odor can be produced. So shake off the misconceptions promulgated by Madison Avenue about perspiration. Deodorants are totally unnecessary. They are a hangover from times when bathing was infrequent and perfumes were used instead. The "deodorant" soaps and detergents used to contain hexachlorophene, which killed many of the bacteria on the skin that turn natural oil rancid. But the FDA has banned this, and those so labelled now contain substances such as trichlorcarbanilide that are limited in their action on bacteria and do not have time to be effective when you bathe before you rinse off. So you are wasting your money on these, too. And the antiperspirants that contain one or more aluminum salts do retard perspiration for a few hours by puffing up the skin around the sweat glands, closing them off. But this results in even more perspiration when the effect wears off. Then you tend to use more of the stuff and make the manufacturers rich. *None* stops perspiration completely—if it did, it would actually be harmful. Far better than paying attention to the ads is to pay some attention to your emotions and physical activity, both of which affect the amount of perspiration, and to your clothing and environment (in terms of temperature and humidity) in order to hasten evaporation. The genital deodorants are also unnecessary and may actually cause irritation. Except for an abnormal vaginal discharge, which a physician should treat, simple soap and water will remove the oils and secretions of both sexes that bacteria act upon, and there will be no odor for hours after each cleansing. Most women know that they should douche only on the advice of their physician.

Nails tend to become more brittle with age, and no substance taken internally, including gelatin, affects this. You can use the many creams and oils on the market that soften nails if you wish, but simply putting your fingertips in warm glycerin for 15 minutes two or three times a week and protecting your nails from hot water and harsh detergents by the use of gloves works much better. The "hardeners" containing formaldehyde should be avoided completely. Nail polishes, especially those with nylon fibers, help by reinforcing the nails.

Corns and calluses occur more frequently in middle age. They are closely related. A callus is a thickening of the skin due to pressure on a bony prominence, and corns form where the tissue permits a deeper penetration of this same sort of thickening. They both occur mostly on the feet and are caused by ill-fitting shoes, poor posture or walking habits, or some abnormality in the foot itself. Although you can obtain temporary relief from trimming, softening agents, or pressure-relieving pads, you should see a podiatrist to have the condition remedied properly. The term *chiropodist* means the same thing as *podiatrist*, but was changed to avoid confusion with *chiropractor*.

Facial "Rejuvenation"

Some time in the later middle years, women might want to consider the process known as thinning. This removes the outer dead layers of skin that have gradually become thicker with the years, resulting in a younger appearance. Chemical thinners containing urea and allantoin are available under many brand names. They take off this outermost layer of dead skin and have the added effect of making the skin swell temporarily, so that wrinkles are less apparent for a week or two after their use. This transient effect is the main reason for their popularity. But these preparations can cause allergic and other adverse reactions. It is best to stay with abrasive thinners such as the loofa sponge or the newer, patented Buf-Puf. Scrubbing soaps containing an abrasive, such as Pernox and Brasivol, work the same way. If you wish, you can use any of these abrasive thinners once or twice weekly after your nighttime cleansing and before applying moisturizer.

Chemosurgery, or a "chemical peel," although it may bear some resemblance to thinning, is an entirely different thing. It is regarded as, and should be performed as, a surgical procedure. It has some effect on the fine "crepe paper" wrinkles around the mouth and eyes, but none upon larger wrinkles or tissue sagging. After appropriate sedation and anesthesia, powerful chemicals such as trichloracetic acid or phenol are used to remove most of the outer layers of the epidermis, often down to the bottom layer. Then either tape can be used to peel off the outer skin layers then and there, or the skin can be kept lubricated, in which case it will peel off by itself in a few days. After the deep redness fades in three to six weeks, the skin is less leathery in appearance, has smaller pores, and the transient swelling for up to three months makes "crepe paper" wrinkles less apparent. But the benefits are rarely if ever worthwhile. There is not only the pain that persists for hours after the procedure, but the possibility of adverse effects from the chemical absorbed through the skin. Fatalities from this have been reported. This procedure *must* be done by a dermatologist or plastic surgeon; otherwise, serious scarring, unsightly changes in pigmentation, and other complications may result. The major reason it is done by them is to improve the appearance of deep acne pits, not wrinkles. Cosmeticians should not do this procedure—ignore their claims of competence, of beauty benefits, and everything else they may say about it.

Dermabrasion is still used sometimes for certain blemishes such as acne scars, but rarely for wrinkles. A sedative is given and the area is chilled with a plastic ice pack or by other means. The outer skin layers are removed with a high speed rotary steel brush or sander and afterwards several weeks are required for the skin to heal and regain a normal appearance. The major problems with this are pigmentation changes, especially in dark-skinned people, and if it is not done carefully a mottled effect may be noted forever after, especially under slanted or bright light. Perhaps half of the acne scars can be removed by this procedure, but it has little or no effect on wrinkles and is therefore not recommended for them.

Before we go on from these two methods rather rarely employed by physicians for treating wrinkles to the one more commonly used that is effective, face lifts, I should say a few words about other treatments that don't work. Some of these are widely advertised and used by cosmeticians. Everyone seems to want to know about facial masques. The simplest of these consist of a wax, clay, or plastic gel that adheres to the skin and hardens. It is then peeled off, and this peeling is claimed to have the same effect as the thinning previously described. It doesn't. Many other claims for masques are made—that they close the pores, tighten the skin, and so on, none of which occur either. However, some masques contain chemical thinners like those mentioned; after the use of this type of masque there is the usual transient swelling and for a time wrinkles are less apparent. But I have already cautioned against such thinners. The action of masques on the skin as they harden—and when they are pulled off—stretches the fine elastic fibers in the skin and also damages small blood vessels. So the word on masques: all peel-offs are rip-offs.

I previously pointed out that no lotion or cream has any effect on wrinkles, despite claims to the contrary. One makeup preparation does *fill in* small wrinkles, making them less visible, but the effect is gone when it is washed off, as it must be every day. Techniques whereby needles are inserted into the wrinkles and electric current is used only cause temporary swelling and are to be avoided. Silicone injection into wrinkles is contraindicated for reasons everyone knows. And diathermy is totally worthless. In fact, it's quite simple—ignore *all* claims made about any treatment for wrinkles except face lifts.

Now let's talk about them. The proper medical term is *rhytidectomy*, which comes from the Greek word for wrinkle. If you think you might benefit from a face lift, there is an easy way to tell: With the palms of each hand placed on your cheeks, draw the skin back and up towards your ears and look at your face in the mirror. If you see a substantial improvement in your appearance, you may wish to consider the procedure. There are basically two types of face lifts, full and partial, which can be done either in a doctor's office or hospital.

For the full or complete face lift, you are sedated and kept under light anesthesia so you feel no pain. Strips in your hair above and behind your ears are shaved. The entire area is sterilized, then an incision is made from the scalp above and in front of each ear down around the ear lobe and up into the shaved strips behind the ear. The facial skin is then undermined and pulled up, and the excess is removed. The suture lines running down the front of the ears are difficult to see, once they have healed, especially in women and in men who wear beards. Stitches are removed a few at a time over the next week or two. You will have an acceptable appearance in a surprisingly short time—two or three weeks—and be able to go about your affairs. This is now done almost as often for men as for women in some areas, so men should be aware of three problems they may have with this procedure besides the scar in front of their ears. The lower part of the ear lobe is often distorted, and this is usually more visible in men than in women. And some of the beard area is pulled up behind the ears, where it is difficult to shave. Men also have to look ahead if they are balding, because when the hair line recedes the scalp scars may be revealed. One advantage men do have, however, is that their skin is somewhat tougher and their face lifts last longer than they do with women.

The second type is a partial face lift or "tuck," in which the surgery is limited just to the area in front of the ear. This, rather than a complete face lift, is sometimes done earlier in life; it affects only the lower third of the face, and produces a less apparent change. Sometimes it is done two or three years after a complete face lift when the skin once again begins to stretch and sag.

The most dramatic advantage of a face life is the emotional lift it provides. Many patients *feel* more attractive, whether they are or not, and their personalities and outlook on life are correspondingly improved. The two major disadvantages are that the skin may be drawn too tight, giving a drawn, expressionless face. And, because the skin continues to stretch, the procedure must be repeated every two to five years if you hope to maintain the effect achieved the first time.

An "eye lift," or blepharoplasty—removal of the bags and wrinkled skin above and below the eyes—may be done at the same time as the face lift or performed separately. Here a careful incision is made close to the edge of the eyelid and through this the underlying fat is removed and then excess skin is trimmed off. The surgical scar cannot usually be seen with the eye open, and its extension at the corner of the eye appears to be a laugh wrinkle. The only possible problems are that too much fat may be removed, which gives the eyes a sunken appearance, or too much skin, which gives the eyes a wide, staring look. However, it is relatively permanent in its effect, in contrast to a face lift.

Plastic surgery is definitely not recommended for removing horizontal furrows of the brow or for "frown" wrinkles. Something can be done by some specialists on the underlying muscles that cause them, however. Surgical procedures designed to attack a second chin directly, or a wrinkled "turkey neck," are not satisfactory, either. Some improvement is obtained in both of these conditions with a total face lift, and one should be content with this.

The price of these procedures at this writing ranges from $3,000 to $5,000 for a complete face lift, $500 to $1,000 for the partial, and $1,000 to $2,000 for the eyelid procedures. Chemosurgery and dermabrasion generally run from $1,000 to $1,500. One thing you should be prepared for ahead of time is that your plastic surgeon will usually ask for his entire fee in advance. The reason he will most likely give is his busy schedule, or the fact that various personnel and facilities must be arranged for ahead of time and a cancellation would be a disaster for him. It is closer to the truth to say that dissatisfaction is frequent enough that some patients would refuse to pay after the surgery has been done. Plastic surgery is rarely paid for by your insurance unless some occupational limitation can be shown: for example, drooping eyelids obscuring the vision of an accountant. There is one happy note, however—the IRS recently ruled that cosmetic surgery is deductible.

If you wish to have any of these procedures done, have your own physician recommend two or three competent specialists. He will have had years of experience during which he has selected the best. Not only must such surgeons be certified by the American Board of Plastic Surgery, but they also should have had extra training is cosmetic surgery as well. Interview them yourself. Evaluate the personality and patience of each, since these are every bit as important as competence. You should not rely upon pictures he shows you or testimonials from his patients unless you can be sure these have not been selected as representing only his best results.

Hair Today, Gone Tomorrow

The earliest change usually noticed in the hair as the years pass is that it seems to be thinning out. In order to understand this, you should know a few facts. The "thickness" of one's hair is determined by several things. The total number of hairs and the diameter of each hair are the most important, and these are given you by heredity. Darker colors appear to be thicker than lighter; waviness (and fluffiness due to various causes) also adds to the effect. Each hair grows from a follicle deep within the skin. It has a growing cycle of three to five years, during which time it grows about one-half inch a month. It then forms a "bulb" on the shaft and enters a resting cycle during which it stops growing for two to four months. Some 10 to 15 percent of the hair is in this resting cycle at any time.

Three things happen that thin hair in both sexes from about age twenty on. One is that the resting cycle gradually becomes longer. The second is that the growth itself slows, and the hairs are therefore replaced more slowly. Both of these would make the hair thinner, even if the total number of hairs remained the same. But it does not. Over the years, some follicles fail to produce hair. So a certain amount of thinning due to these three factors has to be expected by all of us. Fortunately, this much is not usually noticeable until the later years—after age sixty or so.

A fourth effect occurs in women after the menopause, which is much more apparent if they carry the "male pattern baldness' genes, as about 60 percent do. With the loss of female hormones, unopposed male hormones produced by the adrenal glands continue to be present and slowly cause a tendency toward this pattern of baldness over the subsequent years. This was described in connection with the menopause. It can be prevented by early administration of estrogen, as mentioned previously. However, significant reversal once the hair has been lost cannot usually be achieved. A similar process causing outright baldness in men at an earlier age will be discussed later. In a few persons of either sex, certain chronic illnesses and prolonged psychologic stress cause some follicles to be dormant as long as these problems persist. These, of course, should be tended to and treated in the most appropriate way.

What else can be done about thinning hair? Three things. The first is to realize that the hair shaft can be broken off easily below the bulb by any tension during the resting cycle. This bulb is under the surface of the scalp, so the hair that has been broken off is effectively lost until its growing cycle starts again. Therefore tension of any type on your hair must be avoided as much as possible. Women should wear their hair short and not use small rollers (especially the brush type), and avoid buns, tight pony tails, teasing, and the traditional "one hundred strokes" of the hair brush. Choose a style that will involve minimal setting, then use mild cold setting lotions and the largest rollers with the least tension possible. Both men and women should remember that scalp massages do nothing for scalp circulation, just break off more hair. The scalp is one of the most vascular areas of the body.

The second is to realize that your hair tends to become drier with the years, due to the decreasing production of oil by the gland at the base of each hair. This makes it more brittle—and likely to break off anywhere along the shaft. So avoid anything that will damage or dry your hair more, especially dyes, bleaches, strong setting lotions, alkaline shampoos, hot air driers, and strong sunlight. The third thing that can be done has to do with various conditioners and bodying agents that can give the hair a fuller appearance. These will be discussed later.

Dull hair troubles many in middle age. It becomes this way at any age for several reasons. Simple dirt is the most common. Damage to the cuticle, or outer layer of the hair shaft, from sun, heat, dye, setting lotions, harsh alkaline shampoos, or too frequent shampooing is the next most common. Scum from a combination of soap and hard water is also frequent, as is accumulated hair spray. But the one cause that comes with the added years is the gradual lessening in the glandular production of oil that normally coats each hair shaft. Hot oil treatments are not a satisfactory way to counteract this. They leave too much oil, so the hair both looks limp and gets dirty more quickly. Then you have to shampoo most of the oil off, and you are right back where you started. Conditioners are the best answer—we will go into those in a moment.

All of us get gray hair sooner or later. This occurs when some follicles fail to produce pigment. Each of these hairs then is actually white—gray hair is a mixture of these and those that have retained their pigment. The cause of graying is not yet known, although heredity is definitely a factor in determining when it occurs, and certain nutritional and emotional factors also have been implicated. Inasmuch as there is no known cause or cure, no matter what claims you may hear about vitamins, lotions, or potions, the best thing to do when your hair turns gray is simply to accept it and make it more attractive in other ways.

Various substances have been used throughout history in an attempt to hide gray hair; they are at least as old as Cleopatra, who according to tradition dipped a lead comb into vinegar when she combed her hair. The lead salts precipitated onto the hair shaft darken with exposure to the sun. The most popular of the present products that work this way is Grecian Formula. All are limited in their ability to disguise gray hair. Other metallic dyes have long been abandoned, mostly because of their poor results, as have vegetable dyes such as henna, because they are too messy to use. All dyes presently available, whether they are called "rinses," "tints," or "colors" are aniline dyes such as those used in textiles. Dyeing is terribly hard on the hair. It makes the hair dull, dry, and brittle. And when it is dyed, the natural harmony between skin color and hair color is altered, so no matter how well it is done, you can always tell if she (or he) "does" or "doesn't." Approximately 10 percent of people are allergic to hair dyes, and some dyes are presently under investigation as possible causes of cancer. So my advice is to avoid them altogether.

Most shampoos in use today are detergents. Only those that are not clear, that appear milky or are in paste form, contain soaps and other substances—these are much less effective and not widely used. Therefore, the use of rinses such as lemon juice and vinegar to remove soapy residue is no longer necessary. Avoid those that carry labels like "Herbal," "Natural," "Balsam," "Protein," and all other such Madison Avenue verbiage. These ingredients only increase the expense, do not adhere to the hair, and wash right down the drain with the suds. The essential ingredient is the detergent, but unfortunately there is no way you can tell how much you are getting from the label. Even thickness is no guide, because they can be thickened artificially. Just pick a simple inexpensive one that works well for you. Neutral or slightly acid ones are better for your hair. As to frequency, shampoo whenever your hair is dirty, and be sure you rinse completely. If your hair tends to be oily, just shampoo it more frequently. There is no rationale in using different shampoos for "dry," "normal," or "oily" hair.

Conditioners come in several varieties. Three add body to the hair. The best of these contain protein prepared from animal cartilage that coats the hair shaft and fills tiny cracks in the cuticle. Cheaper varieties with synthetic bodying agents are merely diluted forms of hair spray and do not work as well. Those containing balsam are the least satisfactory. Some contain silicone, which tends to retain water in the hair shaft, but this has little effect on body. There are two cautions on all of these— they make the hair less "bouncy," and you will need to shampoo more often, because your hair gets dirty more rapidly. Another type, not really a conditioner but a rinse, contains quaternary ammonium compounds that soften the hair and act as an un-tangler, letting you comb your hair more easily. But these chemicals harm the hair and should be avoided.

Hair growth in certain areas of the body is considered unattractive by many women. Under the arms and on the legs, shaving is still the best answer. A more troublesome problem, occurring mostly in women of Latin ancestry, is growth in such "masculine" areas as the upper lip, face, and chest. This is accentuated after the menopause and is noted in women of all racial derivations then. Some try to pluck out these hairs only to find they return. Shaving these areas daily is a recourse of limited benefit. Such hair can be made somewhat less noticeable by bleaching, but this is not usually very satisfactory either. Depilatories are sometimes used. There are two types and neither is recommended. Chemical depilatories contain thioglycolic acid, which destroys the hair shaft but frequently irritates the skin and causes allergic reactions. The other type uses warm wax or cold plastic, which is applied to the skin, sometimes with a cloth mesh embedded into it, and is rapidly ripped off along with the hair. This is simply plucking on a grander scale. It is painful and can cause infections. Abrasives such as pumice stone are rarely used, simply because they are not very effective.

Women who have this problem should first check with their physician to see if the excess hair is caused by an abnormal production of male hormone by the adrenal glands or ovaries. Tumors that produce male hormone can be removed surgically, or estrogen administration may be considered to counteract excess male hormone or replace that lost with the menopause. Once this step is taken, the physician will probably recommend electrolysis (more properly called electrocoagulation) for the hair that has already appeared. In this procedure, a tiny needle is inserted into each hair follicle until it comes to the end, then an electric current is turned on which coagulates the follicle so a hair can never be produced from it again. That individual hair is then pulled out of the follicle with tweezers. The main discomfort is in the plucking of the hair. Because the follicles that were dormant when a certain area was treated may produce hair later, the same area may have to be gone over more than once. The process removes 100 to 400 hairs at a sitting, is time-consuming and expensive, so is restricted generally to small areas on the face or nipples. It is, however, the only method that is permanent and almost devoid of complications. Be sure you have a person do this procedure who is licensed. A newer method called photo-epilation, using a special light beam, is not nearly as effective, so cannot be recommended.

"Male Pattern Baldness" (MPB) is the principle problem men have in regard to their hair in middle age. It affects two out of every three to some degree. There are three causes of this. The predisposition is inherited in the same proportion by women as by men. As with most genetic traits, there is some variability in its inheritance—it may on rare occasions even skip a generation. It can come from either parent, and if both sides of the family have it, the predisposition is approximately twice as great. The second cause is the male hormone, testosterone, which precipitates the process in those who are genetically predisposed. MPB cannot occur without this influence. And it acts over many years, so age can be considered the third cause.

There is no lotion, tonic, magic light, electrical device, vitamin, mineral, or other nutritional substance that can slow the rate of loss nor restore the hair once it is gone. Well, castration would almost halt the process but one has to consider what would be lost in comparison to what would be gained. There may be hope for MPB in the future, however. No matter how bald a man may become, many follicles still produce a fine fuzz. Research with hormone antagonists and other substances injected into or applied upon the scalp has had some limited success in producing normal hairs. But as yet there is nothing available that works. So don't believe any advertisements based upon "research" by a Finnish physician. Just keep in touch with your dermatologist.

I would like to avoid discussion of hair pieces, weaving, and wigs because they are beyond my competence. Briefly, they can either make you look like you really have hair or are wearing a hairpiece, depending on their quality. However, I should mention one way in which medical science can offer help to a man who is turning bald. Hair transplants have been done successfully for over twenty years now. The process consists of selecting a donor site around the fringe that will not itself be turning bald in the future. This is shaved or clipped, and a small plug is removed from this area containing about twenty hairs. A hole of the same size is made in the bald area to be treated, and then the plug is inserted and sutured in place with tiny stitches. These hairs then grow at a normal rate. To make a hair transplant more effective, the bald area is sometimes reduced by plastic surgery before the transplant is done.

There are a few precautions to be observed with hair transplants. First, the surgeon must be sufficiently skilled to judge which donor areas will retain their hair for the next twenty years or so. If hair plugs are taken from an area due to become bald within the next few years, the transplants themselves will become bald then. Secondly, the estimation will have to be made that the donor area can provide enough plugs to cover the bald areas in a presentable manner. Thirdly, there still must be enough hair left in the donor areas to cover the holes that are left behind, though these do shrink to some degree. Fourthly, the angle of the hair shafts desired in the recipient areas must be estimated; the plugs must be selected to conform to this and inserted accordingly.

The biggest drawback to this procedure is that the hair obviously looks transplanted because it is sprouting out in bunches. Another drawback is the price, averaging $40 per plug, of which 200 to 600 are required. And, because only ten to twenty plugs can be transplanted at one sitting, the entire procedure usually extends over a month or more. There is a relatively new modification known as "strip transplants" that removes the first of these drawbacks. This consists of taking a strip about ¼-inch wide and 3 inches long from the donor site and transplanting it along the border of the area that is to be restored. Then at least the individual, when seen from straight ahead, will have a more normal-looking hair line, and only someone taller than he, who could look directly down on his hair, would know it to be a transplant.

There is one heavily advertised procedure that is *not* recommended. In this, sutures are put into the scalp as a web to which synthetic hair is then attached by technicians. Recurrent inflammation and infection, as well as a cost of $1,000 and up, are the main problems. And the stitches usually pull out over the next two or three years, leaving you right where you were before. Or worse, with a scarred scalp.

With all the information presented here, you probably have come to realize that the changes due to aging in the skin and hair cannot be denied. But they should not be ignored, either. If you give them the attention and care they deserve, a great deal can be done to improve your appearance throughout middle age and the years that follow.

4

The Mind

It is not wisdom to be only wise, and on the inward
vision close the eyes.

SANTAYANA

*T*his chapter will explore those
changes that occur by and through middle age in our mental
ability. Because our senses are the windows of our mind, we
must start with these. The *perception* of the stimuli we receive
through our senses is, however, a mental function. Yet these
two are so intertwined, it is difficult to discuss them separately.
I must warn you in advance that the part on senses and perception
must by necessity be somewhat technical.

Learning and memory are also difficult to dissect one from the
other, but I have tried to. Another *caveat* here—studies in this
area have been both conflicting and confusing. The conclusions
that I attempt to draw from them are not as clear as I would
like, nor as you deserve.

Much more is known about intelligence and its changes with
age. You should be aware before you read the discussion on this
that all of the early studies were disheartening to those of us in
middle age. But with the recognition a decade or so ago of a
methodological error, the newer findings are much more
encouraging—to some, I hope, inspiring. These have to do with
our potentials; the chapter then concludes with what we know
about how the person in middle age is able to utilize these
potentials.

SENSES AND PERCEPTION

It has been said that we swim in a sea of sensations in life, so the changes that begin to take place in our sensory functions by middle age are obviously important to us. Most of us are aware that both the quantity and quality of sense perception diminish by *old* age. Looking more closely at the studies that have been done, however, we find that they provide little data on *middle* age. Most have compared young students with old people who were residents of institutions. Both groups were simply more available for testing. It has also been found that when allowance is made for the physical and psychological health of the older people studied, those factors account for much of the age-related deficiencies reported. This scarcity of solid data presented a problem for me. I have tried to select the most reliable data on middle age where it was available, but at times I have had to average values obtained from testing younger people with those obtained from subjects over sixty in order to arrive at estimates for middle age. With these reservations in mind, let us look at each of the senses, and how they change with the years.

The Senses

SIGHT

The structures through which light must pass to reach the optic nerve are: (1) the cornea, the transparent outer layer of the eye; (2) the aqueous humor, the fluid just behind the cornea; (3) the iris, with its central aperture, the pupil; (4) the lens; (5) the vitreous humor, a jellylike substance filling the eyeball behind the lens; and (6) the retina, the registering surface at the back of the eye. As a person ages, some of these change appreciably and others do not.

The cornea thickens somewhat, but not to the extent that it causes any discernible difficulty. And, although slightly less fluid bathes its surface as the years progress, the middle-aged person is not aware of this either. The pupil becomes smaller steadily but gradually after age twenty or so, and thus less light can pass through it. The effect this has on adaptation to dim light may be noticeable by the fifties or sixties, but usually can be compensated for by increasing the illumination. The decrease in pupil size also reduces peripheral vision slightly, but this is detectable only by special tests. Neither the aqueous humor, the vitreous humor, nor the retina changes in healthy middle-aged people, and overall visual acuity remains relatively constant in good light.

The most significant change is in the lens. It continues to grow throughout life, but because its cells are not shed, like the skin, nails, or hair, it slowly compacts from childhood on. This process eventually affects accommodation, the way in which the lens adapts to near and far vision. Accommodation is achieved by the contraction and relaxation of the lens muscles, flattening the lens or allowing it to become rounder by its own elasticity. By about age fifty-five, this elasticity, which has been decreasing from age five or so, usually becomes stable. But sometime during the decade preceding this, most people begin to be aware that their vision at the usual reading distance of about 15 inches is becoming blurred. For a few years after that, one can compensate by holding objects farther away or by increasing the illumination. But eventually reading glasses are necessary. Another more subtle change in the lens is its gradual yellowing—by the late fifties or early sixties it allows less light through in the blue and violet range, but this can only be detected by laboratory tests.

Thus only two changes in the sense of sight are noticeable in middle age: slightly less effective adaptation to dim light and a loss of accommodation to near vision, which is more significant.

HEARING

The gradual loss of hearing in the high-frequency range that most people experience as they age results mostly from damage due to excessive noise. From occupational causes, men usually lose more of their hearing ability than do women. This loss is more accurately measured in decibels at each frequency, but for our purpose it can be expressed as about 5 to 15 percent for the highest note on the piano by age fifty to sixty for the average person. There is little or no loss in the lower frequencies.

We may be bothered by this decline in our hearing ability in two ways. Since the higher frequencies help us to understand speech and to determine where sound is coming from, we may, when we reach sixty or so, begin to have trouble in these two areas when there is a noisy background. But until then, only music lovers seem to be aware of this high frequency loss; they can compensate for it in two ways. All radios and stereo sets have bass and treble controls, and most of the latter also have a loudness knob which augments both lower and upper frequencies; at concerts, because higher frequencies do not travel as well as lower ones from the source of sound, one can simply pick a seat a little closer to the orchestra.

TASTE

There are four basic tastes: salty, sweet, bitter, and sour. Some evidence suggests that those over fifty begin to lose their sensitivity to sweets slightly; this may be one reason why many begin to prefer tart tastes. A gradual decline in all four modalities after the age of sixty is substantiated by most investigators.

SMELL

Here studies are sparse, but there does not appear to be a significant loss during the middle years, only one paralleling the loss of taste after about age sixty.

TOUCH

Sensitivity to light touch and temperature remain relatively constant throughout life. Vibration sense has been shown to decrease somewhat beginning in the fifties or sixties in those locations where the nerve tracts are the longest, most notably, in the feet. This is never noticed by most of us, however. We lose no sensitivity to pain through middle age, but in those past sixty to seventy, there may be a decrease in *perception* of pain by the brain.

In summary, there are only three decrements in the senses through middle age that need concern us. We undergo a loss of visual accommodation, which requires the use of reading glasses. The diminished light passing through the pupil and lens is noticed only in dim light and, in most circumstances, can be taken care of by increasing the amount of light by which we work or read. The loss of ability to hear higher frequencies is important only for the music lover and can be compensated for as I suggested. So overall, the sensory input we receive from the world around us need not be impaired significantly through our middle years.

I should pause here to point out a concept that may help to clarify much that follows in this chapter on the mind. It is probable that the electrochemical processes involved in intellectual functioning slow somewhat with age at the cellular level in the brain. But we know very little about these processes. We know much more about such gross measurements as loss of brain weight and loss of brain cells—enough to make it clear that such measurements have no relationship to intellectual ability in the normal individual. Only in certain diseases or brain injuries is either cell loss or decreased brain weight correlated with loss of function.

Reaction Time

Reaction times are a good example of this. They have been studied extensively in subjects of all ages. The slowing of the conduction impulses through the nerves themselves, both motor and sensory, is so slight as to be detectable only by special instruments throughout our life span. However, a component in the brain, as suggested above, is believed to be the cause of the slower reaction time seen with aging.

Total reaction time has been studied using many stimuli and variables. One that was rather practical tested the time it took a subject to take his foot off the accelerator and press the brake pedal on seeing a red light. The average time for this total performance was .418 second in the teens and twenties. In the fifties it had increased by .037 second, and in the sixties by .01 second more. These results are similar to those of other studies using different methods. So we are talking about a lengthening of reaction time by late middle age of about .05 second.

Some research has distinguished between simple single-choice reaction times and those requiring two or more choices before reacting. Here there is a slightly greater delay—for example, in the fifty-five to sixty-four-year-old-group, .057 second for two choices and .066 second for five choices.

Such slowing of reaction time is significant only for athletes or others in highly competitive activities involving split-second decisions. It doesn't affect the lives of most of us in middle age.

Perception itself is defined as the processing or interpretation of sense information by the brain. It actually takes two steps to perceive something: first, selection of the stimuli, then summarization of the stimulus patterns. Experimentally, it is almost impossible to separate perception from sensation; most tests in fact incorporate both. There are a few, however, that disclose a slight loss of this processing ability with age. One is the flicker fusion test in which a flashing light is shown to the subject and the duration and frequency of flashes are varied. The point at which two separate flashes are seen as one—the fusion point—occurs at a wider interval between flashes for older people than for younger ones. The loss of this perceptive ability between ages twenty and sixty is about seven cycles per second. Click fusion is an auditory analogue of this test and gives similar results.

Other tests of perception, such as the identification of geometric shapes when only a part of the shape is presented; the identification of objects when presented for fractions of a second; and the spiral after-effect test, are all in accord. By late middle age we need more time—measured in hundredths of a second—for perception to take place. This slowing is only found in the testing laboratory. In everyday life we never notice it.

LEARNING AND MEMORY

The old saying "You can't teach an old dog new tricks" may be true for dogs. But human intellectual equipment is vastly different from that of these and other research animals. So to avoid all the pitfalls of drawing parallels between such animals and humans, I reviewed only studies of the latter for this discussion.

Several problems are involved in assessing changes in learning and memory with age. As is true with the senses and perception, learning and memory also are closely related and difficult to discuss separately—in fact, they are probably two parts of the same process. Also, performance *per se*, that is, the carrying out of psychomotor skills required to express whatever information has been learned, is always an essential part of a test situation. Because this ability does decrease in older subjects, it may affect test results by making it appear that learning and memory abilities have declined when they may not have. Another problem is that older subjects are more adversely affected by such factors as anxiety, meaningfulness of the material, motivation, and interferences in the test situation. These factors have not been controlled adequately in most of the studies reported. Still another problem was noted at the start of this chapter, but is more crucial here than for tests on the senses and perception: For the most part, tests have been performed on school children and on the elderly confined in institutions. Physiological and psychological deficits of the latter—often the reason for their institutionalization—usually have not been taken into account.

The final problem is the most interesting. Using the electroencephalograph with microelectrode implantation, sensory input has been shown to be relayed to different areas along different paths once learning has occurred. *No studies have made allowances for knowledge acquired through the years as distinguished from the effects of age itself.* Categorization and processing of new information may take longer for older people simply because they already possess a great deal of stored information. It should be possible to study this phenomenon. Readily recallable knowledge could be assayed and classified, and the material on each test could consist of two types—one quite similar and the other quite different from that already acquired by the subjects. Using several age groups and age spans, investigators could certainly clarify this aspect of mental ability more than has been done to date.

Learning

It's helpful to think of learning in terms of Jack Botwinick's simple but classic definition, "the acquisition of information or skills." Reviewing the literature on learning, we find that most tests used to measure it have been paired-associate tests, though in recent years, the trend has been toward more cognitive approaches. In paired-associate tests, two words, numbers, or symbols are presented to a subject under varying conditions, then the material learned is assessed.

After a thorough review and consideration of these studies, I find I have to disregard all the methodological problems I just mentioned if I am to come to any conclusions at all. If I do so, then I conclude that in early middle age there is little or no change in learning ability, but by late middle age, a person needs a bit longer to get ready to learn, is slightly slower in learning, tends to persist in a previously learned pattern somewhat longer, and is slower in the performance portion of tests. It is important to point out that nothing in any study indicates a reduced *capacity* to learn, merely that *more time is required to do so* for an older person than for a younger one. That is the best I can do in attempting to summarize the studies that have been done.

James Birren, one of the foremost authorities in the field, offers his conclusions as follows: "At the present time, there is little evidence to suggest that there is an intrinsic age difference in learning capacity over the employed years. . . . Changes with age in the primary ability to learn are small under most circumstances. When differences do appear, they seem to be more readily attributed to processes of perception, set, attention, motivation, and the physiological state of the organism . . . than to a change in the primary capacity to learn." Another eminent authority, Harry Kay, summarizes this way: "To date, the observed relations between learning theory and aging phenomena are tenuous. There is no conclusion which has not been challenged, with the possible exception that the data so far are inadequate to support any firm and general conclusion."

I think we should leave the subject with the inference that we slow slightly in our ability to learn through middle age and let it go at that.

Memory

We know a bit more about the changes in memory with aging than we do about those involved in learning. The current view of memory is that it consists of three distinct processes. The first results from a sensory stimulus, which, when received by the brain, is called a "stimulus trace." Sensory input first goes to the sensory projection area of the brain, with little transmission to other centers. This "stimulus trace" decays in less than a second. The second process is short-term memory. Here an engram, or "memory trace," is involved that varies in duration from a few seconds to several minutes. Data from this holding system are used by the brain for the conscious processing of information. This type of memory has a limited capacity of five to nine items. The third process is termed long-term memory, which includes all longer intervals. In this process, data is apparently categorized and stored subject to search and retrieval, but not much is known about how or where in the brain this is done.

Nancy Waugh and Donald Norman have argued convincingly that some short-term memory is passed on to the long-term system rapidly, so that tests of the former incorporate some function of the latter. They have proposed the terms *primary memory* and *secondary memory*, discarding time intervals and other experimental paradigms. Nevertheless, most of the literature is in the terms I described, so I have to use them.

Having defined these processes, let's see how they change with age. The best evidence available indicates that there is a definite decline in registering and maintaining *visual* sensory traces with age—it is slight in middle age but increases in the older years, after sixty or seventy. However, this is measured in hundredths of a second so need not concern us. Senses other than sight have not been studied sufficiently to come to any conclusions.

As to short-term memory, the consensus of most authorities is that it is changed little through the years of middle age. The rate of retrieval has been found to decline slightly by some investigators toward later middle age, around age sixty, but not noticeably before then.

As for long-term memory, the acquisition, organization, storage, and retrieval processes have been found by almost all who have studied them to slow somewhat with age and to be somewhat less efficient. This can be demonstrated more clearly in late middle age than earlier. Many experiments have shown that any or all of these processes can be improved in several ways, even in those who are quite elderly. One example is the work of Mary Laurence. Using cues indicating categories of information before asking questions, she entirely eliminated differences between young and older subjects. Various other methods—electrical stimulation of the brain and hypnosis, for instance—also eliminate difficulties and delays in retrieving information to the extent that the most minute details from decades past can be recalled. It is entirely possible that we don't forget *anything* we learn. It is simply a little more difficult to recall what we have learned as we grow older, and it takes a little longer.

This is surprising and unsettling. We may have believed for years that short-term memory is the type more affected by age, yet the evidence indicates that it is long-term memory that begins to be impaired. But what most of us mean in a nontechnical sense is that events of a few days or weeks ago may be more difficult to recall than events that happened years ago. By definition, *both* of these are actually long-term memory.

All of us can remember events from our childhood clearly, so we would like to think that our long-term memory is unaffected by age. But we are leaving out one factor. Most of these old memories have been recalled frequently and are therefore more readily retrievable. Botwinick believes that rehearsed old information does not decline with age, but "remote memories that are not practiced are very difficult to examine systematically, and for the most part, they have not been."

Although the studies on long-term memory are convincing to me, two or three criticisms can be made. It should be mentioned first that all of those done on long-term memory so far have been cross-sectional except for two. These had one subject each—the investigator himself. We will see the problem of cross-sectional versus longitudinal studies clarified more when we discuss intelligence. Also, almost all studies fail to distinguish between time that has passed and age *per se*. The most significant criticism is that many tests of long-term memory have not measured the amount of new material actually acquired in the learning phase of the experiments. We concluded earlier in this chapter that we were probably a little slower in learning toward later middle age. Those few studies that have been adjusted for the amount of material initially acquired suggest that long-term memory is not impaired significantly during middle age.

Nonetheless, I think we should accept that a slow but slight decline in long-term memory ability does occur through the middle years. There is a time for gracious yielding to changes brought by aging; this is one. All we have to do is jot down those things we wish to have at hand later, or use some sort of mnemonic system, and not be embarrassed about it.

INTELLIGENCE

So we need a bit longer to learn and have a little more difficulty with long-term memory. These needn't worry us. We can just take our time and use many methods to compensate. What concerns us more is what happens to our intelligence. In middle age we know we must make a shift from "brawn" or "beauty" to "brain" and that this shift is of crucial importance. Therefore any change in our intelligence will have a profound effect upon the quality and value of our lives now and in the future.

What do the studies show? Well, bad news at first sight. I reviewed most of these, and, except for a handful, all showed a steady decrease beginning anywhere from the teens to the thirties. As David Weschsler commented, "Nearly all studies . . . have shown that most human abilities . . . decline progressively after . . . ages eighteen to twenty-five." But there's much more to it than this. Let's look into the subject more thoroughly.

Potential

The origin of the concept of intelligence goes back only to 1905, when Binet and Simon devised the Metrical Scale of Intelligence, designed to predict children who were likely to fail in the Paris school system. They were successful, and the first mention of the term *intelligence* in the psychological literature appeared in an article by Binet in 1908 in which he reported their results.

This test was then modified by Lewis Terman at Stanford, and with the Stanford-Binet Intelligence Scale, the momentum of interest and investigation into intelligence began mounting in the 1920s and 1930s, so that now we can say that we know more about intelligence than we do about any other mental function.

We know more *about* it, perhaps, but are still not precisely sure what it *is*. It is like gravity or light or electricity—we use it and can measure it, but we are not completely certain what it consists of. Wechsler provides one definition: "Intelligence . . . is the aggregate or global capacity of the individual to act purposely, to think rationally, and to deal effectively with his environment." Modern psychologists prefer a more operational definition—the rate of change in behavior of the organism due to experience and practice. Classically, it is the ability to educe and deduce relationships, to abstract the general from specifics, and to detect the specific in a generality. One wit, the late Professor Edwin Boring, concluded reductively, "Intelligence is what intelligence tests measure." Perhaps a germ of truth there.

There are many different intelligence tests, and individuals who do well or poorly on one test show a surprising consistency to do as well or as poorly on other tests. Because of this consistency, a basic quality is believed to be demonstrated. Several statistical methods have been employed to derive this basic quality. These techniques have resulted in a concept of general intelligence, called "g" by Charles Spearman, which is related to all the specific mental functions.

Louis Thurstone then found that these specific functions tended to group themselves into "communal clusters." This meant that individual tests or subtests could be grouped in such a way as to contain common factors of their own. Thus, verbal abilities can be considered one functional unity, as can abstract reasoning, practical reasoning, and rote memory, the usual divisions in a typical intelligence test. These various modalities of mental functioning, however, have not been shown to have any precise physiological or anatomical determination. Their strength is that they hold true in practice.

Before we discuss how intelligence changes with age, we should have some idea of how we start out with it. Most of it, and probably all of our potential, is inherited. Harold J. Butcher, one of the foremost experts in the field, states, "The general opinion of most authorities . . . seems to be that a substantial degree of genetic determination of measured intelligence can hardly be denied." The best estimates of the proportion of our measured intelligence that is inherited range from 50 percent to 80 percent. The remainder is attributable to environmental influences. The inherited basis of intelligence was stressed to the exclusion of all other factors during the period from World War I through World War II, when genetics was in its enthusiastic but crude beginning. But when the world recoiled in horror at the extremes of Nazism, it largely rejected the nature part of the nature-nurture dyad in this as in many other human characteristics. There followed then a strong swing on the part of some to the belief that environmental influences are more important in the development of intelligence. This is where we are now. I would like to ignore both swings and stick strictly to what has been demonstrated by the best available scientific studies: Heredity determines an individual's potentialities, and the environment determines how these potentialities are developed and realized.

We could go straight from this point to our main subject, but we have run right into a horrendous controversy and must deal with it. In 1969 Arthur Jensen, professor of educational psychology at the University of California at Berkeley, after evaluating such programs as Head Start, published a piece in the *Harvard*

Educational Review that has come to be called the "Jensenist heresy." He could not have picked a more inopportune time or theme. His article began: "Compensatory education has been tried and it apparently has failed." This was addressed to educators who were receiving millions of dollars in federal funds for just that purpose. First, he reviewed the known facts about the genetic basis of intelligence. Briefly, he assigned 85 percent of intelligence to heredity, 10 percent to environmental influences, and 5 percent to errors in the testing techniques. He then went on to comment specifically about the genetic differences among various racial groups in a small portion of his paper. There he stated that the evidence indicates Negroes are limited by their inherited capacity, so that when provided with the same environmental influence as whites they still score an average of 15 I.Q. points lower. The reaction among educators and others to this was furious.

I have read the major criticisms of Jensen's work; they are interesting and various. Some lump him with earlier racist authors who knew little about genetics, and make him guilty by association. Some accuse him of advocating a linear hierarchy of inferior and superior races, though he clearly stated that race averages change with time. His coefficient of heritability was attacked as being imprecise, but he had only said that it was the best estimate possible. He was accused of implying that there were inferior and superior races, but he had restricted his comments to one trait, intelligence. Some of his critics admitted that the means vary but that there are individual variations around the mean, which is exactly what Jensen said himself. Another claimed that he assumed an inverse relationship between heritability and improvability, which he did not. Another quoted him as stating that the inherited component of intelligence indicated a *fixed capacity*, but he had clearly said it was an indicator of a *range of potential*. Many laid heavy emphasis on the possibility that one of his sources may have falsified his results. And so it went.

You should read these criticisms yourself—they tell you something about their authors, at least. In *Environment, Heredity and Intelligence*, Jensen's original paper and the seven major critical papers were published conveniently together in book form. You should then also read Jensen's later book, *Educability and*

Group Differences, in which he refuted his critics creditably. There
has been only sporadic objection to Jensen's point of view since
publication of this book, even from educators.

It is curious that the data referred to by Jensen could be found
easily in the professional psychological literature, but they had
not previously appeared in a nonpsychological publication read
by a liberal audience. For example, three years before, Audrey
Shuey, in *The Testing of Negro Intelligence,* reviewed the pertinent
literature to that date—382 references—and had come to a similar
conclusion without causing any stir at all.

A little later, another authority, Hans Eysenck, presented
similar evidence on the Irish and came to about the same
conclusions that Jensen did on Negroes. Now, I am Irish myself.
I have read his book and most of the studies he cites. I accept his
conclusions. I also accept some of the better studies by others that
find groups of Orientals and Jews score a few points higher than
the average for Caucasians. I can't see any reason to get upset over
any of this. There are group differences just as there are individual differences. An inherited genetic basis of intelligence constitutes the range of potential to be realized through environmental influence, and the former is of much greater importance
than the latter; I consider this to be an established fact.

Let's leave this area to those who choose to make it controversial and return to our main theme, the changes in intelligence with
age. All of us are familiar with the concept of the intelligence
quotient, or I.Q. In the original Binet scale, this was arrived at by
dividing the mental age by the chronological age. An early
problem encountered with this approach was that there is not a
linear relationship between mental age and chronological age,
because there are different rates of maturation at different ages for
different individuals. And such a system of deriving an intelligence quotient, of course, was impossible for adults of any age.

The first attempt to solve this problem used the highest
chronological age beyond which observed mental scores ceased to
increase as the denominator. This was done with the assumption
that mental age scores would then remain constant thereafter
throughout life. This resulted in what Wechsler called an "efficiency quotient." He devised statistical methods whereby an
individual could be given a score in terms of his relative standing
among those of the same age.

Then Wechsler devised the Wechsler-Bellevue Intelligence

Scale, which began to replace the Stanford-Binet Test. This permitted testing individuals accurately beyond childhood. In the 1950s he created the first test designed for adults, the Wechsler Adult Intelligence Scale (WAIS). The standardization and wide use of the WAIS in cross-sectional studies is the origin of the concept that the middle-aged individual undergoes a loss of intelligence. For example, the WAIS standard showed a decrease from ages thirty-five to forty-four of 6 points, from forty-five to fifty-four of 8 points, and from fifty-five to sixty-four of even more—16 points. The WAIS had three other major consequences: First, levels of intelligence could from this point on be defined in terms of standard deviation units with the usual statistical procedures; second, no assumption need therefore be made in regard to the relation between the mental age and the chronological age of an individual; and third, his system dispensed with the need of committing oneself to a fixed point beyond which scores were previously assumed to be unaffected by age. His assumption was that all I.Q.'s calculated by this method, if equal, were then identical without regard to the age at which they had been determined.

The original Stanford-Binet Test was arbitrarily standardized assuming adult intelligence peaked at age sixteen. When Wechsler did the standardization of his Wechsler-Bellevue Test in 1944, he found that it peaked at twenty to twenty-four. In 1955, when he standardized the WAIS, the peak was found to be between ages twenty-five and thirty. This was the first hint that some type of "culture change" was taking place. More about this later.

The WAIS has come to be the most widely used and reliable test of intelligence for adults, so a brief description is in order. There are six subtests in the verbal grouping: information, comprehension, arithmetic, similarities, digit span, and vocabulary. In the performance group, there are five subjects: digit symbol, picture completion, block design, picture arrangement, and object assembly. This test has been widely translated and used all over the world, and it has been found to be "culture fair" in all settings. Any arguments that it is not are specious. It has also been shown to be "age fair," so we cannot quibble over the results that show a decline with age. We should remember for the moment, however, that almost all such studies have been cross-sectional—done at one time on individuals of all ages.

In 1955, Jerome Doppelt extended the WAIS norms to include the aged, using 475 people aged sixty and over. He found the decline to be much sharper after that age. Meanwhile, other investigators were exploring various aspects of aging in relation to intelligence tests. James Birren showed that older individuals did as well as younger ones in tests measuring achievement related to general experience in our culture, but did more poorly in those involving manipulative skills, perceptual functions, and processing of new information. Edwin Ghiselli tested 1,400 subjects, aged twenty to sixty-five, put no premium on speed, and found no decline. Sol Garfield tested twenty women in each of three age groups, twenty to thirty, forty to fifty, and sixty to seventy. He found vocabulary scores increased and the abstraction ability to remain relatively constant. These and other investigators were generally consistent in finding a decline with age, but their results suggested that there might be some sort of pattern in the decline.

Jack Botwinick pointed out most clearly what that pattern might be. He observed that intelligence is not a unitary quality and that the WAIS recognized this by its design, measuring the overall factor of intelligence *and* a series of specific factors. He felt that each person has his own characteristic constellation of the various specific factors, but that a decremental pattern with age could be seen in some factors fairly consistently. In breaking the WAIS down into verbal subtests and performance subtests, he found little decline in the verbal subtest until about age sixty-five. But the performance subtests, especially those involving speed and psychomotor skills, declined appreciably before then.

Now, what about the "culture change" first noted by Wechsler and since by many others? The first clue as to its nature and effect was provided by Birren. He used the method of principal component analysis with the WAIS subtests, including age and education in the matrix as if they were scores of subtests themselves. He extracted a general intellective component accounting for about 50 percent of the variance in which age was not at all important. *Education* was important to this component, however. He concluded that education had more influence than age on mental functioning.

Russell Green at about the same time found himself in an embarrassing position. Basing his conclusions upon one cross-sectional study, he reported the usual decrement with aging. But when he did another study in which subjects were matched for education level, he found no decline. So he was caught coming to two opposed conclusions, with the difference due to education.

Through these and similar studies, one element in the culture change was at last clear. Educational level has been rising in our population and recency of education declining. If one were to insist on a twelfth grade education among typical seventy-year-old subjects of one of the earlier cross-sectional studies, he might find as few as 10 percent. But among those twenty years of age, he would find perhaps 80 or 90 percent. All the early cross-sectional studies included older people with a disproportionately high number of immigrants who had received less than an eighth grade education; a long time had passed since their schooling; this schooling had usually been directed toward one practical end; and most had never broadened their lives beyond that end.

Improved health is the second most important factor in the culture change, as has been shown in several studies. Also important are such factors as general improvement in socioeconomic status and greater intellectual stimulation by occupation, travel, the media, and so forth. All of these affect intellectual performance, so in reality a longitudinal study, incorporating all such cultural changes, is the only valid way to determine how much and in what way intelligence changes with age. (Longitudinal studies, of course, involve two or more tests on the same subjects, several years apart.)

To understand how cultural changes can cause conflicting results between longitudinal and cross-sectional tests, we can look for a moment at the example of measuring changes in height with age rather than intelligence. The largest cross-sectional study ever done measuring the height and weight of adults was in 1956, when twenty-three thousand Canadians of all ages were measured. It showed a 3-inch difference in the height of males between ages twenty and seventy, a span of fifty years. These results are compatible with many other smaller cross-sectional studies in the United States. From these findings one *might* conclude that an individual 3-inch loss of height occurs in men between the ages of twenty and seventy. But cross-sectional studies in the United States at the times of the Spanish-American War, World War II, and the Korean War showed a gain in height of nearly 3 inches in recruits over that same span of fifty years. This gain represents several changes such as health care and nutrition over that time. So longitudinal studies have had to be done to determine the *true* change in height of men with age. These have found little or no loss through age fifty, only a fraction of an inch by age sixty, and still considerably less than an inch by age seventy.

Let's return to intelligence and the longitudinal studies that have been carried out on the middle-aged. There are only a handful in the literature, so I will prevail upon your patience and cite each one briefly. One *caveat:* On subsequent tests there seems to be more tendency for the abler to return for the testing.

John Nisbet first tested 141 postgraduate students at an average age of twenty-two and retested them at an average age of forty-seven. In all of the subtests the scores *increased* with age, but the improvement was not as marked in the numerical as in the verbal ones. Nancy Bayley and Melita Oden studied gifted adults at twenty years of age and again thirty years later. They found that verbal concepts and abstractions *improved to at least age fifty*. R. D. Tuddenham gave the Army General Classification Test first used on induction to a group of men about to retire from the army. He found that of the four parts, the only one to show a significant decline was the nonverbal one. William Owens followed 363 male freshmen students of Iowa State College after graduation and was able to retest 127 of them after a thirty-year interval. Their average age was then forty-nine, and their total score had *increased*. Mary Kibler and Lester Sontag found no significant change in a group first in their thirties when tested thirty-five years later. Jeanne Gilbert reported that verbal ability was maintained from the twenties to the sixties in her subjects. Robert Burns tested eighty university graduates when they were twenty-two, when they were forty-seven, and again when they were fifty-six. There was a significant rise in the mean score in the first span and a significant decline over the last, but *the mean was higher at the end than at the start*.

These are the only significant longitudinal studies over the span of middle age that have been done to date. Their consensus needs no comment by me. Best is to quote Botwinick, himself, who after reviewing all such studies through 1977 said, "Decline with age . . . may not be seen before ages fifty or sixty, and even then the decline may be small."

But, although the decline may be small, the longitudinal studies confirm what the cross-sectional studies suggested—there *is* a pattern of change with age. Rather than create confusion by attempting to interpret the subtests and their relative significance, the concept of John Horn and Raymond Cattell can be used in conclusion. They have introduced two terms to describe the kinds of intelligence that change with aging. One is *crystallized*, which comes from the acquisition of certain kinds of information and skills brought to us by the culture. The second is *fluid*, an ability related to the physiological characteristics of the organism. In regard to the changes in each with age, Horn states, "Thus the overall effect may be no loss of ability. What the evidence does indicate, however, is that, with increasing age beyond the teens, there is a steady, if gentle, decline in fluid intelligence. . . On a happier note, and by way of contrast, the evidence also shows that crystallized intelligence *increases* throughout most of adulthood. Here alternative mechanisms come into play. Compensating for the loss of one ability with the surplus of another, the older person uses crystallized intelligence in place of fluid intelligence. In other words, the older person substitutes accumulated wisdom for what might be called brilliance, while the younger person does the opposite."

So it seems that William James' term *sagacity* pinpoints what the middle-aged person reaps from his years—the greater ability to live life fully and successfully using his experience. Intelligence and wisdom, after all, are not the same thing. We *are* wiser now than we have ever been before—and should become more so throughout our middle years. This is the greatest reward life has for us at this time.

Performance

We have only discussed changing *potentials* with age so far. What about actual *performance*? The most frequently quoted authority who studied this is Harvey Lehman. In 1928 Lehman came across an article that claimed individuals were capable of doing excellent work through the age of eighty. He felt that this was just plain wrong. He then started his monumental study, which was published twenty-five years later under the title *Age and Achievement*. In it he reviewed the effect of age upon creativity in the sciences, medicine, philosophy, arts, practical inventions, and other areas. His method was to tabulate the frequency with which productions were listed in various source documents and to show the most "creative" works this way. He then arranged them in tables by the age of the persons producing the works. His general finding was that within most fields of endeavor, maximum production occurred from thirty to thirty-nine years of age. He concluded that "the golden decade for superior creative achievement is the thirties."

Shortly thereafter, Wayne Dennis reviewed this work and raised several objections: (1) Lehman had not differentiated between long-lived and short-lived people, a failure which did not account for potential work by those dying "before their time"; (2) his method emphasized one work of high calibre but not quantities of such work; (3) many of Lehman's tables were based upon a small number of entries, which made conclusions dubious; (4) the tables varied in age intervals; and (5) with improvement of technology and more competition in a field, a later contribution, though perhaps as valuable, would be less likely to be noted.

Dennis documented this latter point in a study of his own on scientists in which he demonstrated that as the total production of scientific work increased with time, the percentage by one person declined, even though his work remained constant in quantity and quality.

I would like to add several other criticisms of Lehman's study that seem significant to me. The criteria leading to his choice of a person's best work were influenced by a tendency to mention a pioneering achievement, then to neglect later less dramatic work necessary to implement or develop it. Also, more recent contributions are more difficult to evaluate—they have not stood the test of time. Einstein's theory of relativity, for example, could not be confirmed until decades later. The effect of time is most noted in the selection of works of art produced and judged during an artist's life, which may be poorly received until centuries have passed, after which they may be recognized as classics. No account was taken of the fact that after producing a major creative work a person tends to be given more administrative responsibilities, to be involved in more scientific and governmental organizations, and to devote more of his time to consultation and teaching, with less time and energy remaining for individual creativity. No allowance was made for the effect of failing health on certain individuals and not on others. And lastly, his overall method of selecting great works was more democratic than accurate—he looked into anthologies of poetry and other works, counted the number of times a certain work had been included in these anthologies, and concluded by this count that a work was "great."

Dennis was apparently stirred, because in 1966 he came out with his own tour de force: *Creative Productivity Between the Ages of 20 and 80 Years*. In this he considered quantity as well as quality of output. He limited his study to those born after 1600 in most cases in order to have a more complete and accurate record of a person's production. He found that historians, philosophers, botanists, inventors, and mathematicians teach their productive peak in their sixties. For scholars as a whole, the seventies were as productive as the forties, and the productivity of artists who hit their peak early was still strong in the fifties. He commented that people in the arts need not undergo a long formal education before they begin production, and the time required to produce a work of art is much less than that of a historian or other scholar. He concluded, "For almost all groups, the period forty to forty-nine was either the most productive decade or else its record was only slightly below the peak decade. In only one field (chamber music) were the thirties higher in output than the forties. In all other cases in which the forties were not the most productive years, this honor went to a later period." This is good news to those of us in middle age, and frankly I have no criticism of his work. But it is strange that Lehman is so widely quoted and Dennis is almost completely ignored.

Other studies on ability and achievement have been on a lesser scale. E. Manniche and G. Falk, studying Nobel prize winners, found that the primary work in physics, chemistry, and medicine was done by those between the ages of thirty-five and forty. C. W. Adams studied 4,204 scientists and found that their chief work was done at the median age of forty-three. In those disciplines in which progress was the result of deduction and intuition, such as mathematics, the median age was thirty-seven, but in those disciplines requiring induction and assemblage of facts, such as anthropology, the median age was forty-seven. Arpad Elo studied chess masters using a complicated statistical analysis noting that intelligence, study, concentration, and performance were all involved. He found the peak performance was at age thirty-five, but that at age sixty-three performance was equal to that at age twenty.

One contribution made by James Birren may be helpful in conclusion. He analyzed the methods used by one hundred successful people and found that those which the older used were distinctly different from those of their younger counterparts. Some of these differences were that the older defined their problems differently, they were more flexible in their approach, they recognized the need for greater discipline and hard work, and that they were more willing to take advice whenever their sphere of competence was exceeded. So perhaps studies of creative ability and mental achievement should not just be concerned with changes in performance as such. We must also understand *how we change and adapt to those changes* or we will miss the point entirely.

5

The Person

He who knows others is clever,
but he who knows himself is enlightened.

LAO TZU

CONSISTENCY AND CHANGE

We have already discussed the physical and physiological changes through the middle years, and also the psychological changes as measured by objective criteria. It would be tempting at this point to adopt the dualistic dictum that these aspects adequately describe the total person, but if we did so, we would fall far short of our goal—understanding the changes that take place in human personality during these years. We *do* change—we know that—but may not understand how or why. Fortunately, more is known now than in the time of Freud and the beginnings of psychoanalysis—when the prevailing tendency was to view personality development as occurring only through childhood or perhaps the early teens. What a gross misunderstanding of the full life of a human being then to view our growth as so grimly bounded! In the long flurry of preoccupation with child development, especially in this country, the possibilities and actualities of a dynamic and mutable adult personality were obscured, even neglected altogether.

Yet now it is somehow vaguely disturbing to learn on the one hand that we never arrive at one "grown-up" self who will be *us* for the rest of the time we live, and on the other hand that we ourselves know too little about the changes that are taking place within us. Once we accept these two facts, that we do change yet are in a way wanderers in the woods, we may search for simple signposts in terms of "stages," "passages," or "seasons," available in the surfeit of "pop psych" books currently being published. In these sophistic summaries we sometimes *see* ourselves dimly, but we never really *find* ourselves. Each of us knows that understanding ourselves and our individual changes throughout our middle years would require close personal consultation over all these years with an expert on the workings of the mind, not to mention considerable introspection and reflection on our own part. Reading even the works of authorities in the field, we often feel we are exchanging such an intimate dialogue for a seat in an enormous auditorium with the authority himself barely visible on a distant podium.

These thoughts presented a problem for me in approaching this chapter. I finally decided to lay out an overview of the main theories of the most significant authorities so you can see for yourself how they regarded the middle years of life, then to follow this with a few conclusions of my own. You will realize at the end that knowledge of our growth and change during middle age is still far from complete. I think, too, you will see that most of the problems *and* the potentials in this area derive ultimately from the values we hold to be true.

For example, if we crystallize our value structure around the age of fifteen or so and don't change it appreciably thereafter, we then pursue fixed goals based upon these values until middle age. We reflect ruefully that we let a *child* do this—what did that child know about life? If we do not attain our goals by then, we feel both failure and frustration. We arrive at a latitude in life where we realize some ports of call not visited never will be; that the course we originally set may have been wrong after all; and we lose confidence in both charts and compass. All too often, even if we achieve our goals and arrive at the destination we set originally our course for, it is no longer there. In the words of Gertrude Stein, we find "there is no there, there." Either way, the reason for our discontent is that while we have changed through the years, our values and goals have not changed correspondingly. Then psychological problems may set in. Since it all began with the formation of our values and the selection of our goals, I've included a chapter about these as the last part of the book.

PSYCHOLOGY

If we're looking for the beginning of the thread of ideas about human personality, we can say that, without realizing it, Empedocles laid the foundation for the first theory in the fifth century B.C., when he held that the world was composed of four elements: earth, air, fire, and water. Hippocrates followed a century later and drew on this concept for his theory of personality as determined by four humors, or fluids. One of these was blood, which contributed to a sanguine temperament that is warm and hopeful. Black bile was the cause of a melancholic personality. Yellow bile produced a choleric, irascible one, while phlegm resulted in a phlegmatic or apathetic frame of mind.

Later, in the chapter on values, I will sketch a bit more in detail the development of our knowledge down through the centuries, but for our purpose here I should start with Sigmund Freud and psychoanalysis in the early part of this century. Although he himself did not allow for any psychological development after childhood, we must look at his theories briefly because they form the foundation for all those that have followed.

Freud believed that human beings possess instincts similar to those of animals. He called them drives and proposed that they are part of our fundamental human self—biologically based, self-centered, and selfish. If man were to exist in a solitary and natural state, he hypothesized, this group of instincts, the id, would operate in accordance with a pure drive for creature comforts, the "pleasure principle." In order to satisfy man's instinctual needs in a way that sets him apart from animals and leads to civilization, the ego developed out of the id. It functions in terms of what Freud called the "reality principle" and is therefore in constant conflict with the id. The superego has to do, he believed, with the introjection of parental influence. The resulting conflict among all three aspects of the personality is constant and coped with through a number of defense mechanisms.

He believed that human personality is formed by age five, and that puberty is the only interesting change left to one until death: "The rest of life is spent playing out dramas of oral deprivation, toilet training and Oedipal rivalry." So adult life was seen by Freud as a plateau, placid or not, until such time as one became concerned with his *Thanatos*, or death instinct.

Of course, many have criticized Freud since his time. He overemphasized the sexual instinct, stressing it to the point of defining our entire development in terms of it, the stages he saw being oral, anal, phallic, latent, and genital. The most serious result of this emphasis is his conclusion that the Oedipal complex is the core of all neuroses. Closer to truth, I think, is that separation from our mother is separation from the source of our life, that our individuation is the greatest task we face, and that it continues *throughout our lives*.

Another criticism is that Freud limits himself too much to considering only parental influence during childhood on ego formation. Other people and our environment certainly contribute, and as adults we may have internalized more societal than parental influences.

Some also find fault with Freud's assumption that man's instincts are identical to those of animals, or nearly so, and that they must *necessarily* be in constant conflict with the interests of society. In fact, society exists so that as many basic desires of the individual as possible may be satisfied without harm to others— certainly far more than would be satisfied society.

To my mind, the most important objection to Freud's theories is that he sees all behavior as essentially defensive. Furthermore, his defense mechanisms are outside our conscious awareness, so we can never discover the truth about ourselves, nor can we be aware of our true desires, motivations, or goals. For Freud, any personality change was impossible except through psychoanalysis. This precludes a significant role for the person himself. And one last comment that is significant to me: Studies of creative people have shown that those who live, in the highest sense, do not adapt to, but transcend accepted norms. For Freud, creativity is on the same continuum as insanity.

No one denies the immense contribution of Freud's work. He broke the ground for modern psychology, and his utilization of free association, dreams, and hypnosis to explore the unconscious was especially valuable. Anna Freud went on to bring more order and coherence to her father's concept of defenses, which he himself had not treated systematically.

Alfred Adler rejected both Freud's biological basis and childhood stages. He separated sexuality from sociability and emphasized that man is characterized more accurately by a setting and striving for goals. He saw the adult as able to control his own life and allowed for the possibility of real change in adulthood. But, except for a brief reference to old age, he provided little material applicable to middle age.

Karen Horney remained faithful to Freud only with regard to

the workings of the unconscious. She doubted the role of instincts, sexuality, the Oedipus complex, and neuroses resulting from childhood traumas. She, like Adler, admitted of change in adult life but did not offer much beyond this.

Among the early psychoanalysts, only Carl Jung dealt in any depth with development during middle age, so I will describe his theories a little more completely. He felt that the early years of adulthood were concerned with acquiring an education, getting married, obtaining a job, pushing for a promotion, and that all of one's energies were put into these endeavors. The time comes in a person's life however, when either he has arrived or never will. Either he is tolerably content in his marriage or never would be. Either he is financially secure or never would be. At this point, about age thirty-five, his earlier "extroversion" begins to shift toward "introversion." Jung coined these two terms to signify the movement of the libido, or life force, first toward the outer world and then toward the inner world. From this point on, an individual becomes more acquainted with inner depths and qualities that had always been there, but which external pressures and distractions had kept from his conscious awareness. And through this inner exploration a person endeavors to find meaning in his or her life.

For Jung, most adult neuroses were an indication that the person was trying to continue to live by the values of his youth past his middle years: "We see that in this phase of life—between thirty-five and forty—an important change in the human psyche is in preparation. Often it is something like a slow change in a person's character; in another, certain traits may come to light which had disappeared since childhood; or again, one's previous inclinations and interests begin to weaken and others take their place . . . we embark on the second half of life . . . with the false assumption that our truths and ideals will serve us as hitherto. But we cannot live in the afternoon of life according to the program of life's morning; for what was great in the morning will be little at evening and what in the morning was true will at evening become a lie."

And he added, "In the second half of life—over thirty-five—there has not been one patient whose problem has not been what life means for him, nor one cured who did not find out." He believed that in order for a person to understand himself fully required approximately fifty years of living. From that point on a person is more sure of himself, accepts himself, and relates better to others and to his own values. His relationships with his children, his spouse, and friends all improve.

We owe a lot to Jung. Another contribution he made concerned the concepts of *Anima* and *Animus*—feminine identification in man and masculine identification in woman. Each of us in midlife and beyond tends to become more aware of and express the internal characteristics associated with the opposite sex. Another is his consideration of the young and old in each of us, *Puer* and *Senex*. We slowly shift from one to the other in middle age by giving up elements of the former and replacing them with elements of the latter. The most important of these is meaning and the search for the meaning of meaning.

If you wish to pursue his thoughts further, the most readable compendium I could find is *The Portable Jung*, edited by Joseph Campbell. Though Jung's most famous concept is that of the collective unconscious—his medium was man's myths—it and others are not directly applicable to our concern here.

After Adler and Jung broke from the Freudian psychoanalytic movement, it formed into a mainstream school totally accepting Freud's methods and principles. Then, over the years, some evolutionary changes occurred—with Otto Rank and his theory of will, Gertrude Klein and hers on aggression, and others. But our interest is middle age, and perhaps the first to admit of an aspect of adult change and yet remain in the mainstream of psychoanalysis was Terese Benedek. She regarded parenthood as a developmental phase and postulated that deep in the parent's subconscious lie his own childhood experiences, which, with the opportunity for intimacy with his own child, reawaken and can be experienced in a new way. She saw this as a kind of limited regression on the part of the parent to the level of the child, as well as an example of emotional symbiosis. She also stated that the menopause was a developmental phase. Other psychoanalysts later seized upon events such as marriage and pregnancy as developmental phases. Elliott Jaques then postulated a midlife crisis that occurs in the mid-thirties, to be resolved in the early and mid-forties. He considered this crisis to be the confrontation with the inevitability of death, the resolution of which depended upon the balance of "life and 'death forces" that were part of the personality structure prior to the crisis. None of these positions need be elaborated upon here. The important point is that there were a few within the psychoanalytic tradition who began to admit of change and development in adulthood.

Some have since gone further in the branch of psychoanalysis known as ego psychology. This school represents a profound break with Freudian theory because it recognizes the ability of man to be rational in life, and for the first time there is something outside the arena of conflict with the instincts in both the self and society. Ego psychologists have broadened psychoanalytic theory beyond its basis in psychopathology, have attempted to account for the normal as well as the abnormal, and to consider how the personality can best maintain its integrity in interpersonal relationships and in cultural settings. They also abandon much of the mysticism of Freud, including his concepts of Eros and Thanatos. Even so, they remain rooted in the rationalism of the nineteenth century—man is still described as a machine with mechanisms. They therefore have little more than the recognition of rationality to offer on adult development.

The most notable—some say notorious—psychoanalyst to consider the entire life cycle is Erik Erikson. In order to put his contribution in proper perspective, one must take into consideration at least two facts: First, he was a lay psychoanalyst—his only professional qualification was a Montessori teaching credential, although he did spend time with Anna Freud. Second, his professional experience was primarily with children—he had next to none with adults. Most of what he did have was in the early years of the Berkeley Study, with young adults. In the light of these facts, we should accept his theories on adults with reservation. In the words of his biographer, Paul Roazen, Erikson's ideas "have often met with uncritical acceptance, among social scientists as well as the general reading public." Educationists have relied heavily upon his stage theory of childhood development, which may or may not be valid—but that is peripheral to our interest here. What concerns us is his extension of this stage theory into adult life:

- Early adulthood, which has to do with the development of a capacity for intimacy versus a sense of isolation from others.
- Middle adulthood, in which generativity versus stagnation is the issue. Erikson refers to the production of something that will outlive oneself, through parenthood or occupation.
- Late adulthood, when the conflict is between integrity and despair. Either one accepts one's life as having been right and

meaningful in some way—and thus accepts death without dread—or feels an existential sense of meaninglessness.

There is obviously *some* truth here, at least in the concept of generativity and the importance of meaning in life. But the real reason Erikson is so widely quoted (and misquoted) is that he was the first to try to offer a theory of any kind on adult personality growth over the entire life cycle. So he certainly has importance historically. Yet in actuality all he has done is present Freud's five childhood stages with less emphasis on sexual content and more reflecting his own adolescent problems with *his* identity. And his adult stages are a lesser version of Jung's thoughts on individuation. The stages of adult ego development as put forth by Erikson are obviously simplistic, vague, and far too general to apply more than partly to each of us. For this reason, I find his implication of universality objectionable. He starts with a semblance of empiricism that has no basis, then goes on to make value judgments without seeming to be aware of the transition. Throughout he remains rooted in Freud's concepts of ego, pleasure principle, and constant conflict between self and society, from which we had hoped we were freed. In fact, *all* his stages are expressed as conflicts. There is no allowance for the possibility that humans can ever have higher aspirations or greater potentials than merely the resolution of these conflicts. And his stage theory requires the satisfactory solution of each before one can progess to the next. This foreclosure of choices later in life because they are totally dependent on choices made early in life seems to me both pessimistic and fatalistic. Culture, class, sex, and the intersection of life span with historical time are all ignored by him. But far more significant than such criticisms are these is the fact that Walter Gruen and others found that empirical research simply did not support his theories. So I need not dwell upon them further here, nor did I feel it necessary to list his works in the Bibliography.

Robert Peck is also a stage theorist, but his stages were crafted more carefully. His first stage occurs at the approach to middle age. One becomes aware then of waning physical powers and begins to value mental abilities more highly. He feels that those who age most successfully in this stage make smooth changes in their hierarchy of values, putting the use of their heads above the use of their hands. Peck's next stage occurs as one enters middle age. Here men and women are seen more as individuals, human beings, with the sexual element becoming less significant. In his third stage, the middle of middle age, a person should enlarge his capacity to shift emotional investments from one person to another, and from one activity to another. He feels this is crucial, because it is in this period that parents die, children grow up and leave home, and the circle of friends and relatives in the same age range begins to be broken by death. His fourth stage, toward the end of middle age, is characterized by mental flexibility versus mental rigidity—"Although one may have worked out a set of answers that were applicable in the past, they will be less so as time goes on, and it is essential that a person remain flexible in his outlook, continue to learn from life and abandon those concepts that are no longer relevant."

Peck also provided three stages for old age. When approaching retirement, a person must seek to understand himself for what he really is, rather than for what his role has been in society. Next, one should avoid overconcern with the physical afflictions of aging. The last stage has to do with the approaching prospect of death. Life is to be lived so that ". . . the prospect of personal death—the 'night of the ego,' it might be called—looks and feels less important than the secure knowledge that one has built for a broader, longer future than any one ego could ever encompass."

I treasure that last thought. And Peck has much more to offer than I could present here. This summary only provides some of the flavor of his ideas. If you read them yourself, you can't help noting the immense improvement over Erikson's stages. Peck adds, ". . . there is far greater variability in the chronological age at which a given psychic crisis arises in later life, than is true of the crisis-points of youth." This is something to bear in mind, because many of the theories that follow are characterized by rigid age-determinism.

The biographical school should be considered next, because all subsequent stage theorists have incorporated its approach. In the 1930s Charlotte Buhler and her student, Elsie Frenkel (later Brunswick), studied four hundred biographies of individuals and conducted interviews with some people living in Vienna at that time. From this, Buhler formed five biological phases, which I will not present here, then turned to consider psychological phases, noting as she did that these are not synchronized with the biological.

Buhler saw childhood as the first psychological phase of

human life when the child lives at home and his entire world for the most part is made up of familial influences and control. The second period begins between fifteen and seventeen and is characterized by exploratory steps into independent activities, most frequently when the youth moves away from home. One formulates goals tentatively at this time in terms of his or her experience until then with prevailing social standards. The third phase begins around the ages of twenty-five to twenty-eight; it is characterized by a more definite selection of life goals, and one then makes choices about vocation, marriage, and establishment of a home. The fourth phase begins around ages forty-five to forty-eight. Negative burdens first begin to appear—sickness, loss of associates, and so forth. One then evaluates his original goals and changes some. The fifth period starts with retirement around sixty-five, or physical disability at an earlier age may bring about this turning point. Retrospection is common at this time, and a person abandons his plan of life with feelings of either fulfillment or failure.

Raymond Kuhlen improved on this growth, culmination, and contraction curve of the biographical approach somewhat by emphasizing self-expansion motives in the first half of life and the roles of anxiety and threat in causing contracture in the latter half of life.

Yet, having read the literature of the biographical school, I am left with a feeling of futility about its conclusions—We know nothing more about adult life than we already knew merely by looking around us. The limitations of this approach are obvious—overemphasis on easily documented external events culturally determined in an ever-changing culture, under-emphasis on the inner change with aging, and almost nothing on the interaction between the changes within the individual and his environment. Still, one thought of Charlotte Buhler caught my eye and is worth noting: ". . . the fact that toward the end people are able, or even feel compelled to, size up the result of their lives indicates that they have followed a directive . . . the human being's *intentionality toward fulfillment*." And she adds; "Our study also shows that only a minority of people has goal patterns that appear to be adequate, effective, and leading to integration. The majority has ideas or goals that seem to be worthless, inappropriate, unrealistic, or internally contradictory."

This is the major theme that has emerged from the contributions of those we have considered so far, and should make all of us in middle age reflect. If it *is* universal, or nearly so, that at the end we look back upon our lives for a sense of direction and accomplishment, then it behooves us to be aware of this *now*, to reselect our values and reorder our goals while we can still direct our efforts toward their attainment, to make, if you will, a midcourse correction.

George Vaillant, a psychiatrist, was influenced by both the biographical approach and stage theory. He and his colleagues first studied 268 Harvard male sophomores and have since followed them past their fiftieth birthdays. He found that from ages twenty to thirty his subjects were careful to follow the rules, were anxious for promotion, and accepted many aspects of "the system." Self-deception about both marital and career choices was common in this period. During this time a man has two major tasks: accepting and adapting to the intimacy of marriage and to the requirements of a career. Incidentally, the Berkeley Growth Studies and the Fels Study show that women are focused at this time also—on marriage and on careers or children if they have them. Vaillant found that the decade from thirty to forty appeared to be more and more concentrated upon career consolidation. Around age forty this "compulsive calm" is left, and the next decade is a time for reassessment of the past and reordering of the future. He concludes, "Perhaps the most important conclusion of the Grant Study has been that the agonizing self-reappraisal and instinctual reawakening at age forty—the so-called midlife crisis—does not appear to portend decay . . . it often heralds a new stage of man." And he adds, "Crisis is the exception, not the rule." To me, these are his most important contributions. His book, *Adaptation to Life*, is well worth reading, despite the fact that it is analytic in orientation and views life as consisting essentially of coping with adversity through defense mechanisms of varying degrees of maturity.

Roger Gould, another psychiatrist under the same two influences, studied all of the patients who were in group therapy at the UCLA Psychiatric Outpatient Clinic in 1968 and divided them into seven age groups with the following characteristics:

Ages sixteen to eighteen—a period primarily concerned with separation from parents. Autonomy then is precarious—these young people rebound from peers to parents for validation and social approval.

Ages eighteen to twenty-two—the theme is the same, but now they are halfway sprung from parental control, and the peer group actually helps them in the process of separation.

Ages twenty-two to twenty-eight—separation from parents is complete and autonomy is established. They have formed an idea of "self" and are beginning to forge ahead without introspection or consideration as to whether their choices in career or marriage are correct or not.

Ages twenty-eight to thirty-four—this group is beginning to question the course of their marriage and career lines now that they are somewhat established and growing young children are now on the scene. Those this age are beginning to become weary of doing what they are supposed to do. They're increasingly conscious that their will alone is not all of them and that inner forces produce patterns of behavior that they can no longer ignore.

Ages thirty-five to forty-three—self-questioning is intensified because of an increasing awareness of the limited time remaining to live. Questions become broader in scope, dealing more frequently with values and the meaning of life itself. Some make a last surge of effort in their careers.

Ages forty-three to fifty—These have accepted their earlier awareness of life's brief span and are resigning themselves to their personalities and lives as they are.

Ages fifty to sixty—people in this group are mellowing and growing warmer. They turn to their parents in a new way, with more affection and understanding of their worth. They no longer regard their children as problems, but as potential sources of close relationships. More conscious of their own feelings, people at this age also now appreciate their spouses more than ever.

This study was supplemented with a questionnaire sent to 524 people and some similar findings emerged: Marital happiness declines in the thirties but begins to pick up slowly in the late forties; the sense of life's finitude comes about somewhere in the thirties; a reconciliation with reality starts in the thirties and forties, strengthening thereafter; and the sense of self appears to crystallize somewhere in the forties.

With just these two studies, based upon *phychiatric patients* and a *questionnaire*, Gould has added little to previous biographical and stage theories except for his attempt to define the age span of each stage more precisely. The course of our development cannot be so constrained by chronology. In his subsequent book, *Transformations*, he states that all of us are born with a biological desire to have what we cannot have—total safety and love—and that life thereafter is a continuing endeavor to eliminate the childhood distortions or "demons" that pursue us because of this through the years until we die. He sees life as little more than the struggle to solve the resultant problems in each stage and offers a seven-step dialogue to aid us in mastering these "demons" that stumbles shamelessly from platitude to platitude. *Transformations* is both psychoanalytic and pessimistic. But once forewarned of its orientation and tone, you might want to search the book for some of the valuable nuggets buried in the stream of Gould's thought, one of them being his consideration of how one's psychological changes through the years can and do affect those closest to him.

Daniel Levinson, a social psychologist, is the last to be strongly influenced by both stage theory and the biographical approach. In 1969, he commenced a study of forty men of various ages between thirty-five and forty-five that terminated in 1975, and he commenced another in 1977 on a group of women. So far, he has reported his findings on the men only. He offers material from such sources as autobiographies, biographies, poetry, plays, and novels in order to augment the findings from his small sample of subjects.

With his concept of individual life structures he endeavors to consider both self and society as well as the transactions between them. He states that a man's life evolves through a sequence of stable periods and transitions. During the stable periods he makes certain crucial choices, constructs a life structure around these choices, and tries to attain his goals within this structure. A transitional point occurs when an existing structure ends and he begins work to form a new one.

The first transition Levinson calls the early adult transition; it lasts from ages seventeen to twenty-two. At this time a man begins moving out into the world of adults, questioning the nature of that world and his place in it, consolidating an initial adult identity.

The first adult life structure extends from ages twenty-two through twenty-eight. To form this structure, a man must make choices regarding occupation, marriage, and life values. In his late twenties, he begins to question these choices.

Levinson's "age thirty transition" lasts from ages twenty-eight to thirty-three and consists of evaluating and modifying the initial adult life structure.

The second adult life structure is called "settling down." This structure takes shape when one is in the early thirties and continues until age forty. A man throws himself into what he builds within this period; he creates his niche in society and a life plan. Late in this period there is a time Levinson labels as that of "becoming one's own man." Although Levinson has overlooked adolescent heroes, he notes that young men often acquire mentors who have profound influence. At thirty-six or thirty-seven, a man casts off his mentor. It would have been interesting to make clear which men acquired mentors and what correlation this acquisition may have had with the lack of paternal influence earlier in life, but this was not done.

During the "midlife transition," which lasts from forty to forty-five, a man questions his second adult life structure and begins to search more earnestly for meaning and value in his life. According to Levinson, these reappraisals inevitably involve emotional turmoil, doubts, and despair. The neuroses a man has carried with him from childhood obstruct change; so do external influences such as his wife, children, colleagues, and other aspects of his occupation. He realizes for the first time that many of his prior choices were based upon illusions. He evaluates the fit between his present life structure and his true self. As the transition ends in the mid-forties, a man must either make new choices, or on new terms, reinforce his commitment to his old choices.

In my opinion, Levinson's unique concept of "life structures" is more comprehensive by including interaction between self and society and achieves more clarity than do earlier descriptions of ego stages. His transitions also give one a more pronounced sense of the dynamic development that occurs in adult life, although he concentrates this development at specific ages.

My main disappointment on reading his papers was over the chronological precision and minutely detailed characteristics of each structure and transition. Such an intricate, detailed, and age-related theory intended to apply to all men based on a study of *only forty subjects for just six years* simply slips off the pages without support. What is worse is that his description of life events prior to age thirty-five depends entirely on the memories of his subjects, and he has not studied *any* men beyond their early fifties, yet in his book, *The Seasons of a Man's Life*, he starts with childhood and continues through old age to death! I was compelled to communicate with Levinson personally to inquire about his data basis for this. He admitted that he had none—only his professional experience—and backed up a step: " . . . we do not claim that these findings have universal validity; we offer this as a hypothesis for further study." I would hope so, yet the implication of universality is a thread running through all his writing. One such statement reads: "We are now prepared to maintain that everyone lives through the same developmental periods in adulthood. . . ." Still, I found his book to be worth reading. At the very least we can derive something warm and human from the biographies he has included.

In the last two decades some child psychologists have begun to call themselves "developmental psychologists," not limiting themselves to the study of the childhood years, but dealing with the changes from birth to death, with sincere attempts to avoid rigid staging. The field is still in its prescientific state; even its methodology is amorphous and under debate. This approach, however, holds much promise for the future.

Existential psychology has one contribution for us in middle age. That is its emphasis on being true to and accepting responsibility for oneself. Beyond this, there is no consistent theoretical form or structure in this school, and it cannot be regarded as a coherent psychological system. But Viktor Frankl did discard Freud's will to pleasure and Adler's will to power. He felt that the will to *meaning* is the essence of human existence.

This brings us to the last psychological school that has something to offer us at this time in our lives. Humanistic psychology started with some observations of Kurt Goldstein followed by Henry A. Murray's historic study of normal individuals. From this, Murray formulated a list of human psychological needs which is still an ingredient in most personality tests, and he also developed the thematic apperception test, which is the most commonly used psychological test, second only to the Rorschach. Murray rejected the past orientation of Freudianism. Instead he felt that a progressively greater differentiation and integration throughout life occurs and that any attempt to explain adults in terms of childhood instincts and fixations missed much of man's being.

Murray was the first to believe that the ego might exist not solely to reduce conflict between self and society. This concept initiated the branch of psychoanalysis known as ego psychology, which I have already mentioned. But while ego psychologists hold that the highest aim of the ego is such synthesis, humanistic psychologists go further. They stress man's purposefulness and that his life's work is to actualize his potentials.

One such humanist, Erich Fromm, emphasized the culmination of human history in a cultural product, human nature. Where Freud saw man as making history, Fromm regarded man as made by history. But man is both created and a creator. He must feel both his rootedness and his individual identity. Ultimately, human values depend upon a knowledge of human nature: "Man's nature is dual. He is at one in union with nature, but too, apart from nature and aware of his apartness." Though the animal in man is gregarious, his reason enables him to be free of the herd. In this dichotomy is his dilemma. But reason alone is not enough—man must not only understand, but *love*. These comments are far too few for Fromm. His major works are listed in the Bibliography for your further reading.

Midway in the continuum of holism and atomism—full integration and fragmentation of the parts of the personality—is the integrative theory of Gordon Allport. He does not reduce all drives to one, nor does he reduce them to the biological, as do the theories of the Freudians and behaviorists. His conception of "functional autonomy" explains how biological needs and cultural-social drives are independent of each other. Allport stressed the uniqueness of an individual in contradistinction to the nomothetic stance of the physical sciences that seek to determine general laws. He also rejected the reification of Freud's personality structure as being more suitable for children and the mentally ill than for normal adults. His *proprium*, or self, is more than biologically based and is *pro*active, not just *re*active. He drew a careful distinction between what *is*, according to statistical norms, and what *should be*, by ethical norms—that is, what a healthy person could and should be through continuing growth and integration of his personality. And he provided some clues as to what such development in an adult involves: an extension of the self into significant areas of life—enlarging one's *"oneliness"*; warm relating to others with an appreciation of the human condition we all share and a respect for all people as people; emotional security or self-acceptance—living within one's emotions without inter-fering with the well-being of others; a realistic perception of skills and assignment and the ability to lose oneself in a truly important task; self-objectification with insight and humor; and the pos-session of a unifying philosophy of life. These are all worth some thought on our part. Again, the full value of his ideas cannot be appreciated unless you read his words yourself.

Abraham Maslow, more than any other, was the formulator of contemporary humanism in psychology. He believed psychol-ogy should center on the human being, and he placed positive value on those capacities and aspirations that distinguish humans from animals. This approach not only sets humans apart from animals, but also sets each person apart from every other. It recognizes the unique quality of each human being and em-phasizes that the full potential of each should be developed rather than continuing in the customary conformity to social norms.

He rejected the idea that man is inherently evil and depraved after tracing the Judaeo-Christian origins of this belief through Freud: "One major shortcoming of research psychology (and of psychiatry as well) is its pessimistic, negative, and limited conception of the full height to which the human being can attain. It becomes more and more clear that the studies of crippled, stunted, immature, and unhealthy specimens can yield only a crippled psychology and crippled philosophy." He added elsewhere, ". . . contemporary psychology . . . has notoriously little to say, for example, about duty, art, fun, play, wonder, awe, joy, love, happiness and other 'useless' reactions and experiences. . . . It offers little to the modern man whose most desperate need is a naturalistic or humanistic end or value system." Maslow also commented that instinct theorists used animal instinct as a model and failed to look for any instincts that might be unique to the human species. He held that our instincts are better regarded as "instinct remnants" that can be modified or disappear altogether, as animal instincts cannot. These and our capacity for reason are *synergistic*, not *antagonistic*.

Central in Maslow's concept of the human personality is his "hierarchy of needs":

1. Survival needs
2. Safety needs
3. Social needs (belongingness and love)

4. Self-respect and esteem needs
5. Self-actualization needs

These will not be gone into here, except to point out that the lower needs are common to all, and their satisfaction depends more on environment and circumstances than do the higher needs. Environment and circumstances can only inhibit, not satisfy, the higher needs; satisfaction of the latter is up to each person himself. Maslow believed that as man ascends this hierarchy in life, he develops from within by an intrinsic drive for growth in the Bergsonian rather than behavioristic sense. For Maslow, human nature is *becoming*, not *being*, as one ascends the hierarchy. This, in my opinion, is his major contribution to understanding how our personalities evolve in middle age.

More time will be devoted to the last step in the hierarchy, self-actualization, in the chapter on values. Although it is our goal in life, according to Maslow, few people arrive there; most stop at steps along the way. Those who stop are limited both from within and from without—by their genes and by society. He commented that even in a totally beneficent society not all would attain self-actualization, nor would all become Leonardo da Vincis or Albert Einsteins—"The culture is sun and food and water; it is not the seed."

Maslow has laid out our course in middle age: "Self-actualization does not occur in young people; they have not yet achieved their true identity; they do not comprehend love other than romance; they have not yet selected their own values; unrealistic idealism still overwhelms realism; they have not leaned toward compassion; nor have they come to terms with their ambivalences toward parents and power." Where before I have suggested that you read an author's works yourself, this time I urge you to.

SOCIOLOGY

Here we leave psychology and look to sociology to offer its insights. But sociologists haven't particularly helped us to understand middle age. For the most part, they are insufficiently concerned with either the continuity or change of personality throughout life, but are content with measuring the effects of life events upon observed behavior. Moreover, most of their studies cover short periods of time and use different bases as well as different methodologies. Each study usually has an internal coherence but doesn't relate to other studies that use their own particular approaches. Most often too, they fix on a single aspect of life and examine it across the spectrum of society. The variety of terms, methodologies, measures, and samples, often without controls, result for our purposes in a meaningless maze. In the last analysis, a sociologist looks for laws, but in reality, each event in life is unique as each of us is unique. Fred Cattrell, an eminent sociologist himself, comments; "We believe that sociological principles will be shown to have considerable worth, but only when they are placed in conjunction with the principles of a great many other sciences."

One exception is Bernice Neugarten, who started with a sociological orientation under Robert Havighurst that gradually became more psychosocial. This evolution resulted in some profound contributions. She developed typology describing "active mastery men," who are self-assertive, aggressive, focused on the environment, and "passive mastery men," who adapt and conform, reshaping themselves rather than their environment. "Active mastery women" are moralistic matriarchs who were once rebellious daughters. "Passive mastery women" are the altruists or the submissive victims of fate. Once this typology was defined, she discovered in her field research that there appeared to be a shift in middle age—men changed to a more passive mastery, and women who were previously passive tended to become more active. As they passed through midlife, men became more tolerant of their nurturant and affiliative impulses, more concerned with others; women became more aware and tolerant of their aggressive and egocentric tendencies.

She found the middle-aged of both sexes to be increasingly aware of the limitation of time left to live and tending to structure time with regard to how much was left rather than in terms of what had passed. She also noted a tendency toward self-reflection and introspection in middle age, which she called "interiority," a concept similar to Jung's introversion.

Neugarten also noted that women passing through menopause or already through it regarded it lightly. This attitude contrasted sharply with the anxiety or dread of menopause frequently found in younger women. She also failed to find any significant spurt of reproductive activity around the time of the menopause—"the closing of the gate"—in contrast to the theories of some psychoanalysts, notably Helene Deutsch.

Underlying the terminological tangle of Erickson and Peck, she concluded that successful people in middle age accepted each change as a challenge and an opportunity for new adventure. And she emphasized that if one can transcend bodily changes at this time, then social and mental activities become even more satisfying than the physical ones were before.

Perhaps Neugarten's major contribution is her demonstration by actual research that personality in adulthood is by no means static, that in fact middle age is characterized by continuing development. So far, however, she says, ". . . we lack a developmental psychology of adulthood in the sense that we have a developmental psychology of childhood." And she admits, "Knowledge of personality changes in the second half of life is meager."

There are only a few major longitudinal sociological studies underway in this country that may have information for us sometime in the future. Two are under the auspices of the Institute of Human Development at Berkeley. The first is the Guidance Study, which originally included infants chosen at random from those born in Berkeley in 1928 and 1929; the second is the Oakland Growth Study, started in 1931–1932 with children from five elementary schools in the area. These two have been combined, are now only into early middle age, and though some of the parents were studied, they were not observed before later middle age. The Duke study has just begun, with only partial reports so far. The Normative Aging Study under the auspices of the Veteran Administration in Boston is still incomplete and mostly unreported. A study on women at the Fels Institute has yielded little data of interest to us so far except what I mentioned previously. Hopefully, these sociological studies will tell us a great deal more than such studies have to date.

ANTHROPOLOGY

We might expect anthropologists to help study changing personality patterns with age. As ethnographers, they have traditionally relied upon the memories and insights of older members of various societies for their cultural data, because most of these societies were preliterate and the adults were their only sources. Anthropologists have long claimed cultural patterns and the study of "rites of passage" as their own province. Nonetheless we look in vain.

Margaret Clark, an anthropologist herself, comments that research by anthropologists in aging has been sparse and, further, that the early psychoanalytic formulations made a greater impression upon them than have recent advances in personality psychology.

An exception is David Gutmann, who is both an anthropologist and a psychologist. He found that the active and passive mastery concept was present also in other cultures, that there was a trajectory of change in men from active to passive and in women from passive to active, only the *manifestations* of this trajectory varied with the culture. In other cultures men change as they do in ours, from trying to control their environment to being more accommodating; they become less interested in power than in love later in life. He also noted that there was a shift in men from phallic sexuality toward a more diffuse sensuality, but that women seem to go in the opposite direction. Even in patriarchal societies, women become more aggressive in middle life. In his studies of other societies he was prepared to accept the emergence of maternal instincts in women early in their reproductive lives, but was surprised by the emergence of certain attitudes toward fatherhood in men, such as increasing acceptance of responsibilities and less self-centeredness. He thought that these changes in both sexes served survival of the species.

CONCLUSIONS

This rapid review summarizes all that I could find in the literature about changes in personality through middle age. Obviously, many mysteries are far from being solved, but we can begin to see some threads; perhaps at the present time we could at least say that there are themes that characterize each time in life, but superimposed on these themes is the infinite variability in each of us and in our relationships with others and with the world around us.

The theme of childhood could be called *introjection*—of the values of parents, peers, and society. The emphasis then is upon conformity and the tempering of self-centered impulses. The child is capable of little introspection and is largely unaware of his own inherent individuality, which consists mostly of potentials, talents, and tendencies. Stages *can* be delineated in childhood, although most of the literature on this blurs maturational and psychological aspects and ignores environmental and cultural influences almost entirely. We see variation upon this theme even here—some older children refuse to accept certain externally imposed rules and values, and some rebel against them all, or try to.

Around adolescence, *idealization* appears to become the theme, and this too can follow many paths. Adolescents take all that has been introjected so far to form an ideological framework, and within this context they begin to form their identity. The search for identity is lifelong; idealization is not. The latter characterizes adolescence far more than the former. Adolescents idealize the opposite sex in romantic love, idealize life values and goals, and form a concept of their idealized self. Again, there is great variability from person to person in the proportions of ideal and real. Only later will each see how much of this idealization was illusory.

In early adulthood, *commitment* seems to be characteristic. This is based upon and receives its impetus from the idealization that has gone before. This commitment can be to education, to a career, or to marriage and procreation, and is still predicated upon the predominant cultural values. In the process of committing oneself in one of these areas, a man or woman inevitably suppresses some of the personality potentials he or she was born with. One wonders if there is not a "great plan" by which each of us is merely an instrument of the species' drive to survive—both woman's historical commitment to a mate and to child-bearing and man's commitment to his mate and the protector-provider role seem to have served the species far more than the individual. Sociobiologists are presently making much of this possibility. If it is true, it certainly need not continue to be so in middle age when the reproductive period is past.

Again, variation on this theme is evident. There are some who drift through the early twenties and delay serious commitments until their thirties. There are still others who never make significant commitments. We must remember that these themes are far from absolute and farther still from any sort of absolute age-determination.

We in middle age are past the period of commitment characteristic of early adulthood, but life is longer now, and many of us tend to drift on with what could best be called *consolidation of our commitments*. We should recognize that our early commitments often remain unchanged, even though the ideals that formed their basis may have been excessively high or inappropriate to our individuality and abilities. Humanistic psychologists show us that throughout middle age change is not only possible, but desirable—even inevitable. We should not have locked ourselves so completely into our earliest choices, nor continue to be prisoners of our past. Throughout early adulthood we should instead have started to listen to our "other voices in other rooms," to use a phrase of Truman Capote, and begun an early exploration of our true selves. We would have done well to heed the wise words of Plotinus: "To the possession of the self, the way is inward."

In middle age, *attainment of our inborn potentials* is, or should be, our theme, instead of a continued consolidation of commitments. When we begin to discover ourselves, we will question our early values and where they have brought us. And we will start a search for what life means to each of us. If we have not done so by midlife, modification of our original values, our goals, and our methods of achieving them is what we must do from here on. We will then be free to grow in both adversity and prosperity. Tusitala, the "Teller of Tales," Robert Louis Stevenson, put it well: "To be what we are, and to become what we are capable of becoming, is the only end of life." It is the *process*, not the *personality*, that lends stability to adulthood.

If there is a theme of later life, it is—or should be—*reaping the rewards* of all that we have done before.

What constitutes the so-called "midlife crisis" would appear to be the result of a failure or delay by some in seeing reality clearly, both in themselves and in their lives. It occurs in fewer than a fourth of men. And although we hear more about the male version, it is as frequent in women, with different and more subtle manifestations. Those of either sex who have been content with consolidation, who have not altered their life course by perceptible degrees up to this point, who have not increased their appreciation of their own potentials nor lived their lives as a process of growth and search for meaning, may become aware of this failure in a number of ways. One may be a gradual erosion of their will or ability to continue fixed commitments, to the point where they cannot carry on any longer. Another may be their meeting with mortality and the awareness of life's finitude, sparked by any number of events, and the despair that frequently follows. A woman who has been committed to being a wife and mother and nothing else, may be jolted by the empty nest into reconsidering her life. (Men, too, are experiencing the empty nest, now that their wives are leaving home more for the working world.) Still another may be the impossibility of continuing to deny the gap between one's initial goals and one's achievements—the goal gap that is almost a congenital condition in our society. Few attain all they aspire to. Even if one reaches the goals set early in life, he or she may feel vaguely discontent in middle age because neither his values or goals changed as he did.

If we encounter such a midlife crisis, there are several paths we can take. The most fortunate of us reevaluate ourselves, our lives, and our goals right then, make our midcourse correction, and continue the process of creative change thereafter throughout our lives. Some postpone this reevaluation for a few more years yet are able to make a later transition, albeit a more stormy one. Some totally deny the inevitable intrusion of reality and commit themselves even more tenaciously to their original goals. This later leads to decompensation, with such manifestations as anxiety, marital discord, depression, or abuse of drugs and alcohol. Others try to return to their younger years in ways that are both foolish and faddish: women with "boob jobs," heavy makeup, and "sexy" clothes; men with long or "permed" hair, shirt unbuttoned, gold necklace—the whole bit. Some escape, or try, to a totally new environment in the Gauguin tradition with the sad results that Gauguin himself experienced. They bring themselves with them and don't realize it until they get there. Or they set out on a "great adventure" characterized more by defiance of death than difference of life. Or plunge into an affair. Still others attempt to pin the blame on their jobs or mates, changing one or both, then again and perhaps again. A few seek a kind of desperately absolutistic solution in religious conversion or through attainment of great power. The point common to all of these unsatisfactory solutions is denial, in one form or another, of their true being.

Awareness and acceptance are the keys to success in this period, success in becoming the person you never became, the person you *can* become. If inner voices are vague and offer no real direction, you should allow time for quiet introspection so they can be heard. Conversation with those who care and in whom you have confidence can help distinguish between values the world has imposed and ones more in harmony with your true self. If you are conscious only of a restlessness and little else, then psychological counseling can aid in breaking down barriers that keep you from looking within and understanding yourself. They keys to failure are reluctance, resistance, and resignation. And those closest must emphasize, not sympathize; help solve, not offer solutions.

At this time in your life, you must come to grips with such eternal questions as time and truth, as well as those closer to home, marriage and mortality. In your favor is knowing that most of the answers you arrive at now will be your last. You have the experience of a lifetime, which you did not have when you first charted your course. You can now recognize externally imposed values for what they are. You are also able to look ahead more clearly and see the futility of continuing in a job or marriage in which you aren't happy and never will be. And you can console yourself that you cannot and need not alter your life drastically. We all do best if we merely *modify* our lives now and as we go on from here. Lastly, you have the satisfaction that the changes you make through the rest of your life will be based upon the truth as you see it, not upon the perceptions of others.

In *Gift from the Sea*, Ann Morrow Lindbergh looks at this in a wonderful way: "Perhaps middle age is, or should be, a period of shedding shells: the shell of ambition, the shell of material accumulation and possessions, the shell of ego. Perhaps one can shed at this stage of life, as one sheds in beach living, one's pride, one's false ambitions, one's mask, one's armor.

"Was that armor not put on to protect one from the competitive world? If one ceases to compete, does one need it? Perhaps one can, at last, in middle age, if not earlier, be completely one's self. And what a liberation that would be!"

6

The Family

"For aught that I could ever read, could ever hear by tale or history, the course of true love never did run smooth.

SHAKESPEARE

At this time in our lives, those closest to us seem to be the source of both more frustration and satisfaction than they ever have been before. And we sense that this contradiction will continue. By now our marriage may have lost much of its early allure, yet we are beginning to feel an increasing need to share life more intimately with someone who cares. And just as we are becoming aware of our identity and it is becoming recognized by the world around us, it may be challenged by our teen-agers, who are in the first throes of groping for theirs. We have long since emerged from the pattern of being a child to our parents and have become accustomed to a relationship with them on an adult basis, yet as they age, we find we are beginning to become a parent to them. There are greater problems as well as potentials in our family relationships now than we have ever known.

But before we can consider the most intimate and meaningful relationship in the family setting, marriage, each of us must explore ourselves as man or as woman—how we became one or the other and how we live our lives as such.

SEX AND SEXUALITY

We all learned long ago that the subject of sex has importance far beyond the physical act itself. During our lives we have been caught up in a time of dramatically increasing knowledge about that aspect, true, and also in a shift in attitudes and morals about it that has been even more dramatic—if not traumatic. But beyond this, we have lived through changes in concepts of sexual *identity* (how we see ourselves sexually; our private experience of our gender role) and sexual *roles* (how society sees us; how we publicly express our private sexual identity). So this section will attempt to touch upon all of these aspects.

Male and Female

To do so, we have to begin at the beginning—the way in which we become a man or a woman. It is not as simple as we might think. There are actually five sexual determinants. As everyone knows, the male sperm contains either an X or a Y chromosome, and the ovum of the famle an X. When they combine, an X and a Y chromosome together determine a male offspring, and two X's a female. But this is only the first determinant of sex, called the chromosomal or genetic.

The second is gonadal. Within the fetus are the primordial gonads, bits of tissue that can become either ovaries or testicles. The chromosomal factor triggers the process whereby either the cortex, the outer part, of the gonadal tissue disappears, resulting in the formation of a testicle, or the core disappears and an ovary is formed from the cortex.

Inside the fetus of either sex at this time are two sets of potential organs: One set can evolve into internal male organs, such as the prostate, and the other can become the internal organs of the female. The external appearance of the fetus is similar then in both sexes. Beginning around the fifth week of pregnancy, the gonads have evolved into either testicles or ovaries, and begin to produce their respective hormones—testosterone or estrogen. The production of testosterone by the male fetus is crucial and overcomes the effects of the maternal estrogen, which is increasing and constantly bathing the fetus. The production of estrogen by the fetal ovaries is not crucial—it is, of course, redundant in the presence of maternal estrogen. The influence of fetal testosterone causes the development of the male internal and external organs, and estrogen from both mother and fetus has the same effect upon the development of the female organs. Therefore this third step is termed the genital.

The fourth step in the differentiation between males and females is cultural. This conditioning occurs through early social influence, first from the family. Studies have shown that it begins immediately after birth, in the hospital, where mothers have been photographed handling boys and girls in different ways.

The last step is largely one of authentication or confirmation. Just before puberty, the respective hormone production increases in each sex, causing accentuation of genital differentiation, changes in body contours, and development of other secondary sex characteristics. Although hormones have already had an earlier role and will continue to be important, this step is usually referred to as hormonal.

Masculinity and Femininity

In talking about masculine or feminine behavior, we immediately get into the classic "nature versus nurture" argument, for which no clear-cut answer has ever been found—nor ever will be. Since the advent of the feminist movement, there has been a lot of controversy about this, so let's review what we do know. In several lower orders of animals such as rats, the hormonal influence upon the fetus has been shown to cause demonstrable morphological changes in the fetal brains that later result in such characteristically masculine or feminine behavior as mounting or receptivity to mounting. The signifiance of this early hormonal influence has been dramatically demonstrated by artifically controlling the hormonal milieu of the fetus of either sex, inducing behavior *opposite* to that expected from the genetic determinant. But in seeking information that applies to man, we have to look at experiments on primates and accept even these results with some reservation.

In primates, without any conditioning, males show a tendency to mount, more assertive or aggressive behavior, a preference for the out-of-doors, territoriality, and a greater tendency toward athletic activity. They also manipulate objects more for utility. Female primates have been observed to be more passive; there is little or no tendency to mount; they use objects less for utility and more for adornment; tend to prefer indoors to outdoors; and show less athletic activity and a greater interest in baby primates, even those not their own.

How or why these differences came about without conditioning was not known until the last few years. Then, as just mentioned, investigators discovered the effects of the fetal production of sex harmones on the forming brains of fetuses in several lower species of animals. The first such experimental work with primates showed only one change. If testosterone was present at a certain critical time in fetal development, then, regardless of the genetic sex of the fetus, the pituitary gland released gonad stimulators at the constant rate characteristic of the male for the rest of its life. If testosterone was not present then (the male fetus was castrated prior to that time), maternal estrogen prevailed and, again regardless of its genetic sex, the fetal pituitary gland would produce the gonad stimulators in the cyclic fashion characteristic of the female for its entire life. This suggested the possibility of other effects of hormones upon the fetal brain of primates, and even man, similar to those found in lower orders, so this was looked into further.

First, the above characteristics of "male" and "female" primate behavior were laid out on a spectrum with the most masculine at one end and the most feminine at the other. Then either testosterone or estrogen was administered to pregnant primates carrying fetuses of either sex. After birth, those offspring whose mothers had been given testosterone, *regardless of their genetic sex*, displayed more "male" behavior. The reverse was not true. As would be expected, estrogen given to the mother appeared to have no effect upon the behavior of the offspring. And genetically male fetuses castrated early invariably behaved as females after birth.

So we do know that there is a biological basis for masculinity and femininity in primates and that this also holds true for all the lower orders that have been studied. The difficulty is in translating this to humans. Man's mental makeup is so different that we can't argue by analogy. Yet no pregnant woman is going to agree to massive doses of testosterone at the critical point in fetal formation or have her unborn baby castrated to clear this up for us.

Fortunately, we have some indirect ways in which the degree of innateness of "male" and "female" behavior in humans can be determined. They aren't as conclusive, but they are strongly suggestive.

One was the wide use in the 1950s of progesterone and similar compounds to prevent threatened spontaneous abortions. These substances are chemically similar to testosterone and their use resulted in a virilizing effect on the genitals as well as the central nervous system of the female fetus. After birth, the girls were found to be more "tomboyish," fantasized more about careers than babies, and so forth.

There are also rather rare syndromes in humans which shed some light. In one, none of the fetal tissue of a genetic and gonadal male has the ability to respond to the testosterone produced by the testicles. In another, neither ovaries nor testes are present at a result of chromosomal error. In both of these syndromes, characteristically feminine behavior occurs from birth on. That it continues throughout life might be attributable to conditioning, however. This latter point is clarified somewhat by a third syndrome. In this, production of testosterone by the male fetus is impaired by the deficiency of a critical enzyme but becomes normal or nearly so sometime after birth. The baby is born appearing to be indeterminant or female and is therefore usually raised as a female. The effects of the small amounts of testosterone produced during childhood are not great, so the child continues to be raised as a female. But at puberty, the production of testosterone becomes nearly normal, producing clearly evident virilization that can no longer be ignored. Most of these individuals change both their sexual identity and sexual roles during or shortly after puberty and live the rest of their lives as males. Their success in doing so depends a great deal upon the social surroundings in which they are born, raised, and live. In most cases, the effects of cultural conditioning in childhood are overcome without serious difficulty.

Another bit of help comes from the study of men who have one or more extra male Y chromosomes. They tend to be more aggressive and more inclined toward violent criminality throughout their lives than males with a normal set of chromosomes. There is also the long-known observation that a high degree of maternal stress while carrying a male fetus tends to demasculinize the behavior of the offspring. The reason for this is that the mother's stress causes the adrenal glands to produce more of a hormone that has incomplete testosterone action, and this is believed to compete with testosterone at receptor sites in the brain at the critical time in fetal development. Richard Restak, in his book *The Brain: The Last Frontier*, has presented much more recent evidence from psychological research that indicates the degree of innateness of behavioral differences between men and women.

So from all such sources we have learned that there is a strong biological basis for masculinity and femininity in the human and that the rest, a lesser part, is learned. We really cannot say more at the present time. But we do have enough evidence so that no one can take either polar position that it is all nature or all nurture.

As knowledge in this area grows, hopefully people will feel more free to be themselves. A "feminine" woman who has been so from birth, and made more so by influences since, should expect less than some assertiveness training courses promise in their brochures. The woman who, from early childhood, has preferred activities that our society considers masculine may also feel more free to do them. And men who lack some of the competitive spirit or "machismo" will be able to pursue some of the quieter paths in life without guilt. We may also become more understanding of at least male homosexuals, who are about four or five times as common as their counterparts in females. Even with our present knowledge, we can postulate that in some a less than optimum level of fetal testosterone may have been present at the critical time in their development in the uterus, or that the receptors in the brain at that point were somewhat refractory. From such considerations there should be more understanding and compassion for them. There is also some comfort here for those of us in middle age who learn that a child of ours is homosexual. Traditionally, psychoanalytic concepts have laid the entire burden upon us, the parents. The more we learn, the less we think of these concepts.

Feminists versus Freud

And now let's return for a moment to an area of confusion and controversy over the third determinant of sexuality, the genital. For some reason, probably his inadequate grasp of the genetics and embryology known even in his time, Freud held that every fetus was innately bisexual. According to him, if a baby was born with a penis, he had evolved in the uterus into a superior being. If the fetus became female, she was obviously inferior and left to her sad lot with "penis envy."

Some feminists are understandably upset by this and have countered Freud's idea with one of their own, based on the fact that for the first five or six weeks of pregnancy every fetus externally appears to be female. From this, they conclude that the female is the original "God-intended" form and therefore somehow superior. However, they ignore the fact that from conception every cell in the fetus can be distinguished as genetically male or female by a chromatin test; they disregard also the primordial elements of the internal sex organs of both sexes that are present then; and finally, they do not acknowledge that the primordial gonads have the potential to develop either into ovaries or testes. Some, like Gail Sheehy in *Passages*, go further, stating that if the testes of a male fetus are removed prior to differentiation it will develop into an anatomically normal female. Although the external appearance would then be female at birth, in actuality such a baby would develop in early childhood so as not even to appear normally female. Without ovaries nor the capacity to reproduce, such a person is not an antomically normal female.

The position of these feminists that the female is superior is as erroneous as Freud's belief in male superiority. Arguments attempting to prove the superiority of one sex over the other seem to me inane, if not irrelevant—the sexes are just *different* from each other. These differences are varied and variable, and *vive la difference!*

The Sexual Act

Although it may be colored by our social conditioning and notions of masculinity and femininity, the sex act itself, *any* sex act, is still the most fundamental way we express our sexuality. If we understand it first from a clinical and scientific perspective, we may be able to have more control over a part of our lives we often feel is fixed and inflexible.

Masters and Johnson, of course, are responsible for the most important pioneering work in the area of sex research and sex therapy. They divided sexual response into four successive stages: excitement, plateau, orgasm, and resolution. Although they talk about the four stages for each sex separately, their use of the same terminology for both sexes tends to blur the fact that some stages are very similar for both sexes, while others are quite different. Consider the resolution stage, for example. Here the female undergoes only partial decongestion and is ready almost immediately for another orgasm, whereas the male usually experiences complete decongestion and a refractory period during which another orgasm is impossible. I don't think the same terms should be used for both sexes without qualification, because they mean different things for each sex. A more accurate way to describe these stages would be to include the sex with each stage—"female excitement," for instance. But the wide adoption of Masters and Johnson's terms in the literature means we must use them, even if modification is necessary.

Although everyone is familiar with these four stages, a brief description of each follows as a basis for our discussion:

1. The excitement stage, characterized by the onset of erotic feelings, as evidenced by an erection in the man and vaginal lubrication in the woman, with localized congestion in the blood vessels and tissues of both sexes. There are other responses involving the entire body, but they are irregular and variable.

2. The plateau, the period between early excitement and orgasm. Again, I have to quibble a bit. This should really be divided into two phases. At first it does resemble a plateau, but once contact has been made with the sexual organ of either partner, the word *plateau* is no longer descriptive for that partner. An ascent of excitement then occurs, even if conscious effort is exerted to reduce it. I think it would be better if from this point the plateau stage were called the ascent or the preorgasmic phase of the plateau stage.

3. The orgasm. This is remarkably similar in its mechanism for both sexes, except, of course, the male ejaculates. It is mediated through the same sensory and motor arcs of the nervous systems; similar muscles are involved, and similar sensations are experienced.

4. The resolution is the last stage, in which the body returns to its basal state.

One last comment: because of the problem mentioned above with the plateau stage the first two stages could be combined, and a much clearer concept could be based upon just *three* stages—excitement, orgasm, and resolution, with the sex specified as I mentioned. But this is enough quibbling—I'm trying to work my way around to discuss sex in middle age.

TEMPEST IN A TEAPOT

Another controversy raging since Freud has been over the nature of the female orgasm. We know Freud believed that the undifferentiated embryo was innately bisexual. He correctly regarded the clitoris as the female version of the penis, but he fell into one of his own fallacies in calling this a "masculine homologue." He also knew that orgasms could be produced by clitoral stimulation alone, but thought that the clitoris was vastly inferior for this purpose to a penis. Little did he know. He went on to conclude that because clitoral stimulation after maturity would not lead to procreation, clitoral sensation must be an immature source of sexual pleasure. He stated that a "vaginal" orgasm was therefore the mature one. This conclusion was reinforced by clinical experience with some of his neurotic patients in Vienna, many of whom had difficulties with orgasm during intercourse but could achieve an orgasm by clitoral stimulation.

Although basic knowledge in anatomy and neurology has not increased that much in this century, most physicians seem to have a better understanding of these subjects than Freud had. When I first read of his distinction between a "vaginal" and a "clitoral" orgasm in medical school, I paid no serious attention to it. Nor did any other students I knew. It was only when Masters and Johnson's first work came out, in which they repeatedly alluded to the distinction, that I began to wonder at their emphasis on this. Then I reviewed the literature and found to my surprise that almost all psychoanalysts had blindly followed Freud. And most popular publications had followed them. No wonder the misconception spread so widely!

During this review, I came across an outstanding article by Mary Jane Sherfey, published in 1966, for which I think she deserves a medal of some sort. As a psychoanalyst, she was in clear opposition to the Freudian postulates in distinguishing between the two, and she presented a well-documented refutation. This must have required the courage of a Christian martyr, for her to publish such heresy in a psychoanalytic journal. And it was considered such in her circles, because the verbal thrashings she received in the editorial comment in that same journal and by other psychoanalytic authors were almost abusive. Once the Masters and Johnson research material became available, however, Sherfey had reinforcement for her position. In 1973 she laid the subject to rest for her colleagues once and for all—"It is a physical impossibility to separate the clitoral from the vaginal orgasm as demanded by psychoanalytic theory." Here is the explanation, which was known since long before Freud. The mucous membrane lining the vagina is supplied with sensory endings only around the entrance and in the outer one-third, and these are sparse. The inner two-thirds of the vagina has none at all. It does contain some stretch and proprioceptive endings, but even these are more concentrated in the outer one-third. The clitoris, on the other hand, has the most intense concentration of sensory endings of any site by far in either sex. No other conclusion was ever even possible—an orgasm is an orgasm is an orgasm. And they all result from clitoral stimulation.

Masters and Johnson's major contribution on this point was to confirm by clinical observation what most of us had only inferred from our knowledge of anatomy and neurology—that the clitoris is the single common pathway of sensation leading to female orgasm. They observed something we did not know, however—the mechanism of its stimulation. During coitus, the clitoral hood is pulled back and forth by traction on the inner labia, causing the orgasm.

They also demonstrated by direct measurement that the rhythmic contraction of the muscles around the vagina was identical whenever an orgasm was achieved, whether by penile penetration or by clitoral stimulation. This cleared up the confusion in women's minds that had let them go along with the psychoanalysts. Although the sensory portion of the orgasm originates around the clitoris and crural areas, the actual motor expression, that is, the muscle contractions of the orgasm, really are mostly around the vagina. Women understandably had difficulty in distinguishing between the two parts of the neural arc—sensory and motor.

Modification in Middle Age

Although we have touched upon the four stages of Masters and Johnson, there is much more about the sexual act itself that we should understand before sex can be as it could be—and should be—in middle age. These other aspects are difficult to discuss because they are so numerous and variable with time, place, and persons. Broadly, they are social, psychological, physiological, and physical. I will go into some of these later, and for the rest, several good references are listed in the Bibliography. But I would like to present one concept that is fundamental by following through a hypothetical sexual act. This must be as simple and shorn of as many subtleties and variations as possible, or we would lose our way. I will attempt to divide an incredibly complex relationship into four rather arbitrary phases and then touch upon only the *differences* in the reactions of each sex. It is an approach you have not seen before. The point is to try to find something "purposive" about each phase, perhaps even some overall pattern to form the framework within which we must make some modifications in middle age.

For the first phase, let's place our abstract man and woman somewhere within sight of each other. Assuming they are reasonably attractive, there will be a tendency for the man to pursue. The woman may slip into certain learned and instinctive patterns that enhance the man's interest while she evaluates both him and his method of approach. She is not usually as sexually aroused as the man is. She is more interested in what sort of man he is—his suitability as a mate. In other words, she not only has slower psychological and physical responses, but a greater tendency toward selectivity. These, of course, have been conditioned by her family and society—they are not all innate. If there is some purpose in this phase, it would appear to be one of mate selection.

Next, let's assume that the woman allows herself to be in physical contact with the male. Another unique difference between the sexes manifests itself at this point—she is more diffusely erotic over her entire body than he is. About 90 percent of a man's sensation is in his penis; his primary desire is to achieve satisfaction through it. While she may want to be held and caressed, he wants his penis to receive this same sort of attention. This difference means he must caress her so that her arousal will approach his—so that she will be lubricated and will allow intercourse to take place. What could be the purpose of this contact and caressing phase? Penile penetration.

During intercourse, the outer third of the woman's vagina constricts around the male organ. This does not enhance her pleasure appreciably, but it virtually ensures orgasm for the man. Her clitoral stimulation is indirect, through the labial folds, while his is direct. This difference means that her pleasure during intercourse is at least sufficient so that she will permit it to continue, while his becomes increasingly intense. Her orgasm is slower to arrive, and even if it should occur first, she still wants to continue, further ensuring his orgasm. *There is apparently no mechanism in this process by which nature provides for—ensures—her orgasm*. Thus, intercourse itself appears to have only one purpose—the man's ejaculation.

If the woman is fortunate enough to have one or more orgasms, the inner two-thirds of the vagina, which had been ballooned out during intercourse, forming an ideal repository for the sperm, collapses in resolution, bringing the cervical opening down into contact with the pool of semen. And if she has not had an orgasm, the same mechanism still operates, but more slowly. In the latter case, the outer third of the vagina stays swollen and acts as a stopper, retarding the loss of semen until the cervix can come in contact with it. The purpose of this phase can only be impregnation.

So, the reactions of each sex preceding and during the act seem to have their particular biological reasons for being: attraction for selection, contact for penile penetration, intercourse for ejaculation, and resolution for insemination. Some conclusions as to an overall "design" are unavoidable. It appears to favor procreation and preservation of the species *whether or not the female is sexually satisfied*. In other words, the male gets his orgasm while the female gets pregnant. Period.

A sad state of affairs for women. But if we see this pattern, then we can alter it in our middle age if not before. Procreation is no longer an issue, biologically or socially, for us.

We can modify it in two ways. The first involves recognition of the strong penis-orientation of the average man. He feels that all the sexual satisfaction a woman could possibly desire can be given her with his marvelous organ. This tends to make women entirely dependent upon penis performance, which serves as a shaky foundation for her sexual satisfaction, especially as a man passes through middle age toward his older years.

The second way is to take cognizance of nature's apparent oversight regarding the female orgasm. It is ironic that her orgasm has been shown to be capable of much more variety, intensity, and duration than the male's. But most important is that she has little or no refractory period after an orgasm and is ready for another almost immediately. Most women report the first orgasm as moderately satisfactory, the second more so, and the third usually as the most intense of all. Masters and Johnson have observed up to fifty consecutive orgasms with the use of an electric vibrator, with the woman stopping only when totally exhausted. And by such objective indices as muscle tension, heart rate, flush, as well as by subjective reports, they found that women have more intense orgasms with clitoral stimulation than through intercourse. Most women do not realize their orgasmic potential. They have been awakened in this century first to the possibility and permissibility of one orgasm if they did not appear to enjoy it too much, then through the period of rigid insistence on simultaneous orgasms, now to expect one for one at any time—*most* of the time. We may be at a true turning point in sexual history in this regard for all women of all ages as they begin to appreciate the potential that is theirs through clitoral stimulation.

From the midpoint of life on, if not before, we should be concerned with the attainment of the total potential satisfaction of both partners rather than persist with nature's biological plan that seems to be designed mostly for the man's. Orgasms, of course are not the only measure, but the enlightened man in middle age should at least back away from his previous penis-orientation and ensure that a woman has several orgasms for every one he has by manual caressing, oral-genital stimulation, the use of a vibrator, or whatever other means his ingenuity can devise in addition to intercourse itself.

Some feminists have sensed this biological disparity and advocate lesbianism as a solution. It's interesting that what we have found missing on the part of most men in the sexual act *is just what is offered by another woman*. Think about that. Another solution proposed by Shere Hite and others is that women "go for their own" by means of masturbation. Sherfey says to this: "However, to . . . argue for the superiority of masturbation, as some have done, is sheer idiocy. Repeated masturbation is a very lonely business." And to quote Eric Berne in *Sex and Human Loving*: "Most people have a hunger for human contact, at least of sight and sound, and in most cases also for touch or stroking." This is an understatement.

Let's expand on these two modifications men must make in middle age, add a few more for both sexes, and end with an ideal example of what sex can be for us that will mention even more. By this time, a man has found it takes longer to get an erection; it is a little harder to keep one and much more difficult to get another soon after orgasm. These are just more reasons why he can no longer continue to be trapped in the concept of penis performance as the "right" way to have sex. He has also by this time become more sensitive to his own feelings and to those of his partner. Inwardly he desires more caressing and closeness, yet he may not express these new needs and continue with the single-minded drive for orgasm he has had since his youth. Still more reasons to change the traditional sexual act. By middle age, a woman has become increasingly aware of her desires and orgasmic potential, more knowledgeable about the ways in which she can achieve greater sexual satisfaction, and inwardly more assertive. Yet she may persist in her passivity and dependence upon the male and his penis. These call for change, too. In fact, with all the elements present for a sex life far more fantastic than either has ever known before, neither partner may be responding to this challenge with change.

Let's look at the biggest barrier first. Some of the suggested variations involve close attention to the woman's genital area by the male. Yet many our age consider this to be taboo. The first hushed mention of cunnilingus in the literature was by Van De Velde about the time we were born—but we didn't hear much about it when we were young. He delicately worked up to what he called the "genital kiss," emphasizing as he did so "spotless cleanliness," and he found it necessary to distinguish it from "pathological practices" in a footnote. In italics he warned, *"Supreme beauty and hideous ugliness are separated by a border-line so slight that our minds and senses may transgress it, unawares!"* Well, things have come a long way since then. Mutual oral sex is now regarded by most of those under thirty as a standard prelude and variation in intercourse. It's time we caught on.

Women of middle age need to surmount several hurdles in regard to this—first, the idea that the area is ugly. Test this out for yourself by standing nude before a full-length mirror. There is actually an exquisite beauty and symmetry about the pelvic area with the legs closed or nearly so. And opening them further just stirs arousal in the man. If you don't believe this, just sneak a peek at any issue of *Penthouse* or a similar publication at your local newsstand. Look at the poses of the models. Why do you think they are posed that way? Second, women who are now in midlife were raised to be extremely modest about this area and many are uncomfortable when their partner pays particular attention to it. This too is due to mental conditioning and can be overcome by patience and persistence—and pleasure. Third, a woman may be afraid of seeming or smelling unclean, a fear that comes from two sources. The menstrual period is one, but this merely involves blood and a small amount of tissue from the lining of the uterus. The odor and taste of the vulva may sometimes be unpleasant for another reason, the action of ever-present bacteria upon natural secretions. All a woman has to do is remove the older secretions and most of the bacteria regularly by washing, and then only a faint muskiness at most will remain. If the area is washed thoroughly just before sex, there will be *no* odor or taste. Some men—but not many—may balk at paying close attention to the female genital area for these same reasons; they should try the same sort of reeducation.

Although any and all ways of stimulating the female genitalia, especially the clitoris, are encouraged, the oral seems to be the best. One reason is that most women are accustomed to the touch of their own hand during masturbation and generally will not respond as intensely to the man's hand, at least at first. It takes some time and sensitivity on his part before his touch can equal hers. Other more exotic forms of clitoral stimulation, such as the tip of a feather, are fine for variation, but are not as satisfying. The major reason the oral way is urged for those in middle age is that it puts no demand on the man for penile performance, yet is so completely satisfying. And just removing this demand will enhance his erectile potential substantially. But don't overlook the possibilities of a vibrator. Many reject its use because it is an artificial device in an act of intimacy. All I can say is, try it.

We have heard for years about the abysmally low percentages of women reported by Kinsey to attain orgasms regularly. Follow the surveys since then. There has been substantial improvement, but still today only about half of women report having orgasms all or almost all of the time. The number reporting mutiple orgasms is minuscule. These are the results you would expect from reliance upon intercourse alone. In *The Female Orgasm*, Seymour Fisher states that 19 percent of the women he studied considered clitoral minipulation essential for an orgasm; 64 percent *preferred* clitoral to vaginal stimulation given a choice; and 30 percent *required* clitoral stimulation even with the penis in the vagina. But, as I have said, using these facts to conclude that "solo sex"— masturbation—is superior, as some do, does not follow . . . for the same reason that massaging your own aching neck doesn't feel as good as when someone else does it. It's the same reason you can't tickle yourself, too. What is this reason? To quote Tevye in *Fiddler on the Roof*, "I'll tell you. I don't know." It just *is*.

Men don't seem to have much reluctance to receive manual or oral stimulation. In fact, studies of prostitutes show that this is one of the main reasons men go to them. We come back again to reluctance on the part of women—this time to perform either or both. Be courageous—try! Women who do so are often surprised by the exquisite pleasure they give their partners. And the man in his turn may be surprised that he can have a satisfying orgasm with only a partial erection—or no erection at all.

Now, at the risk of being accused of voyeurism, let's look in upon a couple our age enjoying ideal sex. Without commenting upon it, we'll assume they love each other and regard each other as unique and special. Each is attuned to the other's emotions and responses. Each responds when the desire of the other is expressed in subtle ways. We need not dwell on other aspects either, such as cleanliness, appearance, or certain courting routines that are familiar and pleasing to both. And we may assume the time and surroundings are chosen to enhance their enjoyment.

Once the two are touching, he would pay much more than absent-minded attention to her uniquely female erogenous zones. He would stroke and kiss her hair, breathe softly on her closed eyes, run his tongue behind her ear, kiss the back of her neck, lips, and nostrils, and touch his tongue to hers. He would massage her shoulder and back muscles, kiss under her arms, nibble at her nipples, and gently caress her tummy and the inside of her thighs with his fingertips.

I wonder if most men realize how sensual a woman's feet can be? He might try probing his tongue between her toes or a firm foot massage with some soothing lotion followed by a very light touch wandering in a lingering way up her legs. The tongue on the small of her back running down into the crack between her buttocks can be tantalizing, too. He shouldn't hesitate to add such variations as scented oils or talcum powder to allow light fingertip caressing all over her body, and a silken scarf that he could trail gently over her abdomen and breasts. She in turn would kiss and caress him, his hair, face, nipples, and abdomen. She should try anything and everything—often a man doesn't even know what he would like. He has been too concerned with pleasing his partner all his life to lie back, receive, and learn.

Eventually, her clitoris would receive his main attention. He can soften the light if she wishes, then bring up her knees and allow her legs to fall apart. This will spread the outer lips of her vagina. It is exciting for her just to feel his breath on her tender parts when they are exposed this way. He could first gently nuzzle her pubic hair with the tip of his nose, then kiss the inside of her thighs nearby, and run his tongue around her inner lips, pausing briefly to flick at her clitoris. From time to time, he could stiffen up his tongue and rub it back and forth over the clitoral shaft or just at the side of the tip. And then, with his arms encircling her thighs, use his hands to pull her lips up and apart and rapidly flick the tip of his tongue back and forth over the tip itself. The clitoral hood is retracted this way, exposing the glans directly to the touch of his tongue. He should be careful not to overdo this, because the clitoris can become numb with such direct stimulation.

All the while, he would be attentive to such signs of her excitement as blushing, moaning, breathing rapidly, thrusting her pelvis, tightening her tummy muscles, clenching her hands, shuddering, even using naughty words. He can use all of these as guides in what he is doing. When he feels she is ready for her first orgasm, he would gently spread her vaginal lips apart, retract the clitoral hood, and place his mouth in a small "O" just over the clitoris. Then he can gently suck her clitoris into his mouth and maintain suction while moving his head back and forth or in a circular manner. This suction will engorge the clitoris and make it much more sensitive. With the clitoris still in his mouth, he can flick the tip of his tongue back and forth very rapidly over it. At this point, most women will have their first orgasm. During the orgasm, he will find it best to maintain suction but stop all other stimulation and allow his head to ride her pelvic thrusts. Following orgasm, after a long period of steady sucking on the clitoris, she may begin to move her pelvis again, and he can do it all over again. And again.

After three or four orgasms this way, it might be time to return to a slow manual caressing of her entire body. Or it might be his turn to receive. His nipples, abdomen, and inner thighs are sensitive, too. And there is nothing like the light touch of her tongue on his testicles. Slow, tantalizing kisses on the shaft of his penis will make him moan for more. And the exploration with her tongue around the head of his penis is exquisite. She may even have a hot cup of coffee nearby, take a sip, and then move her mouth down over his penis. The effect of this can be sensational. At the same time, her hands could stroke his shaft in synchrony with her mouth. The other hand could mischievously tickle his testicles or explore the crack between his buttocks.

By this time, both would be more than ready for intercourse. A leisurely way to begin is in a cross position where she is on her back and he lies at right angles to her on his side with his underneath leg below both of hers and his top leg under her near thigh but over her far thigh. Follow me? In this position, he can see her facial expression and her entire body, and she can also run her hand down to her sensitive areas and caress herself. This can bring her another orgasm. She could also caress him and touch his penis as it enters her. He might massage her clitoris and vaginal entrance with his hand or even use a small vibrator, because by this time she might be getting numb. Usually he will be able to give her one or two more orgasms this way.

Following this, the couple can assume any position in intercourse they prefer, and the man at last can just let himself go. He will have a fantastic orgasm after all this excitement, and, despite the intensity of her previous orgasms, the woman will find this one to be perhaps the most deeply satisfying of all.

As you can see, the two themes throughout this scene are less emphasis on penile performance and more upon the orgasmic potential of the woman.

THE WIDER VIEW

Now, if you will break away from your fantasies, let's take a more general look at what sex can mean to us in middle age. During our lives, changes have been taking place in ourselves and in the world around us that we should look at perhaps more carefully than we have.

Psychology is one. It can cure inhibiting neuroses and has taught us to know what our feelings are and to understand them. It can help us relate to our partner as a person with rights equal to our own, as well as to seek our own fulfillment without remorse. The old dominance-submission relationship is long gone for most of us.

Knowledge is another. We know much more about the subject of sex, and it is less taboo than before. We are also more verbal in middle age and can communicate with our partners more meaningfully. And, in this respect as well as others, women are becoming less constrained by our culture all the time.

Men in middle age are more affiliative and learning to express their feelings in many ways. By this time they have come to desire a relationship with their partners based upon more than such things as sex and social appearance. A man can allow himself to enjoy the prelude of closeness and caressing more. There has been a reciprocal change—her sexual feelings are more focused now, and she can derive more satisfaction during the sexual act itself. Usually, her level of desire has risen by middle age to match his, which has been dropping since the late teens. They are more closely matched in this regard than ever before. The man finds he is able to last longer during intercourse, making possible all the variations I have mentioned. And many more.

At this point in life, both are more willing to experiment and recognize the necessity of variety to alleviate boredom. Contraception has reached a point of being almost perfect—indeed, menopause and vasectomy *are* perfect. Fear of pregnancy is gone. Even messy menses may be no more. Children are older, out of the house going about their own affairs, or are living away from home, providing more privacy. There is, or should be, more time available to be intimate and to express affection in every way. There is also more affluence, allowing weekends away and vacations. In fact, a vacation may be the ideal way to rejuvenate your sex life. Even romantic preludes with dinner out, wine, music, and so on can be enjoyed more often. A man can taper his preoccupation with work, because by now he can see that if he has not achieved his ambitions he never will. For the woman, housework is easier with most of the children grown and gone, and she has already learned to lighten her workload with various household conveniences. If the two have been married for years, they know each other intimately and know, too, what gives each other the most pleasure. Both are less exhausted than they were earlier in their marriage with longer working hours, small children awakening at night, and all the other strains of early married life. Finally, in middle age, both begin to realize that this is the partner who will see them through until the end, no one else. This realization adds a deeper meaning to the sexual relationship than either may have ever known.

So, sex at this time in our lives can be far better than it has ever been before or ever will be again. Nevertheless, there may be one or more difficulties at this as at any age, so let's discuss them, and what to do about them.

Male Sexual Dysfunctions

Men's major sexual difficulties at any age are four. I will mention three only in passing, because they are rare in middle age.

The first is premature ejaculation. This is difficult to define in terms of time—one study found that "normal" intercourse lasted on the average only 20 seconds after penile entry into the vagina! In several studies, most men had an orgasm within one minute. So this difficulty is best thought of in the context of the satisfaction of the two partners. Ejaculation can be considered premature if it occurs before both partners are satisfied. I prefer this simple definition to one specifying any time limit. The cause of premature ejaculation is usually found in early conditioning—by prostitutes in a hurry to make more money, furtive back-seat loving, fear of discovery, and so forth. This pattern is often present from a man's early life, so by the time he arrives at middle age he and his partner either will have adjusted to it or sought therapy. It can almost always be cured, so therapy rather than acceptance is the route to choose.

The second problem is inability to have an orgasm. Most men troubled by this do not have any difficulty with masturbation but find they cannot climax during intercourse. This dysfunction has similar causes as the first, and again, by middle age most couples either have adjusted to the problem or sought appropriate therapy. The recommendation is the same, as are the results.

Primary impotence is the third difficulty males may have. This is most commonly due to early traumatic influences and stems, in general, from deeper psychological origins. It is called primary when a man has never been able to achieve and/or maintain an erection. This is so disturbing that a man will either have sought psychotherapy earlier in his life or have chosen to avoid sex altogether.

SECONDARY IMPOTENCE

The fourth is secondary impotence. All men in middle age experience some form of the faltering phallus syndrome. (One patient of mine thought that all the "saltpeter" they put in his coffee in World War II was finally beginning to work!) This is the physiological equivalent of lack of vaginal lubrication in the woman; it involves the same tissues, the same blood supply, and the same nerve supply. Masters and Johnson use a rather strict and arbitrary definition of secondary impotence: If a male fails in one-fourth or more of his attempts after having been successful earlier in his life, then they consider the term to be applicable.

I prefer to look at it a little more loosely. If you are trying to count, you will never get anywhere. Every man at every age fails from time to time. Far worse than the failure itself is the "fear of failure," when the first failure triggers an anxiety that persists and impairs subsequent performance. Anxiety is one of our ancient defenses against real or presumed dangers, and part of this natural response is an inability to have an erection. So anxiety only makes matters worse. If one allows himself to be locked into this mental set, there is no way he can hope to perform successfully. Trying harder doesn't help—it only hinders. If anxiety is present, it must be recognized and removed first—*it* is the primary problem. A man must realize that his inability to attain and sustain an erection is important to him because he has been conditioned all his life to identify his masculinity and self-worth with his sexual perform-ance. He has to be "reconditioned" to see that they are two entirely different things. This may involve more than introspec-tion or conversation with his partner, although these certainly help. Psychotherapy may be required.

Once anxiety is allayed, the several specific causes of secon-dary impotence and the appropriate therapy for each can be considered:

Discord in the marital relationship. (Suggestions for remedying this are presented in the section that follows.)

Cigarette smoking. This must be stopped because the action of absorbed nicotine adversely affects the mechanism of erection.

Overindulgence in alcohol and food, especially just prior to the act. As Shakespeare said of alcohol, it provokes the desire, but takes away the performance. The solution is obvious.

Obesity. This makes certain positions difficult and leads to excessive fatigue during sex. (See my previous remarks in chapter 3).

Poor physical condition. When any physical stress is placed upon the body, it must be conditioned and prepared for it if it is to be done successfully. If a man has been sedentary for a considerable length of time, any physical stress will be more difficult. Exercise is the only way to increase your potential to respond to any vigorous activity, which the sexual act certainly is. (See the section on exercise in chapter 3.) Although all forms of exercise help, the best for this purpose is often overlooked—frequent intercourse itself. This truism has given rise to the often-heard phrase, "use it or lose it."

Various medical conditions and medications. Your best source of advice and assistance regarding this is your physician. One authority lists over one hundred drugs and diseases that interfere with potency, and it's not even a complete list.

Psychological difficulties. These range in seriousness from preoccupation with career or other concerns through short but intense periods of stress, to depression and psychosis. Your physician will help you here and advise you on any appropriate care he is not able to render.

Fatigue. Rest is the cure.

The decline in testosterone level with age. This is an extremely important topic, so I'll discuss it in more detail. Testosterone is the hormonal basis for the sex drive in both men and women. Young men secrete 4 to 12 milligrams of testosterone per day from both their testicles and adrenal glands, and young women from 0.9 to 2.8 milligrams per day from the adrenals and a trace from their ovaries. In the male, the drop is nearly linear from its level at age twenty to approximately half that by age eighty. So you can easily calculate about where you are at your age. It has also been known for some years that the production of testosterone is reduced in males by psychological stress and increased by satisfactory sexual activity. No significant decline in testosterone production occurs in women, but without estrogen replacement after the menopause, some is lost by conversion to estrone.

The difficulty for men isn't just the slow tapering of their testosterone production, however. There is another facet that has not been adequately investigated: the declining responsiveness of the target tissues to testosterone. There is good evidence that this does occur and plays a significant role. More important than the penis are receptor sites in the brain centers where the primary sexual drive originates. It would seem that the administration of testosterone should be routine to compensate for both declines. But it is not widely used because of one serious drawback. Estimates vary in the literature, but there is about a 5 percent chance that a man in his forties has latent cancer of the prostate. This probability rises with age to about 15 to 20 percent in the seventies and eighties. The administration of testosterone carries the risk, not of causing this cancer, but of enhancing its growth if it is already present. It is much like watering your garden—the flowers benefit, but so do the weeds.

In my own practice, I gave testosterone to middle-aged men quite frequently at low dosages and limited it to those cases where a temporary benefit was sought. With frequent prostate examinations, I encountered no difficulty. Because the liver destroys most of the testosterone taken orally, injections are much more satisfactory. I must confess that I sometimes gave distilled water to be sure the effect was not due to suggestion alone. I also explored the use of an ointment that a man could rub directly on his penis daily. It combined testosterone with a rubafacient (similar to the liniments for aches and pains but milder), which not only provided a warm glow to the area, increasing the man's consciousness of his genitals, but theoretically enhanced the absorption of testosterone into the penis. Again, there was a slight benefit from the rubafacient alone, but with testosterone included the benefit was remarkable. My small study was not continued because there is no practical way to measure precisely how much testosterone is absorbed into the penile tissues versus how much is passed through the venous and lymph channels to the prostate. And very little probably arrived at the brain. Yet this method of testosterone administration deserves to be studied. Consult your physician regarding the advisability of using testosterone in your particular case by whatever route. It is hoped that better tests for carcinoma of the prostate done from blood samples will be developed, because palpation of the prostate is not reliable if the tumor is small. Such tests already contribute greatly to the detection of other cancers. Then testosterone could be used more widely without risk.

Monotony. Boredom in the bedroom is by far the most common cause of secondary impotence, but beyond superficial suggestions of variations in the time, place, ambience, or positions, it is largely avoided in professional and popular literature. Quite frankly, this is because moral considerations are involved, and any other suggestions would be controversial in our culture. Monotony is a far greater problem than just a cause for secondary impotence in the male. It is, in fact, the natural reaction of the human organism, after being exposed to the same or similar stimuli of whatever sort over a long period of time, not to respond as intensely as it did at first. This can be demonstrated experimentally in many ways in every sort of laboratory animal. It is simply a truism for all living creatures. So even though this discussion began as a consideration of the causes of and ways to treat secondary impotence in males, it will be expanded right here to include the woman and the monotony she may feel that can impair her excitement and orgasmic response.

I would like to place these suggestions on a scale of social acceptability. Each of us has, and is entitled to have, a personal moral code; we are free to select and use whatever we wish from this scale and to accept whatever consequences it may bring.

First, most acceptable, and simplest, is to arrange periods of quiet solitude—times by yourself—and use these opportunities to get in touch with your own feelings about your partner, about the sexual act, and about any other aspect that may be inhibiting your enjoyment of it.

Second, an open conversation with your partner, sharing your feelings with each other, can do much to enhance the satisfaction of both.

Third, you can be more open with each other physically as well as verbally. This would include such things as nudity or near-nudity around the home at appropriate times and using a soft light during sexual relations, with one partner communicating but being passive while the other explores. Be as creative with this suggestion as you dare.

Fourth, sharing fantasies and even early experiences with each other. Many women have repressed these, and such books as Nancy Friday's *My Secret Garden* and *Forbidden Flowers* or intimate conversation with their women friends may be necessary to recall them. It is even more exciting to think up new fantasies. The most important sexual organ is the brain. Dr. Robert Solnick markedly enhanced the sex life of men over forty-five at the USC Gerontology Center by enhancing fantasies through a training program.

Men from the age of forty-five through fifty-five had a 42 percent increase in their erectile responses and an increased frequency of intercourse at home of nearly one-third. Men can benefit from Nancy Friday's newest book—on male fantasies—*Men in Love*.

Fifth, is nondemanding sexual play. Here you can use massage of all sorts, gentle caressing with the fingertips, silken scarves, soft fur, and all sorts of techniques that can be described as more sensual than sexual. Take your time with this suggestion.

Sixth, variations in technique other than positions during intercourse. The actual positions possible are really rather few, but much variety can be obtained by exploration with guidance from the partner. Some suggestions have already been given. Again, be creative.

Seventh, and this is the first that may be unacceptable to many, some stimulation may be possible by the use of pornographic literature or movies. Because movies are more graphic, they should have greater potential, but to my knowledge very few if any truly tasteful ones have been made. In pornographic movies, there is rarely any subtlety, sensitivity, tenderness, caring, or, quite frankly, quality (even cinematic) of any sort. And most are strongly male-oriented. Studies show that women respond to tasteful pornographic movies, too. So the possibilities for graphic and glorious sex films are there for some inspired producer, especially now that home video players are becoming more common and movies can be viewed in the privacy of one's own home.

The eighth and still less acceptable way of minimizing monotony is to attend a "soft swing" party or visit a nudist camp once in a while. The point of this is to go one step beyond the two-dimensional figures on the screen to an area where real people are nude or engaging in sexual activity that may be stimulating to you. It is not necessary to indulge—most such places allow you to stay clothed and not participate. The purpose is merely to derive some arousal from the atmosphere. Even so, it is not for most of us.

The ninth method requires more description. This is well beyond the bounds of conventional morality and is called sharing, *not* swapping—sharing your intimacy and feelings with others. For those few who may wish to try this, the most important step is to choose another couple carefully. This is also the most difficult part, because you must come to care for them, as they must for you. All involved have to have approximately the same moral code as well. Once this major hurdle is over, however, sharing can range over a wide spectrum of intimacy. It may only consist of an evening with a quiet meal and good wine in a pleasant environment sharing each person's sexual experiences and fantasies verbally. Or perhaps you could enjoy a weekend at a resort hotel with adjoining rooms. All can relax in robes or even less, sit or lie on a blanket by the fire, and have the same sort of conversations.

How it develops from here is up to the most reluctant member of the group. Caution is the keyword. Again, I stress this suggestion is only for a few. Nude sunbathing could be included with all contact forbidden. The guiding rule is that any contact that does take place has to be with one's own partner. A further step is massage, which can progress to intimate caresses or even to intercourse with one's partner while the other couple is present. The point of sharing is that the emotions and excitement of one couple in whatever they may say or do are transmitted to the other—*shared* with them. But remember, it is easy to get carried away and do something you might regret later, and this would spoil the whole thing. The rule of no contact except with one's partner has to be adhered to, or all sorts of problems can arise.

The tenth way, resorted to by even fewer and still further beyond the bounds of conventional morality, is to exchange partners. I have had the opportunity to talk with some individuals who have engaged in "swapping" and have read several articles on the subject. By its very definition, it takes place solely at the animal level of pleasure, without any involvement of the personalities of the individuals. Those who are well-adjusted and experiment in mate-swapping usually drop out after a few trials, fortunately without much permanent after-effect. Those who continue the practice longer have been found to have a high incidence of underlying psychological maladjustment, and their marital relationship is more often damaged than helped by such activity. So from what I know of "swapping," I cannot recommend it at all.

Nor can I comment on threesomes, because I have met very few with experience in this practice. One thing I do know is that the classic male fantasy of having two women collapses very quickly in real situations, simply because the sexual capacity of two women far exceeds his. An older couple bringing a young man into the circle of their intimacy may have possibilities in the future in view of the woman's greater potential into her later years, but in general the time of threesomes does not seem to have arrived.

You will notice that aphrodisiacs have not been mentioned at all—for the simple reason that none of them work. Well, not unless you *believe* they will. Which brings to mind the story about the fellow who was told by a friend that oysters were an aphrodisiac. He believed his friend, so had a dozen on the half-shell. But his faith must not have been complete, because the next morning he complained to his friend that only eleven of them had worked!

Female Sexual Dysfunctions

There are three important sexual dysfunctions in women. Premature orgasm might be another—but who could complain? One is vaginismus. This is a spastic contraction of the muscles lining the outer third of the vagina upon entry of the penis, finger, or other object. It is only found in women without sexual experience, so is extremely rare in middle age. It has a psychological origin and usually can be handled well by psychotherapy. Another dysfunction is dyspareunia, difficult or painful intercourse. The causes of this are organic, with the single exception of the failure to lubricate, which is related to the degree of a woman's arousal. By *organic*, I mean such conditions as tumors in the pelvis, thinning of the vaginal lining, vaginal infection, deep pelvic thrombosis, endometriosis, and so on. Most of these can be taken care of by a gynecologist.

This leaves us with the major difficulty in women of any age, and that is orgasmic dysfunction—difficulty in attaining an orgasm.

First a word about frigidity. This term, like *impotence*, has been used in ways that are both pejorative and imprecise. It has been used to describe women who do not respond to sexual overtures, who do not respond during the sexual act itself, and also to include women who attain an orgasm easily on masturbation but who have difficulty during intercourse. The term orgasmic dysfunction, although it is somewhat awkward, is better, because it deals just with the orgasm itself. Clinically, this difficulty is divided into two categories. If a woman has never had an orgasm, it is termed primary orgasmic dysfunction. The other category, which describes women who have had orgasms in the past but now can't, is called secondary orgasmic dysfunction.

In general the primary category is more severe, and has three origins:

1. The gender dysphoria syndrome, in which a woman feels that she is a man trapped in the body of a woman.
2. Homosexuality. Although most homosexual women are able to attain an orgasm by masturbation and with other women, some are unaware of their sexual preference and remain incapable of arousal and orgasm in a heterosexual relationship.
3. Beyond the two above, it can be caused by a large cluster of psychological difficulties that are usually characterological and severe, but many respond to psychotherapy.

The primary orgasmic dysfunctions are best handled by a competent psychiatrist, who may suggest additional methods of treating them.

Most orgasmic difficulties of women in middle age fall into the category of secondary orgasmic dysfunction. Some statistics on the frequency of orgasm have already been mentioned, but I only alluded to the changes in them with time. Let's look at these changes more closely. An early paper in 1907 estimated that 75 percent of women usually failed to have an orgasm in intercourse. Another in 1929 stated that 46 percent of women reported either an inferior or no orgasm. In 1938, the *Kinsey Report* indicated that only one-third of the women interviewed failed to have an orgasm, and in Hunt's 1972 survey, he found that 85 percent had an orgasm half or more of the time, and just 7 percent never had an orgasm or almost never had one. This shows what changes in health, culture, and education have accomplished. It also indicates what sexual therapy can do.

Fisher found that the most frequent factor linked to the failure of orgasm in women was the disappearance or unreliability of the father figure during childhood. If a girl felt that she could not depend upon her father's interest in her, she tended to assume conscious control of her own life as she matured. At the start of an orgasm, when external perceptions begin to fade and the world becomes vague, she would sense a loss of this control and react with panic. Already sensitized to the possibility of losing or being separated from her supports and loved ones, she is blocked from release and abandon. Although this may be the major cause, there are, of course, others, and most of them have been mentioned previously in reference to impotence in the male. The causes and the cures are remarkably similar, so they do not need to be gone into again here.

One important contribution of Helen Singer Kaplan should be mentioned, however. This is her suggestion to shift the responsibility for the woman's orgasm from her partner to herself. It is then her concern alone, an idea that leads to more active participation on the woman's part, as well as more communication to her partner about what gives her pleasure.

This is all I have to say about sex in middle age. With this rapid review of the sexual problems that can trouble us, we have found that even most of these can be coped with well. And it is more evident than ever that the way is open to a more satisfactory sex life now than at any other time in life.

For further information on any aspect of sex, there are several good references in the Bibliography. I think the best are those by Helen Singer Kaplan. You can also write to The Planned Parenthood Federation of America, Inc., 810 Seventh Avenue, New York, New York 10019, or to the Sex Information and Education Council of the U.S., 84 Fifth Avenue, New York, New York 10011. SIECUS maintains a list of the best source material available and also prepares some of its own. As to the professionals you can talk to, there are only two: physicians (including psychiatrists) and sex therapists. The latter have come into being only in the last ten years or so. Prior to then people who had questions or were troubled sought out their physicians, even though the subject was not taught as such in any medical school in the United States. However, the better physicians kept up on this as they did with all advances in medicine. There are such courses now in about 85 percent of the medical schools in the country, and most physicians are reasonably competent in this area, with or without psychiatric training. The principal advantage of going to your physician first with a sexual dysfunction is to rule out any physical cause. I have found such causes in about 10 percent of men and 20 percent of women, and most of these can be cured. With these out of the way, your physician is then the best source of information on where you can obtain the type of therapy that is most suitable for your difficulty.

A few comments here on sex therapy. Originally, psychoanalytic treatment tried to reconstruct the patient's personality by resolving his or her unconscious conflicts in order to ameliorate sexual dysfunctions. Then marital counseling found that if the quality of the relationship could be improved, sexual problems would diminish. But both had rather poor results for most people. Sex therapy differs from both these approaches in that it is aimed just at the relief of the sexual symptom and nothing else. It systematically structures sexual experiences for the couple with counseling in between. It resembles behavior modification school of psychology more than it does any other school. Such therapy grew out of recognition by psychiatrists who had left the psychoanalytic mainstream that most individuals with sexual dysfunctions were essentially normal, and that if this one difficulty could be cleared up, they would then function in life satisfactorily.

If you seek a sex therapist on your own, be careful. Dr. Masters estimates that only about 10 percent in the country are competent. As I said, it is best to ask your physician for a reference. If this fails, contact your nearest medical school. Most have a department of human sexuality that will be happy to help you. If both of these methods fail for any reason, you can try writing to the American Association of Sex Educators, Counselors, and Therapists (5010 Wisconsin Avenue N.W., Washington, D.C. 20016) for the name of a sex therapist near you. This is a relatively new organization that is attempting to establish professional standards in the field. When you write, you might also request their pamphlet *The Professional Training and Preparation of Sex Counselors* to see just what those standards are. However, it might dismay you to learn how low they still are. Ideally, sex therapy should be a part of psychotherapy, because a psychiatrist has a good knowledge of the anatomy, physiology, and psychology involved. Although psychiatrists admittedly are scarce, some could receive special training in sexology and establish clinics where paramedical personnel such as qualified sex therapists could interview the couple and conduct counseling under the psychiatrist's supervision. But this is still for the future.

Sexual Morality

We can't leave the subject of sex without touching upon sexual morals, because they influence how we deal with everything that has gone before in this section. Most of the beliefs we have in middle age were acquired early in our lives from our parents and peers, and then from society and perhaps our religion. Few of us have thought these beliefs through since we acquired them. And although we violate these values—most of us do occasionally—we nonetheless hold them out as the true ones for ourselves, for others, and for our children. Thus, uncertainty, guilt, and hypocrisy tend to trouble us.

Many changes have taken place during the years since we acquired our sexual standards. Even if we come back to the same basic beliefs, we should at least take these changes into consideration.

Let me list a few that occur to me; you can delete those that do not apply to you and add others that do. Some of them have been mentioned before, but a list putting them all together may be helpful.

- The religious underpinning that was so powerful in the past began to abate in our parents' time and has largely been lost for many of us in our own time.
- There has during the same period been a fading of the family as a source of our ethical norms.
- Societal sanctions have altered and are now characterized more by confusion than by clear concepts. Surveys of sexual attitudes and acts have made us more aware of these changes.
- Legal sanctions have also changed. Fornication is no longer illegal in many states, and in most others, prohibition statutes are not enforced. Divorce law, which long included adultery as grounds, is changing to hinge on the cruelty concept and further evolving into the no-fault divorce.
- Monogamy has become equated with monotony, as longer lives lead to longer marriages.
- Art and entertainment, seeking dramatic impact in novels, plays, movies, and television, are increasingly free in expressing revolutionary sexual ideas. The media similarly emphasize sexuality in advertising, and all of these have had an effect upon us.
- Where once we were taught that sex was only for procreation to

ensure the preservation of the species, now overpopulation is the greater threat. Sexual relations are presently seen more as a form of interpersonal expression rather than simply a mechanism for reproduction, as with animals.

- The increasing emphasis upon individualism, which originated with the formation of our democratic form of government, has been augmented recently by many minority movements in society. This, too, has had its effect. The women's liberation movement, emphasizing a woman's right to sexual satisfaction and to her equality of opportunity in the work arena, has increased both her sexual expectations and her opportunities to realize them. The increasing movement of women into the work force has lessened their economic insecurity, which has had a twofold effect upon sexual morals. Previously, when she was totally dependent upon her husband for her support, his interest in another woman threatened her much more than it does now. Also, now that she is more aware of her own ability to support herself, her husband's attempts to control her social life by economic manipulation or threat are much less effective.
- Increasing affluence, free time, and conveniences such as telephones and rapid transportation, baby sitters, motels, and many other such changes have made sexual encounters outside of conventional norms increasingly easier. The very anonymity of life in urban (and to some extent in suburban) areas has added further to this. It has also resulted in more contacts with the opposite sex.
- More people remain single longer now, because of a new concentration on careers on the part of women, the steadily rising divorce rate, and the high death rate of middle-aged men.
- The gap between biological maturity and sociological maturity has steadily widened because of our increasingly sophisticated society and prolonged education. This, along with other factors, has increased sexual expression among the younger generation, which has had an influence upon those of us in middle age, whether we are aware of it or not.
- Modern medicine has played perhaps the most important role of all. The lengthening human life span has been mentioned, and it has had multiple and manifold effects. In addition, a higher sexual potential is attainable because of improved health into later years. Medicine has also provided prompt and effective treatment for venereal disease. The most significant

contribution is the development of easy and almost perfect contraception. Another offshoot of medicine is psychotherapy, which can cope with some of the conflicts and guilt that once repressed or inhibited many from expressing their sexuality. It has also led to a greater openness in discussion of sexual problems and an increasing awareness of one's own sexual feelings. In the past two or three decades, the amount of knowledge in terms of sexual techniques and potential for each sex has expanded dramatically.

These are just some of the changes that have taken place in our lifetimes, but they are enough to suggest to you that a reconsideration of your own beliefs is possible—and possibly in order.

But before I talk about sexual morals, a semantic distinction should be made. The word *moral* comes from the Greek *mos*, from which is derived *mores*, meaning customs or manners. The word *ethic* comes from *ethike*, which means the science of character. Ethics is really the study of the right and the good life. I will talk here about morals, the *practice* of what one believes to be right and good.

Although we ourselves may have had little or no direct exposure to religious influence, most of the moral concepts that prevail in society, and which most of us adopted early in life, do in fact come from both the Bible and the "natural law" interpretation of it by the Christian Church through much of our Western history. These concepts have become solidified in secular laws, and they are both pervasive and persuasive in societal norms.

Yet, as you may have gathered, I believe that each of us is entitled to form and follow his or her own moral code. Let me tell you mine, and how I arrived at it. This may help you in rethinking your own.

First, I looked again at the natural law origin of the traditional beliefs in our society. Natural law morality holds that some things are always right and other things are always wrong and that these do not change in a particular context nor in terms of the consequences. In fact, such law morality is held to be unchanged and unchangeable throughout time, being eternal, and applicable in all climates and cultures.

Then I reflected on this. It seemed to me that morality based upon any system of laws is inherently restrictive and pessimistic in its view of human nature. Implied therein is disrespect for each person, with the belief that he is unable to seek moral truths on his own. But law morality is certainly easier. The individual need only apply self-control without thought. This may be the major reason that law morality has prevailed. It is simply easier for both, law-giver and law-follower, whether its origin is secular—arising out of human history—or religious. But it avoids consideration of self, others involved, and the qualities of the interpersonal relationships entirely. And even the consequences. It seemed to me that there had to be something more.

What I did then was return to the origin *of the origin* of natural law—the Bible itself. There I found that the major contribution of Christ was to introduce love into law. In his life and his ministry, he befriended outcasts out of a true concern and love for other human beings. He ate with the unwashed, fed the hungry, gave drink to the thirsty, and clothed the naked. Christ, by his life and teachings, returned responsibility in morality to each of us. Somehow we subsequently lost this. I could see that in a morality based upon love, there is an inherently optimistic view of human nature and the goodness of man. If man himself is good, his sexuality is also good, and in fact its realization in its best sense can be the closest expression between two human beings.

But I could also see that law and love do not have to be in conflict as they so often are. Law can provide general guidelines within which love can be used for the specific application of the guidelines, much as in legal jurisprudence where courts apply general law to specific situations in order to achieve justice. The two positions are actually complementary, not contradictory—each needs the other. Law may be at the boundary of morality, but love is at its very center.

So now I had a framework within which I could construct my own moral code. But I should be clear about what love means to me in this context. It is not romantic love, which is made up of more or less equal parts of fantasy and glandular activity. Love in this sense cannot justify any moral act. What love has to mean here is a deep abiding respect and caring for the essence, the totality, the *personhood* of another as well as oneself. And it seemed to me that this, the failure to consider the totality of the persons involved, is probably the basis of what most of us would agree is immoral. It results in the regard of sexual partners as objects, is the essence of the exploitation of sex by Madison Avenue and of the "*Playboy* philosophy." It is expressed most clearly in prostitution and is at the root of rape. It may also be the reason that, although sex is so heavily emphasized all around us, we are actually starved for true sexuality. Could it be this starvation that leads to its overemphasis?

With love for personhood added to law, I found that my moral code could be stated very simply. One must have love for one's own personhood as well as for that of the other. That's all there is to it. With morality thus defined, however, there is both risk and responsibility. Errors are inevitable. But any such error should not be regarded as a sin, a stigma, or an ineradicable stain—rather, after due reflection, as a way by which one learns. With this as my moral code, I then looked at two or three sexual situations to test it out before I tried to apply it to the most frequent problems we encounter in middle age.

First, I tried it out on the simplest situation of all, no sexual expression whatever. It might seem strange to consider *abstinence* as a moral problem, but hindrance of one's own self-realization and exploitation of others are both possible. Many a lass has led a lad to the altar by teasing and denying him. And even some religious leaders in both East and West abstain to increase the awe in which their followers hold them and thus increase their power. I can't help but regard this as immoral. But abstinence in the absence or illness of one's loved mate is quite another matter. My moral code seemed to work even here. If abstinence denies a portion of either the personhood of one's self or one's partner and is not practiced out of loving concern, it can be considered immoral.

Encouraged, I then tested it on the simplest of sexual activities, masturbation. Based upon a mistaken interpretation of Onan's *coitus interruptus* in the Bible and what was believed to be natural law, masturbation was almost universally condemned until recent years. The last decade or two has seen a swing of opinion by some in favor of masturbation almost without further thought. But in masturbation, there is a certain denial of part of the person and his potential. It is very lonely sex indeed, and for the most part, one seeks in it only a relief of tension. When I applied my code to this, I could see that the morality of masturbation could be positive if done by one love partner out of desire for the other who may be away, ill, or disabled—or if before marriage one partner is strongly opposed to intercourse. But it tends toward the immoral if one's potential for socializing is short-circuited by the more readily available sexual release of masturbation. So the code seemed to be applicable here, too.

I then decided to look at homosexuality with this code, because that seemed to be the most difficult of all. Such activity is found in all animal species and in all societies of man. There is something of the opposite sex in each of us, so there is nothing inherently "unnatural" about it. Therefore, the "natural law" argument has to be abandoned here too. Under my code, I had to admit that if there is true concern and love for the total personhood of one's self and the other, then a homosexual act as such could not be condemned. However, it is sad but true that most homosexual activity occurs between those whose sexual development has been arrested or whose potentials otherwise are not being fully realized. And much homosexuality, especially between males, is not within the context of love, but of isolated, unloving anonymity in which partners are regarded as objects. So I came to the conclusion that it was this social, emotional, and sexual exploitation that is immoral, not homosexuality itself. You can agree or disagree with this, as you will.

And I came to another conclusion with which you need not agree. At the periphery of morality is courtesy. The flaunting of homosexuality when many find it reprehensible is not immoral, merely discourteous. Most of us even resent the flaunting of some heterosexual activity. For example, I feel that someone you are living with out of wedlock should be introduced to those who may be sensitive to the subject by name, not relationship. Anyone whose appearance or conduct might offend others should, out of courtesy, take care to spare their feelings. It's true that many things we could do, such as eating with our fingers, or blowing our nose on the ground, or coughing at a concert may be more comfortable for *us*, but this is no reason to impose such conduct on the sensibilities of others. This wish to feel more comfortable with themselves without regard for the rest of us seems to be the major motivation for "gays" coming out of the closet. If one has a missing eye, wearing an eye patch cannot be considered hypocrisy, just courtesy. As I said, you do not have to agree.

With this, I went on to consider sexual situations that are of more direct concern to us in middle age. Heterosexual morality has traditionally been considered as marital, premarital, or extramarital—and most recently, due to increasing divorce and death of a partner in the later years, postmarital. It is strange that this construct is built around marriage itself. Is early exploratory intimacy between those just into their teens premarital? Are sexual relations between those in their thirties or forties who intend never to marry premarital? Which term is more accurate after a divorce or death and prior to a second marriage, *premarital* or *postmarital*? Nevertheless, these terms are widely used, so I'll use them here.

The solution again seemed simple in both premarital and postmarital sex. It lies in the consideration of the personhood of each involved and a loving concern for the other that transcends one's own physical desire. I could see clearly that the "quickie" described by Helen Gurley Brown and similar activities involve exploitation of the other, exaltation of one's own ego, or selfish satisfaction of one's own desires—something very different from the content of the code I had constructed.

In marital sex, the code should still apply. A marriage license is not a license to disregard the fact that your spouse is a human being with rights equal to your own.

For most of us in middle age, our main concern is extramarital. The ritual and routine of marrige by middle age seem to be leading to more and more extramarital sexual relations. Kinsey first startled us when he found that by middle age about half of all married men and a quarter of married women had experienced at least one extramarital relationship. In 1970, Athanasiou reported that 36 percent of middle-aged women had had at least one extramarital affair. The trend is continuing, according to Morton Hunt's more recent survey, especially in women. This trend would place the respective percentages in the vicinity of 70 percent and 40 percent at this writing. So it is not something we can ignore.

Although fewer women than men now admit extramarital sex, it is interesting to look ahead for a moment. All the surveys have shown that the prevalence of premarital sex in any one age group corresponds with later levels of extramarital sex in the same group. Today extramarital sex stands about where premarital sex did thirty or forty years ago. A little less than one-third of all women had premarital sex in the 1940s, but now that figure is about four-fifths. When the present under-thirty generation arrives at middle age, not only will the percentages probably be higher for both sexes, but the disparity between them may disappear altogether.

There are persuasive influences at work upon us even now in regard to extramarital relations for both sexes from many sources in society. Books such as *The New Intimacy* by Ronald Mazur, with its concept of "supportive intimacies with others," suggest that extramarital sex should become increasingly tolerated. In *The Significant Americans*, Cuber and Haroff commented, "There seems to be a growing tolerance of the idea that some men and women need and want enduring sexual as well as platonic relationships with more than one person concurrently." In her *Future of Marriage*, Jessie Bernard predicted, "It may be that we will have to choose between exclusivity and permanence. A conception of marriage which tolerates, if it is not actually sympathetic with, extramarital relations is on its way. . . ." And in their book, *Open Marriage*, the O'Neills ponder if it is the human being who has failed or the standard of monogamy itself.

I wonder. Perhaps we have failed to understand the human being. The psychoanalytic literature holds that men who have an affair in middle age do so for reasons involving vanity or virility: to try to recapture their youth or to assuage anxieties about their attractiveness and manhood. We know now that these conclusions came from experience only with this sort of man seeking help for these (and other) problems. They do not apply to most men. Nor does the same literature help us much in understanding unfaithful women. We have the answer for some of either sex in a bad relationship, transferred hostility onto the spouse, or revenge for a real or presumed wrong. But for most affairs we have to look elsewhere for the real reasons, and we don't understand them yet. One thing seems to be true, however. Men have had a strong desire for sexual variety throughout recorded history, and probably before that. Eons ago, men may have been scarce in the tribe because of death in wars or hunting, or absent from the tribal home for the same reasons. An evolutionary purpose may have been served by wandering warriors or hunters coming upon new settlements and seducing the willing women there. We really don't know. Perhaps men are just more aggressive. Women have a desire for variety, too, but it's more suppressed than men's— either by biology or society or both. We don't really understand their potential at all. It may in fact equal men's.

The best clue we have at the present time as to the motivation behind most extramarital affairs comes from the studies that have shown, contrary to popular belief, that most do not start with a sexual relationship at all, but with the *search for a sympathetic partner*. Cuber and Haroff, for example, say that enduring affairs have a low sexual component as measured by the frequency or centrality of sex—they are short on sex but long on understanding and empathy. "Typically, it [sex] is not there as sex *per se*; it is more an emergence of human totality." Once again we find that we must face the fact that the totality of the persons involved must be considered, and with loving concern.

Foremost is that of your own spouse. Deception is more damaging than any other aspect of an extramarital affair. Next to deception is the threat of loss, either physical or emotional. An affair, to the uninvolved spouse, represents the loss of trust in and the loss of moral integrity of his or her marital partner. It is also usually interpreted that love has been lost. Neither spouse can predict future reflections, and the marriage itself may later be lost. According to the moral code I have been applying, one must not only understand oneself and the reasons why he or she is becoming involved, but the same would apply to the prospective partner. Then the understanding and consent of the two other spouses would have to be obtained. An affair is not just a triangle—it is a quadrangle and more. The reactions of all members of both families as well as of friends and others in society would have to be ascertained, both now and for the future. And through all this, loving concern toward *all*? This seems to be an almost insurmountable set of difficulties. In fact, it usually is. That is why so much space in this section has been devoted to the ways in which sexual expression can be kept alive and exciting within marriage and, in the discussion that follows, how marriage itself can be made more fulfilling for both, especially in middle age.

MARRIAGE

Marriage, for the middle-aged, can only be understood by exploring its origins. Most of what we have learned in our lives has come from our parents, our peers, and our own experience. Thus we are firmly held in the framework of our own time and culture. We learned when we were young that we could expect to be married, that we would marry for love, that both love and marriage would endure until we died, and that during our marriage fidelity was expected but divorce was not.

Today, all around us, we see others our age having affairs, separations, and divorces. Some seem to be mocking with various alternative life styles the idea of marriage itself. Our own marriage may not have turned out to be all that we had hoped it would be. There is so much turmoil today that we are forced to look back to the origins of marriage in order to understand where it is now and where it may be going. Then we may be able to put our thoughts in better perspective.

Past

Archaeologists have little information for us regarding the organization of the family prior to written record. We do know that, in recorded history, man's intelligence and adaptability to his environment led to several patterns of family organization. Human beings have lived in the constant cold of the poles, in the heat of the tropics, and in the desolation of the desert. Under all these conditions, the consanguine, or extended kinship group, first developed. None of the simpler conjugal arrangements as we know them could have survived. With males absent on hunting expeditions, females and children were prey to animal as well as human enemies. The burden of serial pregnancies, long lactation, and years of child care kept women close to the shelter, grouping for protection and company. In the extended kin group, women were provided for collectively, and there was little or no emphasis on monogamous relationships.

Later, conjugal relationships began to emerge and took four forms:

1. Plural. An arrangement that is seen only sporadically throughout history. Whenever attempted, this form has never persisted for reasons that seem to be inherent in human nature itself.

2. Polyandry. The relationship of several men to one woman. This has been found only when times were extremely hard and the survival of all was threatened. During such times, infanticide of females was practiced, resulting in a higher ratio of providers to preparers.

3. Polygyny. This practice evolved in some societies in which

there was a high casualty rate of males in hunting or in battle. In others it was simply that the strongest and most wealthy males preferred more than one female. Several factors have tended to stifle this type of family organization, the most important of which is the presence of the unrelated males. They can be disruptive and tend to threaten the stronger or wealthier male who has several wives. There are also economic limitations: since men traditionally have been the providers, only a favored few could afford to have more than one wife. But there is one factor that may actually lead to this in the future in our own society, and that is simply that there are more women than men, especially in the middle and later years. A possible trend in this direction should not be overlooked. Otherwise, none of the above relationships need concern us further. They are mentioned briefly because we may tend to think that monogamy is the *only* family structure. We should at least know that it has not always been so. Nor will it necessarily be so in the future.

4. Monogamy is, however, the most common pattern found throughout our Western history and by anthropologists in present primitive cultures.

It is believed by most authorities that women initiated the monogamous relationship for their own protection and that the men acceded primarily for the protection of their property. When agriculture became predominant, there was more stability, both social and economic, and the monogamous relationship evolved to be more formalized. The earlier matriarchal structure that had been characteristic when males were gone on the hunt became patriarchal. Fatherhood, which had been paid little attention theretofore, also began to be formally recognized. Property became even more important and was then inherited in a patrilineal manner. So monogamous marriage had its origin in property. Women themselves were regarded as property, and both they and children were strong backs and pairs of hands— economic assets in early agricultural societies.

At that time fidelity during marriage began to be valued, again primarily for property considerations. At the start, a double standard ruled, with no limitation on male activities whatsoever. From fidelity during marriage grew the concept of chastity for the female before marriage.

We are accustomed to thinking of marriage in religious

terms—or legal ones. It is important that we realize marriages are not made in heaven—they are made here on earth, by people and for people. And the form that marriage takes has evolved through history with the changing needs of those involved and will continue to do so. The earlier forms of the family evolved out of geographical and climatic settings. Over the centuries these became traditionalized, and it was only later that they were made into religious and legal institutions.

Most of us know how these institutions have evolved in our Western history to mold marriage into the form we know today, so this is all I will present of the past of marriage, except for one important point. During the era of feudalism, the idea of romantic love first developed. Marriages at that time were mostly arranged by families, and husbands were gone for long stretches because of almost continual wars. With noblemen absent from their castles, their ladies would entertain troubadours and wandering warriors, and it was their relationships with these men that were idealized and romanticized. It is important to note this— when romantic love first appeared in the Western World, it had nothing to do with marriage. Much later, this romanticization of love spread into the emerging middle class and then to the lower classes. *Only in the past few hundred years has it been the basis for marriage.*

Present

With this much of its history, let us look more closely at marriage as we find it today. By far its most important characteristic is just this basis in romantic love. Our society has replaced race, rank, religion, education, and fortune, as well as societal and sacred rites, all of which function fairly well in other societies, with only one criterion for marriage: romantic love. And on this basis we vow "till death do us part" and actually believe it! As Arnold Nash comments so succinctly, "The modern democratic conception of marriage as a union based on mutual affection and with the intention of permanence is a very recent idea." Romantic love, composed as it is of so many elements of unreality, is doomed to fade in an intimate marital situation. Reality inevitably intrudes. With the coming of the first child, the wife devotes herself more to her role of motherhood and the husband to his role of provider. Romance becomes buried under bills and bicycles. Throughout these years little attempt may be made to develop a more meaningful relationship to replace it. Many husband and wives gradually cease doing things together and grow apart, and both then live on in loneliness after the children have left. *This is the very loneliness that marriage should prevent.*

We need to look more closely at this basis for marriage—romantic love. No one really understands it. We seem to know a great deal more about sex than we know about love. Nevertheless, let's see what we do know. Authorities in child development believe an infant's first sensations are visceral, and that if the constellation of these can be labeled anything, it can be called self-love. Some self-love remains as long as one lives, mostly in the unconscious. Soon, an infant becomes aware that he is the center of his mother's concern and that many of his gratifications relate to his relationship with her. He then begins to feel love for her as an extension of self-love. Soon, the father begins to operate as another such satellite. As the child develops, he acquires a relationship toward his siblings that he later extends to his peer group. This still has strong elements of self-love in that whatever empathy a child has toward other children is usually directed toward that which is like himself in them. Throughout his development, especially through puberty, an idealized self is being formed from many sources including society at large. An ideal of the opposite sex develops from the same sources.

Romantic love appears to be a fusion of three things. The first is self-love extended as a love for the elements that are like oneself in the other. The second is the transferred portion of love for the parent, especially the parent of the opposite sex, that has by this time become separated from the parent himself. The third and most important element, idealization, exists only in societies such as ours, because there must be an appreciable difference between a person's actual self and his ideal self. As Philip Solomon says, "In societies where ambition and competition are at a minimum, romantic love is virtually unknown." Before the personality is mature, the gap between the actual and the ideal self is severely felt. The object of one's romantic love fills this gap, and essential elements of the idealized opposite sex are projected upon the partner. This is the closest we can come to understanding romantic love at the present time.

However, it is a powerful thing, and no one underestimates the chemistry when these three elements are combined. With sexual desire added to the formula, we experience perhaps the most powerful emotions we will ever have in our lives. But *as a basis for marriage*, it has to be questioned. It is well-documented that when marriages at midlife are evaluated, there is little or no difference in the happiness present in marriages that were originally based on romantic love from those that were based on more pragmatic considerations. In other cultures such as parts of China, Africa, and the Middle East where tradition is strong and marriages are still arranged, it is surprising how well most of them turn out. The same was true in our own Western past before romanticism in relationships emerged. To me, two conclusions are inescapable: Romantic love need not be an essential ingredient at the start of marriage, and even when present, it inevitably fades thereafter.

Yet the rapture and intensity of romantic love abounds in our literature and fascinates us—Hero and Leander, Tristan and Iseult, Romeo and Juliet. Even in *Love Story*. It is unbearably sweet and transfiguring, but note that it usually ends in tragic death. The theme of *thanatos* may be a metaphor for the necessary end of romantic love, which cannot possibly be sustained in its illusion and utterly consuming intensity.

But we should not avoid such early love experiences. We learn from them. Each time we find out more about ourselves and the kind of mate we need and the kind that might need us. Hopefully, each time we choose a little more wisely, coming ever closer to loving on the basis of reality rather than imagined perfection or projection. Such love would seem to be a far better basis for marriage.

Besides its beginning in romantic love, the second most important characteristic of modern marriage is the persistent concept of permanence in view of our longer lives during this century. Since its origin and through most of its history, monogamous marriage was never intended to bind two people together for the length of time we now live. The vow to remain together "till death do us part" was not difficult to keep in the past when death was not far off.

The third characteristic of marriage today is the exalted expectation we have of it in view of its origins as a biological and economic entity. The media, the arts, and particularly popular entertainment have enhanced these expectations beyond any possibility of reality to fulfill.

The fourth is the influence of technology that has lessened a family's dependence upon the woman's traditional functions in the home, lessened her burdens there, and at the same time increased her occupational opportunities. The latter has also decreased the wife's economic dependence upon her husband.

There are many others: increasing emphasis upon the individual and his own fulfillment; the weakening of legal, religious, and social barriers against divorce; the suffrage movement of the nineteenth century, which has culminated in the women's liberation movement; the sexual revolution that began with Ellis, was carried on by the *Kinsey Report*, then by the findings of Masters and Johnson, and finally with the advent of "the Pill." Not only has contraception increased women's sexual freedom, but more favorable family planning is also now possible, lessening her reproductive burden. There are many more characteristics of marriage today that make it different from our past. Even our increasing social and geographic mobility cause those with very different backgrounds to meet and marry, producing greater difficulties in adapting to each other than ever before.

Yet all the societal norms to which we are expected to adhere in marriage are derived from the past. Then most were valid in a stable and rural environment; where the roles for each sex were determined biologically; many were even necessary for survival. Religious tenets were adhered to in practice, if not in belief, and the patriarchal organization of the family was not questioned. Now production is in the factory, education is in the school, religion is in the church, recreation is outside the home, sex is easily available all around us, and protection is vested in the police. This historical functions of the family have been reduced to little more than rearing children and providing affectionate companionship. When we face these changes squarely, we can understand better how and why alternative relationships are arising.

As Anne Morrow Lindbergh said, marriage in its present form may be "a fortress which has outlived its function." True, if it is regarded as a fortress. But looked at in other ways, the potential is there for far more. Let's see what the possibilities are at this time in our lives.

Marriage in Middle Age

First, a look at the literature. The most comprehensive and informative study, in my opinion, was by John Cuber and Peggy Harroff. They found five kinds of relationships in effect at middle age.

The first is the "conflict-habituated." In this type there is a great deal of tension and conflict, but it is controlled or channeled. The partners are content in their discontent. The second kind they call the "devitalized." These mates have lost the intimacy and close identification that they knew early in their marriage. They do not share each other's lives but do depend upon the fruits of the other's activities. The third category is the "passive-congenial." This has much in common with the devitalized, with the essential difference that the passivity that pervades this association has been part of the relationship from its start. The fourth mode is the "vital." Here the two are intensely bound together psychologically in relation to the important matters of life. Their sharing and their togetherness are genuine. They really enjoy doing things together rather than alone. They are a minority and seem to know that they are a minority. Their chief characteristic is that they have found how to resolve conflicts quickly and satisfactorily. The last category is called the "total." It is similar to the vital relationship, but it is more multifaceted. There are more points of significant sharing and togetherness between the two people involved.

Note that the individuals themselves are not described by this typology—the relationship is. A vital person can actually be living in a devitalized marriage and express his vitality in some other way. Cuber and Harroff leave it to the reader to decide the degree of happiness in each relationship, but they do come to the conclusion that the most prevalent types in middle age are the devitalized and passive-congenial. But they also observed that mobility from one category to another was possible.

In their work, the authors used two terms that tell us something of mechanisms involved by which couples arrive at one of these five categories—*utilitarian* and *intrinsic*. Both the passive-congenial and the devitalized are utilitarian marriages because the goals are set primarily *outside* the relationship itself. The former is utilitarian from the start and the latter becomes so. The conflict-habituated marriage comes to this end for the same reason. In the intrinsic marriage, the most important goals are set *within* the relationship. Outside goals come later. In the intrinsic marriage there is both sunshine and shadow, but characteristically there is a growing and deepening involvement in the other person's physical and psychological presence. The essence of an intrinsic marriage is the centrality of the mate's welfare in the other mate's scale of values. It is because of this that such marriages become vital or total. Such a relationship does not come about by drift or default.

Several studies have been done on satisfaction over the married years. Two comments should be made before I describe these. There have been far too few studies of happy marriages— most have concentrated on what makes marriages unhappy. Also, the emphasis until recently has been on attempts to predict adjustment in early marriage, proceeding under the assumption that if one could select a compatible mate and both were ready for marriage, that both would then "live happily forever after." Only in the past decade have some investigators looked beyond the original choice into the changes that occur in individuals throughout the life span and into changes in the relationship itself. Cuber and Harroff themselves observed, ". . . correct choice is not the whole story . . . there is also the crucial change in the mate with the passing of time." Choice may have been paramount in the past, with shorter lives. Far more important today are awareness of change in self and partner and the adjustments in the relationship required as our lives go on.

Almost all investigators who have studied the whole span of marriage agree that both partners report their happiness and satisfaction to be at a peak during the first year or two of their relationship. But the initial satisfaction drops to a low point about five years after the marriage. Peter Pineo was the first to use the word *disenchantment* to describe this phase. Boyd Rollins and Harold Feldman assembled a dozen such studies, some of which were longitudinal, and added one of their own. From these they concluded that the satisfaction curves were different for men and women. Men become disenchanted within a year or two; and then their satisfaction remains at that low level with minor fluctuations until just before retirement. This suggests more emotional investment in their careers than in their families. Women, on the other hand, become disenchanted when the first child arrives, remain at a low level of satisfaction until the last child leaves home, and at that point they diverge according to their methods of coping with their new freedom. Ernest Burgess and Paul Wallin came to similar conclusions. Douglas Kimmel found it was worse for the man. Robert Blood and Donald Wolfe disagreed—they saw a similar decline for both, but noted that it was slightly worse for the woman than it was for the man. After 20 years of marriage only 6 percent of the wives were "very satisfied," while 21 percent were "conspicuously dissatisfied." Their overall comment was, "As individuals, middle-aged husbands and wives may find satisfaction elsewhere—in friends, the husband in his work, the wife in her children—they seldom find as much in each other." And they add that the low divorce rate in this period (about twenty per one hundred marriages) is no real measure of the satisfaction that prevails. Rather it is a reflection of other factors that tend to hold the couple together.

In most such studies, the dissatisfied women of middle age were those who had concentrated their thoughts and efforts in the home and had not extended themselves into other activities. They were trying to hold onto the secure social role of homemaking, which was disappearing as the children left home. (So-called "accident" children near the menopause often turn out not to be accidents at all.) Following the life cycle through its course, most authorities agree that satisfaction of both partners usually increases after retirement, once the adjustment of the retirement itself has been passed.

The evidence for this curve of disenchantment is undeniable. It applies to most of us. So now, at middle age, we must set about counteracting this curve—it is the last chance we have. Each has to redesign his or her life, take up new roles in the relationship, and alter old ones. Robert Havighurst offers some suggestions on the tasks at this time: "adjusting to the loss of a parental role, achieving new friendship with married children, accepting the role of grandparent, extending one's network of friendships, joining organizations, accepting the physical and psychological changes with age, acquisition of other interests and hobbies and establishing a life pattern that will form the foundation of retirement." Blood and Wolfe also provide clues: If the marriage is to be satisfactory from this point on, each must reach out to the other and develop a new intimacy. Then the relationship can be even *better* than at the start of the marriage. They point out that persistence of the wife in her role as mother with her married children can only alienate them and disrupt her relationship with them, as well as with their husbands. Persistence of the husband in over-concern with work also results in disaster.

In all these studies, the clues are there for us. If we can resolve our conflicts with our spouse successfully, keep our concern for him or her above that for career and children, and work on the relationship while extending our activities into the community and larger spheres, marriage in middle age can not only be successful, but more satisfying than at any other time of our lives. This is when our previously acquired values and views of marriage, as well as other aspects of our lives, may have become somewhat worn and lost their luster. They must now be re-thought, restructured and refurbished for the last half of life. I will have something to say about how we can go about this later. Let me first point out the new opportunity that is ours to do so.

Ruth Cavan first coined the term *postparental* to signify that phase of marriage after the last child has left. This phase is now emerging as a new one in human history. Jessie Bernard comments, "People did not live long enough in the past to reach it . . . one spouse or the other had died long before the youngest child had left home or was married." This is due to two demographic shifts: longer life expectancy and fewer children over a shorter span. Irwin Deutscher notes that parents now have more than one-fourth of their married lives still to come when the last child leaves home. "This phase of the family cycle is seen by the majority of middle-aged spouses as a time of new freedoms: freedom from the economic responsibilities of children; freedom to be mobile (geographically); freedom from housework and other chores. And, finally, freedom to be oneself for the first time since the children came along." Bernard adds, "To women for whom the wife role has remained salient, taking precedence over the maternal role, this segment of her marriage can be the best of all. . . . We're only now beginning to recognize the importance of this wholly new form of marriage; its potentials for happiness have hardly been explored."

Before I offer some suggestions on how to make the most of this new phase, I would like to review with you some of the difficulties encountered in marriage at midlife among my own patients. Some may apply to you, and on reading them, the first steps to take in coping with them will come to you. In discussing the difficulties, I find it helpful to consider marriage at this time from two points of view, "his and hers," like bath towels, because, as Jeanne Mueller has pointed out, there are really two marriages operating at every point in the marriage cycle, that is, a tendency on the part of each partner to perceive the relationship in terms of role models rather than reality. And there is more disparity between these two in the middle years than at any other time.

HERS

A woman's marriage can be considered in terms of herself, her husband, her children, her parents, and society.

First, herself. All of a woman's life to this point has seen encouragement to become more attractive in order to get a man, to marry the man of her dreams and to raise children, but no one has told her what lay beyond. Now that she is middle-aged, her husband may be preoccupied with his career and his own problems, the children either have left home or are ready to leave, and there is no clearly defined cultural role for her to assume. Alternatives are emerging all around her, but she had no model in her parents or grandparents. If she devoted the previous twenty years to her family, her intellectual development probably was arrested somewhere around the birth of her first child, and her range of interests by now has narrowed even more. Meanwhile, her husband has moved on, becoming more sophisticated in several areas while she remains on her plateau. As her beauty in terms of contemporary criteria wanes, and as her figure becomes more rounded, she may become somewhat depressed in our youth-oriented culture. Her gray hair at this time may arouse associations in her mind of those she knew when she was younger who were impossibly old when they had gray hair—in reality, they *were* a great deal older physiologically than she is now. The gradual decline of her husband's sexual drive does nothing to allay her own self-concept of vanishing attractiveness.

Feminists are absolutely correct in describing the intellectually dead-end quality of homemaking—it does not have the intellectual stimulus to prod anyone's personality to grow. A woman has to be directed from within herself. If she is successful in this, she finds that her opportunities actually are greater than those of her mate. As the last child goes off to school, she has the time during the day to read, to attend theater matinees, to visit art museums, to go to lectures, and to participate in community activities, if she will only do so. When the children leave home for good, her time is even more her own. Except for the early years of child rearing, she need not remain on an intellectual plateau—she can match or surpass her mate, who is confined to the relatively narrow range of stimulation provided by his job, which, as the years go on, inevitably declines. Somewhere Shakespeare says, "The fault, dear Brutus, is not in our stars but in ourselves." She should remember this, and if she has not done so before, *get going herself* to create a wider range of interests.

In the next chapter, "Labor and Leisure," I talk a bit more about the situation of women who are trying to modify their lives from a fairly solidly traditional base to one of more unfamiliar possibilities. One of these is a career of her own. If a wife wants to enter or reenter a career, one word of caution. She is no longer single. She has to consider the effects upon her husband and children. She should start a career only after consulting with her husband and older children. Together they should concentrate on discussing the goals of all of them and arriving at a clear consensus. The decision should be a cooperative one as much as possible. By way of guidance, most studies have shown that when there are preschool children, all are happier if the wife stays home—and the children turn out better. But when there are grade school children, most studies favor work for the wife as being best for all concerned. If the husband's income is low, the wife's augmentation contributes to the family and often more than compensates for her absence from the home. However, as the husband's income rises, a point of diminishing returns is reached. Above that point the husband may resent both the pressure her work puts upon him and the children, as well as the lack of time and attention he receives from his wife. Outside work for wives in families of high economic status is frequently associated with disgruntled husbands and disappointed wives. So a word to the wise. Perhaps self-fulfillment in some other way?

Next, lets look at "her" marriage in relation to her husband. A wife really has three roles here: mother, daughter, and mistress to him. He has three roles with her also: father, son, and lover. Both partners should feel flexible moving among these roles. When one partner shifts roles, ideally the other partner should shift to a complementary role. Throughout marriage the mistress-lover roles should predominate. If not, one or both may turn from the chill to some new thrill.

Most women know that romantic love is doomed to fade by middle age and wonder what will take its place. And he in his turn, too, wants to know. Something has been said about this in other parts of the book. More will be said when we discuss our values in life. For now, let's listen to the words of those who are wiser than we. True love, mature love, is a "real conscious devotion" in the words of Karl Jung, who adds, "To be sure, it takes a lifetime to arrive at this stage." Abraham Maslow observes that in true love there is "an affirmation of the other's individuality" and adds that "we have customarily defined it in terms of a complete merging of egos and a loss of separateness, a giving up of individuality rather than a strengthening of it." He affirms that attraction of mature people for each other is less on the basis of such characteristics as appearance, and more on qualities such as goodness, decency, and other character traits. Harry Overstreet says in *The Mature Mind*, "The love of a person implies, not the possession of that person, but the affirmation of that person. It means granting him, gladly, the full right to his unique manhood," (Read *person*hood). Erich Fromm defines mature love as "a spontaneous affirmation of others, as the union of the individual with others on the basis of the preservation of the individual himself." Most simply put, friendship is the finest relationship between humans, and love is the most meaningful form of friendship. Beyond being a man or woman, each is *human*.

Now let's look at the woman's marriage in relation to her children. She may have realized all of the satisfactions promised her in motherhood when the children were small and absolutely dependent. But the strife and stresses during the middle years with adolescent children contrast greatly with what whe was taught to expect. She may even be bothered by guilt now because at times she wants to reject her role of motherhood. The attractiveness of teenage daughters may be a threat to her at the time when her own beauty is fading. Even the sexual experiences of the younger set nowadays may arouse in her old conflicts and feelings of envy that she tries with difficulty to repress.

All that I can say is that this period of strain with adolescents will change to one of growing appreciation of her children for their own emergence, independence, and accomplishments as they mature. A time of serenity and satisfaction lies ahead if this period can be surmounted. Relating to a child when he or she becomes an adult is immensely more satisfying than relating to a child ever could be. Children themselves become more realistic in regarding the parents for the qualities they possess as time goes on. More will be said about this when I discuss adolescent children.

Lastly, a few words on her marriage as it pertains to her—and often his—parents. The increasing incidence of illness in parents, their financial insecurity, loneliness, and emotional problems are all brought to bear more upon a daughter than upon a son. When she has emotional crises in her own life and cannot talk to her husband, she might turn to her parents to find that they have ceased to care—they are now involved in their own activities and relationships and may have regressed to the point where they are almost obsessed with the minutiae of their own existence. Worse yet, both his and her parents were raised at a time when they were led to expect that they could depend upon their children in their old age. On the other hand, we have been raised in a time that taught self-reliance as well as overindulgence of our children. Women, more than men, are caught in this two-way trap.

In all of the aspects of "her" marriage, a woman is fortunate in one respect. She encounters most of her difficulties earlier than her husband does. Her appearance is essentially unchanged through her twenties and early thirties. Her marital and parental roles tend to remain the same. Her interactions with society may be unchanged, but somewhere in her late thirties, changes begin to occur which she can no longer ignore: first in her attractiveness, then in her relationship to her children, and then in the possible alienation from her husband if he becomes overly immersed in his career. So she has several years during which she can reconstruct her values and goals and have her own adjustments in these respects well under way before her husband is moved to begin his. If she has not faced up to this until her husband finds he can no longer ignore his changes, usually about ten or fifteen years later, the occurrence of two crises simultaneously is too much for many marriages to survive. On the other hand, if she faces them when they occur, her husband is there to help—as she will be later to help him.

HIS

His marriage is different from hers, although it operates around similar factors: himself, his wife, children, parents, and perhaps most of all, his career. Sexually, too, he is experiencing a waning interest and potential.

A man has molded himself from his early years to be husband, father, and provider. Some degree of boredom in his career probably has set in by this time, and he may see himself in a trap from which there appears to be no escape. He may project some of this boredom upon his mate in the marital relationship. His wife's expectations and those of his children and colleagues also seem to him to stifle his search for himself. Even time, if he allows it to, limits him from exploring his true identity beyond these roles. Sometimes, for her own security and stability in the relationship, his wife tries to manipulate him into maintaining the identity she has known all along. If she does, he will see her as the symbol of all his restrictions, and his frustrations may explode against her. The oft-heard male complaint "She doesn't understand me" is sometimes true. But truer still is that he usually doesn't understand *himself* very well at this point.

The two things a man must have at this period are time and room—time for reflection, to stand back, to be objective, and the freedom to explore the emerging aspects of his personality. The tendencies of those around him both at home and at work too often constrain him. Out of a greater freedom allowed a man in the marital situation at this point will emerge a closer union later. He will then recognize the value of his family in a new light, and the rewards to all, although delayed, will be ample. His new autonomy and confidence in himself will evolve into a more open expression of his affection and need for his family, if they can but withstand the stresses and strains of this change.

The increasing independence and assertiveness of his wife, added to the changing roles of women now, calls for another adjustment on his part. Society tolerates the emergence of certain masculine traits in women far better than it does passive or feminine qualities in a man, so hers tend to emerge more than his. A man who cannot tolerate this independence on the part of his wife, who longs for the days when she was dependent, may end the marriage and take a younger woman who once again will reassure him by being dependent—until she too grows older. This starts the roulette wheel turning, and he may repeat this pattern until old age or accumulating alimony payments force him to stop.

On the job, he finds that his own and his family's demands for material goods and status press him for increasing production just as boredom and fatigue begin to set in. He may see at this time that whatever salary he attains will never satisfy his family's desires. He is also becoming aware that he will not become the top man on the pyramid—there is room for only one stone at the top. At work he has found that the best way to manage other people is to suppress his inner feelings and to wear a mask. But he may not have learned that this doesn't do well in intimate relationships at home. Instead of getting in touch with himself and expressing his true feelings, he may turn to divorce or drink. A man must now reassess his immense investment in his work, the rewards of which his wife and children have come to accept as their due, as he, himself, may have. The decline in his energy, the changes in his physical appearance and health, and the possibility of disability and death all have to be reckoned with.

Too often at this point he reaches out for his children just as they leave him—emotionally, in terms of their interests, or from the home entirely. When he would like to lean upon his parents as he did long ago, he finds that they are now leaning upon him.

These, then, are some of the most frequently encountered difficulties in "his" and "her" marriages during the middle years. I have not gone much beyond mentioning them—and to imply that a new relationship must be arrived at. This is because each of us is different and has different difficulties that we see in our own ways. The solutions have to be our own. We must remember always that we are not the same persons who entered into the marriage, nor do those closest to us remain unchanged. Nor is society itself the same. Our relationship in middle age must be a new one. And, like life, this cannot be static—it is a *process*. The choices are three: drift, with increasing distance; divorce, with another marriage to follow that will itself be a new relationship; or revitalization of the present relationship. Which will you choose?

THE NEW RELATIONSHIP

The revitalization of marriage in middle age is best based upon three principles: commitment, communication, and compromise. A fourth "C," counseling, practiced in a preventive way, will be mentioned when we discuss divorce.

Any two humans involved in an intimate relationship are subject to reactions in the heat of the moment. Commitment adds security to the relationship at the cost of only a little freedom. It means the willingness to understand the other, to take the time and try. It means dealing with the here and now, not with what has been or might have been. In the ancient Ketuba, or Hebrew marriage document, the patriarchal orientation demanded not *commitment* on the part of the woman, but *consent*. Her only reward for this consent was security. Symbolically, in modern marriage ceremonies there is an increasing elimination of the promise to obey.

Reflection will show that no matter how a marriage was begun, if it has survived to middle age, each partner has much to match the other, and each has helped to develop enough common areas of interest to neutralize most of what may make the marriage difficult at this time. There is a great deal to build upon. We realize that we cannot go back to the beginning and do it all over again. Unless a reconstruction is begun now, for many only a miserable marriage or the lonely single world is waiting.

The new relationship involves the systems concept. The classic marriage puts forth that *one and one are one*—fused, a dyad, with the same tastes and activities. *One plus one are two* is the philosophy of Fritz Perls—"I am I and you are you." This is more suitable for the single life. Best of all is when *one plus one are three*, including the matrix for a dynamic relationship between the two. Most middle-aged couples have a closed contract resting on the norms of society, parents, religion, and habit. A closed contract implies possession of the mate, denial of self, presenting a couple-front to the world, with rigid roles, including fidelity and exclusivity. The new relationship should recognize the uniqueness and freedom of each partner and the right of each to grow in flexible roles. There should be, as Kahlil Gibran said, "spaces in your togetherness." Commitment on this basis has real meaning.

Communication is perhaps the most important component in the new relationship. We all enter marriage with different backgrounds and expectations. The male especially has been molded to silence and stoicism. This may constitute a barrier that is difficult to break through. On the other hand, the female has usually been raised to dissimulate. True communication inevitably involves risk as one expresses feelings and inner needs. The first step is to try to get in touch with your own emotions. The next is simply to ask when the other would be receptive and try to express them then the best way you can. The third is to *learn to listen*, not only with your ears but with your heart. Most of us spend the time while the other is talking thinking about what we want to say next. Some listen selectively, hearing only what they want to. A simple exercise to start with is for one person to state how he/she feels as clearly as possible, then for the other to try to rephrase it in his own words to make sure he has understood. Two simple rules to follow are to always tell the truth, and to tell the other only as much of the truth as he or she needs to know. More advice on communication can be found in Lederer and Jackson's *Mirages of Marriage* and other references listed in the Bibliography.

Compromise is an essential ingredient in any intimate relationship. In his books *The Intimate Enemy* and *Creative Aggression*, George Bach has set forth several rules for the satisfactory resolution of conflict. These are well worth reviewing. Bach may err a bit in emphasizing the ventilation of anger almost to the exclusion of all other emotions, but at least he gives some good advice on how to modify and channel it and avoid destructive or vengeful behavior. Briefly, he urges that both partners choose a mutually acceptable time and place for their discussion of differences and confine themselves to the issues at hand. These must be the real ones and not subterfuges. He emphasizes being candid and open as well as listening and understanding. Neither should ever try to win. It is here that compromise comes in. If one loses a discussion or an argument, both lose eventually. Ask yourself, should you hang on and hate—or negotiate?

As I emphasized before I outlined some of the difficulties, marriage in middle age can be the most thoroughly satisfying aspect of our entire lives. For the most part, I have presented only some of the problems and potentials. The solutions I offered were few—call them clues. The rest is up to you. I'll close with a quote—and still another clue—from Ann Morrow Lindbergh as she writes in *Gift from the Sea*. "The tide of life recedes. The house with its bulging sleeping porches and sheds begins little by little to empty. The children go away to school and then to marriage and lives of their own. Most people, by middle age, have attained or cease to struggle to attain their place in the world. That terrific tenacity to life, to place, to people, to material surroundings and accumulations, is it as necessary as it was when one was struggling for one's security or the security of one's children?"

ADOLESCENT CHILDREN

Well, here we are in middle age with children who are either adolescent and at home, or a little older and recently departed. Let me ask you a question calling for an honest answer. Do (or did) your adolescent children contribute more happiness or more unhappiness in your life? If your reluctant answer is the latter, cheer up, you have a lot of company. Sociological studies show that the same is true for most middle-agers with children this age.

We have already noted that such studies found *marital* satisfaction to dip at the birth of the first child, continue to descend to reach the lowest point in the years when the first child is adolescent, remain low, and rise again only when the last child leaves home. *Parental* satisfaction shows a similar but slightly different curve. It is at its peak when the first child is born, remains fairly high for a few years, but then it too descends to reach its lowest point when the children are adolescent. It drops more rapidly the more children there are, and to lower levels. And parental satisfaction does not rise again either until the last child has left home. Of middle-aged parents interviewed, three-fourths or more report "significant conflict" *at the present time* with their adolescent children—more with sons than with daughters. And older couples looking back characteristically evaluate their years with teen-aged children in the home as "especially trying" —more so than the earlier years when the adjustments of marriage and economic difficulties were greater. Such findings are surprising enough, but it is astounding to learn that these studies, most of them done during our lifetime, also report that *childless couples are the happiest of all* despite the disapproval with which society generally regards such marriages. Even a recent survey of fifty thousand parents by Ann Landers found that 70 percent, given the choice again, would not have children—it just wasn't worth it.

The birth rate in our country is telling its own story. Starting in the sixties, the average family size began to go down, and this decline gained more momentum in the seventies. Family size is now less than half what it was two decades ago—in fact, it is at an all-time record low: less than two children per couple. Among younger parents, the reasons given range from the realistic to the idealistic, from the heights of "environmental concerns" or "world overpopulation" down to "we want to do our own thing." Whatever the reason may be, The Pill is providing the means. Does this "birth dearth" mean that the generation of parents behind us knows something we were not told?

Are we learning too late, caught once again between the past and the present? When we were young, we tended to mold ourselves on our parents and grandparents. Most of them had large families—they were the last generations who lost many children to disease and for whom children might have been an asset, economic or otherwise. Or perhaps they, too, were caught, having based their ideas on the example the generations before them. Children *were* an asset in many ways throughout our agrarian history, and even through much of our early industrialization. Customs favoring large families were deeply ingrained in our country and tended to persist past the point when children began to become more of a liability than an asset. The *ideal* of large families lasted longer than the *idea*—the real reason for them. It was in this milieu that we were raised and learned what we did of family life.

The truth is that we *were* trapped between the past and the present. Between an idea and an ideal. The studies that I referred to were done too late to help guide us when we were having children. And the studies that should be done to help us now haven't been. Look in the libraries—you find shelves of books for our use on child development and how we as parents should treat our teen-agers. Where are the works advising us, in middle age, how we can hold *our* lives together with teen-agers in the house—or even one for teen-agers telling them how to treat their middle-aged parents?

Those of us who with adolescents in the late sixties and early seventies had dutifully raised them till then according to the childhood authorities of the time—Gesell, Dewey, Watson, and Spock—and knew that during adolescence we could expect the children to test the limits of parental discipline as part of their search for their own identity. But we were not prepared for them to go beyond this to the actual abuse characteristic of that period. If you had adolescents then, you learned as no other generation has how much children can hurt their parents. And there is no greater hurt than from those you love. The authorities had told us all along to allow them room for their own development, and we tried to. But they did not warn us that this could result in such an all-consuming self-interest, in such an absolute intolerance of others and all views other than their own.

Our children even blamed us for all that was wrong with the world—a world not of our making and in which most of us had done and were continuing to do our best. In their violent demonstrations against the Viet Nam war, they did not realize that they were damaging the democratic process itself, even though that process resulted in the decision to enter the war that may have been a mistake. They did not recognize that they were sapping the source of our strength as a nation, which may have catastrophic consequences in the 1980s, or that they were destroying the validity of international treaties that have protected millions throughout history and that one day they might want to protect them. They knew too little of reality and history —or simply didn't care. And they refused to see that their rebellion *prevented* a rapid and favorable end to that war, causing many more casualties—even ensuring that the casualties themselves were to be in vain. The resultant slaughter and starvation in Southeast Asia have been and remain appalling. Where are these protestors and their "ideals" now?

We were told, too, that we could expect our children to use our values as a basis to form their own, rejecting some and modifying others. We were not told that they would reject all of them while living off the fruits of them. They burned draft cards, not credit cards. Nor did we know that this total rejection would come at a time in our lives when we ourselves would begin to have doubts about our values and be in the process of rethinking them, and thus be especially vulnerable. This total rejection was in effect a rejection of all that we had lived our lives by, and therefore a rejection of us and our worth as human beings. As soon as we got them up on their own two feet, they began walking all over us. And the advice the authorities and their books gave us for guidance: "There isn't a single problem that will arise during your child's adolescence that calmly sitting down and discussing it won't ameliorate." The advice was right except for one word— substitute *aggravate* for *ameliorate*.

And when the loud parties and horrendous music of that time (even worse than now) drove us to distraction, we were past the point where we could tell them to "play outside, dear," or put them to bed early. The Pepsi generation created a peptic generation—us.

We as parents in those times also had other new and greater worries: our adolescents' experimentation with the pleasures and dangers of drugs and sex. One day we were casually informed by our daughter at college that she had taken to living with someone to make ends (and presumably other things) meet. And, "But, Dad—*everyone* smokes pot!" We who had teen-agers then truly bore a special burden. All parents expect some anguish with their adolescents. But we suffered far more than our parents did—or their parents. One would have to go back in history to times when more children died than lived to find anything comparable. We can at least hope our children do not suffer so with their children. Times are improving somewhat now, and adolescents are, too. They are actually coming closer to what we were taught to expect.

However, those of us who have adolescents now have our own problems. Some are a hangover from the stormy sixties and seventies. Some are new. For example, we knew something of the expense of rearing children when we conceived them. But we did not know the cost would ascend to become astronomical. It now costs over $100,000 for a middle income family to raise a child from cradle to college. And the expense of college is approaching $10,000 a year at a time when the way in which we will provide for our own old age is considerably less than certain. What is worse is that the middle-agers of today were raised during the Depression and knew times both lean and hard. As a consequence, we worked and saved and tried to give our children all we could. Few adolescents are threadbare or hungry today, as many of us were. Most have known nothing but plenty all their lives and have come to expect affluence as their due, with no appreciation of what we went through in order to provide for them. And heaven help us if actuality falls something short of their expectations.

Yet a lot of things we were told to expect are turning out to be true today. We see our teen-agers' erratic and sweeping swings of emotion, their infatuation with fads, their repeated lack of effective solutions to their problems, their overbearing cocksureness when they feel they have found them, and their despondent gloom when they realize they haven't. These are just part of growing up. Then there is the process of "letting go," which we knew ahead of time would be difficult. But no matter how hard we try, somehow we always seem to be out of phase. The moment we allow greater independence, they come rushing back to us, and if we are startled, they berate us for "not understanding." When we try to hold them close and comfort them, we are apt to be rejected and admonished that they are "grown up now." The only rule we can follow through this confusing time is that the best way to hold on to our children *is* to let go.

I'm not going to make this section longer by giving you any "words of wisdom." As I mentioned before, ample advice can be found in any library, and there are numerous agencies, counselors, and other sources you can turn to, for what they are worth—which isn't much. But at least we can be comforted by the knowledge that adolescence is one mental malady that cures itself as the years pass.

So by middle age, we had hoped to see in our children the realization of all our hopes and dreams; some reward from late-at-night bottles, changing diapers, bandaging skinned knees, and comforting them when they cried; the results of all those investments in lessons, vitamins, braces, and camps. And for the most part, we are doomed to disappointment. But things will get better—what other direction can they go? Our children will mellow as they mature, and there are always grandchildren to look forward to.

Through it all, remember a bit of sage advice from Carl Jung: "Nothing has a stronger influence . . . on their children than the unlived life of the parents." Think about that. And live a little yourself.

AGING PARENTS

One reason we are called middle-aged is that we are in the middle, between our adolescent children and our aging parents.

Few things occur at this time in life that are more disturbing—even devastating—than a telephone call telling us of the first failing or infirmity of a parent. This triggers a surge of emotions. A sense of impending or inevitable loss and loneliness, a reawakening of old filial love (perhaps conflicting with hostility buried since childhood), resentment, even anger and fear. But

worst of all is guilt. I will have some advice that will help you with
the latter, but throughout, remember that although the problem
may be yours, the fault is not. You have divided responsibilities at
this time—to yourself and your family as well as to your parents.
You can only do the best you can, although it may be less than
they expect or than you feel you should.

Be ready for this call—it will happen to all. And the better
part of being ready is *having taken steps to prepare*. I would like to
suggest a few you can do now. First, work out your area of
responsibility clearly with the others concerned. Then, knowing
this area, look in the white pages of your telephone book under
the following code words that are applicable to your area of
responsibility: *Community Service, Health, Human, Housing, Legal
Aid, Senior, Social Service*.

Then look under religious and fraternal organizations and
governments—city, county, state, and federal—for the same
code words.

Call and ask each, not only for the information you need, but
about sources for more. Write to those that are distant from you.
Request whatever printed material any of these sources has to
offer.

If your parents live far away, one call to the Family Service
Association office where they live is all that may be necessary.
This will put you in contact with a social worker who already has
this information and can apply it where your parents live.

The next step is to get your parent or parents under the care of
a good physician, preferably a certified internist. Find out from
him all you can about their health and his best estimate of medical
expenses that may be expected in the years ahead. Then check on
their medical insurance and Medicare coverage.

You will be surprised how much just these few steps taken
ahead of time will help when the call finally comes.

As you have the time and opportunity, try to acquire at least a
rough idea of your parents' financial situation, and talk to an
estate attorney. Armed with his advice, have a conversation with
your parents at a time when it is convenient for them about their
will and where it is kept, who their attorney is, and federal estate
and state inheritance taxes. If possible, find out also about their
insurance policies, Social Security and veterans' benefits, who
their insurance agent and accountant are, where their bank
accounts and safety deposit boxes (and keys) are located, and any

other pertinent financial matters. This step is usually difficult, but you will be saving yourself much more difficulty later on.

One way I can help you prepare is to present some of the problems middle-aged patients of mine have had with their parents, problems my patients had not expected or even thought of, because they arise from social changes that are somewhat subtle in their effects. The solution to each depends, of course, on the circumstances at the time. But to be forewarned is to be forearmed.

Ours is the first generation to have the degree of mobility we have, to be able to move a nuclear family around virtually at will. We can break family connections more easily than ever before. The result is that many of us are separated by great distances from our parents; often, we see them only in times of crises or ceremonies. Our focus is on our work and our own families, not on them. Yet we might have grown up believing we would live near them and continue to relate closely to them, and they may have believed this, too. So we may feel vaguely guilty about the distance between us, literally and figuratively. Actually, the surveys that have been done show that most older parents prefer their autonomy—to live their own lives and to see their children when and where *they* choose. Remember this word *autonomy*. It and the word *activity* are two keys that will guide you when your parents begin to fail.

The traditional role of the parent as teacher is, in the case of older parents and their now middle-aged children, not just gone, but in many cases reversed. This is due to many changes in our society. However, our parents may not recognize this, but tend to carry on the same way they did when they *were* guiding our lives. And related to this, another role reversal occurs as they age—in terms of authority. When we begin to have to make decisions regarding their futures, long-buried conflicts and hostilities within us may emerge. Parents in their turn may be uncomfortable with this new relationship and feel powerless in a way they never have before.

Still another role reversal occurs in their lives, this one with respect to each other. Our fathers are no longer the all-powerful figureheads we knew when we were growing up; our mothers now tend more and more to be the dominant ones. This may be more difficult for us than for them to accept and affects the way we relate to them as a pair.

How one lived in retirement was different for our grand-parents than it is for our parents—recreation was more home-centered then. Now there is a wide variety of recreational patterns, most of which are away from the home. The lack of this focus on the family as a source of entertainment and emotional support may be difficult for them to adjust to and leave them feeling stranded and at loose ends. This feeling may be compounded by the traditional belief that their children would provide for them financially as they aged. But we are experiencing at this time the most severe financial demands in our own lives, trying to provide for our own retirement and for our children's college education. This may tend to produce both guilt on our parts and resentment on theirs. We must recognize that our resources—and therefore our responsibilities—are limited, and we must be realistic.

Our fathers' fathers lived in a time when most men were self-employed and retired gradually of their own volition, with economic independence. The period of retirement was shorter, and less money served the retired couple. But our own fathers have been working, for the most part, in corporate enterprises in which retirement has been mandatory at age sixty-five; their economic security depends entirely on Social Security income, a pension plan, and savings. Inflation has often rendered such provisions inadequate, to say the least, especially in view of the longer life expectancy now. Closely related to this situation is the fact that increasing socioeconomic upward mobility has brought most of us to a higher level in society than our parents. They may be looking back with bitterness on the more limited opportunities they had in their times.

For several decades, young people have left parental homes while their parents were still vigorous and capable. The nuclear families we formed have led independent lives for twenty or thirty years, during which time our parents remained capable. By middle-age we are accustomed to assume only obligations to our immediate family. Thus the imposition of the burdens of an aging parent has much more impact upon us than it had upon our parents. They assumed these burdens sooner, often before they were married, and for them the burdens did not last as long.

There are obviously many more potential problems with aging parents. These, however, are some of those which have come about because of social and cultural changes, largely during our own lives, and often were not foreseen for this reason.

But consider the advantages we have now in handling problems with our parents. We have more resources of all sorts. We have more experience than we would have had, had they occurred earlier in our lives. And our better education certainly helps. Our greater knowledge of psychology also enables us to understand them—and ourselves—better. Information about aging and the aged has increased enormously in the past two decades. Governmental agencies and other organizations for the aged have multiplied in recent years.

Once you have contacted the resources I suggested, you might also look in your local library for more information, or write to the National Council on the Aging, 1828 L Street, N.W., Washington, D.C. 20006, and to the Administration on Aging, U.S. Department of Health and Human Services, Washington, D.C. 20205. You can also obtain the address of the state agency on aging in your parents' state capitol by writing to the Administration on Aging. The National Council of Senior Citizens, at 1511 K Street, N.W., Washington, D.C. 20036, too, has helpful information. One of the best sources is the American Association of Retired Persons, 1909 K Street, N.W., Washington, D.C. 20049. The AARP has pamphlets on many aspects of aging and retirement, and you might even want to buy your parents a membership. Suggest they contact their nearest senior citizen center, where friends, activities, and still further resources are available. You can find the address of the center nearest them in the telephone book or in the *Directory of Senior Citizens Centers*, obtainable from the Superintendent of Documents, U.S. Government Printing Office, Washington, D.C. 20403. This office also produces many helpful booklets for the aging—ask for a list when you write.

While your parents are still vigorous, there are many community service organizations that they can join, such as Senior Opportunities and Services (S.O.S.). Their senior center maintains a list of several such organizations. They should contact their church or synagogue for others. They may be unaware of the various governmental programs that assist the elderly in remaining active. The federal agency ACTION administers such programs as Senior Companions, Foster Grandparents, Retired

Senior Volunteer Program, and Volunteers in Service to America. Its address is 806 Connecticut Avenue, Washington, D.C. 20325. SCORE, the Service Corps of Retired Executives, can be contacted through the Small Business Administration, 1441 L Street, NW, Washington, D.C. 20005. The two themes from this point on are autonomy and activity. Because your parents have the right to choose how they are going to live—and die. And they should keep as active as their physical and psychological limitations will permit.

If the time comes when either one is more restricted to home because of physical limitations, the scene shifts. You will already have a lot of information to help you with this phase. Their local library may have a book-by-mail program or might deliver books, paintings, and records. Light housekeeping and shopping services—even transportation and escort services—may be available. Call the department of social services nearest them. A Ring-a-Day service may ease your anxiety considerably—call the American Red Cross or the local commission on aging. Simple home health care is a coming concept, and you should call the health department in their area for information, or write the National Council for Homemaker-Home Health Aid Services, Inc., 67 Irving Place, New York, New York 10003. Their local senior citizen group and agencies such as the United Fund/United Way, Community Chest, and American Red Cross may also be able to help you. A commercial organization with branches in over two hundred cities is the Homemakers Home and Health Care Services, 3651 Van Rick Drive, Kalamazoo, Michigan 49001.

Day care centers for the elderly are developing in many areas. They provide recreational, educational, and social services as well as lunch for the partially disabled. And they offer transportation to and from these locations. Call the local health department or the local senior citizens center for more information on these centers. There is also a hot meal program (National Nutrition Program for the Elderly) that serves at least one hot meal per day, five days a week, in centrally located buildings such as schools, churches, and senior citizen centers. Participants pay what they can afford. Meals on Wheels and similar programs bring prepared meals to those who cannot leave their homes and are eligible.

When health problems are serious, you should first consider

having a reliable paid live-in companion, who can be instructed by your parents' physician. Again, preserve autonomy. Many of these companions can carry out the required care very well. If necessary, the local Visiting Nurses Association will send a registered nurse as often as may be required to assist. You can find the closest VNA in the telephone book.

Although autonomy in their own home should be preserved as long as possible, at some point you might want to consider a senior residence, where more care is provided, or a home for the aged, where there is even more personal care.

Two methods of care from this point on have not been mentioned yet. The first is taking one or both of your parents into your home. In my experience, this has almost always been disastrous for all concerned. The second is nursing homes.

Before I discuss them, I have two suggestions that have not yet become part of our society. Perhaps someone will read this and take up the suggestions. One would be a *medical* day-care center patterned after the social ones that I already mentioned. With the part-time services of a physician, registered and vocational nurses, occupational and physical therapists, these could complement the facilities offered at the social day care centers at less than half the cost of a nursing home.

The second suggestion is one that would work well in combination with both the medical and social day-care centers, and would be especially valuable in cases where only one parent remained. Where there has been nuclear fission, that is, when the older nuclear family has been broken by death, nuclear fusion could be considered. The remnants of nuclear families and compatible couples could form cooperative households. Economically, they could function like any other consumer cooperative, thereby lowering costs and improving quality of the food. Benefit would accrue to the man who is still able to work even part-time, because he would have to devote less time and effort to home tasks and could concentrate on providing income. The women could pool their efforts in home tasks, and assignment of tasks should be made on the basis of both ability and health. The emotional and social benefits would be immense.

One of the first difficulties that would be encountered in setting up such an arrangement is that architecture has not yet conceived of this. The living unit should provide for the privacy of the various members and couples, as well as have a central area for socialization and meals. Apartment houses could be utilized as a transition step, where each person or couple could spend private time in a small apartment but the members could jointly rent a larger one to use for communal activities. It would seem that in all of the retirement communities being built, some imaginative architect could construct at least one such unit as an experiment. This sort of an arrangement would put off the time that an older person would have to be confined in a nursing home, with its consequent isolation and depersonalization. Care, especially of the more personal type, would be provided by those whom one knew and liked rather than by paid help.

The decision to have your parent or parents enter a nursing home is a serious one. Proceed cautiously. Again, try to preserve their autonomy and activity as much as possible. First consult their physician to see if it is absolutely necessary. While talking with him, discuss the various ones available. They can be grouped into two major types, but there are shadings in the degree of care within each type. One is the Intermediate Care Facility (ICF), in which the patients are ambulatory and require little care. The other is the Skilled Care Facility (SCF), with constant nursing supervision, more personal and medical care, and often other rehabilitative services. Ask his advice as to the most appropriate. You can also obtain a list of nursing homes from the local health department, state branches of the American Nursing Home Association and the American Society of Homes for the Aging. The Social Security office maintains a list of homes approved for Medicare, and the county department of social services has a list of those approved for Medicaid. Each state office on aging in the state capitol also keeps a list of facilities.

Once you have chosen the best possibilities, you should visit them yourself—at unexpected times. Get the "official tour" later. Use your eyes *and* your nose. Ask to see the nursing home license issued by the state, as well as the federal certificate indicating the home is a licensed provider of Medicare or Medicaid. The administrator should have a nursing home administrator license (except in Arizona). Talk to the residents there; ask them privately about the care. Observe the activity room in session— and its atmosphere. Sample the quality of the food—this is extremely important for the elderly. Try to pick one nearby to facilitate your visiting. If possible, let your parents participate in the entire process. Be sure to discuss costs clearly—with your parents and the administrator—before making your final decision.

A pamphlet entitled *Thinking About a Nursing Home?* is available from the American Health Care Association, 1200 15th Street, N.W., Washington, D.C. 20005, and this may help you. You can also write to Consumer Information, Public Documents Distribution Center, Pueblo, Colorado 81009 for the pamphlets *"It Can't Be Home"* and *"Nursing Home Care."*

Look for deficiency reports on the particular nursing homes you are considering in the local Social Security office; government inspection reports, too, are available to the public at the local department of health as well as at welfare offices.

When a parent dies, it is usually a profoundly disturbing event, whether the relationship was close or not. But there have been few studies on the effect of a parent's death on *adult* children, so not much is known about it. The problem is particularly traumatic, because the death of one elderly parent leaves the other in an increasingly lonely and dependent state. You must guard against becoming a surrogate spouse.

One thought that may help you at this time is that older people do not fear death in the same way you and I might. Almost all have prepared themselves in ways we cannot conceive. It is almost as if a greater wisdom than ours is present as death approaches. When it comes, it is almost always accepted with serenity. If there is fear, it is more often a fear of dying than of death—the process, not the result.

If you are concerned about your parents lingering on in a terminal illness with tubes in every orifice and machines sustaining their lives, look into the California legislation on the "right to die" and the "living will." Similar provisions have been enacted in other states. Information can be obtained from the California Medical Association, 731 Market Street, San Francisco, California 94103, and elsewhere. See if there are any hospices near your parents—they are scarce, but compassion and care for the dying is unequalled there. A few are now opening to those who are dying from lingering illnesses other than cancer.

When the death of a parent occurs, you will find that after the grief has run its course, there is then a period of profound growth within you. A link with the past is broken forever. Somehow you know down deep that you are no longer a child. As you grapple with the dismay that comes with your increased awareness of your own inevitable death and your undeniable isolation in the world without the lost parent, you adopt a more mature attitude toward your own mortality and, perhaps even beyond that, to your own immortality. You find that from your parents' aging and deaths you learn a great deal about your own—before it happens.

In one way, the problems you encounter with your aging parents are similar to those you have with teen-age children— both need you and yet don't need you. Both want you and don't want you. You do have your own life, and it is best to live it while *caring*—for all concerned; to be aware all the while of the increasing number of options and possibilities open to all of us. We don't need to be locked in by the customs that bound and served us in the past; we can examine our own situations and, with the help of others, invent ways to make the lives of our adolescent children, our parents, *and* ourselves far more fulfilling than the traditions of the past could ever allow.

DIVORCE

During middle age, disruption of the marriage is dreaded by both partners more than ever. The husband, concerned with his career, recognizes the advantages—including the respectability— of continuing even a bad marriage. There are always certain creature comforts in the worst of marriages, and he especially wants to avoid the alienation from his children that divorce usually entails. The wife may not have done much to discover or develop herself and may fear solo contact with the outside world. As she contemplates her three alternatives on divorce— a career for which she may be unprepared, remarriage, or permanent singlehood—it comes to her that all three involve immersion at least for a time in a single world that is vastly different from the one she knew before. She has heard about the new morals of those who are single and feels sadly out of step. She has also heard that men her own age prefer women ten to twenty years younger, and she calculates that those who might be interested in her would be in their dotage. And she has been told that all the single men out there have serious personal problems anyway—they are either loners or losers.

Even if very little else is shared, some of the couple's fears are. Both are concerned about the effects of the divorce on their children and of the unknowns in the lives they themselves would live. They both fear their own disapproval, as well as that of their friends and society. Considering all of this, it is not surprising that many in middle age hang on, come what may. After all, isn't that the right thing to do?

Yet divorce is on the increase at all ages. In this country there were seven million divorces in 1978, a sevenfold increase since 1900. And during the past two decades there has been an approximate doubling of divorces involving those in middle age. One-fourth of marriages that have lasted more than fifteen years now end in divorce. We in middle age are not immune at all. Bargains made in our teens and twenties often backfire in our forties and fifties.

What is truly tragic, however, is not these statistics, but the vast numbers who are unhappy in their marriages and lack the courage to divorce. Two *can* be lonelier than one. Throughout, we should have practiced preventive maintenance on our marriages. Fortunately, for most of us, it is still not too late. We have long been accustomed to this with our cars and other machines and devices. We have even come to accept periodic physical examinations in order to maintain our health. But the idea that marital counseling should start before marriage and continue throughout it still seems strange to us. Most couples wait until their marriages are in serious trouble before seeking professional help, and the data show that intervention then does not do much good. Counseling at that time prevents divorce in only about 10 to 15 percent of cases even when measured over a short period of time—five years or so—and succeeds in converting miserable marriages into reasonably happy ones in less than 5 percent of cases. Conciliation courts report even worse results. At the present time, professionals are merely witnesses at the wake. Yet this need not be.

We do not have to look far to find the major reason for the lack of preventive counseling. The discipline of psychology, on which counseling is based, is young. It is not even a science as such. Rather it has evolved in the form of "schools," which have a certain coherence within themselves but not with each other. And most professionals in these schools are not only crisis-oriented, they concentrate more on individual psychopathology than upon intimate relationships between two relatively normal people.

There are four ways in which you can practice preventive maintenance in your marriage. One you can do yourselves. The book *Mirages of Marriage*, by Lederer and Jackson, contains a self-check that either spouse can do alone, another checkup the two can do together, and one to be done with the aid of a nonprofessional third person. Many such "self-help" systems are available. The other three ways each involve professional counselors of various backgrounds, so you should know something about them.

The first is the marriage counselor. In some states a counselor is not required to have any training at all before setting up practice. In others, the standards vary widely. In most, a Bachelor's degree in divinity or a medical degree without any other training is considered sufficient. The better counselors have a Bachelor's degree in a behavioral science such as psychology or sociology and several years of experience. The best go beyond this basic education to have a Master's degree in social work and one or more years of professionally supervised experience before they set up shop. Because of this variety of backgrounds and the difficulty you may have in determining the competence of any one counselor, it's a good idea to contact a Family Service Association office. These are staffed by trained social workers and maintain a list of other competent professionals for referral. A list of over three hundred accredited agencies can be obtained from the Family Service Association of America, 44 East 23rd Street, New York, New York 10010, or you can consult your telephone book for the office nearest you.

The second type of professional who can provide marital counseling is a psychologist. First, be warned that almost anyone can call himself a psychologist or psychotherapist. And many with little training do. Licensing is lax in most states. Be sure you select one with a Ph.D. in psychology at least. He or she will have completed some forty semester hours of graduate work and prepared a doctoral dissertation. But remember that this kind of education has consisted primarily of reading textbooks, work in the laboratory with animals, and listening to lectures. The program leading to the doctoral degree is directed toward research and teaching the subject, not toward treating patients. In the last several years, the subdiscipline of clinical psychology has developed. Here a person with the above education also receives an internship of one or two years in supervised clinical work with patients. In this time, he or she also has the opportunity to associate with sociologists, psychiatrists, and other professionals and is much more qualified to care for people than those who have only obtained a doctorate. The American Psychological Association, 1200 Seventeenth Street, N.W.; Washington, D.C. 20036, publishes a national directory in which you may look up the background and training of individual psychologists.

The third type of professional is a psychiatrist. He or she is usually a college graduate in biological science and has then gone on to complete four years of medical school, one year of internship, and three or four years of residency in psychiatry in a hospital or similar institution. Thereafter, two or more years in practice and successful completion of written and oral examinations are required for him or her to be certified in this specialty. Although, again, almost anyone can call himself a psychoanalyst, the term is more properly reserved to a psychiatrist trained as above who has gone on from this point to take training in traditional Freudian concepts, undergoing analysis while doing so. Although psychiatrists are by far the most competent and can prescribe medications when indicated, there are two disadvantages in seeking help from them of which you should be aware: They have been trained to treat the mentally ill and to deal with individuals, not couples. There are published guides available listing psychiatrists, but because of the nature of their in-depth interpersonal therapy, the best source of referral is your own physician.

The best is yet to be: family therapists. Some professionals with the above backgrounds have both interest and experience in the relationship between relatively normal individuals in the marital situation and are comfortable in dealing with both husband and wife simultaneously—even with children. Some use a team approach, with a male and female therapist working together, which has immense advantages in marital counseling. But family therapists are still in woefully short supply, so this still must be considered the wave of the future in most areas.

When we have given it all we have, and even the best preventive or remedial therapy has failed, the fearsome spectre of divorce seems to offer the only way out. Let's take a look at the origins of the negative views attached to divorce. They can be grouped best as *historical* and *actual*. The former should be gotten out of the way first so we can come to grips with the latter, which really matter.

We have already touched upon the historical origins when we discussed the evolution of marriage itself. As we saw, marriage originated to protect private property and to ensure patrilineal inheritance. During the Talmudic time of Hebrew history, divorce first came to be condemned and this was reinforced in the early Christian era with stress upon the statement of Jesus in the Gospel of Matthew: "What therefore God hath joined together, let no man put asunder." The Council of Carthage in 407 A.D. crystallized the doctrine of the indissolubility of marriage, and in 1154 A.D. the Council of Trent proclaimed marriage to be a sacrament, with separation possible only on the grounds of adultery, apostasy, or cruelty. Annulment was similarly restricted.

During the Renaissance and the Reformation, many medieval customs relating to divorce persisted. The Protestants, with their insistence on obedience to the word of God as revealed in the Bible, used Matthew as their basis. English law gradually incorporated this divorce doctrine. The early Protestant colonists brought with them to the New World both the religious and legal sanctions of the Old World. The value of women as property and their function in ensuring survival of the family enhanced these customs here. Children were economic assets, too, and society sought to protect them for this reason, as well as for more humanitarian ones. Thus social mores were added to the religious and legal factors to become a third factor mitigating against divorce. Literature, and later the media, reinforced these mores, dwelling on the disaster of divorce. One rarely reads stories, for example, of healthy people of strong character who have the courage to dissolve an unsatisfactory relationship, cope with the stress, and emerge from the situation happier and able to do a better job with their children and with themselves. In our time, sociologists have been more concerned with poverty, racism, and other problems than with the prospect of divorce and what happens to those who divorce. Nor are long and successful marriages the stuff of which many sentimental stories or sociological studies made. As usual, the education establishment accepted without question the views of the sociologists and those of psychoanalysts who consider those who divorce to be hopeless neurotics and in need of prolonged psychoanalysis. Paradoxically, the latter with their reliance upon the medical model, may have contributed to the casualty rate of marriages. The therapy of one "sick" partner inevitably tends to exclude the other.

These are the historical origins of our negative views on divorce. You can see that they are no longer relevant nor valid reasons to preserve marriage at all costs, to make divorce legally and socially so difficult as to be prohibitive. Instead, in our history, marriage should have been seen simply as one possibility in the search for a fulfilling life. Stop and think about this for a moment. If divorce had evolved to become simpler and easier, *it would not have affected happy marriages at all*. But unhappy marriages would have been dissolved with much less scarring and agony. And with remarriage, the total number of happy marriages could only have been increased. Somehow we took a wrong turn in our history.

What are the *actual* reasons for the prevailing and persistent negative view of divorce in our culture? They pivot around three points: the effect upon your own happiness, that upon the one with whom you have shared your life, and that upon the children born of the relationship.

This last is by far the most important. The well-being of children can be affected in many ways by divorce and, it is true, often adversely. But we should bear in mind that most of the dismal data presented to us has been the result of research done on children in mental health clinics during the first few years after divorce. Until recently, the long-term effects of a divorce upon children and, conversely, the effects upon them of a continued, but bad, marriage, have received little attention. And those children who coped well after divorce were almost entirely ignored. Recent studies have shown that most children are actually relieved when the prolonged conflict has come to an end. Surprisingly, they also show that once the initial trauma has passed, children after a divorce are actually no worse off than those from intact families—rather, it is the *quality of the marriage* that determines their happiness. The emotional divorce is far more important to them than the legal divorce.

When a divorce occurs, children between the ages of two and four may tend to feel they have caused the divorce—that *they* have been bad. The same is true for those between six and eight, but they also fear loss of love and even abandonment. The effects of divorce are usually more severe at this age than any other. Later, between nine and twelve, children have begun to develop a capacity for coping, but it is still immature; anger is added to their fears. This anger is directed at whichever parent they believe is responsible, although they have no way of understanding the situation. Teen-agers have lost the infant's feelings of blame but retain much of the other immature reactions through most of the teen years. The fears fade in the later teen years, and anger tends to dominate thereafter. They also encounter the "loyalty dilemma" between the two parents, more than younger children, which frequently leads to cruel rejection of the parent no longer in the home. All of these reactions at any age are lessened if the children are properly told about the divorce and reassured that the parents are not divorcing *them*, that they are still loved by both and will be cared for. If parents continue to parent well, disturbance to their children can be minimal. Sometimes a couple that fails in marriage can do far better at divorce—and with their children.

The first two factors I mentioned, your happiness and that of your spouse, can be considered together. It is my experience that once the adjustments to the divorce have been made, both become far happier people. They begin to find themselves once again in their uniqueness as individuals; thereafter they grow emotionally, are warmer, relate better to others, find sources of strength within themselves of which they were unaware previously, become more involved with careers, and in many cases, even more involved with their children than before the divorce. And I have found, too, that the reasons people have for divorce are almost always sounder than those they had for marriage in the first place. Those who divorce, are, in truth, those who have not had good marriages. But they are also those who would not settle for a bad one.

Thus the actual reasons divorce is feared are not enough to remain in a miserable marriage. In *Gift from the Sea*, Anne Morrow Lindbergh wrote words in another context that also apply here, "Parting is inevitably painful. It is like an amputation. A limb is being torn off, without which I shall be unable to function. And yet, once it is done, I find there is a quality to being alone that is incredibly precious. Life rushes back into the void, richer, more

vivid, fuller than before. It is as if in parting one actually did lose
an arm. And then, like the starfish, one grows it anew; one is
whole again, complete and round—more whole, even, than
before, when the other people had pieces of one."

A marriage that ends with divorce in middle age can never be
counted as a total failure. Looking back over the years, one sees
there were many good ones; usually, only the recent few were
bad. The divorced person has learned a great deal and knows
many more of the pitfalls and problems in relationships and
knows better how to avoid them in future ones.

Actually, for the mature person, the perils and problems of
divorce are fewer and less complicated than they are for a younger
person. Mature people have more resources in many ways. There
may be fewer disagreements over possessions, simply because
there are more of them and the couple no longer needs the big
house that was purchased for a growing family now that the
children are on their own. It's often best to sell it at this time
anyway. The children themselves are better equipped to handle
the divorce of their parents now, too, than they were when they
were younger. Each partner has a better understanding of himself
and herself, and of their emotions, than was possible earlier in
life. Each may be—and should be—searching for himself or
herself at midlife, and that search may best be made unencum-
bered by a bad marriage. And for the woman, the educational and
occupational opportunities she has now are greater than they ever
have been in our history.

It is because of the divorce procedure itself that most of the
trauma occurs to the two involved. Fortunately, divorce proceedings are currently coming under greater scrutiny and change.
Centuries ago, legislatures enacted statutes giving the courts
jurisdiction to dissolve marriages largely on the ecclesiastical
grounds I mentioned. The unfortunate result of this has been that
the proceedings were then cast in the mold of the classic legal
battle between two adversaries. Inherent in this model is the
plaintiff's attempt to prove the defendant at fault in order to
recover damages. The outcome is that one party must be proven
"guilty" and the other "innocent." As adversaries, each party is
set up to get "his" or "hers," and the attorneys to get theirs. There
is little consideration of what would be fair or just. The difficulties between the two are thereby enhanced enormously.

Oddly enough, the state, which once was only a keeper of

records at the marriage, now enters fully into the divorce proceedings. The decision to marry is a personal one, but that right is revoked when the decision to "unmarry" is made. Obviously, courts and legislatures can legislate neither love nor happiness, yet they become intimately involved in the divorce procedure. Ideally, the divorce should be left to the individuals themselves, with nonjudicial arbitration where necessary. There are legal grounds by which this could be brought about—in the right of privacy and the right of association. Legislators could easily enact laws giving the right to divorce to the individuals, but they have not done so. In the last analysis, how can a court decide which one of the parties is at fault? Is there ever only one to blame when a marriage fails? Laws and courts may have a role in establishing the framework of arbitration to settle property disputes, child custody, or child support, but they should not enter into the dissolution otherwise. This should be the domain of the two people involved. If any attorneys are involved, *they should represent the children*.

Some small steps have already been taken. "Do-it-yourself" divorce kits are now available from several sources. This can be a satisfactory solution if there are no serious disputes. On November 23, 1970, the California legislature passed a law (California Civil Code 4101) which made possible the first truly no-fault divorce. In this act, the word *divorce* itself was eliminated and replaced by *dissolution*. Almost every state has adopted some form of the no-fault concept in its divorce laws by now. Only Illinois, Pennsylvania, and South Dakota have rejected such legislation. But even in some of the states that have adopted the no-fault concept, the idea of someone being to blame when divorce is at hand persists. For example, some states legally equate simple incompatibility with cruelty.

It will be a long time before judicial proceedings are removed from the divorce process. Because lawyers profit and most legislators are themselves lawyers, significant reform finds resistance with them. In the meantime, it seems that the system by which we form and dissolve marriages can make sense only if the two processes are in some way made legally consistent with each other, with terms specified and all possible eventualities foreseen and provided for as in any contract. Having a contract from the start would require an attorney, but the trauma presently caused at the time of divorce by attorneys would be greatly reduced.

Although an attorney would be necessary in preparing such a contract, the roles of attorneys and courts would be greatly reduced at the time of divorce.

Alimony is another anachronism that needs revision, a revision that is all too slow in coming. The word itself derives form the Latin *alimonia*, which means sustenance. It is a relic from the Middle Ages, when a husband owned all family property, *including his wife*, and when women were rarely, if ever, employed. At that time, the ecclesiastical courts granted *alimonia* with a legal separation, and it was appropriate then—especially considering that upon marriage, the husband assumed full possession of all the property that was the wife's prior to marriage and that it remained with him after the ecclesiastical separation! A wife's only protection then was *alimonia*. Now wives can keep the property that was theirs when they married. They are usually awarded much of what was the husband's as well, because during marriage it is almost impossible for the husband, the principal wage earner, to keep his income separate from the financial resources he had when he entered the marriage. In theory, the setting of the alimony is supposed to consider the wife's assets and earning ability, but in practice this is rarely done. Most states do have modification statutes, but almost all modifications are upward. The strange reasoning behind this is that what was fair at divorce when all facts were present and under consideration is somehow not fair a few years later when they both have gone their separate ways. The wives thus share their husband's good and bad fortunes during marriage but only their good ones thereafter! If he is unable to work, he is usually required to liquidate assets he had *prior* to marriage to continue to pay alimony. Often his payments are set so high that they prevent him from marrying again. The wife, however, is taken care of financially either way, whether she marries or not. Little wonder that a large proportion of divorced men fail or flee such a system.

The custom of alimony encourages the wife to have live-in lovers rather than marry, with a deleterious effect upon the children. She is also discouraged from continuing her own education or pursuing a career, because her payments might be lowered. Alimony also encourages her to emphasize her motherhood role, which is disappearing at middle age, when she should be seeking to express herself in other ways.

The reasons for alimony that are valid today come down to

two: A woman is less employable a number of years after her education than she was before, and there are no retirement rights in marriage. Therefore, alimony should be considered as *rehabilitative*. Archaic ecclesiastical and punitive aspects should be dispensed with. Divorce insurance taken out at the time of marriage is one way in which the acrimony of alimony could be lessened. If not needed, the insurance could be converted into an educational fund for the children or into a fund for the couple's retirement.

The present tradition of awarding custody of the children to the woman is another that is all too slow to change. Grant for a moment that the man has been a bad husband—is he therefore necessarily a bad parent? He may in fact be a better parent than his former wife. Where is the justification for depriving him of his children? Even if the divorced wife avoids "poisoning" the children against her former husband—and few do—her continued close association with the children often causes them to develop some of the same traits that he may have left her for. Her bitterness after the divorce all too often unconsciously promotes patterning of the children contrary to the former husband's beliefs and values. And, although his *obligations* are clearly spelled out in the divorce document, his *rights* rarely are. For example, even though the father is allowed rights of visitation, his former wife has all too many ways to frustrate them or use them as a weapon, and he has little legal recourse. Most important is that *there is no legal provision whatever for his decisions regarding his own children*. Much more could be said, but enough already has been to suggest that the new concept of joint custody can be the only just one for the future. The children do belong to both parents and no court should take them away from either one unless it would be in the best interests of the children to do so. Four states—California, Oregon, Iowa, and Wisconsin—now have joint custody laws, and joint custody can be requested in all other states.

Let's go on to consider briefly what happens to the two who divorce at midlife. This has been researched by many investigators. Much more has been written about what happens to women than to men after divorce, and perhaps rightly so. In many ways, the woman loses far more, especially if she has had no career besides that of being a housewife and mother. She finds her social life is changed drastically. Once it was organized around other couples; now she finds herself excluded more and more by them. She is often reluctant to extend herself socially, and in our society it is usually more difficult to do so. As a consequence, she finds herself more frequently in the company of other women. She has to bear the strains of her children's adolescence more directly than her former husband does, and more of the care of her aging parents usually falls to her than that of his parents to him. And we have mentioned that the difficulties of adapting to the single world are usually more difficult for her than for him. She is still bound to home and all of its practical problems, but without the support, assistance, and comfort of her husband, which made those burdens lighter before.

She can help herself first by taking renewed interest in her appearance, allowing herself new clothes, exercise, makeup, and whatever other indulgences may make her feel more relaxed, buoyant, invigorated, and self-confident. As quickly as she can, she must try to find ways to form new interests and find a career, for all too often recently divorced women live off just two things: alimony and bitterness. Above all, she must cast off the feeling that she alone has failed—or that her former husband was entirely to blame. *Two* made the marriage what it was. *Two* made it fail. What blame there is should be shouldered and shared by both. She must face her loneliness as *aloneness*, with an eye to its unique value. She cannot prevent pain, but she can reduce its duration and intensity. And at the worst times, she can ask herself if she misses the reality of her married life or the fantasy of what it might have been.

Her former husband will be suffering his own burdens, too. Instead of coming home to comfort and routine, he may find himself living with other transients in hotel rooms or lonely apartments. He will miss a great deal of what he liked about his marriage, especially seeing his children in the evenings and on weekends. He may even encounter subtle ostracism at work. He will almost certainly be discontented at first with the means of finding feminine companionship; the early relationships he develops will probably seem shallow and cheapening. And his financial loss is severe. He is often left with less than half his after-tax income.

There are many resources available to help both partners when a marriage ends. Read some of the references given in the

Bibliography. Browse in your local library. The counselors already mentioned can help in their ways, as can ministers, rabbis, and priests.

When you are ready to socialize, the best rule to follow in meeting someone of the opposite sex who could be a potential partner is to pursue your own interests. A woman, especially, must go beyond children, church, and charities. Go to concerts, plays, museums, and art galleries. Linger there. Join ski or soaring clubs. Reawaken your literary interests and join an organization with tastes that parallel yours. Attend wine-tastings or gourmet dinners. Become active politically; pursue some cause you believe in—join the Sierra Club or another ecology group. Take up an art class or an extension course in geology, astronomy, or psychology. Travel. Take that tramp steamer or the long-deferred visit to your dreamed-of resort. The list is endless.

Two cautions in this. You must first decide that you are really ready to meet someone. Then your appearance and manner will reveal your decision. There is no purpose making yourself available when you send signals that you are not. Secondly, whatever you do must be done for its own value *because you enjoy it*. Meeting someone must always be a secondary consideration.

As to singles clubs, caution again. Select the ones that will be compatible in age, socioeconomic stratum, and the type of persons there. Put on your best appearance, project confidence if you can, and try to enjoy both the activity that is planned as well as the competition that is inevitable. Learn to cope with rejection. The most widely known such group, Parents Without Partners, was started in 1957 and now has over 100,000 members in nearly a thousand local chapters. Check your telephone book or write: Parents Without Partners, Inc., 7910 Woodmont Avenue, Washington, D.C. 20014. Ask for their monthly magazine, *The Single Parent*. Another more exclusive social singles group that has branches in most major cities is Who's Who International. Write to 4337 Marina City Drive, Marina Del Rey, California 90291, for information. Divorced Anonymous is another one. There are many such singles organizations, and one or more are certain to be in your area and acceptable to you.

Beyond the books I have listed in the Bibliography, you may be interested in a divorce survival kit available from NOW's New York Chapter, 47 East 19th Street, New York, New York 10003. Excellent pamphlets can also be obtained from the Public Affairs

Committee, Inc., 381 Park Avenue South, New York, New York 10016. Ask your physician for other sources of information and assistance available in your community.

Divorce is the end of one life, true. It is also the start of a new one.

Statistics show that remarriage is in the cards for about three-quarters of divorced men and two-thirds of divorced women, regardless of age. But a man at forty might have two or more chances in his life to form a happy, intimate relationship. A woman of that age may not have more than one. Although statistics do not tell you how your own life will go in regard to remarriage after divorce, it is true that they are disheartening for middle-aged women. A divorced woman who is forty years old has less than a 3 percent chance of remarrying within a year and about a 20 percent chance of ever remarrying. A fifty-year-old divorced woman has less than 1 percent chance of remarrying within a year and a 6 percent chance of remarrying later in her life. But these statistics are not really as grim as they appear to be. Many prefer to remain single after their adjustment. If you want to remarry, the statistics should spur you to make more effort than those surveyed did.

It is a truism that previously acquired children cause most of the problems in second marriages. The new partners themselves seem to have learned by experience and do far better than they did in their first ones. Dr. Paul Glick, chief of the Population Division of the Census Bureau, said, "Those who remarry are much more likely to remain in their second marriage than persons married only once are to remain in their first." Look at it this way: If you were divorced, you belong to a group of which 100 percent of marriages ended in divorce. Yet in second marriages, nearly three-fourths of the marriages last for life and seem to be satisfactory. That's quite a shift in odds. They're just one more example of the value of looking to the future's possibilities rather than to the pains of the past.

WIDOW OR WIDOWER

Few of us who are married ever stop to think about the possible death of our mate or the time thereafter when we must go on alone. Wives especially must give this some thought now, because ahead of them lies an average of ten to twelve years of widowhood. The gap between the life expectancies of men and women widens throughout the middle years. Male mortality is more than twice that of females during this time. The disparity is not dramatic when both are in their early forties, but by the decade between forty-five and fifty-four, 1 percent of males are widowers and 8.2 percent of females are widows. And, again according to the latest census figures, in the decade of late middle age, between fifty-five and sixty-four, the percentages are 3.5 and 20.6, respectively. Look at that figure again. *More than one-fifth of all American women in late middle age are widows.* So most of what follows will be for them. Women since childhood have often thought of themselves as brides, wives, and mothers in the marital setting, but rarely if ever as widows. Now, in middle age, you must.

There are four suggestions I wish you would take in order to prepare yourself for the possibility of widowhood.

The first sounds almost philosophical, but is fundamental. You have to *think through your own attitude towards death.* Death is the natural end to life and should be accepted as such. It cannot be avoided—nor can consideration of it, if we are to face it well. As Rabindranath Tagore said, "Death belongs to life as birth does." Somehow we have become separated in our society from the *idea* of death and even from the *fact*, the reality, of it. We try to keep thoughts of it away from us and arrange for the event itself to occur at a distance—in a hospital or some other institution. When you've begun to work this out in your own mind and have accepted it as natural, as the last phase of life that we all must pass through, then find a time when you can share your thoughts with your husband. Learn his thoughts, too. Your talk will quite easily turn to the reality that death some day will separate you from each other.

The second step requires more effort. Several times in this book I have stressed how important it is for you, the woman in middle age, to *develop your own potentials and interests.* If you have not done so already, now is the time to begin or resume a career, to join a club that really means something to you, to become an influence in the community, a good friend, an art lover or collector, or a worker for a favorite political group—whatever you wish. You *must* become something besides a wife and mother *now.* Otherwise, when your husband dies and your children have left, what will you be? A nonwife and a nonmother. And what is that?

The third step is to *work on developing your practical skills around the home.* If you've never taken part in home maintenance of the traditionally masculine sort, begin by hanging a picture, trimming a hedge, changing a fuse, or unplugging the toilet. Your husband will usually be glad to help you in this, if not, there are all sorts of manuals and classes to guide you.

The last step may be the most important: *Understand your financial situation.* Begin now to manage money on your own. Set up your own bank account and handle your own investments. Make sure you and your husband both have wills, that you know their provisions, and that they are kept up to date. One comment on wills: Originally they were intended to provide for children when they *were* children. Now they will be adults when we die. Or they were to provide for spouses who could not provide for themselves. Now, in many cases, they can. Or a will provided for aged parents, for whom society has now largely taken over. You should discard these preconceptions when you prepare your will. In your own old age, additional financial resources can make all the difference. Don't cling to them just to pass them on at your death.

Make a list of all your present assets and another of your liabilities. Keep these lists current. Check all insurance policies carefully. Adjust them if necessary. Make sure from this point on that the premiums are paid on time. Look into both of your retirement plans, and note especially if either spouse is entitled to benefits if the other dies. Contact your local Social Security office now and periodically for pertinent information. There are probably provisions at the present time of which you're unaware, and they are changed frequently. Locate all bank books and keep them in a safe place. Find out where the safe deposit box is, and become a coholder if you are not already. Know where the key is kept. Review the contents with your husband, and discuss the securities, real estate deeds, and anything else that is kept there. Keep enough money in your own bank account to handle expenses for at least a month or two in the event of his death, because in most states all liquid assets, even joint bank accounts, are frozen until the will is probated. And Social Security benefits for widows are almost always delayed for four to six months.

You might even prepare your own "survival kit," containing

birth certificates, marriage license, Social Security number and information, military discharge, deeds, title to automobiles, insurance policy numbers and other pertinent information, pension provisions, deposit box contents and account numbers, and a complete list of assets and liabilities. Add whatever you wish, but keep it up to date.

Then you are ready to consult financial experts directly. Go with your husband or by yourself to see your stock broker, the investment advisor at your bank, your attorney, insurance broker, and anyone else who plays a significant role in your finances. Lynn Caine, in *Widow*, suggests a "contingency day" every year for a complete review of all financial matters with your husband. This review is a good opportunity to start including your children. Beyond finances, it is also an opportunity for you and your husband to share your thoughts with them to help them learn gradually and naturally about the realities death brings. One subtle result of such sessions is what psychologists call anticipatory grieving—both you and your children come to face the prospect of the death of your husband and, without realizing it, make many inner adjustments a little at a time. When he dies, the shock is then not as great as it would have been otherwise.

In any discussion of death, the stage theory of dying must be mentioned, if only to dismiss it. Many look to it as a known and well-established structure from which they hope to derive guidance and comfort at a terribly trying time. In 1965, Elisabeth Kubler-Ross, a psychiatrist, began interviewing terminally ill patients in Billings Hospital in Chicago. In 1969 she published *On Death and Dying*, in which she held that five stages occur in those who are dying: denial, anger, bargaining, depression, and acceptance, in that order. This stage theory was then widely publicized in the lay press and accepted by many who have no experience with the dying. However, in reaching her conclusions, she disregarded all the variables that enter into the process, such as age, sex, personality structure, and even resources of the dying person such as religion or personal philosophy. She also ignored the nature of the disease and the effects this would have upon her stages, as well as the degree and kind of pain that may be involved. The environment in which death takes place was not considered, although this has been shown to be a significant factor in how one reacts to his impending death. Nor did she consider the contributions of those who are close to the dying person, either as friends, relatives, spouses, or professionals providing care. Most important is her disregard for the duration of the dying process. She did not even attempt to standardize the interviews so that any reasonable conclusions could be drawn.

I know of no clinician who has extensive experience with dying patients who subscribes to her stage theory. I myself have treated many more dying patients than Kubler-Ross interviewed, and I have yet to have a single one go through the five stages she describes. If she had called them *emotional states* that those who are dying *frequently experience in various sequences*, her research would have had some value. As a matter of fact, if I were a stage theorist, I could add several more "stages" to her list: fear, resentment, reassessment of life, self-pity, concern for others, and so on. But I would certainly not attempt to place them in rigid order nor claim that all those who are dying must pass through all. An excellent recent review of all the literature on dying by Richard Schultz and David Alderman found no evidence of any such "stages" in dying. E. Mansell Pattison, professor of psychiatry and editor of *The Experience of Dying*, concludes, "There is really no clinical evidence to support the concept of a series of emotional stages. . . ."

If the so-called "stages" of dying are of no use to you with your husband lying in the hospital gravely ill, what do you do? Here are a few suggestions:

• *Candor.* I have yet to find a person who is dying who did not know it, whether told or not. Be truthful and face the issue with him.

• *Contact.* Almost all those close to death hunger for the touch of those they love. Yet you may, without being aware of it, withdraw because down deep you fear the death the dying person symbolizes for you. He is still the one you love—reach out, touch, caress, and hug him.

• *Communication.* A dying person wants—needs—to talk about his impending death with someone who cares. Be honest about your own fears of death, but do not burden him with them. Rather help him with his. Listen. You may be surprised to learn that more of his concern is for you and your children than for himself.

• *Compassion.* Ensure that all that can be done *is* done to relieve his pain and anxiety. Physicians are trained to cure and, when that is impossible, may be remiss in the little things that matter.

They and other professionals may need reminders from time to time. Let your husband know that you yourself care. Do not be content with words—your presence, your manner, and what you do are far more important.

- *Continuity*. Tactfully let him know what is going on in the world outside with the ones he loves. Those who are dying know that they cannot take part, but frequently resent being closed off from all outside events. There is no purpose pretending that you and others have ceased to live because he is doing so. Reassure him of your resources, that you and yours can carry on when he is gone.

- *Completion*. As his life draws to a close, it is comforting to review what he has accomplished and the worthwhile things he leaves behind because he has lived. This is a time when his values or his religion can come in. And herein lies hope for a hereafter with many.

As for yourself, review and muster your own inner strengths. Come together with your children for comfort. Rely upon your friends and physician at this time. Lean, too, on your minister, priest, or rabbi. They will be there for you.

When you make arrangements for a funeral, respect both his wishes and those of the ones who remain. Accept the ritual. Since the dawn of man, a ceremony has been found to be comforting to those who live on, and it serves as a coda-like close to the dead person's life. Elements of the Irish wake and Jewish sitting *shiva* may be incorporated before or after the ceremony. An amazing amount of healing can occur when friends and relatives gather together, work their way through sorrow, and reminisce about the life of the deceased. Reality is faced and accepted, and even humor may enter in to help assuage the grief.

Always ask a good friend to come with you when you go to arrange for the funeral. At least one of you might read *Funerals: A Consumer's Last Rights*. You may be told that embalming is necessary, but in most states it is mandatory only if death was due to a contagious disease, if the body must be kept for several days before burial, or must be transported by common carrier. With immediate cremation there is no need for either embalming or a casket, no matter what you are told. A simple cremation costs as little as $300, but the usual funeral and burial expenses advocated by most funeral directors can total $3,000 or more. In 1976, the

Federal Trade Commission held public hearings on the practices of funeral homes, and stricter regulation of funeral practices would have followed except for effective lobbying. One excellent solution is to join a memorial society ahead of time. They offer the simplest and least expensive arrangements and are usually sponsored by a church or other nonprofit organization. A list of these can be obtained from the Continental Association of Funeral and Memorial Societies, 1828 L Street, N.W., Washington, D.C. 20036.

After your husband's death, you will probably pass through several emotions. But we still don't know much about them, because psychologists have concerned themselves with the bereaved only in the last few years. Again, as with the emotions the dying person experiences, there are no "stages." Nor do they necessarily occur in any particular order.

Shock is the most frequently felt, and usually is first. It prevents you for a time from realizing that a real and disastrous event has occurred. While experiencing this, you may feel somewhat detached and even be more capable than usual in dealing with details. Reality is prevented from intruding for a while. Allow the shock to pass of its own accord. It will.

Realization occurs sooner or later. Friends crowded around to comfort you while you were in shock, and you probably were not able to appreciate their comfort then. But now the pain penetrates, and they are no longer there. You may be restless, purposeless, and less efficient at this time.

Anger almost always occurs at some point, yet it is almost as frequently repressed. It is only natural to feel resentment because you have been left in this situation, and that resentment may easily burgeon into anger. It is similar to the feeling a divorced person often feels toward the former mate. But in that case, the person at least has someone else toward whom to direct this anger. Do not hold it in or be ashamed of it.

Guilt may arise when you have time to consider the past and whether you did everything you could have done. It shouldn't trouble you too much if you remember that you are a human being, fallible as all of us are, and probably did all that could have been expected of you. But you may feel guilty for being angry, and this guilt is harder to contend with. You must go back to your anger, get in touch with it—cry or scream, but somehow let it out. Express it to a friend, religious counselor, or psychotherapist. Or try to pretend your husband is there—talk to him and tell him about it.

Fear is another common reaction and often a well-founded one. It can also fuel your anger if you haven't been well provided for. Assay your resources and opportunities. Make lists if this helps. Fear usually fades substantially when faced with these.

Grief, of course, is common to all. Face your feelings, let yourself have them. The worse you allow yourself to feel, the sooner you will feel better.

You may experience other emotions besides these. Try to avoid denying or repressing any of them. They must be worked through as soon as you are able to; otherwise they will emerge later in some more damaging way. Those who fail to deal directly with these emotions have a greater incidence of illness, accidents, and even suicide during the six months to a year following the death of a spouse.

When your emotions permit, it may help to analyze your loss logically. You might try breaking it down into its parts. You've lost financial support, true. But if you and your husband have worked out financial matters beforehand in ways similar to those I've described above, this is not usually an insurmountable problem. You miss your spouse as a companion, as a person who shared much with you and comforted you. Others can partially serve as substitutes in this regard. Parents, children, friends, and associates can all help. You miss your husband sexually. But wait a while before looking for another relationship. You will know when the time is right. Continue this way, considering each of the elements you have lost and what you can do about each one.

When you begin to recover, be good to yourself in ways only you know. Start to build your new independent identity. Get involved with persons and activities that interest you. Remember not to make any major decisions about finances, moving, or anything else for a year or so. And when you feel you are ready to begin a relationship with another man, look back to the discussion on divorce for clues on how to start.

Although the scar may never vanish, the wound will heal. The first year is the hardest. After that, most widows make a satisfactory adjustment to their loss. Treasure your memories, but as soon as you can, set about making new ones.

7

Labor and Leisure

Blessed is he who has found his work.

CARLYLE

Far too frequently, modern man is both bored in his work and restless in his play when he reaches the summer of his years. You have heard the phrase "too busy making a living to live." But "making a living," for most Americans, is much more than supplying the necessities of life. We work for reasons that are beyond these and rarely wonder why. Only a few of us can claim that our work fulfills personal or philosophical ideals. Generally, we work for less worthy but no less compelling goals: wealth, status, and power.

These three are at once separate and inseparable. Wealth procures the things we must have to survive and also luxuries as far in excess of those needs as we can afford or care to have. But we sometimes obtain a sort of status with wealth, and power, too. Status, by itself, is a fragile thing. *Sic transit gloria mundi* has sounded in our ears for centuries. The status of a judge is usually high in relation to his income; that of a lawyer low, even if he makes a great deal of money. A powerful political demagogue is admired by some, and a quiet poet by others. A scientist acquires his status—but little wealth—through the number and value of his contributions to human knowledge, while a rock musician acquires both his status and wealth by the number of records he sells, regardless of their quality. A tobacco-chewing baseball player is often more famous than a Nobel laureate in our country. And the desire for power, whether we admit it or not, motivates many of us. With it often comes wealth—status too, in certain circles. This drive for power remains as an atavistic persistence of aggressive instincts that once were essential for the survival of primitive man. We no longer live in such a world, unless we make it so.

These few thoughts on wealth, status, and power are offered with the hope they will cause you to pause and evaluate your motives and methods, your satisfactions and dissatisfactions in your occupation. The middle years too often are disgruntled ones for us at work, whether we have attained our goals or failed to. This chapter will take a long look at this, then try to find out how we got here and how we can get out.

The solution lies in understanding the evolution of work— more importantly, of the work *ethic*—in our country. But first we have to look a little farther back in history at both.

THE WORK ETHIC

The ancient Greeks did not even have a word for work. In fact, they had a word for leisure, *skole*, but their closest word for work actually meant "unleisure." Their beliefs conformed to their vocabulary. One should be "unleisurely" only for the sake of leisure. And this idea—that work was done only to make it possible to live a worthwhile life—continued into the early days of Christianity. Augustine modified this somewhat with his injunction that leisure was to be used, not for its own sake, but for the contemplation of the divine. Aquinas modified it still further. He believed we must work to have the time and physical security needed to worship God, such worship being the highest human activity possible.

Nor were work or the work ethic as we understand them widely present through the Middle ages. Then life was agrarian and rural for the most part, and though a difficult, ceaseless struggle, it was satisfying in a tangible way—one could see the direct connection between daily toil and survival. Plowing a field in the cold spring months meant one could eat the following winter. Even as serfs began to move into towns, work could still be seen as connected with daily survival. All the urban trades, secular or religious—butcher, blacksmith, carpenter, weaver, welder, wood-carver, builder and decorator of the great cathedrals—allowed man to see and feel pride in his accomplishments. And holidays, centered around the agricultural calendar, afforded ample free time for leisurely pursuits.

The work ethic that we later inherited is found first in the monasteries of the twelfth century. Medieval Christians were then beginning to realize that Christ's second coming was not imminent, so work itself became a form of self-purification, helping to create a certain kind of millenium here on earth. However, this ethic remained confined within monastery walls for most of the next five centuries.

In the fifteenth century, some Renaissance men turned to the arts for their life work. Transforming the world with the images of art, they were bringing to it products having nothing to do with physical survival. They were concerned rather with the satisfaction of spiritual and aesthetic longings.

Then, during the seventeenth century, with the Reformation, leisure lost both value and stature. The Protestant movement adopted the work ethic of the medieval monasteries. Even Sunday, the traditional day of rest, became a day to *work* at worship. The Protestant attitude toward leisure was harshly disapproving: leisure was slothful, and sloth was a sin. An ascetic life of hard work was for them the only right or moral way of life. Whereas man had only worked to live before the Reformation, now he worked in order to earn the *right* to live.

Long before the Pilgrims landed in America, Calvin and then Knox had set the Puritans apart even from other Protestants in terms of their ethical philosophy. Puritans had only two major tasks in life: One was to follow and obey God; the second was to choose a calling and pursue it diligently. In America, Cotton Mather and others of the cloth continued to emphasize this belief, urging hard work, thrift, frugality, sobriety, honesty, and stressing the quality of the product of one's endeavor. Not only was success thus clearly defined, but its pursuit was reinforced by divine sanction. This emphasis on hard work and the loss of leisure denied a place to art and the crafts in the New World. The aesthetic did not thrive among ascetics. American Puritans were hostile to anything that seemed extravagant and sensual. These qualities reeked of the ceremonies of the Church of England, the church they had rebelled against and left behind.

In our country, the first settlers had a hard time keeping the Indian from the window and the wolf from the door. Neither the climate nor the soil was friendly. Labor was necessary to survive; leisure was not. The Puritan work ethic prevailed. Those who risked a life in this new country had to be adventurous, and after their arrival a continuous process of selection went on in which the industrious succeeded and the indolent did not. The settlers here had left behind the burden of a class structure, and over the next century they and their descendants were free for the first time, not only to move horizontally across the country, but vertically in a new social system as well. And they were blessed with virtually unlimited resources, although the treacherous winters of the wilderness harboring these resources were challenges for the American Adam.

Even those who chose not to follow the work ethic of the religious leaders espoused the same code, giving it a secular basis. This secularization of the Puritan work ethic was actually the beginning of our modern dilemma. One of Benjamin Franklin's maxims was "Early to bed, early to rise, makes a man healthy, wealthy, and wise." Healthy, *wealthy*, and wise. The original Puritan work ethic did not embrace wealth, but despised it as worldly and sinful.

Inherent in the ethic itself was a duality that posed a dilemma not easily solved. If one diligently pursued material success he would produce wealth, which in turn might tend to provoke sloth, pride, ostentation, and other traits not in keeping with Puritan tenets. This dichotomy was patched over for a time with the admonition that once wealth was acquired it was the individual's duty to tithe and to give generously to charity. More briefly put, do good for yourself so that you may do good for others.

Pursuit of wealth was the first change in the work ethic in our young nation. It was further fueled by a desire to show Europe that in America it was possible to go from rags to riches and from riches to respectability. The first settlers were demonstrating to the aristocrats of Europe that the lower and middle classes were not inferior nor somehow defective.

By the nineteenth century, the Puritan philosophy had accustomed Americans to working hard and resting little. When the Industrial Revolution reached these shores, man was taken away from his life in the fields and matched to machines. Later, many were assigned cubicles in corporations. The effect was the same. Men lost the independence they once had when they labored on the land. Instead of a finished product that he could see, feel pride in, or that would feed and clothe him, the only tangible result of a person's labor was a pay envelope. So, by the end of the century, meaninglessness and monotony had begun to creep into work. Women's work in the home began to be denigrated because it didn't even produce a pay envelope. The major impact of industrialization was upon the conditions of work itself, not upon the ethic, which continued with its one modification, the more open pursuit of wealth for its own sake.

By this time, religious influence had begun to wane, at least in urban areas. One effect of this fading of the faith was an increasing tolerance for enormous fortunes and for whatever methods, fair or foul, by which they were acquired. Other influences in the latter half of the nineteenth century further encouraged the pursuit of wealth. One was the ever-widening impact of Adam Smith's *The Wealth of Nations*, written in 1776, with its thesis that man should take raw material and convert it to something useful and thus produce wealth. The novels of Horatio Alger had their influence as well, as did the advent of social Darwinism as an acceptable philosophy. John D. Rockefeller, Jr., was heard to use the phrase "survival of the fittest" on more than one occasion, and Andrew Carnegie expounded this philosophy in his *Gospel of Wealth* published in 1889. The accumulation of immense fortunes brought with them the accumulation of great power. And, after a generation or so, when the memory of the Robber Barons' methods began to fade, status followed power and wealth. For the first time, these three were held out as goals for all. Thus a drastically altered ethic, with only its roots in the Puritan principle of hard work, began to spread across the land and down into every class.

Around 1900, some opposing tendencies were developing. Populism was born among agrarians, muckrakers began attacking the trusts, and unionism was rising to correct the abuses of some large corporations and what David Ricardo called the "iron law of wages." The thoughts of Karl Marx were even gaining acceptance in some quarters. And sociological literature, such as Thorstein Veblen's *Theory of the Leisure Class*, was challenging those committed to success in these terms. During these years, the classic conflicts between emerging unions and expanding corporations were raging. But battle done by these behemoths in the name of the common man lost him even more autonomy, industriousness, and pride in his work—his compensation consisted of improved conditions, financial benefits, and shorter hours.

Then the Depression hit and government intervened. The triumvirate that has troubled us ever since—big business, big unions, and big government—was then formed. The theories of John Maynard Keynes were used to excuse this governmental intervention. His belief that "we shall be absolutely dependent for the maintenance of prosperity and civil peace on the politics of increasing consumption" ignored the discouragement and ulti- mate decline of supply that follow such an emphasis on artificial increase of demand. Human nature being what it is, productivity inevitably falls when one is rewarded with no relationship to what he produces. Since then, government has promulgated an unbal- anced federal budget, inflation, increasing money supply, bur- geoning social benefits, confiscatory taxation, discouragement of research and investment by business, manipulation of bank and consumer credits, and a maze of restrictive regulations and edicts—all stifling enterprise and productivity in the private sector.

Emphasizing consumption not only discouraged pro- ductivity, but resulted in more workers in distribution and sales. There was less and less *real* work geared to creating something; we were consuming more and producing less. Mass production by then had standardized the worker, the product, and its price; all that was left was to deceive and standardize the consumer himself. Salesmanship and advertising set about to do just that, and in the process, those in this field identified with their products and did the same to themselves.

During World War II, there was a brief resurgence of some of the earlier values of the Puritans. Production was emphasized, the people frowned upon profiteering, and believed briefly again in quality and individual enterprise. It also brought forth such literature as Arthur Miller's *Death of a Salesman*, Sloan Wilson's *The Man in the Grey Flannel Suit*, William Whyte's *The Organization Man*, and John P. Marquand's *Point of No Return*, which ques- tioned the values we had by then acquired relative to work and the distortion to that date of the Puritan ethic. Then, after the war, we all settled back in. Our children rebelled against some of the values during the stormy 1960s, but we did not stop then to think them through, let alone alter them, and this is where most of us find ourselves today.

Frugality was the first part of the Puritan ethic to fade, then satisfaction from hard work, then pride in making a product of high quality, then independence, then honesty (with the growth of advertising), and finally even thrift (when credit and installment plans were urged upon us). Although vestiges of these lost values linger, we have replaced them almost entirely with the goals of wealth, status, and power without questioning these deeply. And we feel a measure of discontent that is especially acute in middle age. We have been at this sort of thing longer than any generation before us. Let's look at the dimensions of our dilemma.

DEALING WITH DISSATISFACTION

Pick up the classic book *Working* by Studs Terkel, and leaf through it. You will commiserate with most of those between its covers. Psychologist Herbert Greenberg, head of a marketing and research firm in Princeton, New Jersey, recently interviewed 250,000 white and blue collar employees from 4,000 firms. Four out of five workers said they were dissatisfied with their occupations. A task force of HEW set up to look into this problem concluded that "significant numbers of American workers are dissatisfied with the quality of their working lives. Dull, repetitive, seemingly meaningless tasks, offering little challenge or autonomy, are causing discontent among workers at all occupational levels." And the American Management Association states that among the 3,000 American businessmen who responded to their survey, 40 percent of all middle managers and 52 percent of all supervisory managers described their work as unsatisfying. So it isn't just blue collar blues. It permeates all levels. And it seems to strike us hardest in middle age.

Through all of this, the leisure that some of our forefathers knew in the Old World never really recovered from the early Puritan influence. Free time now is mostly an extension of work. Our parties always seem to have some underlying business purpose. Martini lunches, too. On weekends, our golf game is often more an extension of the office than it is a pleasant sport in its own right. Country clubs and other recreational facilities are frequently used for business—and deducted. Our free time is also encroached upon by the need we feel to refurbish the status symbols we earned at work. We polish our cars, manicure our lawns, and repair our homes. Or we merely recuperate so that we can work more efficiently the following day.

Leisure as the Greeks knew it and as it was lived by the favored few throughout most of Western history was not lost in the U.S.—it was never here at all.

If you find yourself in this situation in your own middle age, it seems to me that you have four alternatives: Stay at your job and alter it as much as you can to obtain greater satisfaction; leave to take up a second and more rewarding career; retire now to pursue other interests; or gradually blend in more satisfying leisure time to compensate for your dissatisfaction at work. Some who are more fortunate can combine two of these.

Modifying Your Job

If you have resolved to keep working at your present job but would like to derive more satisfaction from it, you need to analyze your sources of satisfaction thoughtfully. I have already suggested something of the shallowness of money, status, and power—now. I'd like to suggest the following as far more meaningful sources:

1. *Plan.* Is the idea entirely your own, or did your own creativity play an important part in the conception of it? Second best, is the concept in accord with your own values even if someone else thought of it, that is, do you believe in what you are doing?
2. *Process.* Are you autonomous in the work itself, and is it under your control? Does your own creativity continue to be as fundamental in the carrying out of the plan as it was in its conception?
3. *Pace.* Can you vary the intensity of your labor—speed up, slow down, stop, or shift to another process if and when you wish?
4. *Product.* Is the quality of the finished product such that you feel pride in it? Is it considered worthwhile by those whose opinion you value?
5. *Potentials.* Do you learn and grow in your work? Do you feel you are discovering and developing talents hidden within you? Are your skills and abilities increasing so that you can change to other plans, processes, and products?

These five are the most important, but there are others:

6. *Recognition*. Do you receive appropriate appreciation for your role, from inception to completion, from your associates and superiors? And from your spouse?
7. *Income*. Is the income enough to let you and your family live comfortably?
8. *Convenience to home*. Can you live where you want to, and is the place of your work reasonably close and convenient to your home?
9. *Free time*. Do you have enough free time for creative leisure? Is the intrusion of your work into your free time minimal?
10. *Environment*. Is it clean, comfortable, and cheerful where you work?
11. *Colleagues*. Are your associates compatible and cooperative? Do you enjoy their company?
12. *Spirit*. Do your close associates believe in the work as you do, without being bribed or manipulated?

These are enough to consider, but you can add more of your own. If you answered "yes" to all twelve questions, you are truly fortunate—your work is ideal. Few of us are. Look at your "no" answers—the questions are listed in approximate order of importance—and think carefully about which ones you can change and how.

You will notice that money appears far down on the scale. (And it is not expressed as "security" for a reason I'll touch upon in a moment.) Power does not extend beyond that necessary to produce the product—never to the manipulation of others. And status as such does not appear at all—instead, your own pride in what you are doing and recognition of your true worth by those whom you respect do.

Another Career

If a modification in the directions suggested above is impossible or nearly so, you might consider another occupation using the list as a guide in your selection. When you stop to think that a person's work career now spans forty to fifty years—and in the past it was perhaps half that—such a possibility seems less improbable than at first glance. Except in rare circumstances, one career over such a span of time cannot help but be stultifying.

If a career change can be brought off, you will find a new surge of energy and efficiency—your zest for life itself will be en-hanced. You will, of course, be concerned about security in such a shift. Remember, *opportunity* may be found outside ourselves, but *security* lies within. It depends on your health, energy, concentration, dedication, and ability to adapt to technological changes. Those who seek it in their work steadily descend from more worthwhile sources of satisfaction to this or never rise above it in the first place. Even if you do not actually take the step, preparation for a second career can only enhance your sense of security, so why not at least go this far?

What are the difficulties? There are several. One is that our educational system prepares us only for single careers. Another is that we are not psychologically tuned to the possibility of a second career. Still another is that pension plans and seniority rules encourage workers to remain in one career. If a middle-aged person wants to change jobs, he finds that employers may be reluctant to hire him because of higher Workmen's Compensation rates and higher pension costs. Employers also often feel that their investment in training an older worker is not as profitable for the few years of production he has left. Furthermore, salaries tend to be higher for the older worker than for the younger one, and this may deter the employer. He may have other concerns about lack of flexibility, slower learning, lower production, increased absenteeism, and higher turnover in older workers, although most of these are not true. And the public seems to prefer younger people in contact work. You can add other difficulties to this list that apply more personally to you. But we all run the risk of a double disaster—criticism implying that we are irresponsible and a period of continued economic demand without income.

What are the solutions? First, you need a solid financial base. Personal savings and liquidation of such assets as equity in your house may be enough if you modify your standard of living. It would be far better if retirement plans could be altered to include the possibility of a second career. A portion of the accrued benefits could be paid early to provide a bridge between careers, and the longer period of two careers would more than compensate for the loss. Better yet, a contributory plan much like an insurance policy could be devised for just this purpose and started on the first day of employment. Unions, which should be concerned with all needs of workers, are strangely remiss in providing for this. So far, management has evolved most of the plans for financing and educating workers for second careers. And pension programs have to be portable from one career to the next. An excellent example is the Teachers Insurance and Annuity Program permitting college professors to transfer from one institution to another with no loss of pension benefits.

Second, assess your strengths and weaknesses accurately. This includes not only employable skills, but personality factors—persistence, courage to change, ability to withstand the initial psychological stress, and your potentials in the new area you choose. What have you done in the past that was most satisfying to you? A career counselor can be of great assistance in this step.

Third, set realistic goals *in terms of the work world*, matching your personal assessment to actual job possibilities. There is much more to it, of course, but these three steps are a way to start.

Employers could do more than they have. But first they have to change their thinking. There has been some effort to train established employees for jobs that open up in new areas of production. Instead of hiring new employees to perform these jobs, companies have found that their tried and reliable employees can learn the skills necessary to perform the new jobs and do as well or better. There should be more of this. Employers are beginning to recognize that continued training in almost all fields is necessary in order to keep up with advancing technology. Much of what many of us will need to know about our jobs a decade from now has not yet been discovered; half of the labor force then will be working with skills and on jobs that do not now exist.

There are several sources as yet untapped that could aid in the practical expansion of job opportunities for middle-aged employees. Universities should supply more weekend and mini-residential courses. Instructors from all kinds of educational facilities could take practical programs into the community or present them at job sites after working hours. Psychologists, in particular, should do more to evaluate and expand the few studies that exist on second careers. Those that have been done have only demonstrated that success depends for the most part on the resources and goals of the individual. Yet there have been too few studies even on this, and very little analysis of the findings.

The government at both state and federal levels could do far more than it does now. Present programs such as State Disability, Workmen's Compensation, and so forth, should be made less burdensome for employers hiring part-time employees so that a person could phase into a new job gradually. As a worker approaches his level of peak earnings in one position, he finds he is spending a great deal of time and energy avoiding exorbitant income taxes. If our government is truly "of the people, by the people, and for the people," shouldn't it relax its regulations for a person preparing for another, more fulfilling career? Because it is more satisfying, the second career might well bring in more money and generate more taxes than continuation of the first. Certainly, taxation over the longer span of both careers would result in greater income for the government in the long run. About the only beneficial action the government has taken in the entire area of second careers is to pass the Age Discrimination Employment Act of 1967, which with its extension in 1974, has made it somewhat easier for middle-aged people to get new jobs.

Already, some developments in the private sector are favoring second careers. There are more organizations with "head hunters" who assist individuals in middle management and above in finding new positions. They offer career counseling, psychological tests, and extensive consultation. One of the most famous of such counselors is John Crystal, whose Crystal Management Services, Inc., in McLean, Virginia, has helped over three thousand middle-aged men and women with midcareer changes. His course requires a 25,000-word autobiography about one's working career, and sixteen three-hour sessions, preferably spread over twenty-one weeks. His book, *Where Do I Go From Here With My Life?*, and Richard Bolles' *What Color Is My Parachute?* are both used in this career reevaluation. You can purchase these books and administer the course to yourself, but it is best conducted by a career counselor, who can minimize frustration, confusion, and trial and error. Many other helpful references are listed in the Bibliography.

The work week that has shortened over the past fifty years or so may be as few as thirty hours by the year 2000. But this trend is slowing. The major reason for this is that workers almost invariably prefer income to fulfillment because they really don't know how to use more free time! Also, more flexible retirement means that one can leave a first career as early as age forty.

Vacation time, too, has increased and will continue to increase. All of these changes allow more time to prepare for a new career.

Another encouraging development is the sabbatical being instituted in certain firms. This concept comes from the ancient Israelites, who allowed their fields to lie fallow every seventh year to make them more fertile. The same principle applies to the human being. U.S. Steel has a program in which senior employees are entitled to three months off with pay every five years. IBM has gone one step further, providing tuition-aid plans and fellowships for employees during their sabbaticals.

Women are adding impetus to the second career movement. Although they may be biologically restricted to a career of motherhood for a number of years, after that more and more are pursuing a second one. Not only their example, but their financial assistance can be of great help to their husbands. Their own rapidly changing career roles are so important that I'll devote a separate discussion to this later in the chapter.

Two other factors are favoring second careers now. Our longer lives is one that was mentioned, but our health is better than ever in our sixties and beyond, enabling us to continue to work vigorously and productively in these later years. The second is that jobs are becoming more service-oriented, and there are more opportunities than before for one to initiate some service enterprise. In fact, until the work world becomes more favorably disposed to second careers, some form of self-employment in the service area may be the best route for most of us who wish to take up another occupation in our middle years.

For more help and information on second careers, you can write to the American Personnel and Guidance Association, 1607 New Hampshire Avenue N.W., Washington, D.C. 20009.

Early Retirement

Those who have enough capital to quit working completely, or those who have been cured of their depression hangovers by working wives and children now out of college, may elect the third alternative to a dissatisfying work life: early retirement. This more often than not turns into a second and more rewarding career or into the problem of improving the quality of leisure, which I'll discuss shortly.

Retirement, and especially early retirement, frightens many of us because our society is still so strongly work-oriented. And it is a relatively new phenomenon. Only since the 1960s has retirement while one is still in good health begun to be a significant movement.

I have mentioned that most working people now have the time necessary to plan and prepare for a second career. The same is true for early retirement. The steady increase in free time lets one explore other interests, and longer weekends and vacations now actually allow a person to rehearse for retirement.

Some of this time should be set aside for quiet contemplation, thinking back over your life, your early ideals and goals, the things that have given you the greatest satisfactions, the talents that you never developed, and the person you never became. Remember that during our working years a lot of recreation is just restorative, resting us just so we can work more efficiently. For the most part, we have chosen recreation only as it relates to our work. When we retire, this is no longer true; we then need activities with a worth of their own. We should measure them in terms of what they do for us.

Most of the suggestions I made in regard to second careers are applicable to early retirement also, so no more will be said here. Many people, despite their fears, have retired early both successfully and happily. Sociologists have begun to study this over the last ten to fifteen years, and most of their reports are favorable. As an example, thirty-seven "career dropouts" were recently interviewed at the University of Southern California, and all expressed happiness with their new way of life. With more preretirement planning and financial preparation, early retirement most likely will increase in the future.

While we are on the subject of retirement, I should point out that in my experience most in middle age have not gotten around to thinking about it much or preparing for it at any age. Many are vaguely looking ahead to the usual age of sixty-five—or even seventy with the new 1978 retirement law—but have done little beyond hoping their company pension plan, Social Security, and savings will take care of them. Now is the time to make your plans and act on them. The rewards you reap in your sixties and beyond will depend directly upon what you do in your forties and fifties.

First, two myths should be dispelled. Older data told us those who retired dwindled out their days in misery and died before their time. This information was based upon cross-sectional studies on retirees with poor health, limited education, and little in life beyond their work. All recent longitudinal studies show that most of those who retire are content, enjoy much better health than in the past, and have normal or longer life expectancies. At sixty-five, the average male can now expect at least fifteen more years of life on retirement; the average female at the same age, nineteen more. The second myth is that income begins to taper off after about age fifty, so if you haven't set something aside by then it's too late. Again, recent longitudinal studies show that income continues to increase until retirement, as does net worth. In fact, there is an increasing spread between income and outgo between fifty and sixty-five, as children finish college and home mortgages are paid off, that is ideal for retirement preparation. As more people learn this themselves, they are retiring earlier and enjoying it more. In 1975, nearly two out of three—64 percent—of those eligible for Social Security were retiring before age sixty-five. This year, 1980, fewer than 20 percent will continue working past age sixty-five, according to projections. The only complaint about this trend is from wives who find they have twice the husband with half the income, who often may be heard to lament, "I married him for better or worse, not for *lunch!*"

The first thing you should do now, no matter when you plan to retire, is to gather as much information as you can on retirement. You will find several good books in your local library. One of the best organizations to contact is the American Association of Retired Persons at 1909 K Street N.W., Washington, D.C. 20049. Mention that you are interested in their division called A.I.M.—Action for Independent Maturity, which is made up of those individuals over fifty who want to prepare for retirement. Join, and subscribe to their magazine *Dynamic Maturity*. The AARP has excellent pamphlets on all aspects of retirement. In addition, your local community college often will have a worthwhile extension course on retirement, or hold seminars on the subject. Call and ask.

Now is also the time to look into your Social Security benefits. Approximately half of my middle-aged patients found errors in their records when I urged them to do this. Do it now while you still have substantiating documents. You can obtain a postcard titled "Request for Statement of Earnings," form OAR-7004,

from any post office or Social Security office and mail it to the
Social Security office nearest you or to the Social Security
Administration, P.O. Box 57, Baltimore, Maryland 21203, to
receive a complete record of your eligible earnings. At the same
time, request two pamphlets: "Estimating your Social Security
Retirement Check" and "Social Security Credits—How You
Earn Them." These are free and will enable you to estimate your
income from this source when you retire. In planning, remember
that Social Security benefits are tax-free and that they are indexed
to increase with the cost of living.

You might also ask for a copy of "Your Medicare Handbook"
when you contact your Social Security office. Note the present
provisions carefully. They will be changed between now and
when you retire, but it is well to become acquainted with them as
they are today. There is still time to arrange for your company
health insurance or private health insurance to dovetail with the
provisions of Medicare when you retire.

Veterans of the United States armed forces and their families
may be eligible for benefits. If you were disabled or ill while in
active service, you may qualify for a pension. Contact your
nearest VA regional office, your state department of veterans
affairs, or one of the veterans organizations for information. A
publication called "Federal Benefits for Veterans and Depen-
dents" covers many of the salient points and can be obtained from
VA offices.

Private pension plans should also be investigated now. Later
may be too late. One of the best booklets to use as a guide is
"Know Your Pension Plan," prepared by the United States
Department of Labor and available from the U.S. Government
Printing Office or the Consumer Information Center, Depart-
ment 534H, Pueblo, Colorado 81009.

The 208-page pension law passed by Congress in 1974, the
Employee Retirement Income Security Act, or ERISA, although
unreadable itself, requires most employers to give their employees a readable explanation of their pension plans. This
legislation has many flaws. It is complex, expensive for
employers, and discourages the formation of new plans, especially by smaller companies. The three vesting plans set forth are
inadequate, and funding for pensions can even be waived if an
employer demonstrates hardship. Portability is dealt with
poorly—the transfer of benefits is permissible only when the old

and new employers both agree to do so. Since the former employer would lose money, transfer can rarely be managed. There still is no protection against the firing of an employee in order to defeat his pension expectations. But the law is at least a step in the right direction. Efforts are needed to have a better law passed, with the rights of both employers and workers respected.

Private pension plans will become even more important in the future as the Social Security system comes under greater strain. The ratio of contributors to recipients in 1945, for example, was 35:1; today it is 3:1; sometime around the year 2000 it will be 2:1. Fortunately, private pension plans are on the increase. Nearly one-half of the labor force is now covered by some form of pension or profit-sharing plan. In firms with fifty or more employees, over 70 percent now have pension plans and another 10 percent have profit-sharing arrangements.

If you are self-employed, contact an accountant for details on a Keogh plan. If you do not participate in any pension or profit-sharing plan, you may be eligible to set up your own Individual Retirement Account (IRA). Again, your accountant can give you information on this and keep you up-to-date on the rapidly changing provisions of both plans. Helpful pamphlets on either can be obtained at banks and savings and loan institutions.

The above sources of information will help you with the how of your retirement. The when, where, and why are up to you. The best attitude is not to think that you are retiring *from* your work, but to look forward to what you are retiring *to*.

Improving Leisure Time

The fourth alternative, perhaps the most practical for most of us, is to try to make better *leisure* of our free time. It may seem strange that I distinguish between free time and leisure. There is a difference. According to Aristotle, leisure is "a state of mind or a quality of feeling . . . a state of being in which activity is performed for its own sake or as its own end." We should perceive it qualitatively, not quantitatively. True leisure allows us to know ourselves, to know our fellow man, and to know nature. Previously we urged ourselves to *do*; now we can allow ourselves to *be*.

We know about the greater time now available within the span of a working career. But there is much more time available to us than this. Greater longevity during this century has given a man about twenty to thirty years outside his average work life of forty-one years. The average woman's work life is about twenty years, and that outside of work about fifty-three. An infant born today will actually spend more of his waking life in free-time activities than at work!

Yet surveys conducted on Americans show that nearly half their free time is now work-related or spent around the home in activities that enhance status in much the same way as their work does. Nearly another half is spent passively watching television, spectator sports, and so forth. *Less than 3 percent of our free time is spent in active or creative pursuits.* We simply don't know what to do when we have time on our hands.

In *Self-Alienation and the Loss of Leisure*, Alexander Martin comments that modern man is not well adapted to this increase in his free time. Throughout his life he has repressed his true self; his spontaneous feelings, thoughts, and actions cannot emerge. This alienation from himself leads to despair. Thoreau's words come to mind: "The mass of men lead lives of quiet desperation. What is called resignation is confirmed desperation."

This is not surprising. For the majority, free time is a relatively new phenomenon. As Margaret Mead said, "Such opportunities have never before been experienced by the large majority of the people of a great civilization." And we have no models for this new way of life. In the past, those with free time of the sort we have now were the aristocracy of the Old World, against whom we rebelled; before that there were the Greeks, whose leisure depended upon slave labor.

In preindustrial culture, recreation depended upon the season and was integrated with agricultural production through pagan rituals, festive celebrations, and religious ceremonies. In the industrial age, work became separated from the home and family, and the leisure enjoyed in the home workshop or as an artisan then became separate from work, with most of it distributed before and after working careers. Leisure needs to be both improved and interwoven with work over our entire life span. In our society, free time is wasted by those who have the most, our young. In middle age we have too little. And in old age it is too late—many have forgotten how to take advantage of it or never knew how.

Julian Huxley states, "The leisure problem is fundamental.

Having to decide what we shall do with our leisure is inevitably forcing us to reexamine the purpose of human existence and to ask what fulfillment really means. . . ." Staffan Linder goes further in *The Harried Leisure Class:* "In practice, not even those endowed with the necessary intellectual and emotional capacity have shown any propensity for immersing themselves in the cultivation of their minds and spirit. The tendency is rather the reverse. . . ."

How can you bring more value to your leisure and thus compensate for an unfulfilling situation at work? Learn to listen to yourself. An activity is truly leisure only if it comes from one's true self and desires. You must choose it yourself, for yourself. You may have to look back to your childhood for help, because by middle age you've probably been suppressing for the sake of more "mature" goals the capacity for spontaneous play, humor, and sheer joy in the wonders of the world you had then. There is truth to the old maxim often attributed to Mark Twain: Work is what you *don't want* to do; play is what you *want* to do. In a way, it's almost that simple.

When you choose a leisure activity ask yourself these questions: Do you enjoy it? Does it stretch your mind and teach you more about life? Is there something creative about it? Does it express some part of you? Is it seen by others as worthwhile? Does it help others in some way? Does it involve sharing with others? Most importantly, does it develop latent potentials in you?

Colleges and universities could really help now. The post–World War II "baby boom" is past for them, and college enrollments are declining. These institutions should address the leisure problem and develop courses to help middle-aged and older people enhance their lives. And by these I don't mean the "nonsense" courses most provide or classes on hobbies we can develop ourselves. The really substantial courses we need should come to grips with the meaning of life, human origin and destiny, and explore the best ways to live the life we have left. They should delve into the arts, philosophy, literature, and religion to find *meaning*, and they should do this in ways suitable for us at this time in our lives.

Higher education must reach out to adults. In our early education, there was much emphasis on conformity for the sake of discipline. We all had to sit at our desks and do things as everyone else did. For the most part, we were discouraged from independence, individuality, and creativity. It's no wonder we're reluctant at midlife to return to the classroom. And it's no wonder instructors are reluctant to allow individual talents and the varying experiences of adults to emerge. It's more work for them, and it tends to undermine their power. But it could be a rewarding experience for all. Instructors might even learn something from *us!* We've acquired a lot of knowledge from life by now. We have matured in a variety of ways; we have acted independently in real situations; and we have accumulated experience far greater than anyone could hope to gain through books and lectures alone.

But still, in most adult education programs we are herded into large classrooms and condescended to by professors—if anything, even more than are undergraduates in their teens and early twenties. Such passive attendance at a lecture is not the way to educate adults. We must be actively involved. Those of us with relevant skills must assist in the programs. Because adults are accustomed to a great deal of personal contact, we should have less paperwork than we did in school and more seminars in which we participate. Attempts to use the mass media are easier for the educators but are doomed to fail also, because these programs don't and can't incorporate this idea. We should also be encouraged in independent work. After all, we've been doing it for much of our lives. The professors must leave their ivied halls and ride the rural circuits. The open university in Great Britain first developed along these lines, and it's a good model to look to.

On the other hand, if we are to expect educators to guide us in our leisure, we must change our own orientation. Sometimes we say we "*had* philosophy in college," much like we had a case of measles we hope never to have again. Our own minds must open, and we must be prepared to try the new. Remember that most regrets in life are not over the things we tried and at which we failed, but over those things we never tried at all.

As Erwin Edman said, "The best test of the quality of a civilization is the quality of its leisure." The test of a civilized person is not what he does when he must, but what he does when he has the free choice.

WOMEN AT WORK

Much of the foregoing has necessarily been directed toward men. But there are now over forty million women in the labor force, and the number is increasing by about one million a year. This increasing interest and participation of women in work deserves discussion all by itself. The increase derives from several sources: the desire for more necessities and luxuries than a husband's single salary can provide, the need to prepare for joint retirement, the likelihood of widowhood, and from the increasing amount of time available to women, especially in the postparental period. Most important of all, it comes from a thrust by women toward self-fulfillment that has gained much momentum from the women's liberation movement. I think a brief review of the movement is necessary to understand this. Most of us at our age, men *and* women, have heard a lot about it but have not looked into it, or what it means and might mean in our own lives.

What has come to be called the "new feminism" arose in the early 1960s and reached a peak during the last two years of that decade. The origins, however, go back to the older feminism concerned with property and suffrage, of which a good account is given in Eleanore Flexner's book *Century of Struggle*. The impetus for this second phase came from the experience of women employed alongside men during the Second World War. About a third of them stayed in the labor market after the war, and they became increasingly conscious of and angry about the discrepancies in status and pay between them and their male counterparts.

In 1961 President Kennedy appointed a President's Commission on the Status of Women, with the task of reviewing employment practices in the federal and state governments. Several state commissions were set up following this, but popular fancy first took fire in 1963 with the publication of Betty Friedan's book *The Feminine Mystique*.

In 1964, Congress added the word *sex* to Title VII of the Civil Rights Act. This prohibited discrimination in employment, not only on the basis of race, color, religion, and national origin, but also on the basis of sex.

In 1966, under the auspices of the United States Labor

Department, a conference was held in Washington, D.C., for representatives of the several state commissions on the status of women. The enthusiasm at this time was soon seen to be somewhat misdirected in hoping the government could cure all ills. Later that year the National Organization for Women was started by Betty Friedan. The original concepts of NOW were these: to combat discrimination in hiring and promotion; to oppose abortion laws in several states; to advocate free birth control clinics; and to promote free day-care centers for children. Through all of these ran the theme of more career opportunities for women. Resistance arose to the latter two because of the demand that they be financed by taxpayers, and to the first because the stated goals were in fact a form of reverse discrimination. That is, a law requiring that 52 percent of all positions in employment *must* be held by women would be antithetical to the spirit of free enterprise, with its reward for excellence regardless of any such criteria as age, sex, color, or religion. Resistance on the abortion position was encountered especially from Roman Catholics.

The National Women's Political Caucus was formed in 1971 in Washington, D.C., with the intent of promoting more participation by women in politics. Because of pressure from this and other groups, the Equal Rights Amendment passed Congress in 1972 and went to the states for ratification, where it remains, three short of the number needed for adoption at this writing.

In the last few years, the movement has burgeoned far beyond what can be touched upon here. However, a few works should be mentioned that you might wish to read. For a brilliant but somewhat warped view of power and politics in "patriarchy" read Kate Millett's *Sexual Politics*. Her advocacy is of a revolution against domination by males, but she is unclear about what ultimate relationship between the sexes would follow such a revolution. If it would be one of female domination, we'd probably be no better off than we are now and, ethically, right where we are now. A more fundamental theorist is Shulamith Firestone in *The Dialectic of Sex*. Her thesis starts with Marx and Engels, but she states that the most oppressive class system—that of men and women—is not based on production but reproduction. She advocates artificial reproduction and wants to remove the "barbaric biology" that has subjugated women. Humanism is strangely absent from her feminism.

Many of the early feminist works discouraged marriage as a career; others advocated other approaches. Germaine Greer's *The Female Eunuch* protested against the "male" standards to which females have been forced to submit. Roxanne Dunbar argued against marriage, because the sexual revolution should be a full-time occupation. Beverly Jones stated, "The inequalitarian relationships in the home are perhaps the basis of all evil." Judith Brown saw marriage as an "unnecessary and bizarre heritage of oppression"—it maintained the dominance-submission game by indoctrinating children in it and thus "served the savage society well." One splinter group advocated elimination of men, as Hitler did the Jews. And Dana Densmore advocated complete celibacy for both sexes.

Frenetic feminism began to shift toward more moderate views during the 1970s with Friedan's essay in the anthology *Voices of the New Feminism*. For the first time, she allowed women the choice to enter sexual activity and motherhood if they find it meaningful, and if for them it is fully creative. Carolyn Bird, in *Born Female*, used the hopeful and helpful term *androgyny*. This word is a combination of *andro*, meaning male, and *gyn*, female. It suggests a pattern of men and women *together*, with the consequent freer development of masculine and feminine traits in either sex. The implication here is cooperation with a rational approach—an affirmation of *human* freedom, not that of only one sex. Underlying the use of this term is the philosophical assumption that the common qualities shared by males and females, their humanity, is much more than the smaller area of sexuality. An excellent exponent of this position is Elizabeth Janeway in her book *Man's World, Woman's Place*. Another fine work is Carolyn Heilbrun's *Toward a Recognition of Androgyny*. She states, "Androgyny suggests a spirit of reconciliation between the sexes; it suggests, further, a full range of experience open to individuals who may, as women, be agressive; as men, tender; it suggests a spectrum upon which human beings choose their places without regard to propriety or custom," and, "I believe that our future salvation lies in a movement away from sexual polarization and the prisoner of gender towards a world in which individual roles and the mode of personal behavior can be freely chosen."

Feminists recently have begun to shift their attack from men *per se* to institutions. More women are coming to recognize that men have been oppressed as much or more than they have, but in different ways, by the same institutions, an understanding that promises dialogue between the sexes and portends well for the future.

Although I am heartily in favor of the women's liberation movement, I can't help commenting on what seem to me to be a few serious mistakes that have been made along the way—for example, the initial reliance upon government to put everything right. Another was the loud emphasis on lesbianism, which was poor public relations for the movement as a whole. Another was the close association with and imitation of the Negro civil rights movement. Women's traditional position in the home may bear some relation to that of chattel to the man, but the differences are far greater than the similarities. And the early association with black militance and violence that then deteriorated into riots and looting has created a backlash among concerned citizens that will still take some time to overcome.

Another major mistake was the use of the male role model without thinking through what the female role should be. This not only overlooked or denied what unique qualities and virtues women may have, but put the two sexes directly in competition. The male himself needs liberation in his own way, and the masculine mystique also needs exposure and analysis. A philosophy that women should be equal to men the same way that men are equal to each other seems to me inherently wrong. There is a fallacy in this functionalism.

But the movement has changed a lot since the first days of its contemporary phase, and its accomplishments are many. Laws are becoming more fair, and all of us are more conscious of our prejudices. As a man not connected with the feminist movement, I can't discuss the subject any further, but I know that now men and women alike are making more serious efforts to be themselves, regardless of given social roles. And those roles themselves are breaking down a bit more all the time in our daily lives. Women's liberation will come close to reality as more of us aim for "human liberation."

As I see it, in their working careers women now have four options, or various combinations of these: a career before marriage; a career instead of marriage; a career during marriage; or a career after marriage. For most women, all but the last two are impossible from the midpoint in life on. And a woman of middle age embarking upon a career encounters double discrimination—that of both age *and* sex. This is true whether she was previously well-qualified for a position or only recently has become qualified.

Yet middle-aged women now comprise a surprisingly large segment of the working force. In the age span thirty-five to forty-four, nearly 50 percent of women are at work, and in the span of forty-five to fifty-four, the percentage is well over 50 percent and climbing. But the U. S. Department of Labor's *Handbook on Women Workers* clearly indicates the disparity between men and women in occupation as well as in income relative to education in these age ranges.

Permit me a moment on a soapbox. Something must change this. Women who are middle-aged need to adopt an entirely different tack from that of seeking a job in a firm and forcing it to treat them fairly. Double discrimination cannot be legislated or demonstrated away. The rule of the marketplace historically, since the agora of ancient Greece, has been competition. Everyone who enters the marketplace has sought to do what he does best and thereby to succeed. I don't see why these fundamental ground rules should change, nor even how they could be.

All businesses are started with an individual's idea and with the initiative and industry to develop and market that idea. Women should concentrate on developing the ideas, the initiative, the organization, and the effort that brings success in the best traditions of our free enterprise system. What this means for most is some form of self-employment, at least at the start. For some inspiration and ideas along this line, read Sandra Winston's *The Entrepreneurial Woman*.

Why shouldn't a woman conceive a new idea and develop and market it, and if it enhances her enterprise, hire only women in her organization? If she were to market a product that is used by women, she could realize a success that no male could hope to duplicate. Her advertising approach could counter what NOW's media monitoring kit so eloquently discloses—the denigration of women.

In short, I think women in middle age—and all women wanting to work—need to concentrate on developing a more positive approach to finding and developing their own talents and skills, and on gearing their careers more to themselves as individuals and to the realities of the marketplace, rather than diffusing their energies in conflicts, confusion, and counter-productive causes. After all, haven't we just seen that what our world of work needs is the infusion of more individuality, creativity, and self-determination? And our world in general certainly won't improve with more of the same conformity, tedium, and despair that has been with us for so long.

Now down from the soapbox for some practical steps to take. Write the Women's Bureau, U. S. Department of Labor, Washington, D.C. 20210 for their booklet *Careers For Women in the 70's* and *Job-finding Techniques for the Mature Woman*. Ask for other pamphlets about women at work today. Send for the pamphlet "A Working Woman's Guide to Her Job Rights" from the Superintendent of Documents, U. S. Government Printing Office, Washington, D.C. 20402.

If you want to start your own business, write the Small Business Administration, 1441 L Street, N.W., Washington, D.C. 20005, for valuable assistance and information.

If you haven't finished college and need further education in your chosen field, you can take the College Level Examination administered by Princeton University at various locations around the country—you may be surprised to find that you can reenter at a higher level than you left. Many colleges and universities have a similar "CLEP" plan of their own. For a high school diploma equivalent, if you have not graduated from high school, you can take the General Education Development Examination and then go on. Many institutions of higher learning give "life experience" credits. Ask about this possibility. Don't hesitate to start in a community college. Transferring to a university with a good department in your field of interest is relatively easy after two years in such a college.

Some states are passing bills creating centers for displaced homemakers. Look into this if this kind of program applies to you.

For all sorts of ideas, as well as job counseling, write: Advocates for Women, 256 Sutter Street, San Francisco, California 94108; New Directions for Women, 2515 North Charles Street, Baltimore, Maryland 21218; Career Services for Women, 382 Main Street, Port Washington, New York 11050; Catalyst, 14 East 60th Street, New York, New York 10022; the Task Force on Older Women of the National Organization for Women (NOW), 3800 Harrison Street, Oakland, California 94611; Career Planning Center, 1623 South La Cienega, Los

Angeles, California 90035; Options for Women, Inc., 8419 Germantown, Philadelphia, Pennsylvania 19118; The Women's Opportunity Center, 148 Administration Building, University of California Extension, Irvine, California 92664; Prime Time, 420 West 46th Street, New York, New York 10038; and the Civic Center and Clearing House, Inc., 14 Beacon Street, Boston, Massachusetts 02108. Write to Women's Work, 1649 K Street N.W., Washington, D.C., for their informative magazine and to Interface Bibliographers for their *Age is Becoming*, which has a far larger list of helpful publications than I could include in the Bibliography. Their address is 3018 Hillegass Avenue, Berkeley, California 94705.

One last thought: At middle age a woman's task is less to *change* the world, than to *confront* the world. Believe in yourself and you can.

8
VALUES

"Into this Universe, and *why* not knowing,
nor *whence* . . .
And out of it . . .
I know not whither . . ."

EDWARD FITZGERALD

THE SOLITARY SEARCH

Most observant readers have realized by now that this book is laid out like a lengthy office visit with their physician. But it's the type of visit that doesn't seem to take place much any more, and that's really the reason for this book. At one time or another, I've heard almost every middle-aged patient say something like "Doc, I don't know what's been happening to me, but . . ." This is why I wrote the sections on myths versus truths about aging. And the lament usually ends, ". . . I've got this particular problem that's starting to bother me now." So there were several sections on some of the common medical problems in middle age. I wish I could have covered more, but the book would have been too long.

Often, when whatever brought a patient in is taken care of and we are sitting together in the office afterward for a few moments, I hear an almost rueful "You know, I sometimes wonder if I still have it up here." This is the reason for the parts having to do with learning, memory, and intelligence in middle age. Some patients who are more perceptive tell me, "I seem to have become a different person over the last few years, in ways I can't understand." I tried to help here with the chapter "The Person." And how some of these changes within us during middle age affect us at work and at home was discussed in "Labor and Leisure."

More important are the ways in which these changes and those in one's spouse alter the relationship between the two—"My marriage used to be great, but things have gotten sort of ho-hum in the last few years." The section on marriage in middle age was about this. Many patients add, "My kids aren't a source of satisfaction any more—in fact, most of the time now they are just a pain in the ass!" There was a discussion on adolescent children, too. Or I'm told, "Our parents seem to be causing no end of trouble as they grow older. I didn't expect this sort of thing at all!" This is the reason for the section on aging parents. And most middle-aged men at some time or another confide, "I know I can't keep it up like I used to, but when it comes to sex, sometimes I can't even *get* it up!" So there was something on sex and sexuality.

It is only during a later office visit that the subject of this last part of the book comes up, if at all. But is is more important than all the others taken together. Except for those few who manage to avoid them by denial or distractions, certain questions emerge for all of us in middle age in a way that is more urgent and insistent than ever before: "What is my life for? What have I done with it so far that is truly worthwhile? What should I do with what I have left? And, above all, *why?*"

These are questions not easily answered, so they are not easily asked, either. The physician, in fact, does not usually hear them as such. Nor all too often, does anyone else. But every person in middle age must at least ask them *of himself* if his life is to have meaning or purpose from then on. Once the questions are asked, each person then has to start his own search for the answers, because ultimately they are personal ones. The search is therefore a solitary one, although those who are closest and physicians and other counselors and religious advisors can certainly help along the way.

The questions are neither easily asked nor answered, and some of the answers themselves can only be tentative ones that change with the years and the circumstances. Because the answers sought are both personal and partial, this chapter will have more to do with the search itself than with answers that may be found as the search goes on.

Earlier I mentioned that Charlotte Buhler, on interviewing people toward the close of their lives, reported that a reevaluation at the midpoint of life was crucial. In fact, this has been found to be true by every major investigator who has considered the whole trajectory of human life. Those in middle age who fail to do this tend to end their days feeling empty, cheated, disappointed, and discouraged. But those who *do* complete their lives with a sense of fulfillment and a conviction that it was all worthwhile after all. The latter half of life has at least been lived on their own terms.

My role in your search must be a limited one. But there are three things I can do. The first is to ask you to ask yourself the questions, if you have not done so already. Set this book aside and take out a pad of paper. Allow a quiet hour or so to make a list of those values by which you are presently living your life. Opposite these, put the corresponding ones you feel you *ought* to be living your life by. Compare the two lists, and reflect on the differences. Take your time with this reflection, perhaps an entire weekend. As you do so, look back in your life and try to recall when and where you acquired each value and why. Write this down next to each. Note which have changed and the reasons you changed them. Put down also those you once believed in but no longer do, and why you abandoned them.

Over the next several days, think about what you have written and on the worth the values you now hold have for you at this time in your life. Reflect on why some may not have the worth you assumed they did before you took the time to think about them deeply, or why a few may not be as clear as they should be, or how certain ones conflict with others on your list. And lastly, consider the disparity between your life as you believe it ought to be and as it is. Is the difference great enough to warrant a reconsideration of your values at mid-life, and possibly a continuous reconsideration for as long as you live? Should *you* start a solitary search?

If you do, you will find as you go on that you will not be changing all of your values, or even most of them. Nor should you. At most, your "midcourse correction," to borrow a term from space age technology, will merely be a modification of the original course you set for your life. Each of us must maintain some—if not most—of his beliefs to give him confidence, balance, and guidance, while holding others tentatively to allow for adaptation to a rapidly changing world. As I said, the search is more for a valuing process than for a strict structure of values to which one can adhere from then on without change. But the first result of such a search is a clearer understanding of the values you hold—and of those you have to let go.

A second way I can help is to present a few of my own thoughts on how most of us acquire our values and about some of the prevailing ones in our society. These thoughts are offered with the hope that they may stimulate you to return again to your list and think about what you have written. Of course, you need not agree with what I have to say—it might even be better if you don't.

All of us are alike in one respect. Early in life, we acquire our first values from our parents, then from our peers. These are various versions of the values of our culture. We have little choice in this, because as children we are not critical. This characteristic of the human being may have served the species well in the past, and perhaps still does around the world today, because the child thereby absorbs whatever values are necessary to survive in various cultures and conditions. In our own country, formal education in elementary and high school reinforces these values in us, and approbation continues to be dependent upon conformity. For many, church and then college continue the process, although we may begin to question some of the values we have acquired to that point. As adults, laws and social influences of all sorts strive to make us conform to the same predominant values. Perhaps the worst such influence is that of the mass media, which treat us like Pavlovian dogs to make us purchase a product. Even most of the noncommercial content of newspapers, magazines, television, and radio is directed at the mass market, the lowest common denominator.

What are some of the values that prevail in our culture? Materialism is the first to catch the eye. Most of us spend a great deal of our time and energy accumulating things that rust or rot. And all of us are aware how shallow this endeavor is, whether we admit it openly or not. In the chapter "Labor and Leisure," I tried to indicate what I thought of wealth, status, and power, the three goals toward which so many mold their lives. You might want to thumb through that chapter again, because no more will be said about them here. There and in other parts of the book I discussed values that are not so shallow, and you might wish to review these too.

Some in the modern world seem to have found values in

science and the wonders of modern technology, or at least live their lives as though they had. But reflect on this for a moment. In science there *is* an open stance toward knowledge, and truth itself is sought. This much we all acknowledge. Since the shift from the deductive method to the inductive, knowledge has accumulated enormously in all areas. Thus absolutism has become relativism, magic and superstition have been rejected, diseases are cured, and starvation prevented. Our lives are now improved in innumerable ways. But one must eventually face the fact that this tremendous body of knowledge is neither moral nor immoral in and of itself, only as it is implemented. At the most, science can only tell us *how*, never *why*. Science itself has tried to come to grips with values, first in an indirect way, through such disciplines as anthropology and sociology, and then directly in the formalized study of values known as axiology. The results have not been encouraging. The only conclusion one can come to is that at least in our lifetimes there will be no science of values, only the value of science. But because science seeks the truth, or a portion of it, a nexus of social values can be formed. To seek truth, freedom of thought is a necessity, and originality and creativity are desirable as means toward that end.

Some have a vague concept of evolution that is rather different from what Darwin had in mind, believing that somehow we have evolved a society based upon true values and that for this reason alone our traditional social values should be accepted and lived by. And they seem to have the same faith in this sort of evolution for the future. But there is a fundamental flaw in this thinking. Biological evolution is based on mutation, which is opportunistic. It happens by chance, and thereafter natural selection exerts its influence based on the conditions that exist at that time. There is no way such evolution can look to the future. The biological nature of man has been shaped by conditions that have long since come and gone. Man's present state has come about much more by adapting his environment to him than by his adapting to the environment.

There *has* been a cultural evolution in our Western tradition, and it is continuing, but it is not based upon biology or biological evolution. Neither this basis or any other can be brought forth to justify a claim that our present social values are necessarily true ones. A look through anthropology at the many other cultures around the world today that function effectively, or back in time through history and archeological evidence to others that apparently did so is enough to confirm this. Social changes have been and continue to be so rapid that the best we can do is understand some of the biological bases, depend heavily upon our intelligence, and rely upon an increasing understanding of our emotions. Man has come from Adam to atom much too quickly.

Some are still guided in their lives by religion. However, since the Renaissance, the Reformation, and the advent of science in the Western world, religious dogma has deteriorated for many as a source of values to live by. There has been a recent resurgence of faith among the young, and the elderly tend to remain traditionalist in this as in other ways. But a lot of middle-agers have abandoned formal religion in this mechanistic, materialistic age. They may attend synagogue or church because it is the acceptable thing to do, for their families, or for reasons of sociability, but not as many as in the past live their lives in absolute adherence to the values of any religion today. But I must tread cautiously here. In fact, I should stop with just that one observation. Under the simple term *religion* can be included the entire spectrum from atheist to fundamentalist. And an essential element in most religions is faith, total and without compromise. Those who believe so completely in any religious value system should close this book right now. The rest is not for you, unless you want to have some of your beliefs challenged, to be stimulated either into making a stronger commitment to them or into changing some of the beliefs you now have. The search is for those of us who are not as sure.

There is no need to mention other value sources and systems in our society. It is enough to note that many have lost their luster. My purpose was to interest you in looking again at them, go on to consider others, and then return thoughtfully to your own list.

The third way I could help in your search would be to tell you the story of my own midlife search. This might give you clues, a sense of some directions to take, and certainly some to avoid. It should at least get you started on your own. You will see many of the answers I found for myself along the paths I took. But they will not be the answers for you. Yours must be your own. Unlike all of the preceding parts of the book where I have tried to give answers to the questions most often asked in middle age, this chapter will offer none. But my story might form the foundation and framework for your own inquiry.

My search started one night when I tucked my daughter Ruth in bed and sat with her awhile, as I used to do when she was small. She looked up at me with her trusting brown eyes and without warning popped this question: "Daddy, why is everything?" Of course I couldn't answer her. I said, "It just *is*, that's all," and told her to go to sleep. But a question like that can't help but start you thinking.

Over the next few years I looked at my work more closely. I had tried to do all the right things, had worked hard, and was busy in a rewarding, respected profession. But I felt trapped on a treadmill. My reasons don't really matter to you, so I won't bore you with them here. If you feel this way, you have your own reasons, and they *are* important. Later this led me to leave my practice, write this book, and do other more worthwhile things with my life. That was the second best decision I ever made.

Then I began to look at my marriage the same way. It had been miserable almost from the start. And it got worse from there. I didn't know why, either—I just kept hanging on because of the children. In the worst of times, my former wife would offer her explanation: "I guess I'm just a bitch and can't help it." Well, that may or may not have been true. I might have been something worse. In either case, it was certainly more complicated than that. But a year of counseling failed to turn up much else, so we agreed to keep the structure of the marriage together simply because we had five kids, and each go our own way discreetly without questions. I don't know or care to this day what she did, but I had a relationship for nearly two years with someone I came to care for a great deal and will always remember. Then one night my wife brought the whole house of cards down in a terrible scene in front of the children. Which led to our divorce, and *this* was actually the best decision I ever made. I should have made it long before. For several years now I have been in another marriage, and with Bea I now know how fulfilling a fine marriage can be.

Then I looked further into my life. I was surprised— shocked—to discover that many of the principles by which I had lived so far were of dubious value. They consisted of a hazy blend of a few Christian principles I had been taught in childhood with some utilitarian "greatest good for the greatest number" concepts

I had picked up in college. The former just didn't work by themselves for me. Far too often when I turned the other cheek, that one got hit too. Christian principles did work if the other person had some decency, but that is not always so in life. I concluded that they couldn't be the only ones for me to live by. The "greatest good" philosophy goes a bit further in some ways, perhaps, but when I thought about this, it seemed to end on an empty note. The plan was there, but no purpose. For the most part then, I was living according to the values of society, by habit, and without thought.

My search then got going with random reading and reflection on what I read. I had no system other than tending to select works from the Great Books list. I was moved to do this in part by a quotation I remembered of C. Hartley Grattan: "Out of a systematic investigation of what wise men have said about the issues of life, one can, in middle age, slowly fortify a position of one's own toward life." I hoped that out of such reading some shapes, or even shadows, of values appropriate for me might emerge. This turned out to be true to some degree—the biographies and autobiographies of the great and near great were especially valuable. But I had neglected one word in that quotation—*systematic*. I really didn't have any system at all. True, I learned a lot from writers such as Ovid (when he could get his mind off sex), Erasmus, Montaigne, Bacon, Shakespeare, Franklin, Emerson, and literally hundreds of others. But sometimes I made the mistake of wandering into a bookstore and buying one of those brightly jacketed "pop psych" books there. This was simply ridiculous. I didn't waste much time learning to look out for Number 1, or feeling around for my erroneous zones, or letting loose with a "primal scream." I wonder if those who do ever find that anyone is listening?

It was obvious that I had to have a system. No one should spend so much time reading about values in life that he isn't able to live.

This called for some thought on my part. I wondered where values—any values—come from in the first place? In the dim dawn of man's history here on earth, it was probably easy to know what to believe in and what to do. Some things were self-evident in the struggle to obtain food, shelter, and clothing. In interpersonal relations, there must have been a time when Ug told Og what to do and that was that; otherwise, Og got bashed in the head with a club. Such a system was certainly easy for Ug—not as much fun for Og perhaps, but at least he didn't have to agonize over decisions. Later in the course of man's evolution, there also must have been a time when he did come to agonize over decisions. This was when man became unique among animals because of his intelligence, and consequently became concerned not just with being, but with meaning. He then became aware of himself and of an orderliness—even a certain purposefulness—in nature around him. This awareness gave rise to a faith in a Supreme Being and of a relationship between himself and a deity that has been present in all cultures and in all times. Yet I have just said that formal religious systems are thought of now by many of us in middle age as consisting of a few tarnished symbols and tattered threads. But I decided I should look once again at our religious heritage. For example, respect for the individual, a value we all cherish today, arose first in the Old Testament with a positing of man's one-to-one relationship with God, and this was strengthened by the New Testament. It certainly wasn't apparent in most of man's history in the Western world before the Bible. And the words of the many prophets that inspired and led millions of followers must contain some truths. So this seemed warranted as the first part of my more systematic search, and I will share this with you in the next section.

Further thought led me to a second source of values that followed closely on the first. It had its origin with man's awareness that he himself was rational, that he was capable in some limited way of understanding nature and perhaps why life has meaning. Thus his early wonder evolved into formal philosophy. It had been a long time since I had studied philosophy, so I decided to see what meaning it might hold for me now. I'll share this with you, too, later.

Although few would deny the power of man's reason, fewer still would give it either an exalted or exclusive role. I found that philosophy was inherently limited because of its reliance upon reason. So I thought I would explore psychology as a third source of values. Through this we have not only learned to understand ourselves and others better, but more of religion and philosophy as well. Although I was not aware that a search for values through psychology had ever been attempted before, it seemed to be worth a try.

So, rather than wander through a large library at random, I decided that I would begin with these three: religion, philosophy, and psychology. From there, one can easily branch out in any direction one wishes. It seemed to be a good system to start with. Let me tell you first what I learned when I looked again at religion.

RELIGION

This was the most painful part of my search. I had been raised in a family that had been religious for generations; many had been ministers and missionaries. As a child I had said bedtime prayers and grace at meals, and somewhere I still have a ten-year Sunday school pin. But about the time I went off to college, I rejected it all, bag and baggage. Ever since, I had carried with me some sort of gray cloud composed of guilt, doubt, and conflict between the world I was in and what I had been taught then. When I returned to consider religion again in my middle age, I did so in the same way I had been living my life—rationally. With religion, this also means historically. I met both success and failure—success in dispelling the gray cloud, failure to find anything more. The rational and historical part takes up most of this chapter, and you should read it only if you have a gray cloud of your own. But at the end, I realized that instead of looking for values in the wrong place the right way, perhaps I had been looking in the right place the wrong way. There is a page or two at the end in which I tell about some of my thoughts then, and these may be of interest to all.

First, I tried to find a satisfactory definition of religion. This is not as simple as you might suppose—most definitions hang between a platitude and a paradox, and all are somewhere in a spectrum ranging from the cynical to the thoroughly theological. The one that I settled upon is that religion is a link between the finite and the infinite. The religious quest in this context is an endeavor to relate one's self to reality and eternity. Religion in all its forms has tried to perform this essential function for man and thereby satisfy some essential human need. It seeks to explain that which cannot be explained, by a "leap of faith" beyond reason, to use Kierkegaard's phrase.

Next, I explored the historical roots of all religions as set forth in the references in the Bibliography, and others. Lucretius, for example, thought the origin of religion was fear. This may be true. Man is apparently the only animal aware of himself as an individual. He is also aware that he can never completely understand the universe around him, where he came from, why he is here, nor his destiny beyond death. Early man, faced with the sun and the sea, *Sturm und Drang*, and all the problems of life—birth, puberty, marriage, sickness, war, and death—sensed his finitude. It was because of and around these that he first built his religions.

I then went on to read about the earliest forms that religion took. In all of these, man regarded everything in the world as possessing a spirit or life like that of his own. This was the only way he could explain the world then, in terms of his own experience. To him, someone more or less like himself, but far greater in power, was accountable for everything that happened. Thus, all of nature was alive and filled with spirits. Early man believed these spirits could be made friendly in the same way *he* could be pleased, through rituals, prayer, or pleading. In time, a shaman took over much of the ritual. It was only a step from here through a charm or good-luck piece to set up an idol or totem. When the idol was housed, we had our first church, with the shaman as its priest. The shaman then complicated the ritual and kept much of it secret to enhance his power and position. Gifts to the idol (and the shaman) of greater value than words were then in order, so offerings and sacrifices were added to prayers.

This brought me to the beginnings of formal religious systems. I had to pause here to decide just how large a scope to take. Although I was raised an Episcopalian, I had become fascinated with Oriental religions when I lived in China and Japan, and later I did graduate study in the religions and philosophies of East and West at the University of Hawaii. I would like to have looked at all of them again. But, clearly, going into any religious system other than the predominant Judeo-Christian one of our culture would have been beyond my purpose, as well as yours in reading this.

Even in this one tradition I found that I had to narrow my focus. Fortunately, all formal religions can be dissected into three parts: theology, ritual, and ethics. The first two are more determined by climate, culture, and history; ethics are less so. Man is man, and there are fundamental and enduring qualities in his relationships with his fellow man in whatever time and place. So it is not surprising that all religions are similar in their ethical principles. As Lewis Browne reminds us, "Men may be divided by that which their priests assert to be divine, but not by what their prophets prescribe as humane." I am indebted to him for proving his point in *The World's Great Scriptures* with the following versions of the Golden Rule found in several religions:

- *Brahmanism*: "This is the sum of duty: Do naught unto others which would cause you pain if done to you." Mahabharata, 5,1517.
- *Buddhism*: "Hurt not others in ways that you yourself would find hurtful." Udana-Varga 5,18.
- *Confucianism*: "Is there one maxim which ought to be acted upon throughout one's whole life? Surely it is the maxim of loving-kindness: Do not unto others what you would not have them do unto you." Analects 15,23.
- *Taoism*: "Regard your neighbor's gain as your own gain, and your neighbor's loss as your own loss." T'ai Shang Kan Ying P'ien.
- *Islam*: "No one of you is a believer until he desires for his brother that which he desires for himself." Sunnah.
- *Zoroastrianism*: "That nature alone is good which refrains from doing unto another whatsoever is not good for itself." Dadistan-i-dinik, 94,5.
- *Judaism*: "What is hateful to you, do not to your fellowman. That is the entire Law; all the rest is commentary." Talmud, Shabbat 31a.
- *Christianity*: "All things whatsoever ye would that men should do to you, do ye even so to them: for this is the Law and the Prophets." Matthew 7:12.

These were presented to you because they brought me a sense of the brotherhood of man. I would like to think that religion would be the bulwark of individual freedom first and foremost, and allow each of us to practice the Golden Rule in our relations with our fellow man. But read on with me. Man is less than his religions. Throughout history he has ritualized and dogmatized them with time. The ritual and dogma inevitably become concentrated in the hands of the few, where it becomes crystallized, sacred, and eventually claimed to have been revealed to them as law by God. From that point, God is invoked as the irrefutable source of power transmitted only by these few, and this law is then imposed upon the remainder of the people—whatever that law may be. Such authoritarian religious systems functioned fairly well for thousands of years in societies in which education and communication were limited, and paralleled the political systems of their times. They only began to fail a century or two ago in our Western world. Sacred authoritarian norms have since begun to crumble, leaving only secular law, behind which the Church once stood. And it might be added that although both are effective, punishment here on earth has never been quite as effective as the threat of punishment in the hereafter for the believer.

With these thoughts, I turned to our Judeo-Christian tradition. In doing so, I tried to ignore theology and ritual as much as I could, because in a search such as this my principal concern was ethics. I knew I could always return to the other two later. The first task I set myself was to read about the Bible and its origins. If you wish to do this, too, the best references I could find are listed in the Bibliography. I wanted to do this before I reread the Bible itself. It had been a long time since I had done that, in fact, not since my childhood. I was interested in different things now as an adult. You may be, too. For example, I wanted to know more about the origin of the concept of one god or spirit, which arose relatively late in human history. I found that the earliest known belief in monotheism was in Egypt in the fourteenth century B.C. Then the pharoah Amen Hotep IV came to worship the sun god Aton, and changed his name, which meant "Amen is satisfied," to Ikhnaton, meaning "profitable to Aton." That such a belief should arise at some time in history would seem inevitable, since the sun is the source of all life sustenance. Ikhnaton commanded his people to give up their beliefs in their many gods. They did so during his life, but when he died the old priesthood and polytheism once again regained control. The Semites were in Egypt at that time, and they carried the concept of one God with them out of Egypt in their Exodus. This is the origin of the great tradition we have inherited: "Hear, O Israel: the Lord our God, the Lord is One."

The early Babylonian writings also interested me because of their influence upon Hebraic scriptures, so I read about these next and found them fascinating. In them there is a creation, a temptation, a deluge, a casting of Satan out of heaven, a hell that burns, a resurrection of Ishtar, and many other elements that became part of Judaism. The Jews resided in Babylon from 586 to 536 B.C., when final form was given to their Mosaic books. They turned these Babylonian myths into moral preachments, and Babylonian magic rites into religious symbols.

I was beginning to find that reading about the Bible was so interesting that I kept putting off reading the Bible itself. If you follow my path, I think you may, too. But wander where you will. I learned a great deal, but the reading took a lot of time—time not many of us can spare. So I would like to set out a few salient points I learned with the hope this will save you many hours of reading—or perhaps stir you to more. You may know most of this already—if you do, just skip the next three paragraphs.

After the Semites returned to the Holy Land, their religion, with its roots in a primitive polytheism, was forged into one of the most creative creeds in the history of mankind. One of the Gods of Canaan, Yahu, the god of thunder from the hills, was renamed Yahweh and became a stern warlike god typical of the times. Yahweh was first under Saul, a demanding deity in defense against surrounding cults and had such human characteristics as wrath and jealousy. It was only in the time of David that Yahweh began to become a loving father. Much later, by the time of the second Isaiah, Yahweh had evolved to become the God of all tribes and richer in kindness, love, and mercy.

The Hebrews divided their sacred books into three parts: the Law or Torah, the Prophets, and the Writings. The Torah, which means direction or guidance in Hebrew, contains the five books of Moses. These are now known not to be Mosaic, but rather a mosaic. Moses was already dead several centuries before the appearance of the books bearing his name. These first five books were written between 1000 B.C. and 300 B.C. They are mostly tribal reminiscences of a preliterate society, consisting of tales of battles and great men, ballads, and folk songs. The prophets flourished principally between 750 B.C. and 450 B.C., and their words were added as the second great division around 200 B.C. The third and final section, the Scriptures, or Writings, were added just prior to the Christian era, about 100 B.C. Because the sacred scriptures needed interpretation for practical and homiletic purposes, the Talmud, the great codification of Jewish law, both civil and canonical, became part of this. Later, less respected texts are grouped as the Apocrypha, which fills the gap between the two Testaments.

The Old Testament was originally written in Hebrew, with a few portions in Aramaic, and underwent many subsequent translations. When Alexander the Great conquered Jerusalem in 334 B.C., the Diaspora started, culminating with the second subjugation of Jerusalem by Rome in 130 A.D. This dispersion sent the Jews into many countries where colloquial Greek was the most common tongue. In the fourth century, the Greek version of the Bible was translated into Latin and became known as the Vulgate version. With some revision, this is still the official Bible of the Roman Catholic Church. The King James translation into English was accomplished in the seventeenth century and is undoubtedly the most beautiful in literary style. More accurate translations than either of these have appeared since. These are the minimum historical facts to know, I think, before one begins to read the Bible itself.

My next task was exactly that. If, in your search, you wish to follow my route, I'd recommend that you read the Bible with any standard commentary—it brings light to many obscure passages, and life to others. I would also suggest that you use one of the more accurate recent translations to avoid as many errors in transcription and translation as possible—such as the one in the Vulgate version that put horns on the forehead of Michaelangelo's Moses!

Even so, I was immediately faced with innumerable difficulties in the Old Testament. For example, there are two different versions of Genesis; Cain gets a wife from the land of Nod when there was no human life on earth other than Adam's family; Joseph is sold as a slave to caravans of two different tribes; Noah at one point takes one pair of each type of animal into his ark, and then again seven pairs; and even the narrative of the conquest of Canaan in Joshua does not match the description in Judges. I encountered many conflicts and contradictions such as these, and you will, too. So my gray cloud began to be dispersed. I could only come to the conclusion that *not every word in the Bible can be true*, despite the claims of those who wave it in the air and claim this to be so. In fact, even mathematical law is defied when the circumference of the great basin in Solomon's temple is stated in the Bible to be three times its diameter. Any child who has studied arithmetic in school knows about *pi*. As I said before, this part of the book is not for those who have faith. I do not wish to disturb those who do. And those who are not as sure can come to any conclusions they wish. These are merely mine.

But I also found that as an adult I could regard the Old Testament in a different way, a way that is less rational perhaps, but more meaningful. For example, Genesis would invite us to contemplate the wonder of the created world, with God as its creator. And man truly *does* have a status different from any other living creature on earth. Behind the story of the Garden of Eden and man's temptations and his fall, one senses the truth that knowledge destroys both our childlike innocence and happiness, replacing them with responsibility. I think that when we read the Bible today, we should try to see the world through the eyes of the people then, when much more of it was mystery than now. There was no science as such—minds were more mystic than rational, and truths were *revealed*, not sought for by man. Tales were told to enhance principles and people, not truth as we think of it today. When, too, we understand that men in those times often thought and spoke in terms of poetic symbols and images, much more of the Bible can be understood and accepted by the modern mind. At this point in my search, still more of my gray cloud was going away. I did not have to believe every word, yet I could still accept much of the Bible.

To me, the most remarkable contribution of the Old Testament is that it takes from a Mesopotamian background many myths and legends with a wealth of polytheistic imagery resting upon a primitive cosmogony, and establishes one single living and active personal God. The belief in a God who hates sin and loves righteousness is the foundation of the Hebraic and Christian religions. Wherever this belief spread, it profoundly affected human relationships, gave sanctity to the home, and dignity to the individual. It has made prayer and praise a constant practice of the Jewish people and has held them together throughout their troubled history.

The next task I faced proved to be much more difficult. I had read the Old Testament through. Now I had to read it once again and attempt to derive some system of ethics from it. Frankly, I was not very successful in this. I'll tell you what I found, but it reflects more of a lack on my part than any lack the Bible might have. You may find more, and I hope you do.

Originally the religion of the Semites was simple and happy. Sin was not stressed, and there was no concept of an afterlife. The relationship between Yahweh and His people crystallized into a covenant or agreement, and the conditions which the people had to fulfill were those of rigid adherence to specific moral principles. From the time of the return from Babylon, the religion gained in moral fervor, leaving behind the ritual and joy of the Babylonian influence. It became stern and somber, a religion of fear rather than love, with a central theme of sin. Reward and punishments were still confined to this life—there was as yet no idea of a hereafter.

The moral principles themselves range from those of primitive tribes, through statements against oriental despots to include such disparate and conflicting elements as parts of Roman law and Greek philosophy. Read, for example, the books of Ezra and Ruth. Both talk about the marriage of Jews to non-Jewish women, but the statements are diametrically opposed and supported by different principles of logic. Another example is the conflict between Deuteronomy and Ecclesiastes—the first calls for complete obedience to the sacred laws, while the second counsels not to be overly righteous in conforming to them. Still another is in the early books where specific proscriptions against afflicting a widow or orphan are given very clearly. Here for the first time in our culture we are enjoined to have concern for our neighbors. Then we take a large step from these books to the prophet Amos. In doing so we also take a large step from an agrarian society to a more complicated urban society. With Amos, for the first time, concern for all of mankind, not just for one's neighbor, is urged. This ethical progression here and elsewhere helped to dispel still more of my gray cloud—the part that came from hearing hundreds of conflicting sermons, each based on a passage in the Old Testament. I would suggest that you, too, try to see this ethical progression and not let your way be cluttered by contradictions.

From Amos to the New Testament there began to be more concern for the individual than for the social unit. This is most evident in Jeremiah and Ezekiel. Some of the difficulties of divine justice—retribution for evil acts—also emerged during these eight centuries. The problem of divine justice has not been settled to this date. The struggle is first seen in Jeremiah and the second Isaiah, continues in the book of Job, runs through some of the

Psalms, and continues into the New Testament. The problem, simply put, is that living correctly should receive its own rewards and evil should be punished, but experience does not confirm this. However, the subtle transformation that I mentioned from a God of divine justice to a God of mercy and forgiveness evolved from this struggle.

Although I found all of the Old Testament fascinating on rereading it as an adult, the prophets inspired me most. They elevated the piety and propriety of the Jewish religion to its greatest heights. The first prophet Amos issued a call to morality and nobility, which is the true start of the gospel of Christ. Later, when the Assyrians were at war with Israel, Isaiah, the prophet of this period, presented Yahweh as omnipotent, omnipresent, and omniscient in defiance of the Assyrian god Assur. Isaiah issued the messianic hope that a redeemer would come to relieve the people of their subjugation and misery and establish a dictator-ship of the dispossessed. These prophets and others promoted brotherhood and love for one's fellow man, which Jesus was later to incorporate in his teachings.

At this point I made a decision that was necessary for me, but may not be for you, because I am far from being a theologian. Although there is a large body of Jewish theological literature in which ethical systems emerge more clearly, I concluded that it was beyond my ability to extract more from the Old Testament and decided to go directly to the New—to use the former mostly as a basis for a more thorough consideration of the latter. You may take another path. If you are following mine, I would again like to set out some of the more salient things I learned from reading *about* it that one needs to know before reading the New Testament itself. I will try to be brief, but this time these will take two or three pages, not just a few paragraphs. As before, you might want to skip them entirely if you already know this much or more.

The New Testament contains twenty-seven documents pro-duced over a period of one hundred years beginning soon after 50 A.D. Although not in the order in which they were written, they appear in the Bible beginning with the four Gospels that recount the life and sayings of Jesus. Following the four Gospels, the Acts of the Apostles is the part that recounts the expansion of Christianity into the Mediterranean world and the origin of the early Christian Church. Then follow twenty-one epistles, or letters, written by several early missionaries, and finally there is Revelations, a book of apocalyptic visions.

The earliest documents written were some of the epistles Paul wrote to various churches from A.D. 50 to 60. The first Gospel put into writing was that according to Mark, probably written in Rome soon after the year 70 A.D. for the gentiles there. Mark apparently knew Peter and tried, after the latter's death, to set down what he remembered of the fisherman's reminiscences, which were largely confined to the deeds rather than the words of Jesus. If Mark were our only Gospel, we would know nothing of the beauty of the beatitudes, the Lord's prayer, the Golden Rule, or the parables.

In Matthew and Luke, approximately 610 of the 661 verses in Mark's Gospel appear, but these two Gospels also contain about 200 verses which are not found in Mark. In these there is a close correspondence pointing to a common origin, called by biblical scholars "Q" from the German *Quelle*, meaning common source. This source has long been lost. The Gospel ascribed to the apostle Matthew was not written by him, but by another writer, probably Jewish, in Syria, about 85 A.D. or a little later. He obviously had Mark's writings to draw upon. The purpose of his presentation comes through to present Jesus to the Jews and assure them that he was not overthrowing, but rather fulfilling Jewish law and prophecy. The Gospel according to Luke may not have been written by Luke but by an unknown gentile convert about the same time.

These three gospels, because they have so much in common, are known as the Synoptic Gospels, *synoptic* meaning they share a common view. But there are some differences. Those between Matthew and Luke are illuminating. The former, written by a Jew, traces the descent of Jesus from Abraham; but the latter, written by a gentile, traces it from Adam. Mark is regarded as a more accurate historical record, and between Matthew and Luke the author of the latter has a higher regard for his early sources than that of Matthew, who had a tendency to embellish and add arbitrary details. It is in Matthew that most of the miracles ascribed to Jesus appear.

The fourth Gospel, traditionally attributed to John, was written about 110 A.D. and must be regarded not as historical but doctrinal. This is a presentation of Christ from a theological point of view as the Logos or Word. Not only is the authorship doubtful, but it contradicts the Synoptic Gospels in more than a hundred details. As an example, for a point I want to make later, it is the only Gospel that tells of a spear in Jesus' side upon his crucifixion. It is the product of a later generation in an alien soil, and therein Jesus is already divine and described in terms both mystical and gnostic.

It is curious that except for brief references elsewhere, the Gospels are our only source of substantial information about Jesus. For this reason, some people doubt that he ever existed. These skeptics are referred to secular works such as those of Tacitus and Suetonius, where he is mentioned briefly but unmistakably. As everyone knows, Jesus himself left nothing in writing, and reports were by word of mouth for the greater part of the forty to sixty years after his crucifixion.

Some modern scholars believe that Jesus was born in Nazareth, not Bethlehem, as is the tradition. Even the year of his birth is an estimate—about 6 B.C. The day is not known at all. In 345 A.D. the Church designated December 25 as the day because the early Christians had come to use this, then the calculated date of the winter solstice, as a defense against persecution. When Diocletian proclaimed himself a god, he declared his birthday to be at the time of the winter solstice, the central festival of Mithraism. The Christians could then appear to conform in the celebration of the Roman ritual.

The virgin birth is not mentioned in either Mark or John, and although Matthew and Luke tell of it, they both trace Jesus back *through Joseph*. That is a point to ponder. It is evident on reading all sources about this that the Davidic descent was more important earlier, the virgin birth became of concern only much later. In fact, some authorities present convincing evidence that Jesus had four brothers and at least two sisters. After looking at all the evidence as objectively as I could, I came to the conclusion that Jesus was the son of Joseph by normal processes and that this was accepted and recognized by his contemporaries. This conclusion, of course, is mine and should not influence you in your own. If you wish, disregard mine entirely.

As you can tell from the above, I was not content to read about the New Testament without beginning to read it concurrently. If you are following my path, you will probably be doing the same. I found I could not resist going back and forth from the scholarly sources to the Bible, checking one against the other.

Before I go on to tell you what I found in the ethical teachings of Jesus that had meaning for me in my middle age, which was the purpose of this part of my search, I have to comment upon one epochal event, the crucifixion. My conclusions stunned me, and they will almost certainly shock you. But bear with me. They may also stir and stimulate you in your own search to arrive at completely different conclusions.

I first passed over the event without much thought, but then was caught by some contradictions in view of what I now know as a physician and returned to it. In fact, I spent weeks studying all that is known about crucifixions then, the causes of death, and everything else I could find. A few of these points should be mentioned if only to give you some idea of why I reached the conclusions I did.

The crosses used by the Romans were T-shaped; the form we know is apparently anthropomorphic in origin. Platforms were provided for the crotch, the feet, or both. Nails were not used. Instead the victims were tied to the cross hand and foot. The first mention of nails in regard to Jesus was in the apologetic period of the second century. Victims frequently fainted in a few hours due to the accumulation of blood in their lower extremities, but death did not come for two to three days, or occasionally two or three weeks, depending upon climatic conditions. When it did, it was apparently due to a combination of dehydration and exposure. The size of the stones used then to close the opening of the sepulchre easily allowed one man to move them—as Joseph of Arimathea apparently did.

All this and much more led me to the astounding conclusion that Jesus may not have died upon the cross in 6 hours, as the Synoptic Gospels indicate, but may have been carried away in a faint. I would like to emphasize that this is my conclusion alone, and of course I am responsible for it. I have not read it anywhere. Here, more than on any other conclusion of mine in this chapter, I would urge you to arrive at your own and discard mine completely if you wish. And you probably will. I was absolutely staggered by this possibility and returned again and again to the Bible to try to restore my previous belief. But I could not. Mark, recognized as the most accurate historical record and the account I relied upon most, from the description of the crucifixion on (16:8) was clearly written by another hand. Each Gospel then goes its own way—even the Synoptic Gospels are no longer synoptic. I was simply left with this awesome doubt, and I really don't know what to believe from that point on about subsequent appearances or anything else.

If there *were* no death on the cross, there could have been no resurrection! Yet for nearly two thousand years the resurrection has been central to Christian theology. It is strange that in none of the earliest documents is there any mention of such an amazing event. Acts, written 70–90 A.D., describes the early ministries—including Paul's first missionary sermon at Perga—without mentioning it. In his own writing, Paul does not refer to it until his first Letter to the Corinthians, and then he emphasizes its theological importance, that Christianity as a religion would be meaningless without it.

As I said, my thoughts and doubts about the traditional birth and death of Jesus are my own, and you will almost certainly reject them outright. But they did inevitably led me to doubt the traditional divinity of Jesus. I went back then to the Synoptic Gospels to note that Jesus did not clearly identify or equate himself with God but rather used the phase, "Son of Man," by which he meant the Messiah. He believed that he had been sent by God to prepare man for the reign of God here on earth, a concept that was then more than a century old among the Jews. Much of his ministry was to make men worthy of the Kingdom of Heaven. Jesus made no claims of divinity for himself in his own right, but at the same time, he made astounding claims about what God was doing *through* him. He did not claim to *be* God but to *bring* God. Later, I'll describe how the Church dealt with the question of his divinity. But for me, although I was considerably shaken, still more of my gray cloud had cleared.

I'd like to leave this point and go on to a less controversial area, the ethical teachings of Jesus. In general, he accepted the Mosaic commandments and believed in the prophetic influence upon the Law. However, he went beyond the fatherhood of God to the brotherhood of man. Except for the brief references I cited previously, this is the first statement of such a philosophy in the history of humanity. Prior to that time, love was confined to one's family, tribe, or fellow believers. Now, as God so loved men, they should love him *and* one another. This love for God and one's fellow man was far more important for Jesus than the outward conformity to ritual that characterized the Pharisees and Sadducees. He taught that God's mercy and love are given without the requirement of virtue of the individual, as is his forgiveness. Throughout his ministry Jesus stressed the intrinsic value of every human, and he especially endeavored to elevate the status of women and children. Briefly put, he transformed religion from ritual to righteousness.

The best summary of his teachings is the Sermon on the Mount, and you are referred to the most eloquent version in Matthew—I would urge you to read it there, and will not quote it here. The Sermon was probably a collection of the sayings of Jesus at various times and various places. I was struck by the fact that although these are imperatives once again, they now come from Jesus the Son of Man rather than from God, as in the Old Testament. A second unique quality I noted is that they are not directed to the powerful, enjoining them to be just to those under their authority, but to the poor, the hungry, and the meek themselves. He exalts humility, poverty, gentleness, peace, and love and is indifferent to economic gain and high position. To the sinners he promised forgiveness, to the doubtful he gave a doctrine, and to the miserable a hope of heaven.

Here I had to pause. I recognized that these ethical principles constituted perhaps the greatest step forward in the history of the human race. But I could not do otherwise than approach them in terms of my own experience, with my own limited reason, and with some knowledge of psychology. In this way I could accept most but not all. Each of us has to decide what he will or will not accept and live by. I would rather not impose any more of my conclusions on you, but let you come to your own and go on to tell you in a paragraph or two some other things I learned. My cloud was almost gone by now—if I could not believe Jesus was divine, I didn't *have to* accept those parts of his teachings I couldn't agree with.

Christ's ministry left little to support a systematic theology. Much of the remainder of the New Testament tells how Paul strove to rescue Christianity from the oblivion of the many mystic and messianic cults of that time. To attract the intellectuals, including the Greeks, Paul used the idea of the Logos, borrowed from Philo. This is the concept that God had contact with the earth and man only through an intermediary known as the Logos or the Word, or the Son of God. Paul took over the Mithraic sun-day rather than the Hebrew Sabbath, and the Mass from the Mithraic Taurobolia. The spring festival of Ostara became

Easter. When he came to use the concept of the resurrection, he adopted the traditions of other gods that had died to relieve mankind, such as Osiris, Attis, and Dionysus. In fact, the word he used to refer to Jesus which was *Kyrios*, the original term given to the dying and redeeming Dionysus.

In order to enhance the growth of the young church, Paul intermingled much of his rabbinical background with the simple faith and love that Jesus had taught. He took the concept of moral evil, which had its origin with Adam in the Garden of Eden, and upon this laid the foundations for subsequent Christian theology —that all men inherit "original sin" and that they can be redeemed only by God's grace through faith in Christ. This was the reason that the resurrection became so important theologically for Paul. Christ's death and resurrection were necessary for a world lost through Adam's sin. And when Christ broke the bonds of death, heaven was opened to all who had the grace of God.

It was about here in my reading and thinking that I realized my gray cloud had cleared completely. I felt an intense relief, but also a profound sense of something lost. However, I persevered, because what I was now reading was more history than mythology—more verifiable and amenable to rational inquiry. And the sources to which one can refer that cover the next thousand years of Christianity expand almost exponentially. For these reasons, I would like to leave this period entirely to you in your own search. But I have to pause to present some thoughts on Thomas Aquinas because he was so important to me in mine.

Around 900 A.D. scholastics began to systematize and rationalize religious dogma. The premise of their philosophy was a complete acceptance of the conclusions of the Christian Church to that date, and their purpose was to justify these dogmatic dictates. Among the important scholastics were Erigena, Anselm, and Abelard, but the greatest was Aquinas. He wrote at the peak of the power of the Church in the thirteenth century and incorporated much of the thought of the Greek philosophers, especially Aristotle, whose writings had been returned to the Western world by the Crusades.

He recognized that some happiness, although imperfect, *was* attainable here on earth, but held that the true goal of the soul was the contemplation of God. Perfect happiness was attainable only in heaven. He combined the four Aristotelian virtues of prudence, temperance, justice, and fortitude with three theological virtues—faith, hope, and love—to form seven cardinal virtues. Missing are some of Aristotle's virtues such as humor and friendship.

Aquinas distinguished four types of laws: eternal, or God's regulatory reason; natural, based upon man's reason and his perception of eternal law in nature; human civil law grounded in natural law; and divine law as revealed in the Bible. Of these four, only natural law, according to Aquinas, could be subjected to rational analysis.

These two brief paragraphs on Aquinas are all that I can offer here. He wrote volumes, and more volumes have been written about him. If his works are as important to you as they were to me, you will have to read them yourself. I must tell you I reflected a long time on his contributions. They have had a profound effect upon Christian thinking and upon the Christian world. I would like to tell you some of the conclusions I came to, which you can accept or reject as you will.

It seems to me that there are several inherent problems in basing an ethical system on "natural law." First of all, it rests upon man's perception of nature, which is far from perfect. Isn't the world *obviously* flat? Doesn't the sun *obviously* revolve around the earth? Even in modern science, the Gaussian principle of indeterminacy in the outer reaches of space has its counterpart in a similar principle of Heisenberg in the inner space of the atom. Secondly, man's reason is far from perfect, and reliance upon it often results in erroneous abstractions. And thirdly, the abstractions thus derived are thereafter applied to all specific situations. Through time and tradition, such rules become absolute. When new knowledge contradicts, as it inevitably does, the only resort is a retreat into the Magesterium and infallibility. Lastly, this thinking always ascribes the moral quality of an act to the act itself without any consideration of its consequences. More will be said about this fatal flaw when I discuss Kant.

The Thomistic synthesis of reason and religion, held together by papal authority, was incorporated as the official philosophy of the Roman Catholic Church by the papal encyclical *Aeterni Paternis* of Leo XIII in 1879. Catholicism today is still set in the framework of Thomism, as is the Anglican Church and my own Episcopalian Church.

After Aquinas, the doctrine of twofold truth arose. That is, a thing might be true according to reason but not according to theology. With this then, theological truth was placed higher in the hierarchy than truth according to reason. Reason was still restricted to the lower or natural world and prevented from entering the realm of ultimate reality. Deism then attempted to reconcile the contradiction between revelation and reason. Unfortunately, this attempt to apply reason to religious doctrine inevitably emphasized the value of reason. Therefore Deism was doomed, but it did initiate once again on the part of man an attempt to find a basis for morality other than through theology.

No further attempt to change this authoritarian religious position was made for the next five hundred years. This was largely due to the intrinsic nature of this philosophy as it had been stated by Aquinas. If Thomism is true, then no further progress is possible; in fact, progress *itself* would be evil. Therefore the philosophy had only two choices: to stagnate or deteriorate.

As I said, the period past Paul to Aquinas, and that to the Reformation are left to you and your own reading. I would like to take up the thread with the Reformation. Then, the absolute authority of the Church was replaced with another, the infalliable Bible. Martin Luther, the author of the Reformation, was struck by the similarity of those who sought saintliness to those who pursued pleasure and power in more worldly spheres. He felt that the grace of God was something given to man rather than a goal toward which man should strive himself. He restored some of the quality of earlier, pre-Thomistic Christianity and was honest in accepting the inner or animal nature of man. But at the same time he was concerned with how reason could control this. Luther was well aware of the limitations of man in doing so. I like to extrapolate his thought in my own way—that good works do not make a good man, but rather a good man produces good works.

Luther may have been the prophet of the Reformation, but Calvin certainly did more to organize it. He emphasized divine sovereignty and acceptance of hardship, rejection of luxury, and living laboriously in this world. The last was in contradistinction to the other-worldly asceticism of monasticism.

The Puritan movement arose when the Presbyterians, in attempting to use both the Bible and Calvin as their guides to reorganize the Anglican church and dissect the Church from the state, were opposed by the Anglicans. The word later came to be used in a wider sense as an ethic of reform pervading English culture at that time.

The Puritan was in the world, not of it, and the concept of a vocation as a role to fill in God's plan was emphasized. Hard work, honesty, and avoidance of idleness were all parts of this ethic. This was a time when there was a shift from agriculture to a capitalistic economy and mercantilism. The outer life of Puritans was characterized by hard work, simplicity, and frugality; their inner life by honesty and diligence. I dwelt on this earlier in the book when I traced the origin and development of our work ethic.

In the eighteenth century, Joseph Butler introduced rationalism into the Anglican church, and Puritanism itself mellowed somewhat. Bibliolatry began to be countered by a type of pragmatism, relying upon human nature as the basis of a moral system interpreted by reason. At the same time, an evangelical revival led by John Wesley and others was taking place in England. The Church of England had become complacent, and urbanization with industrialism had pervaded society.

These last few paragraphs probably contained nothing new for you. But they and the next few are offered here to lead into more current Christian thinking. What I found there was of profound importance to me in my search.

From the midpoint of the nineteenth century, the Bible began to be analyzed rationally by critical scholars. Notable among these has been Rudolf Bultmann. He stated that the New Testament writers used a mythological language of preexistence, incarnation, ascent and descent, miraculous intervention, cosmic catastrophe, and so on, which made sense only when based on a world view that has long since become antiquated. He therefore advocated "demythologizing" the Bible. It has become accepted by most that the Bible *does* contain many myths, but that these, too, can be an important form of religious truths.

Karl Barth in his despair in the disorder of man at the time of the first World War reached back to Paul, especially the epistle to the Romans. Barth continued the tradition of Luther, with his "justification by faith" and his disparagement of external acts in favor of a reliance upon the grace of God. This theme was continued in the United States by Reinhold Niebuhr. He differed in many respects from Barth, but shared the latter's despair in the disorder of mankind. Niebuhr believed that man in his social unit is more inhumane than man alone, and he attempted to find Christian solutions to the problems of current civilization by being realistic, that is, by not hoping for an ideal social structure. If the Christian could but have contrition, he would not then lose his conviction, but could find his way in faith through the realities of modern life. Niebuhr had faith in God's ultimate victory.

Dietrich Bonhoeffer held that the Church was based upon the fact that down deep every man feels the need for religion. But he raised the question, "Suppose men feel they can get along perfectly well without any sense of sin or desire for salvation?" His answer is that, in this twentieth century, we must have a more modern form of Christianity that does not depend upon these premises.

I come now to a point that means a lot to me. I had long ago ceased to believe in God in the traditional sense. I had faith in a certain order in the universe, but that was all. In order to believe *in* God, one must first know what he believes to *be* God. Traditional theology is based upon "proofs" for the existence of God. A presupposition for these proofs is that God might or might not exist, and they all argue from something which everyone admits exists, the world, to a being beyond it, to a God "up there." It always seemed to me that if such an entity as God could be proved by any of these methods, it would not be God, it would merely be a further piece of existence. God must be everywhere—or nowhere. Paul Tillich helped me immensely when he said that God is part of the whole of reality in a way that is somewhat like the relationship between a cause and its effect. To him, as he said in *Religion Without Revelation*, God is "the *natura naturans*, the creative nature, the creative ground of all natural objects." Tillich goes on to say in the *Shaking of the Foundations*, "The name of this infinite and inexhaustible depth and ground of all being is God . . . if that word has not much meaning for you, translate it, and speak of the *depths* of your life, of the source of your being, of your ultimate concern, of what you take seriously without any reservation." That is, God is not "out there" at the limit of our lives, but at its very center and can be found, in Kierkegaard's phrase through "a deeper immersion in existence." Martin Buber helped me also in *I and Thou*: "When he, too, who abhors the name, and believes himself to be godless, gives his whole being to addressing the *Thou* of his life, as a Thou that cannot be limited by another, he addresses God." So, after much more thought, I came once again to believe in God in this way. And prayer, too, now has meaning for me. Not as supplication, but as a means of inner exploration.

From this, I turned to try to reconcile the conclusions I had come to earlier about the divinity of Jesus as they conflict with traditional theology. For the first few centuries of the Church, Christology was dominantly docetic—that is, in viewing the incarnation, Christ undeniably *appeared* to be a man but somehow he was also divine. These conflicting concepts were wrestled with at the first council of the Church held in Nicea in 325 A.D., but the problem continued unresolved. Finally, in the famous definition of Chalcedon drawn up in 451 A.D. it was decided that he was man but more than man. He was at the same time truly God. I have some difficulty in grasping how a group of men sitting down in a conference then or at any time could take it upon themselves to decide that Jesus was God. Be that as it may. Earlier I explained why I doubted the divinity of Jesus. But if the two traditional concepts of a God "up there" who sends his son "down here" are abandoned, what is left? For me, a great deal remains. Once the dogma of his deity is discarded, a surprisingly sympathetic and humanistic picture of Jesus comes through. The key is love over law: "Thou shalt love the Lord thy God with all thy heart, and with all thy soul, and with all thy mind. This is the first and great Commandment. And the second is like unto it, thou shalt love thy neighbor as thyself. On these two Commandments hang all the Law and the Prophets." For me, this serves as the simplest summary of his entire ministry.

Although the Church reverted from love to law with Paul, papal authority, Augustine and Aquinas, through Luther and the Puritans, the humanism of Jesus' teachings has been reintroduced in our time. Read the works of Hans Kung and Edward Schillebeeckx. Tillich, too, searched for a solution between the absolutism of the Church that breaks down with every change of history and a relativism that makes change itself the ultimate principle. He returned to the *principle* of love, which gives an eternal quality to ethics that is unchangeable, with the *expression* of love as dependent on continuous acts of creative intuition. "Love alone can transform itself according to the concrete demands of every individual and social situation without losing its eternity and dignity and unconditional validity." This is *person*-centered, not *principle*-centered, and is, in essence, humanistic. Similar threads of thought are found in the writings of Professor John Fletcher, Bishop J. A. T. Robinson, and many others today.

If this trend towards humanism is disturbing to you, let's go back for a moment to the most authoritative laws of all, the bedrock of the Bible, the Ten Commandments. I'd like to tell you how I have come to see even these in a new light. One is "Thou shalt not kill." This was originally applicable only to other Israelites—the Old Testament abounds with accounts of killing those outside the tribe. Further, even the killing of fellow tribesmen was not always regarded as murder. One could, for example, avenge himself for the murder of one of his kin. The *lex talionis* (the law of retaliation) pervades Mosaic ethics. So even this commandment can be regarded in the context of its time as a movement in the direction of humanism. Before then there were *no* limits to vengeance.

And "Thou shalt not commit adultery" was given at the same time that a man was enjoined to take in the wife of his brother if the latter died and have children by her. Humanism again.

Another states, "Thou shalt not take the name of the Lord thy God in vain." This had its origin with the revelation to Moses of God's name as just four letters, Yhwh, and prohibited the utterance of this as a word because of its holiness. It does not mean, as most of us think, that we should not refer to God in swearing or blasphemy—we must not speak his name *at all*. Absolutist at the start, but this commandment has undergone an evolution through the centuries in the direction of humanism both within and without the Church.

Still another commands, "Thou shalt keep holy the Sabbath day." Almost none of us today do this. The Sabbath is really Saturday. We rarely even keep Sunday holy. Christ himself said the Sabbath was made for man, not man for the Sabbath. What could be more humanistic?

My point is that even laws such as the commandments, in fact many of the most authoritarian statements in the Bible, can be looked at in a new way. Many were not absolute nor universal then and many of those that were have evolved to become less so since.

So today the sanctions of Sinai have largely lost their terror. Both Reform and Conservative Jews have become extricated from an authoritarian framework. Only the Orthodox remain. Catholic casuistry has always had intricate systems for avoiding its own "natural laws." Most of Protestantism, too, is moving away from an authoritarianism based upon the Bible toward a new humanism that holds the matrix of morality to be man.

This is as far as I could go in the religious part of my midlife search on a rational basis. I hope it has been of some help, at least suggested some routes to take or not to take in your own search. Where you disagreed, and I am sure this was often, it may have served this purpose, too. But even this called for a lot of afterthought on my part. Much had to do with the ancient origins of religion and its existence ever since—the *need* for it if not the living of it by all men in all time. Even to the present—I have seen few atheists remain atheists on their deathbeds. When I wrote the Psychology section that follows later, I browsed once again through Jung and reflected on the subconscious origins of all myths and about his concept of the "Collective Unconscious." Could this be the cosmic imprint, the infinite in all of us, below our conscious minds? At that time, I happened to have the chance to visit some of the caves in Spain where man painted the walls some thirty thousand years ago. The caves themselves were a refuge and place of renewal, and the paintings a plea for help on the hunt. Was not this religion for man as he could conceive it then?

In fact, is not religion something that comes from that part of our minds that corresponds with the level of consciousness that man had then and long before? Has all of our attempt to apply reason to religion since the time of the great Greek thinkers somehow been a perversion of something purer? Perhaps there *are* no "proofs"; perhaps there should be none.

The first function of religion was irrational—why should it not still be so? Early man's mind was simpler, in tune with nature and the seasons. He was not concerned with an afterlife, but with life itself. He was more intuitive than rational. We are more rational, true, but at the same time we have lost touch with some of our inner selves and with nature. Why not set aside some of our rational being if doing so brings us peace and hope? Within us we all have the need for solace, refuge, renewal. This need may be more real in a way than our reason. And around us in life we see that there *is* everlasting renewal. The myths of Isis and Osiris, Demeter and Persephone, and the Eleusinian mysteries arose from the eternal return of spring and life. The return to life in all these myths was through love. Why not, in a way we cannot comprehend, for man?

Is not the meaning of life itself inaccessible to the rational mind? And death? These are the problems that are paramount in middle age. Reason alone can never give us answers that are completely true or truly complete. Why not turn back at this time in our lives for another try in another way? Why *not* believe in some of the answers religion provides where there are as yet no other answers? Religion in all its forms does give us ancient answers to unanswerable questions, and these do satisfy our inborn desire to perceive a pattern, a purpose in our lives.

So the religious part of my search is not ended. It will continue the rest of my life, but in a way that is less rational than it was before. And ultimately, I believe, more satisfying. As I go on from here, the words of the old hymn come to mind:

Hast thou not seen
How all that thou needeth
Hast been granted?
Ponder anew
What the Almighty can do . . .

PHILOSOPHY

As you could tell, my return to religion as an adult was something of a struggle for me. I hope reading of it was not as disturbing for you. If it was, that was not my intention. Again, you are urged to continue to hold sacred whatever you yourself believe to be true.

Admittedly somewhat staggered, I entered next into the realm of philosophy, as I had originally set out to do. Religion, after all, is more of the heart than the head, beyond reason's reach. Faith is there or it is not. This is not so with philosophy. Here man has used his reason to its very limits in an endeavor to understand life and its meaning.

When I was younger, the term *philosophy* itself tended to awe me. It brought to mind those wisest of men, "the sages of the ages," who lived a very long time ago. I couldn't help feeling that their thoughts would be both too difficult for me to understand and inapplicable to life as it is today. But the word *philosophy* merely means love of knowledge. Thought of this way, all of us are philosophers in some sense. And the broad field of philosophy can be made much more comprehensible by dividing it into its four major parts: logic, esthetics, metaphysics, and ethics. Fortunately for our purposes, the first three can be left to the philosophers themselves or returned to later.

As in religion, ethics are the primary concern in a search such as this. Ethics, in the philosophical sense, has a broader meaning than in religion or than we are used to in everyday life. We usually think of it as meaning the moral choice between right and wrong behavior. Ethical philosophy is really a great deal more. It concerns itself with the way of life that is open to man, the good life, the life worth living.

I have always been fond of philosophy, especially ethical philosophy. I said before that man has similar feelings and failings in relation to his fellow man whenever and wherever we find him. And the more I study, the more I can see how each thinker has built upon the thoughts of those that came before him. This time, I found that three coherent ethical systems emerged that touched upon my life today. The rest could be set aside with only a brief comment on each. I'd like to tell you how I thought these three systems through, but first, because it may have been about as long for you as it was for me since you studied philosophy, a bit of history by way of background.

Philosophy began with the Greeks in the city of Miletus, in the early sixth century B.C. At this time, science and philosophy were one, and both had their origin in the contemplation of cosmology. The Milesian school came to an end with the fall of Miletus in 494 B.C., leaving behind a heritage of mysticism and mathematics.

Heracleitus, an Ephesian, made what I believe to be the first ethical contribution in philosophy when, in answer to the static formulations of the Milesian school, he replied that there is no permanence: "You cannot step twice into the same river, for fresh waters are ever flowing in upon you." He held that nothing ever *is*; everything is *becoming*. This is a thought to remember. Perhaps because of the way the brain is constructed, we somehow find it easier to accept a static view of things. The concept of change is vaguely disturbing, and this is especially true as we grow older. However, the theme throughout this book is that if we accept change as a challenge and respond to each challenge with change, we are dealing with the very stuff of life.

Next in history came Democritus and other philosophers oriented to the physical who, having reduced the natural world to the smallest conceivable particle, the atom, reached the end of an era and the end of the extension of man's experience into the physical world that would be possible for the next thousand years.

So from this time, philosophers turned more toward the consideration of man. Even the historians of that epoch, Herodotus and Thucydides, and playwrights such as Aeschyus and Sophocles, turned their attention toward man. One incidental result of this trend was the undermining of the status of the Grecian gods. They and their lives began to become the myths we know today. In the fifth century B.C. there arose in Greece a group of men called Sophists, who wandered from place to place making their living teaching young men of good birth how to participate in politics. In Plato's dialogue the *Protagoras*, there is an interesting portrayal of what the Sophist and his life must have been like. Protagoras himself exemplified the trend of philosophy toward the contemplation of man with his famous quotation, "Man is the measure of all things."

Socrates was the greatest of the Sophists. He lived in Athens at its Periclean peak. Socrates himself left no written word, so what we know of him comes from the historian Xenophon and Plato. His most famous statement is "Know thyself," which he took from the temple of the oracle at Delphi. His own words were "The unexamined life is not worth living." In the *Phaedrus* of Plato it is perhaps more poetically expressed: "May the outward and inward man be at one." The thought—and truth—behind all three quotations struck me as especially important to carry with me in my search.

That's all the history I'll present as such. For more, you are referred to Will Durant's timeless *The Story of Philosophy* and other sources in the Bibliography. But before tracing the three ethical systems I mentioned, I would like to mention a few others briefly. You know them or have heard of them, so this is more of a reminder than an exposition, in case you wish to pursue them on your own.

Taking one part of Socratic thought, Zeno founded the Stoic

school in Athens in the fourth century B.C. This ethical philosophy persisted over a period of only five hundred years in Greece and later in Rome, but because it underwent many variations, it is difficult to define its principles with precision. In general, the Stoics held that although man could not control the circumstances which affect him, he *could* control his reactions to them. Its strongly ascetic quality, reflective of an oriental passivism, probably can be traced to the fact that Zeno himself was of Phoenician stock.

The Stoic ethics turned on two concepts: nature and virtue. They regarded nature as a unitary whole in which all events, even human acts, are subject to laws that are to be accepted. Virtue is to be obtained by subjecting natural impulses as well as reaction to external events to the rule of reason. This led to a law of duty that was accepted by many Romans, most notably Marcus Aurelius and Seneca. An egalitarian influence was introduced by Epictetus, perhaps because of his status as a slave.

The school of the Stoics eventually came to the position that emotion was not a natural part of man but a perversion of reason itself and entirely to be eradicated. Virtue and vice thus became polarized. For a time, Stoicism was a counterpoint to the sensualism of Rome, but as a philosophy in and of itself it ceased with the *Meditations* of Marcus Aurelius and his death in 180 A.D. It lived on only as a part of Christian theology when Aquinas melded some of the Stoic concepts with the philosophy of Aristotle.

Although there are elements of Stoicism in us all, it was not a complete ethical philosophy and so perhaps deserved to die. Even theoretically, we know it is impossible to banish *all* desire and *all* emotion—nor is it even desirable. Practically, with our newer knowledge of psychology, we not only recognize the value of some emotions such as fear and love, but we know that anyone who came close to realizing perfection in the Stoic ethic would be schizophrenic. Perfect attainment is possible only in death. It is interesting that several Stoics, including Zeno and Seneca, left this life by their own hands.

The Cynics of ancient Greece formed another short-lived school, not only rejecting all knowledge, but even the possibility of knowledge. However, they had their counterparts in more recent history in pessimism and existentialism. Arthur Schopenhauer, in the words of Will Durant, was the prince of pessimists. He was a product of his time. Waterloo had come and gone, the revolution had failed, Napoleon was rotting on a rock in a distant sea, and death was the only visible victor. Schopenhauer felt that the world was all misery, but that a force of will drove us on. Happiness was to be found only in the brief absence of pain if the striving were for the moment successful, but then we must once again strive. The reach of Schopenhauer's will was greater than its grasp. He wished to escape desire, but this too is a desire.

Existentialism had its origin with Søren Kierkegaard in the middle of the last century, when science had seemed to replace religion. He felt that reason was useless—life had to be "lived forward and understood backward." His emphasis on pessimism was overwhelming, as was his deprecation of society, but more crucial was his emphasis on the irrational. He used irrational criteria to defeat reason as a test of truth and then used the same irrationality to evaluate truth. Either path leads to absurdity. From this point, existentialism splintered into the various philosophies of Heidegger, Jaspers, Camus, Sartre, and others.

Two more subsidiary schools arose in history that deserve mention. Evolutionary ethics had both its birth and death in the second half of the nineteenth century. It was patterned upon the evolutionary principles of Charles Darwin and was espoused first by Herbert Spencer, then by Thomas Huxley. It soon became apparent that it was founded upon an inaccurate analogy. The essence of man is unique and different from that of plants and animals. Not only was this analogy erroneous, but the system had to invoke the Lamarckian theory of inherited acquired characteristics to explain the "evolution" of ethics. This implied that the laws of logic as well as of morality that have been found to be conducive to society survive in subsequent generations as inherited traits.

The last of the lesser schools I will mention is the nihilism of Friedrich Nietzsche. He combined the pessimism of Schopenhauer with elements of Darwinism. His conclusion was that the history of man has shown that there are two moral codes: the master morality, which is the natural one, and a slave morality, which is artificial. Might makes right is the undisputed verdict of nature. The traditional Judeo-Christian culture was appropriate only for slaves and was created by slaves for their own protection. Religious leaders had inverted the natural moral values so that they themselves could become the masters.

In my opinion, the value of Nietzsche rests solely on his caustic criticisms of Judaism, Christianity, and democracy, which were a stimulant to all three. He himself steadily deteriorated from this iconoclasm to insanity.

Authoritarianism

If you have a stronger philosophical bent than mine you may have winced at the foregoing dismissal of so many ethical systems, or at the failure to mention many other minor ones. But, as I have said, this is the story of my own search. Yours is your own. The three systems that follow are the only ones that hold meaning for me—each for a different reason, as you will see. As you read, I hope you will both agree and disagree. Write your thoughts in the margins. Go on to read the works of the philosophers who interest you. My purpose is to stir you to *think about* the points I touch upon, not to persuade you to accept them yourself.

Authoritarianism as a philosophy probably arose from man's earliest contact with his environment. When he found he was able to manipulate material things successfully, it would have been a simple step to extend this method to his relationship with his fellow man. I postulated before how Ug presumably got along with Og by means of a club. As social organizations became larger, some customs evolved that were successful by their very expediency, and they then hardened into moral codes. These were often reinforced by punitive legal systems, and many even received religious sanction. Of course, other elements contributed along the way—exaltation of ego, hunger for power, greed, fear of departing from the status quo, and so forth, but the root of all such systems seemed to me to be simple expediency.

Man has been under the burden of many authoritarian systems throughout his history, and I found it interesting to trace the origin of them all back to just this—simple expediency. Simple systems do work well for simple people, but they fail when the people are not so simple. Few of us are so simple today.

The major manifestations of authoritarianism became cloaked in religion very early in our Western world and were incorporated in the organized Christian Church nearly two thousand years ago. In the last section I followed this from parts of the Old Testament through Paul; left papal power, Augustine, and monasticism to you; and paused at Aquinas. Even the Reformation failed to reform this aspect of organized Christianity. Bibliolatry was substituted. As I indicated, much of the exposition of the humanism of Christ's ministry was left to a later theology.

The earliest positions of authoritarianism in secular philosophy are peripheral to my purpose here. So I will pass over them to present a few thoughts of its principal proponent, Immanuel Kant. His approach was unique, in that the source of the authority was within, not without. He started with an intuition in man of a moral sense, traced this to metaphysical heights, and then came back again to man with his categorical imperative, "Act as if the principle from which you act were to become through your will a universal law of nature." By categorical, he meant unconditional, but he allowed for another class of imperatives as well, the hypothetical. The hypothetical are binding only conditionally—that is, if a certain condition is to be accepted. For example, if you wish to be believed, do not lie. Man's duty is to obey these imperatives in each and every act. And this duty must be done for duty's sake, not for the sake of happiness or any other goal. It is rather through the performance of duty that one becomes *worthy* of happiness in Kant's scheme.

This is only a cupful from the ocean of his writings. I would refer you from here to any one of a number of excellent sources—with one admonition: The last person you wish to read on Kant is Kant himself. But that much was necessary in order to present a few of my arguments against him. These, I believe, are some of the major reasons authoritarianism has lost its hold upon us as an ethical philosophy—or should:

1. He discounted the role of empirical observations and based his ethical system on an *a priori* principle, conscience. We now know enough about psychology to realize that this intuitive moral sense arises from an introjection of societal values early in life and is therefore relative to the particular culture being considered. Therefore, both his categorical imperative and its universal extension rest on a faulty basis.

2. Application of his categorical imperative is unclear. Does the universality test apply to each particular situation or problem as it arises? If it does, then when we come to decide upon a certain act we can easily rationalize that this act should then *become* universal when that situation arises for another. And no two situations are ever identical. Chaos would be the conse-

quence. But if Kant meant his principle to apply to *classes* of acts, this would lead to rigidity and moral fanaticism. Either way it fails.

3. He stated that because every man *can* conform to his moral law he therefore *ought* to. This does not follow at all.

4. He so polarized duty and desire, duty and reason, duty and experience, that these conflicts cannot be resolved in this life. He therefore had to postulate an afterlife in the hope that in immortality justice would triumph.

5. Kant's system constituted only a negative guide to conduct. Morality in its highest sense has to be positive.

6. In defining virtue as obedience to moral law, Kant reconciled it with freedom because he conceived of freedom as submission to law. I find this difficult to accept.

7. There is no guarantee of happiness in his system. He stated that it is only just, that we *ought* to obtain happiness by being worthy of it in doing our duty. He failed to suggest any means whereby happiness could be assured.

Above all, in Kant's system, such elements as warmth, love, kindness, and compassion are missing.

These are enough. I don't want to bore you as badly as Kant did me. Instead, I would invite you to browse through the works of Georg Hegel, who followed Kant. His works are a true delight. He believed that anyone who obeyed a moral law such as Kant's without reason was simply a slave to a self-imposed law. He emphasized that all aspects of man's nature, including passion, love, desire, and sensuous experience must be included in any ethical system. Higher than Kant's law was Hegel's "reconcilability," a loving disposition. He sacrificed the universality of an abstract law for the richness and reality of love, and in so doing reconciled desire and duty, restoring the unity of man. Hegel also stressed the freedom of the individual, returning once again more closely to Aristotle. He felt that with freedom the individual would develop, that his desires would then come to include a desire for the happiness of others. Rather than to an afterworld, he looked to world history for justice.

Joseph Butler, James Martineau, and Jacques Maritain have been the main advocates of authoritarianism from Kant to our own time, but they were lesser lights and in my opinion have failed to resurrect this philosophy from its deserved demise.

I would like to close this brief discussion of authoritarianism with a few further thoughts about it. As I write, I read in the papers of the denial of human rights all over the world, of the suppression of free theological thought by John Paul II, of hostages held, and of the Soviet invasion of Afghanistan, so I realize this philosophy is not dead for all. Let me put it another way. As a philosophy, I believe it *is* dead, but the lack of theoretical validity does not stay those whose interest is practical expediency.

In all its theoretical formulations, I found one element to be consistent in this philosophy. No matter whether its origin comes from without—divine or natural law, empiricism, or history—or from within as moral intuition or conscience, authoritarianism invariably comes to regard each moral act as a discrete and self-contained unit with intrinsic characteristics of rightness or goodness. If any act is judged to be good, then this judgment is extended to a class of acts so that any further act in that class is good without regard to circumstances or consequences. This fatal flaw of secular authoritarianism was mentioned before when I discussed Aquinas and religious authoritarianism. In life, one is simply unable to escape the necessity of evaluating acts in terms of consequences, so all such systems fail.

The one positive thing I can say about the absolutism of authoritarianism is that it does provide us with general principles within which we are better able to understand particular situations. Perhaps the most pervasive and persistent form of authoritarianism is in our legal structure, which limits man's range of actions. But even our laws have their origin in the collective expression of individual wills in a democratic society. I can only conclude that the development of science, industry, commerce, individualism, and especially education, along with our increasing reliance upon reason and understanding of our emotions, have all brought us beyond the scope of any authoritarian philosophy, religious or secular. But as I have said so many times before, you are as entitled to your own conclusions as I am to mine.

Yet now you can see the reason I presented it. I wanted to point out its origin, describe its manifestations here (and in the previous discussion of religion) so that it can be recognized more clearly in all of its forms, and then give reasons why I feel it should be rejected. Obviously, I believe that the time is long past for its burden to be lifted from humanity. For an ethical philosophy to guide my own life, of course, I had to look elsewhere.

One caution as I turn to two systems that emphasize individualism: One must be careful not to substitute absolutism of the individual for absolutism of law. Conscience is fallible, and conscience without conscientiousness is unforgivable.

Hedonism

The second ethical system I followed through history has been called many things in many times. Its most persistent quality has been hedonism, so I have chosen to call it that. Again, if you are a purist, you may wince as I select quotations from some philosophers whose principal positions were not hedonistic. And some subtle shadings between pleasure and higher forms of happiness will only become clear as I go along. I must confess that before my own midlife search, I was an altruistic hedonist. You will see here why I changed.

Aristippus, a student of Socrates, started the trickle that was to become a stream. A native of the city of Cyrene, he advocated pleasures here and now as the chief and only goal in life. The past is no longer, and the future is yet to be. This was the start of hedonism as an ethical philosophy.

At about the same time, Epicurus founded his school of philosophy in Athens, promulgating the conviction that the study of ethics is man's most important concern. He modified the Cyrenaic philosophy of the pleasure principle in three ways. First, he included mental as well as sensual pleasures—he felt that the former were higher and should be preferred. Second, he included future as well as present pleasures. That is, certain immediate pleasures should be forgone in order to obtain more meaningful pleasures later. And third, he emphasized avoidance of pain, which he called negative pleasure. So you can see that when we talk about someone who overindulges in food, drink, or other sensual pleasures, we may *say* Epicurean, but we *mean* Cyrenaic.

After the Cyrenaics and the Epicureans, hedonism flourished in Rome, but it declined with its fall and with the advent of Christianity. It was partially resurrected in the late sixteenth and early seventeenth centuries by Francis Bacon, but his contribution lies less in ethics than in other areas. Benedict Spinoza, later in the seventeenth century, declared happiness to be a goal of conduct. He defined happiness simply as the presence of pleasure and the absence of pain. But he introduced a note of altruism by stating that men, under the guidance of their reason, seek what is useful not only to them but also to the rest of mankind. Thomas Hobbes observed that man loved only himself and cared for others only as they contributed to his own pleasure. He concluded that if man were allowed to remain in a state of nature, a condition of chaos would result. This fact gave rise to society. The state, in his view, should be supreme, constituting a covenant of the people with one another. The power of the sovereign, or Leviathan, is given him by the people to enforce that covenant. This was one of the theoretical foundations for the establishment of modern democracies.

David Hume, the great skeptic of the next century, started as an empiricist. He observed that men pass moral judgments and found that in all things that men considered good, there was a common quality known as utility—that is, they are good because of their consequences. In counterposition to Hobbes, who endeavored to reduce every human motive to self-love, he stated that there was a capacity in man for being affected by happiness other than his own and that the morality of an action can be measured by its contribution to the happiness of all.

Then Jeremy Bentham came on the scene. His goal was to make ethics as precise as the new science of physics was then becoming. He attempted to quantify pleasure, and in the formation of his hedonistic calculus, restricted his concern to physical pleasures. He put forth seven criteria to facilitate a correct choice among pleasures—criteria such as intensity and duration. To this method of calculating pleasure, he added four sanctions, so that a person would not exceed the grounds of propriety in pursuing pleasure. The first is physical, whereby a person learns from nature which action is harmful and which is beneficial; second is the political, in which he is guided by the laws of the state; third is moral, whereby he is guided by the pressure of public opinion; and the fourth is religious, with reward and punishment not only in this life, but also in an afterlife. He felt that since these sanctions were in operation, we were not required to compute the effects upon others of every act.

In the nineteenth century Thomas Carlyle tried to make hedonism more altruistic. He called Bentham's philosophy a "pig philosophy" and rejected porcine pleasures for man. He urged in his "greater nobleness principle" that we look to heroes for our ideals and stressed the difference between mental and physical pleasures.

It remained for John Stuart Mill to state that the greatest good for the greatest number should be the goal of life, thus firmly adding altruism to hedonism. He took something from both Plato and Aristotle in emphasizing the qualitative difference of pleasures, and went on to state that the ingredients of happiness are each desirable in and of themselves, not necessarily as a sum or aggregate resulting from a calculus. One of the other advances he made over Bentham was his rejection of psychological hedonism, that is, the doctrine that an individual has *no choice* except to seek pleasure and to avoid pain. Another was his reiteration that those pleasures derived from our human qualities have a value surpassing those from the animal qualities within us. Still another was that he recognized the existence of an internal sanction— conscience—over and above the four sanctions of Bentham, thereby returning some autonomy to the individual.

After Mill, the theological utilitarians took up the thread. Henry Sidgwick fervently wished that egoism and altruism could be brother and sister but came to the conclusion that the only way to guarantee that a good man would receive his just reward would be on the theological assumption of another life after death. George Edward Moore, a disciple of Sidgwick, held that a right action is one which gives the best consequences possible from any given act, regardless of the doer's intent and the probable consequences known at the time. The paradox in his position is that this can never be known until after the action is taken.

There, all too briefly, hedonism is today. Let me present some of my criticisms of this ethical philosophy, and you will see why I moved on to another.

A philosophical point, perhaps, but pleasure cannot be the *same* as good. If it were, this would imply a higher criterion whereby pleasure is determined to *be* good. So pleasure itself, no matter how defined, cannot be the greatest good in life. And if only pleasures of a lower order were to be sought, several difficulties would arise. How would a hedonist seeking only those explain self-sacrificial acts? Pure pleasure also tends to be all-absorbing, which would interfere with the ability to make choices among such pleasures. They are also short-lived. Man desires more. We must include higher pleasures—for want of a better word, *happiness*.

With our knowledge of psychology, we know now that all of our choices are not made deliberately—many are impulsive, not purposive. Reason is never in total control. There can be no perfect prediction, so we are plagued with the problem of consequences. Most importantly, the hedonistic paradox persists unsolved. That is, our experience in life teaches us that happiness is not attained by direct pursuit.

But there were some contributions made by hedonism in its course through history. One is that it did recognize happiness as a valid goal, and another is that it distinguished between pleasures of an animal order and uniquely human happiness, emphasizing the latter without excluding the former. Most important, it has brought us face to face with the paradox that happiness, even if it is a valid goal, is not to be pursued directly. Nor is it to be found without, in things. It resides within us; it is an *accompaniment* of acts which this philosophy leaves undefined. So from here, let's go to the third system to see if something is said about what such acts may be.

Self-realization

Self-realization is the ethical theory that a person's purpose in life is the realization of his highest potentials. Implicit in this theory is that a person can somehow become aware of his potentials, develop them, integrate them harmoniously within himself, and then integrate himself similarly in society. To me, this had always seemed to be a somewhat selfish system. This is why I had never accepted it. But I learned more about it when I thought it through again. Let's see where it came from and where it leads us.

The origin of self-realization is found once again in Socrates, in the *Timaeus*, *Protagoras* and the *Laws* of Plato, where it is stressed that ignorance of oneself results in evil, but that with knowledge of self will come both virtue and happiness.

Plato went on to develop this ethical system further. He was twenty-eight when Socrates, his master and mentor, took the hemlock. Afterwards he wandered the world for years, absorbing knowledge from every fount and sitting at every shrine before he returned to Athens to write and teach at his Academy. In order to understand Plato's presentation of this ethical system, I first must touch upon his metaphysics. To Plato, human *perception* revealed phenomena in terms of only a superficial or transient reality, but *reason* was able to detect the absolute and universal reality beyond perception. This may best be comprehended by considering mathematical principles. Although you may see a triangle or an algebraic equation, the principles of these themselves are beyond the figure and the equation—they are universal and intangible. Therefore, for Plato, the idea or the form of good must then be the ultimate good, or God. Inasmuch as man is made in the image of God, man's task is then to perfect himself to approach as closely as possible this ideal. Only thus can he find happiness here on earth.

In analyzing man, Plato went beyond the dualistic concept that posited the animal and mental as being the only aspects of the human being. Between the animal and the mental he added a third, the energetic part, which he called the spirit, where the heroic virtues reside. Both of the lower faculties must be subordinate to and in the service of the highest. In the *Phaedrus*, he reiterated that desire is always in need of restraint and that reason will always be in the right. His conception of human nature prefigured Plotinus and Augustine in Christian theology. To me it also sounds somewhat like Freud.

In *The Republic*, Plato conceded that all men desire happiness for its own sake and that for different men happiness may take different forms. In the *Philebus*, he allowed a place for lower pleasures only insofar as they do not interfere with the higher functions of man. But throughout his writings, he emphasized that the function of the mind brings man true virtue and therefore the highest happiness.

You can already see why I felt the system to be somewhat selfish. There is little concern for others or one's relationships with them. But for me, there are other flaws as it was expounded by Plato. To him, life lacks the Heracleitean sense of flux and change, and there is no room for such things as humor or love in his world. Another, to me, is his statement that virtue *necessarily* results in happiness. This was inadvertently admitted by Plato himself in his concept of "the noble lie" in *The Republic*, whereby the rulers of the state must impress upon the citizens that virtue is for their own good and will lead to happiness, even though the citizens themselves may not believe this. His emphasis upon order also seems excessive when you think through his idea in

The Republic that all should occupy themselves in the task for which they are best fitted. A shoemaker's son would be best fitted to be a shoemaker, unless other educational opportunities were provided, a point he fails to clarify. If this idea were carried out, his wise philosopher-kings would continually control a totalitarian state, with all occupations and classes fixed apparently for eternity.

Aristotle objected to Plato's distinction between the ideal form and the actual thing experienced. He thought that the form existed *in* the thing, not outside of and apart from it. This is his concept of *entelechy*, where the form is the meaning expressing itself in material shape. Therefore for him, the good is not a single entity and universally present—he allows for differences among situations as well as among the people encountering them.

He, like Plato, believed that happiness is the goal of life, but he went beyond Plato's position in a manner consistent with his naturalistic bent to state that man has three natures: the vegetable (physical), the animal (emotional), and the rational. He acknowledged that on the vegetable level good functioning of the body can give a sense of well-being, and he accepted this. He also acknowledged a place for the satisfaction of our animal desires on the second level. However, it was on the third, or rational, level that supreme happiness was to be attained. Here he is more consistent with Plato. The function of human reason, fulfilling the potentials of the mind that is unique to man, constituted for Aristotle the greatest good in life.

These conclusions are for the most part found in his *Nicomachean Ethics* (named after his son, Nicomachus), which ends with a discussion on friendship and happiness that serves as a transition into his *Politics*. In the latter he stated that beauty, art, literature, and even humor may be appreciated and contribute to happiness. He admitted that man—even a philosopher—must have food, shelter, clothing, and other certain vital needs met, but once these requirements are assured, the wise man will go on to seek happiness as a whole and in proper proportion. The common run of man, however, will see happiness distorted and emphasize instrumentalities such as wealth and other lower-order pleasures instead of the life of reason. But Aristotle believed that education could elevate this sort of person. An essential part of his ethical system is that happiness is found in activity—it is not a static state. He also believed that the soul is as inseparable from the body as wetness is from water and that the soul dies with the man, so happiness is to be found in this world alone. Throughout his thinking he seemed very much aware of the hedonistic paradox: Happiness must not be pursued directly. He often referred to moderation, which has come to be called the Golden Mean. This was not a rigid mathematical average of extremes, but fluctuated with the collateral circumstances of each situation, discernible only to mature and flexible reason.

After Aristotle, self-realization continued in a different context with Paul, Augustine, Anselm, and others in the Christian tradition. As a secular philosophy of life, however, it lay largely dormant until the last century. Thomas Green, Francis Bradley, and Brand Blanshard then made minor contributions that do not need to be elaborated upon here.

Just as the atomistic philosophy of Democritus came to an end until man could devise the tools with which to explore his physical world further, the ethical philosophy of self-realization did not advance significantly after Aristotle until some twentieth-century philosophers who were also psychologists began to learn how to heed the admonition of Socrates to look within man.

Before we see what they had to say, I'd like to tell you what I derived from this philosophy. First, some of its contributions. Like hedonism, it accepts happiness as the goal of man. I think we all pretty much accept thus, albeit with certain modifications and conditions. It is congruent, too, with its emphasis upon the higher forms of happiness over the lower forms, without excluding the latter. This, too, is acceptable to most of us. Its most singular contribution is its resolution of the hedonistic paradox, in emphasizing *activities* in accordance with a hierarchy of values. Highest is the activity of the mind, and the greatest happiness attainable *accompanies* such activity.

To me, the main fault of self-realization, aside from its overconcern with the individual, is that it is theoretically vague. It leaves the definition of perfection—the qualities it consists of—undefined. It also leaves the *process* of perfecting unclear, and the *purpose* of the perfecting process is either not stated, not stated clearly, or given simply as happiness.

It was within some of the university departments of philosophy around the world at the turn of this century that psychology as a distinct discipline began to emerge. However, I find it fascinating to look back in philosophy to the more remote roots of psychology. At the very beginning, Anaxagoras, Empedocles, and Hippocrates had thoughts that could only be called psychological. Socrates, Plato, and Aristotle all dwelt on the mind of man. In the seventeenth century, Rene Descartes, with his statement, "I think, therefore I am," emphasized the mind and not the theological soul as that part of man distinct from the matter of his body. Gottfried Leibniz also believed that the mind and body were distinct but acted harmoniously. His concept of degrees of consciousness even foreshadowed the concept of the unconscious as developed by Herbart and then Freud. John Locke devoted a great deal of his thinking to the analysis of sensation, perception, and ideas. His emphasis on empiricism also laid the groundwork for experimentation in psychology. Henri Bergson was concerned with the instincts and intelligence of man, and Hegel held that man had "drives" rather than instincts as in the animal model presupposed by Bergson. But I won't go on. Let's just say that all of the sciences arose from philosophy, that psychology is the latest to do so, and return to our subject.

Foremost among the modern philosopher-psychologists was William James. He dealt first with truth, stating that it was related to human judgment and human needs. Its verity lay in its verification. In his *Ethics*, he stated that static perfection was not the final goal, but that perfecting is a process. "The ever enduring process of perfecting, maturing, refining, is the aim in living." Again, the theme of change and adjustment to change. With this he brought philosophy down from the outer reaches of space to the homes and hearts of men.

The pragmatism of James continued on the strength of John Dewey's dialectical skill. Dewey also acknowledged that happiness was not to be pursued as a direct goal. It was the result of an active process, not a passive outcome, and it was different for every man and every situation. Dewey believed that intelligent inquiry must have a role in moral situations, and that each situation must be treated in terms of its own attendant problems. There can be no fixed rule applicable to all cases as authoritarianism holds—again a theme we've encountered before. Both James and Dewey are well worth reading in your own search.

With these two as transition, I would like to explore psychology further to tell you what elements of ethical philosophy I found there. I am not aware that this has been done quite in this way before. But bear with me—I think you will find it interesting.

PSYCHOLOGY

Although I learned a lot from rereading the works of the great philosophers, I constantly encountered the inherent limitation of philosophy in answering my questions about values in life. This is its reliance upon reason. Reason may be the rudder by which we consciously control our lives, but the sail exists, too—and the ship itself and the unseen effects of wind and water upon it. Few of the philosophers address such everyday events in life as friendship, fear, humor, loving and being loved, the pride we take in our children as they grow and mature, the satisfaction from work well done, the mystic experiences we may have had, or even orgasm, with its infinite intimacy. Obviously a lot of life has been left out. With this reliance upon reason, ethical philosophy has "gone about as fur as it can go." In fact, there has been little contribution from philosophers over the past century or so in this area. Most are mired in metaphysics.

I have described how the discipline of psychology began to emerge from various departments of philosophy in universities in the Western world around the start of this century. In the words of Ruth Monroe, "its full liberation is a matter of recent decades."

Out of the influence of Bruer, Janet, Bernheim, and Charcot, Sigmund Freud's work in psychoanalysis developed. He coined this term, which is used to this day by proponents of his theories. His biologically based system was discussed in a previous chapter, "The Person," and as it makes no allowance for ideals, altruism, or any value system, I could not derive anything from it in my search.

Alfred Adler was the first psychoanalyst to make some contribution to our understanding of values. As I noted previously, he rejected the biological basis of Freud's work, with its mechanistic causation, and felt that the human being moved in the direction of finality. Causality does exist in the natural sciences, but man moves *toward* goals. He conceived of man as having inborn potentials rather than biologically based drives and stated that society helped men realize their potentials. He changed his early "will to power" concept later in his writings to a more Aristotelian one—realization of a person's potentials—which he called perfection. In his scheme, arrival at perfection required the setting of goals and then, through discipline and hard work, the achievement of them. Each person sees perfection in his own way and strives for it in his own way. While Freud saw man "goaded on by the id, hemmed in by the super-ego and rebuffed by reality, with the ego struggling to cope," or torn between Eros and Thanatos, Adler at least saw man as capable of forming his own values and acting upon them.

Carl Jung also felt that the sexual emphasis in Freud's theory of libido was excessive. He described the libido more broadly as the "energy of the processes of life." This energy is undifferentiated and can be used in many ways, the first of which is self-preservation. Once survival is ensured, the energy can then become transformed into cultural or spiritual pursuits. Jung believed that individuals were constantly evolving throughout their lives just as the human species has evolved throughout history. He combined causality, that is, the past influences that act upon the present, with teleology, wherein there is a futuristic orientation for man. About values *per se* he was only sketchily descriptive. But one point of his deserves reiteration: Man is more concerned with outward affairs early in life, but by midlife becomes more concerned with his own true self, others, and life itself—in particular its *meaning*. Jung believed that this inner exploration could help the person find a significance in his life that would make it possible for him to accept the finality of death with equanimity.

So with Adler and Jung I saw that we are able to rise above the Freudian biological basis, look to the future, set goals, strive toward them, and have a clearly defined energy source with which to do so. Jung also tells us that middle age is the time to search within to find our true selves and meaning in our lives.

Karen Horney emphasized the self as a whole person, in contrast to Freud's theory of the subdivided personality. She felt this "real self" was inborn. Although a child would early mold himself upon other's values, at some time this inborn self must be realized. Thus later life, if not the best chance, was certainly the last chance to realize this inborn identity. But I did not learn much from her about how one is to find out what this self is nor how to go about realizing it.

Carl Rogers helped me more on this. He also believes that the core tendency of a human being is the actualize his potentials and, further, that this actualization brings happiness in life. He conceives of actualization as a fulfillment of a genetic blueprint and stresses that self-actualization does not *aim* at pleasure or happiness but that it is *accompanied* by happiness. His psychology is set in the context of therapy, and central to his approach is his concept of an ongoing valuing process. He notes that a child introjects value patterns from many sources and then regards these as his own. Because of the variety of the sources, there is inevitable conflict. His client (as he calls his patient) has unknowingly relinquished his right to judge and determine values to others and has lost touch with his own valuing process. In therapy his client is encouraged to sense and feel what is going on within him, to use this experiencing as direct reference to which he can turn as a guide in his behavior. It is through this valuing process that the individual actualizes his true self. He states that a person should trust this internal wisdom but do so knowingly, using both reason and experience. As a person matures, a certain commonality of values within the self will then emerge; he then tends to move away from facades, "oughts," "shoulds," and pleasing others. Universal values "out there," imposed by philosophers, priests, or politicians, are but background guides for such an actualizing person.

Where others had been concerned with the self or lifted our sights to society, Erich Fromm related man to the reality of humanity. Man alone of all animals is aware of himself and his destiny. Primitive man tried to escape this awareness through myth, religion, and a closely knit social group. Through the Middle Ages man continued to have such security and stability, but the Renaissance and the Reformation destroyed these. Man found freedom, but its price was the loss of this security and stability. Fromm commented that some men still tend to "escape from freedom" by returning to totalitarianism or authoritarian religious systems.

Throughout his writings, Fromm disparaged the supernatural origin of our ethical system and deplored the emphasis on evil and guilt of our Western religions. He noted that Lao-tzu, Buddha, and even Isaiah and Jesus were humanistic. Fromm spoke out for humanity rather than humiliation and for reasons rather than rationalizations. He recognized the importance of society in allowing man to achieve the free and harmonious development of his personality. In a "sane society," man would have the possibility of transcending nature through creativity rather than by conformity. Since most societies are not sane, only the conformist would be adjusted. *Society* is either sick or sane, not man. Fromm stated that the only way man can achieve happiness is to realize his potentials: "The aim of man's life, therefore, is to be understood as the unfolding of his powers according to the laws of nature. . . . The whole life of the individual is nothing but the process of giving birth to himself; indeed, we should be fully born when we die—although it is the tragic fate of most individuals to die before they are born."

Maslow's Theory of Self-Actualization

I have come a long way in just a few pages setting forth what I learned so far about values from psychology—ignoring behaviorism and mental measurements, vaulting over Freud and many others to trace the development of humanistic psychology to its foremost proponent, Abraham Maslow. Maslow's theory of personality structure was described in "The Person." Briefly, he set forth a hierarchy of needs with self-actualization being the highest in the hierarchy. His is a philosophy of ascending the hierarchy—becoming, not being. I would now like to go further into what he meant by self-actualization.

In trying to determine what a self-actualizing person was, Maslow kept a notebook for years, his "GHB Notebook" (Great Human Being). He started keeping notes on his students and those he knew and then included great people from history whom he thought were self-actualizing. He then sought certain threads of similarity. These characteristics were so important to me in my search that I have listed them here in detail. I tried to use his own words as much as possible in order to convey his thoughts more accurately, although nearly two dozen pages in his *Motivation and Personality* are condensed to the following:

MORE EFFICIENT PERCEPTION OF REALITY AND MORE COMFORTABLE RELATIONS WITH IT

Self-actualizing individuals have an unusual ability to detect the spurious, the fake, and the dishonest in personality and to judge people correctly and efficiently. Perception in all areas is less distorted by wish, desire, anxiety, fear, optimism, or pessimism. This results in a superior ability to reason and to perceive the truth. The consequence is that they live more in the real world than in the man-made mass of concepts, abstractions, expectations, beliefs, and stereotypes that most people confuse with the world. They are less threatened by the unknown and often are more attracted by it than by the known.

ACCEPTANCE (SELF, OTHERS, NATURE)

These individuals accept themselves and their own nature without chagrin or complaint. They see human nature as it is and not as they would prefer it to be. They do not feel guilty about their own shortcomings or those of the species or of the culture or of the group with which they have identified, but they are aware of the discrepancies between what is and what ought to be.

SPONTANEITY, SIMPLICITY, NATURALNESS

Self-actualizing people are relatively spontaneous in behavior, but far more spontaneous than that in their inner life, thoughts, and impulses. They recognize that the world in which they live could not understand or accept this, so they conform to the ceremonies and rituals of convention with a good-humored shrug and the best possible grace. They have codes of ethics that are relatively autonomous and individual, rather than conventional, but are the most ethical of people even though their ethics are not necessarily the same as those of the people around them.

PROBLEM-CENTERING

They are in general more focused outside themselves, with some mission in life, some task to fulfill, some problem outside themselves that enlists much of their energies. These tasks are nonpersonal and unselfish, concerned rather with the good of mankind in general, of a nation in general, or even of a few individuals in his or her family. This seems to impart a certain serenity and lack of worry over immediate concerns that make life easier not only for themselves but for all who are associated with them.

THE QUALITY OF DETACHMENT, THE NEED FOR PRIVACY

They can be solitary without harm to themselves and without discomfort and prefer solitude to a greater degrees than the average person. They have the ability to concentrate to a degree not usual for ordinary men. They make up their own minds, come to their own decisions, are self-starters, and are responsible for themselves and their own destinies.

AUTONOMY, INDEPENDENCE OF CULTURE AND ENVIRONMENT, WILL, ACTIVE AGENTS

They are relatively independent of their physical and social environment. Rather, they are dependent for their own development and continued growth on their own potentialities and latent resources.

CONTINUED FRESHNESS OF APPRECIATION

Self-actualizing people have the wonderful capacity to appreciate again and again, freshly and naively, the basic goods of life, with awe, pleasure, wonder, and even ecstasy, however stale these experiences may have become to others.

THE MYSTIC EXPERIENCE, THE PEAK EXPERIENCE

These experiences, described so well by William James, are a fairly common experience for self-actualizing persons, though not for all. Maslow makes the point that it is important to dissociate this type of experience from any theological or supernatural reference, even though for thousands of years they have been linked. It can occur to a lesser degree of intensity than the theological literature would indicate. There is no absolute, qualitative difference between the mystic experience and all others; it can be placed on a continuum with them.

GEMEINSCHAFTSGEFÜHL

This word, invented by Alfred Adler, is the one chosen by Maslow as the best one to describe the flavor of the feelings for mankind expressed by self-actualizing subjects. They have a deep feeling of identification, sympathy, and affection for human beings in spite of occasional anger, impatience, or disgust. Because of this, they have a genuine desire to help the human race.

INTERPERSONAL RELATIONS

Self-actualizing people have deeper and more profound interpersonal relations than others. They are capable of more fusion, greater love, more obliteration of the ego boundaries than other people would consider possible. One consequence of this is that they have especially deep ties with rather few individuals. Their circle of friends is small.

THE DEMOCRATIC CHARACTER STRUCTURE

They are democratic in the deepest possible sense. They can be and are friendly with anyone of suitable character, regardless of class, education, political belief, race, or color. As a matter of fact, it often seems as if they are not even aware of these differences, which are for the average person so obvious and so important. These individuals, themselves elite, select for their friends the elite, but this is in terms of character, capacity, and talent, rather than birth, race, blood, name, family, age, youth, fame, or power.

DISCRIMINATION BETWEEN MEANS AND ENDS, BETWEEN GOOD AND EVIL

They rarely show the chaos, the confusion, or the conflict so common in the average person's ethical dealings, although very few of them are religious.

PHILOSOPHICAL, UNHOSTILE SENSE OF HUMOR

Their sense of humor is not of the ordinary type. They do not consider funny what the average man considers to be funny— hostile humor, superiority humor, or smutty humor. Characteristically, what they consider humor is more closely allied to philosophy than to anything else.

CREATIVENESS

This is a universal characteristic of all self-actualizing people. There is no exception. Each one shows in one way or another a special kind of creativeness or originality or inventiveness.

RESISTANCE TO ENCULTURATION, THE TRANSCENDENCE OF ANY PARTICULAR CULTURE

Self-actualizing people get along with the culture in various ways, but all of them resist enculturation and maintain a certain inner detachment. Their yielding to convention is apt to be rather casual and perfunctory, and when this is too annoying, the apparent conventionality is tossed off as easily as a cloak.

When compared with the awesome act of constructing this list of attributes, my comments are minor, minuscule. The characteristics, of course, were not derived in a truly scientific way. There seems to be both incompleteness and redundancy in his list. It also appears to be a series of static pictures. It would seem evident, for example, that a self-actualizing individual could be compassionate and empathetic at one moment and at another, inner-directed, but this is not brought out well. Although he lists these as *the* characteristics of self-actualizing persons, it is less than clear that *all* of them must be included in any one person. The implication is that they are not. Lastly, there is no attempt at weighting the value of one relative to the others.

I would like to emphasize one point. Maslow's self-actualization has nothing in common with the self-gratification so prevalent today. In fact, one ascends through his hierarchy, *which includes loving others and being loved*, before he begins to actualize. And as we have seen, an actualizing person has greater love for others and concern for all of mankind than most. The "doing your own thing" philosophy of some of our younger set is not what Maslow means at all.

I have the feeling as I read these descriptions that I am looking at the initial sketch of a great painter who died before he could complete his masterwork. Someone must continue to develop these ideas now that Maslow is gone. One approach would be to agree upon a simpler set of attributes and specify a range of attainment within each attribute. Then the attributes themselves could be arranged in an order of desirability or significance as determined by actual studies. Another way to develop Maslow's characteristics could be to group them under perception, cognition, conation, and action, which would render them more susceptible to analysis and experimental verification in psychological studies.

No matter how these qualities are dealt with in the future, Maslow has made a profoundly important contribution. *His is the first coherent statement about human potentials in history.*

I do not believe we will ever be able to find or form ultimate human values until we fully understand the human being. Psychology is still far from this, true, but it *has* set down the first few stepping stones, and these show us the way. Our task from here is to lay down more and not use those that are there as stumbling blocks.

One wonders even at this point along the path how self-actualization differs from the tradition of Aristotelian eudaemonism that of other self-realization philosophers. Maslow himself says, "We may agree with Aristotle when he assumed that the good life consisted in living in accordance with the true nature of man, but we must add that he simply did not know enough about the true nature of man. . . . The only thing that Aristotle could do was to build a picture of the good man in his own culture and in that particular period of time." Many of Maslow's self-actualization characteristics have to do with social interaction. This, too, is a very clear departure from some of the narrowly constructed self-realization theories. He also puts more emphasis on a natural process of allowing one's inborn potentials to unfold, rather than on making a conscious effort to achieve them. These are the major differences between self-realization and self-actualization as I see them. The former incorporated the better elements of hedonism but went beyond them. Self-actualization goes beyond both in giving us goals and telling us more about how we are to arrive there. Humanistic psychology, with its insight into man, has brought us to the point where the two great extant ethical philosophies, hedonism and self-realization, are seen to touch and the three *even begin to form a continuum*. This is truly a remarkable achievement.

Of the future, Maslow says, "I should say also that I consider humanistic, Third Force Psychology to be transitional, a preparation for a still 'higher' Fourth Psychology, transpersonal, transhuman, centered in the cosmos rather than in human needs and interests, going beyond humanness, identity, self-actualization, and the like."

This sounds a lot like religion. Is it possible that the two great extant ethical philosophies and humanistic psychology will fuse in the future with the ethical elements that are common to all religions?

THE MIDCOURSE CORRECTION

This was my route—through religion, philosophy, and psychology—in a search for values on which to base an alteration of the course of my life, now that it had reached its midpoint. And my search will continue from here as long as I live.

On returning to religion I came to abandon absolutistic views for relativistic ones and the divinity of Jesus for his humanity; to hold man high; to reject sin and shame; to find God *within* as well as without; and to love my fellow man as myself. Much of this I had lived and believed before. In a sense, my search here only helped me see my own values and some of their origins more clearly.

In rereading philosophy I learned that I must know myself; that happiness, not pleasure, is the *summum bonum;* and that this happiness comes through realizing my inborn potentials, not by direct pursuit.

And in turning to psychology I learned more about how to attain this realization and some of the characteristics of the person who has done so. This was rather awkwardly termed self-actualization. Why not simple fulfillment of what a person is meant to be?

I traced these three historically for a purpose: From the ancient answers of religion, through the cultural middle of intellectual history when philosophy vied with religion to define life and living, to the insights of modern psychology, to show why I believe that we are almost at the point in history where the three can be seen in synthesis. Reflect for a moment on some of the same truths as viewed from these three vantage points. Psychology would help us know ourselves as philosophy had urged from its beginning and, further, to love ourselves and others, as would religion. Modern psychology stresses individuality, and current Christianity tells us that love is the simultaneous surrender and salvation of our individuality. Existentialists and other nihilists even now can be given the answer that there *is* an essential structure of being but that most human existence is an incomplete form of this essence. Man has a path to follow toward the unity of essence and existence.

We also know now that we are one with the rest of the world of nature, and we are able to turn away from Cartesian chasms between mind and matter, from theological schisms between the "natural" and "supernatural," and psychological separation of cognition and conation. The false dualism of desire and duty is also transcended, because desire is recognized as the motivating force of human action—in the course of our individual development, reasons become part of desires, and desires then become desires *for a reason*. And the dilemma of egoism versus altruism can now be transformed in the expansion of the self to include a true concern for others.

Above all, with the sources of values set in historical perspective, I hope you can see that they change as the world changes. People change them; people created them in the first place. When we are aware of the incredible volume and variety of thinkers and their systems that have arisen, prevailed, and died out or endured in whatever form and by whatever means, we are freer—freer to understand ourselves and to determine our own values more autonomously. When we see the possibility, necessity, *inevitability* of change in our own lives, we realize that this is a form of freedom, too.

Yet the predominant values of our culture have not changed rapidly enough to give us guidance in our middle age, because this time in life is a new phenomenon. These values guided us when we were younger, true. We needed them then. Some conformity is essential if a society is to survive, is to have continuity. Even the elderly have some guidance from our cultural traditions—old people have been with us throughout history. But there is little or none for us. This is a task we must take on for ourselves. Although our culture may not help us much, but if we take on this task, we can certainly help our culture.

Youth is a time of exploring, testing, developing. Yet as we enter adulthood we are *not* fully formed. Nor are we in middle age. Like all of life, the process of human development continues—into old age, to death. Some our age who sense the failure of our culture to provide direction revert to the fun and games of youth. Some ignore the changes taking place within and the potential for more and plod on in an unexamined life. Some give up and grow old before their time. Never has the need for values been more urgent than at this time in our lives.

Each of us, like a leaf, a flower, like any creation of life, is unique. Why not look within? Why not "know thyself"? The purpose of this chapter has been to encourage you to do so, to start your search, to bring yourself to your own fulfillment and find out what your life is for. Then you can make a statement to yourself and to the world of who you are. This, I believe, is what the middle years are all about. Paradoxically, the first sign of aging is a signal for the start of your true birth. But if you don't begin now, you never will—and your future can only be your past, happening over and over.

Bibliography

PREFACE

Chew, Peter. *The Inner World of the Middle-Aged Man*. New York: Macmillan, 1976.

Davitz, Joel, and Lois Davitz. *Making it From 40 to 50*. New York: Random House, 1976.

Hunt, Morton, and Bernice K. Hunt. *Prime Time*. New York: Stein & Day, 1975.

Le Shan, Eda J. *The Wonderful Crisis of Middle Age*. New York: David McKay, 1973.

Lindbergh, Ann Morrow. *Gift From the Sea*. New York: Pantheon, 1955.

McLeish, John A. B. *The Ulyssean Adult*. New York: McGraw-Hill Ryerson, Ltd., 1976.

Neugarten, Bernice L. (editor). *Middle Age and Aging: A Reader in Social Psychology*. Chicago: University of Chicago Press, 1968.

Simon, Anne W. *The New Years*. New York: Alfred A. Knopf, 1968.

Taylor, Robert B. *Welcome to the Middle Years: A Doctor's Guide*. Washington, D.C.: Acropolis, 1977.

Troll, Lillian E., et al. (editors). *Looking Ahead: A Woman's Guide to the Problems and Joys of Growing Older*. Englewood Cliffs, New Jersey: Prentice-Hall, 1977.

MYTHS OF MIDDLE AGE

Aldridge, John W. *In the Country of the Young*. New York: Harper & Row, 1970.

Barron, Milton L. *The Aging American: An Introduction to Social Gerontology & Geriatrics*. New York: Thomas Y. Crowell, 1961.

Bier, William C. (editor). *Aging: Its Challenge to the Individual and to Society*. New York: Fordham University Press, 1974.

Butler, R. N. "The Facade of Chronological Age: An Interpretive Summary." *American Journal of Psychiatry* 119:721–728, 1963.

Cameron, P. "Age Parameters of Young Adult, Middle Aged, Old and Aged." *Journal of Gerontology* 24:201–202, 1969.

Clausen, H. A. "Glimpses into the Social World of Middle Age." *International Journal of Aging and Human Development* 7(2):99–106, 1976.

Drevenstedt, J. "Perceptions of Onsets of Young Adulthood, Middle Age, and Old Age." *Journal of Gerontology*. 31(1):53–57, 1976.

Gardner, L. P. "Attitudes and Activities of the Middle-aged and Aged." *Geriatrics* 4:33–50, 1949.

Gunn, A. D. "The Middle Years." *Nursing Times* 66:1043–1044, 1970.

Hargreaves, A. G. "Making the Most of the Middle Years." *American Journal of Nursing* 75(10): .71772–1776, 1975.

Jackson, D. W. "Advanced Aged Adults' Reflections of Middle Age." *Gerontologist* 14(3):255–257, 1974.

Jaffe, A. J., and Gordon, J. B. *Demography of the Middle Years: An Interim Report of the Highlights*, New York: Bureau of Applied Social Research. 1968.

Kimmel, Douglas C. *Adulthood and Aging: An Interdisciplinary Developmental View.* New York: Wiley, 1974.

Lesnoff-Caravaglia, G. "Editorial: Senescence and Adolescence: Middle-age Inventions." *Gerontologist* 14(2):98, 1974.

Maas, H. S., and J. A. Kuypers. *From Thirty to Seventy.* San Francisco: Jossey-Bass, 1974.

Neugarten, B. L. "The Awareness of Middle Age," in: *Middle Age and Aging,* Neugarten, Bernice L. (editor). Chicago: University of Chicago Press, 1968.

Nydegger, C. N. Middle Age: Some Early Returns—A Commentary. *International Journal of Aging and Human Development* 7(2):137–141, 1976.

Rose, A. M. "Factors Associated with the Life Satisfaction of Middle-class, Middle-aged Persons." *Marriage and Family* 17:15–19, 1955.

Tibbets, Clark, and Wilma Donahue (editors). *Aging in Today's Society.* Englewood Cliffs, New Jersey: Prentice-Hall, Inc., 1960.

Tuckman, J., and I. Lorge. "Classification of the Self as Young, Middle-aged or Old." *Geriatrics* 9:534–536, 1954.

United States Bureau of the Census. "1970 General Population Characteristics Final Report." PC(I)-B1. U. S. Summary. June, 1973.

Woodruff, Diana, and James E. Birren (editors). *Aging: Scientific Perspectives and Social Issues.* New York: Van Nostrand, 1975.

MAN AND MORTALITY

Alexander, P., and D. Connell. "The Failure of the Potent Mutagenic Chemical, Ethylmethanesulphanate, to Shorten the Life Span of Mice" in: *Cellular Basis and Aetiology of Late Somatic Effects of Ionizing Radiation.* R. J. C. Harris (editor). New York: Academic Press, 1963.

Andrew, Warren. *The Anatomy of Aging in Man and Animals.* New York: Grune & Stratton, 1971.

Bakerman, Seymour (editor). *Aging Life Processes.* Springfield, Illinois: Charles C. Thomas, 1969.

Brady, R. O., *et al.* "Replacement Therapy for Inherited Enzyme Deficiency. Use of Purified Glucocerebrosidase in Gaucher's Disease. *New England Journal of Medicine* 291:989–993, 1974.

Brues, Austin Moore (editor). *Aging and Levels of Biological Organization.* Chicago: University of Chicago Press, 1965.

Curtis, Howard J. In: *Symposium on Topics in the Biology of Aging* (Salk Institute for Biological Studies, 1965). Peter L. Krohn, editor. New York: Interscience Publications, 1966.

Ebbesen, P. "Papilloma Induction in Different Aged Skin Grafts to Young Recipients. *Nature* 241:280–281, 1973.

Finch, C. B., and L. Hayflick. *Handbook of the Biology of Aging.* New York: Van Nostrand Rheinhold, 1977.

Gold, P., and Freedman, S. O. "Specific Carcinoembryonic Antigens of the Human Digestive System." *Journal of Experimental Medicine* 122:467–481, 1965.

Goldstein, S. "Biological Aging: An Essentially Normal Process. *JAMA* 230:1651–1652, 1974.

—————. "The Biology of Aging." *New England Journal of Medicine* 285:1120–1129, 1971.

Gordon H. A., E. Bruckner-Kardoss and B. S. Wostmann. "Aging in Germ-free Mice: Life Tables and Lesions Observed at Natural Death. *Journal of Gerontology* 21:380–387, 1966.

Green, J. "Vitamin E and the Biological Antioxidant Theory." *Annals of the New York Academy of Science* 203:29–44, 1972.

von Hahn, H. P. "Age-related Alterations in the Structure of DNA II. The Role of Histones." *Gerontologia* 10:174–182, 1964–65.

Harman, D. "Prolongation of the Normal Lifespan and Inhibition of Spontaneous Cancer by Antioxidants." *Journal of Gerontology* 16:247–254, 1961.

——————. "Prolongation of Life: Role of Free Radical Reactions in Aging." *Journal of the American Geriatrics Society* 17:721–735, 1969.

Hayflick, L. "The Limited *in Vitro* Lifehime of Human Diploid Cell Strains. *Experimental Cell Research* 37:614–636, 1965.

Hollingworth, J. W., G. W. Bebe and M. Ishida *et al*. *Medical Findings on Atomic Bomb Survivors: the Uses of Vital and Health Statistics for Genetic and Radiation Studies*. New York: United Nations, 1962.

Jarvik, L. F. "Survival and Psychological Aspects of Aging in Man." Symposium of the Society for Experimental Biology 21:463–481, 1967.

Kallmann, F. J., and L. F. Jarvik. "Individual Differences in Constitution and Genetic Background." in *Handbook of Aging and the Individual: Psychological and Biological Aspects*. J. E. Birren (editor). Chicago: University of Chicago Press, 1959.

Kohn, Robert R. *Principles of Mammalian Aging*. Englewood Cliffs, New Jersey: Prentice-Hall, 1971.

Krohn, P. L. "Aging Symposium." *Science* 152:391–393, 1966.

Lansing, Al. "General Biology of Senescence." In: *Handbook of Aging and the Individual: Psychological and Biological Aspects*. J. E. Birren (editor). Chicago: University of Chicago Press, 1959.

Madigan, F. C., and R. B. Vance. "Differential Sex Mortality: A Research Design." *Social Forces* 35:193–199, 1957.

Martin, G. M., C. A. Sprague, and C. J. Epstein. "Replicative Life-span of Cultivated Human Cells: Effects of Donor's Age, Tissue, and Genotype." *Laboratory Investigation* 23:86–92, 1970.

McCay, C. M., *et al*. "The Effect of Retarded Growth upon the Length of Life Span and upon the Ultimate Body Size." *Journal of Nutrition* 10:63–79, 1935.

Medvedev, Z. A. *Protein Biosynthesis and Problems of Heredity, Development, and Ageing*. New York: Plenum Press, 1966.

Orgel, L. E. "Ageing of Clones of Mammalian Cells." *Nature* 243:441–445, 1973.

——————. "The Maintenance of the Accuracy of Protein Synthesis and Its Relevance to Aging." *Proceedings of the National Academy of Science* 49:517–521, 1963.

Ostfeld, Adrian M., *et al*. (editors). *Conference of the Epidemiology of Aging*. Elkridge, Maryland: U.S. DHEW Publication No. (NIH):75–711, 1972.

Packer, L., and J. R. Smith. "Extension of the *in Vitro* Lifespan of Human WI–38 Cells in Culture by Vitamin E." *Journal of Cellular Biology* 63:A255, 1974.

Palmore, Erdman (editor). *Normal Aging II; Reports from the Duke Longitudinal Studies, 1970–3*. Durham, North Carolina: Duke University Press, 1974.

——————. *Prediction of Life Span: Recent Findings*. Lexington, Massachusetts: D. C. Heath, 1971.

Pyhtilä, M. J., and F. G. Sherman. "Studies on the Histones and DNA of Calf and Old Cow Thymus." *Journal of Gerontology* 23:450–453, 1968.

Rockstein, Morris, and Marvin Sussman (editors). *Theoretical Aspects of Aging*. New York: Academic Press, 1974.

Samis, H. V., Jr., and V. J. Wulff. "The Template Activity of Rat Liver Chromatin." *Experimental Gerontology* 4:111–117, 1969.

Shock, N. W. "The Physiology of Aging." *Scientific American* 206:100–10, 1962.

Smigel, J. O., J. Piller, C. Murphy, *et al*. "H-3 (Procaine Hydrochloride) Therapy in Aging Institutionalized Patients: An Interim Report. *Journal of the American Geriatrics Society* 8:785–794, 1960.

Stein, G. S., J. S. Stein, and L. J. Kleinsmith. "Chromosomal Proteins and Gene Regulation." *Scientific American* 232:46–57, 1975.

Szilard, L. "On the Nature of the Aging Process." *Proceedings of the National Academy of Science* 45:30–45, 1959.

Walford, R. L. *The Immunologic Theory of Aging*. Baltimore: Williams & Wilkins, 1969.

Wheeler, K. T., and J. T. Lett. "On the Possibility that DNA Repair is Related to Age in Nondividing Cells." *Proceedings of the National Academy of Science* 71:1862–1865, 1974.

Whitten, J. M. "Cell Death During Early Morphogenesis: Parallels Between Insect Limb and Vertebrate Limb Development." *Science* 163:1456–1457, 1969.

Williamson, A. R., and B. A. Askonas. "Senescence of an Antibody-forming Cell Clone." *Nature* 238:337–339, 1972.

Wright, W. E., and L. Hayflick. "Nuclear Control of Cellular Aging Demonstrated by Hybridization of Anucleate and Whole Cultured Normal Human Fibroblasts." *Experimental Cell Research* 96:113–121, 1975.

Wulff, V. J., H. V. Samis, Jr., and J. A. Falzone, Jr. "The Metabolism of Ribonucleic Acid in Young and Old Rodents." *Advanced Gerontological Research* 2:37–76, 1967.

THE BODY

YOUR HEALTH

A New Survey on Access to Medical Care (Special Report No. 1). Princeton, New Jersey: Robert Wood Johnson Foundation, 1978.

"AAFP Report. Official Definition of Family Practice and Family Physician." *AAFP Reporter* 2:10, 1975.

American Medical Association. *Physician Distribution and Medical Licensure in the United States, 1976*. Chicago: American Medical Association, 1977.

Belloc, N. "Relationship of Health Practices and Mortality." *Preventive Medicine* 2:67–81, 1973.

Citizens Commission on Graduate Medical Education: *The Graduate Education of Physicians*. Chicago: American Medical Association, 1966.

"Conflicts of Interest in Fee For Service and in HMO's (editorial). *New England Journal of Medicine* 299:1071–1073, 1978.

Delbanco, T. L., and W. C. Taylor. "The Periodic Health Examination: 1980." *Annals of Internal Medicine* 92(Part 1):251–252, 1980.

Directory of Medical Specialists, 19th Edition, 1978–1979. Chicago: Marquis Who's Who, Inc., 1978.

Enthoven, A. C.: Shattuck Lecture—"Cutting Cost without Cutting the Quality of Care." *New England Journal of Medicine* 298:1229–1238, 1978.

Feldstein, P. J. "Research on the Demand for Health Services." *Milbank Memorial Fund Quarterly* 44 (supplement): 128–165, 1966.

Fuchs, Victor R. *Who Shall Live?* New York: Basic Books, 1974.

Institute of Medicine. *Advancing the Quality of Health Care: Key Issues and Fundamental Principles*. Washington, D.C.: National Academy of Sciences, 1974.

Institute of Medicine Ad Hoc Advisory Group on Preventive Services. "Preventive Services for the Well Population." In: *Disease Prevention and Health Promotion: Federal Programs and Prospects. Report of the Departmental Task Force on Prevention*. Washington, D.C.: U.S. Government Printing Office: Appendix 1–30. (USDHEW Stock #017–001–00418–9), 1978.

Knowles, J. "Wiser Way of Living, Not Dramatic Cures Seen as Key to Health. Preventive Care to Become More Important." *Wall Street Journal*, March 23, 1976.

Lewis, C. S. "Characteristics of Non-board-certified Internists." *Forum on Medicine* 2:817–818, 1979.

Linn, L. S. "Factors Associated with Patient Evaluation of Health Care. *Milbank Memorial Fund Quarterly* 53:531–548, 1975.

Luft, H. S. "How Do Health-maintenance Organizations Achieve Their "Savings"?: Rhetoric and Evidence." *New England Journal of Medicine* 298:1336–1343, 1978.

McDermott, W. "General Medical Care: Identification and Analysis of Alternative Approaches." *John Hopkins Medical Journal* 135:292–321, 1974.

Mendenhall, R. C., A. R. Tarlov, R. A. Girard, *et al.* "A National Study of Internal Medicine and Its Specialties: II. Primary Care in Internal Medicine." *Annals of Internal Medicine* 91:275–287, 1979.

National Center for Health Statistics. Health in the United States, 1978. Hyattsville, Md.: National Center for Health Statistics, 1978. (DHEW publication no. (PHS)78–1232).

Noren, J., T. Frazier, I. Altman, *et al.* "Ambulatory Medical Care: A Comparison of Internists and Family-general Practitioners. *New England Journal of Medicine* 302:11–16, 1980.

Petersdorf, R. G. "The Doctors' Dilemma." *New England Journal of Medicine* 299:628–634, 1978.

Preventive Medicine USA. Theory, Practice and Application of Prevention in Personal Health Services: Quality Control and Evaluation of Preventive Health Services. Task Force Reports sponsored by the John E. Fogarty International Center for Advanced Study in the Health Sciences, National Institutes of Health and the American College of Preventive Medicine. New York: *Prodist.* 36–56, 1976.

Raccella, E. J. "Potential for Reducing Health Care Costs by Public and Patient Education." *Public Health Reports* 93(3):223, 1976.

Riley, Matilda White, and Anne Foner. *Aging and Society, Vol. I.* New York: Russell Sage Foundation, 1968.

Scheffler, R. M., N. Weisfeld, G. Ruby, *et al.* "A Manpower Policy for Primary Health Care." *New England Journal of Medicine* 298:1058–1062, 1978.

Shenkin, B. N. "Medical Education, Medical Care, and Society in Sweden." *Journal of Medical Education* 49:357–67, 1974.

Taxay, E. P. "The Health Care Team." *JAMA* 239:1137, 1978.

"The Public's Need for Information about Health Problems." A Louis Harris study for the Blue Cross Association, Washington, D.C., 1971.

United States Department of Commerce, Bureau of the Census: *Statistical Abstract of the United States, 1977.* Washington, D.C.: U.S. Government Printing Office, 1977.

United States Department of Health, Education, and Welfare. *Access to Ambulatory Health Care: United States, 1974* (advance data No. 17, February 23, 1978). Washington, D.C.: U.S. Government Printing Office, 1978.

——————. *GMENAC Staff Papers: Supply and Distribution of Physicians and Physician Extenders.* Washington, D.C.: U.S. Government Printing Office, 1978.

——————. *National HMO Census of Prepaid Plans, 1978.* Washington, D.C.: U.S. Government Printing Office, 1979.

United States National Center for Health Statistics. *Health Survey Procedure* (Publication No. 1000, Series 1, No. 2). Washington, D.C.: U.S. Government Printing Office, 1964.

——————. *Origin, Program, and Operation of the U.S. National Health Survey* (Publication No. 1000, Series 1, No. 1). Washington, D.C.: U.S. Government Printing Office, 1965.

Walker, A. R. "Survival Rate at Middle Age in Developing and Western Populations." *Postgraduate Medical Journal* 50:29–32, 1974.

Watts, M. S. M. "Health System Agencies and Local Physicians. *Western Journal of Medicine* 128:337–338, 1978.

Wersinger, R., K. J. Roghmann, J. W. Gavett, *et al.* "Inpatient Hospital Utilization in Three Prepaid Comprehensive Health Care Plans Compared with a Regular Blue Cross Plan. *Medical Care* 14:721–732, 1976.

HEART ATTACK AND STROKE

Ahrens, E. H. "The Management of Hyperlipidemia: Whether, Rather than How." *Annals of Internal Medicine* 85:87–93, 1976.

Barndt, R., Jr., D. H. Blankenhorn, D. W. Crawford, and S. H. Brooks. "Regression and Progression of Early Femoral Atherosclerosis in Treated Hyperlipoproteinemic Patients." *Annals of Internal Medicine* 86:139–146, 1977.

Basta, L. L., C. Williams, J. M. Kioschos, *et al.* "Regression of Atherosclerotic Stenosing Lesions of the Renal Arteries and Spontaneous Cure of Systemic Hypertension Through Control of Hyperlipidemia." *American Journal of Medicine* 61:420–423, 1976.

Blankenhorn, D. H., S. H. Brooks, R. H. Selzer, *et al.* "Rate of Atherosclerosis Change During Treatment of Hyperlipoproteinemia." *Circulation* 57:355–361, 1978.

Coronary Drug Project Research Group. "Clofibrate and Niacin in Coronary Heart Disease. *JAMA* 231:360–381, 1975.

Doyle, J. T., and W. B. Kannel. "Coronary Risk Factors: 10-year Finding in 8600 Americans—Pooling Project, Council on Epidemiology, American Heart Association." Paper presented to the Sixth World Congress of Cardiology. London, England, September 1970.

Freis, E. D. "Salt, Volume and the Prevention of Hypertension." *Circulation* 53:589–595, 1976.

Gordon, T., W. P. Castelli, M. C. Hjortland, *et al.* "High Density Lipoprotein as a Protective Factor Against Coronary Heart Disease: The Framingham Study." *American Journal of Medicine* 62:707–714, 1977.

Hurst, J. W., S. B. King, R. B. Logue, *et al.* "Value of Coronary Bypass Surgery: Controversies in Cardiology: I. *American Journal of Cardiology* 42:308–329, 1978.

Hypertension Detection and Follow-up Program Cooperative Group. "Five-year Findings of the Hypertension Detection and Follow-up Program. I. Reduction in Mortality of Persons with High Blood Pressure, Including Mild Hypertension. *JAMA* 242:2562–2571, 1979.

——————. "Five-year Findings of the Hypertension Detection and Follow-up Program. II. Mortality by Race, Sex and Age." *JAMA* 242:2572–2577, 1979.

Kannel, W. B., and T. Gordon (editors). *The Framingham Study: An Epidemiological Investigation of Cardiovascular Disease.* Section 30: "Some Characteristics Related to the Incidence of Cardiovascular Disease and Death: Framingham Study, 18-Year Follow-up." Washington: DHEW (NIH) 74–599, 1974.

Kannel, W. B., W. P. Castelli, and T. Gordon, "Cholesterol in the Prediction of Atherosclerotic Disease: New perspectives Based on the Framingham Study. *Annals of Internal Medicine* 90:85–91, 1979.

Kerschbaum, A., R. Khorsandian, F. Caplan, *et al.* "The Role of Catecholamines in the Free Fatty Acid Response to Cigarette Smoking. *Circulation* 28:52–57, 1963.

Larsen, O. A., and R. O. Malmborg (editors). *Coronary Heart Disease and Physical Fitness.* Baltimore: University Park Press, 1971.

Levy, R. I. "Stroke Decline: Implications and Prospects." *New England Journal of Medicine* 300:490–491, 1979.

McIntosh, H. D., and J. A. Garcia. "The First Decade of Aortocoronary Bypass Grafting, 1967–1977: A Review." *Circulation* 57:405–431, 1978.

National Center for Health Statistics. *Blood Pressure Levels of Persons 6–74 years: United States, 1971–74.* (Vital and Health Statistics. Series II: Data from the National Health Survey, No. 203). (DHEW Publication No. (HRA) 78–1648). Washington, D.C.: U.S. Department of Health , Education, and Welfare; September 1977.

National Heart, Lung, and Blood Institute. *Proceedings of the Conference on the Decline in Coronary Heart Disease Mortality.* National Heart, Lung, and Blood Institute, 1979. (NIH publication No. 79–1610).

Relman, A. S. "Mild Hypertension: No More Benign Neglect." *New England Journal of Medicine* 302:293–294, 1980.

"Report of Inter-society Commission for Heart Disease Resources: Primary Prevention of the Atherosclerotic Diseases." *Circulation* 42:A-55–A-95, 1970 (revised April 1972).

Stamler, J., and F. H. Epstein, "Coronary Heart Disease: Risk Factors as Guides to Preventive Action. *Preventive Medicine* 1:27–48, 1972.

Stern, M. P. "The Recent Decline in Ischemic Heart Disease Mortality." *Annals of Internal Medicine* 91:630–640,1979.

Veterans Administration Cooperative Study Group on Antihypertensive Agents: "Effects of Treatment on Morbidity in Hypertension: II. Results in Patients with Diastolic Blood Pressure Averaging 90 Through 114 Mm. Hg." *JAMA* 213:1143–1152, 1970.

Wilber, J. A. "The Problem of Undetected and Untreated Hypertension in the Community. *Bulletin of the New York Academy of Medicine* 49:510–520, 1973.

Wissler, R. W., and D. Vesselinovitch, "Regression of Atherosclerosis in Experimental Animals and Man. *Modern Concepts of Cardiovascular Disease* 46:27–32, 1977.

Wright, I. S. "Correct Levels of Serum Cholesterol." *JAMA* 236:261–262, 1976.

NUTRITION

Alfin-Slater, Rosyln B., and Lilla Aftergood. *Nutrition for Today*. Dubuque, Iowa: William C. Brown, 1973.

American Medical Association: "Diet and Coronary Heart Disease: A Joint Policy Statement of the AMA Council on Foods and Nutrition and the Food and Nutrition Board of the National Academy of Sciences—National Research council." *JAMA* 222:1647, 1972.

Bogert, L. Jean, and George M. Briggs. *Nutrition and Physical Fitness*, 9th edition. Philadelphia: W. B. Saunders, 1973.

Blackburn, H. "Book Review: W. E. Shute and H. J. Taub. *Vitamin E for Ailing and Healthy Hearts.*" *New England Journal of Medicine* 283:214–215, 1970.

Calloway, D. H., and S. Margen, "Human Response to Diets Very High in Protein." *Federal Proceedings* 27:725–729, abstract, 1968.

Chaney, Margaret S., and Margaret L. Ross. *Nutrition*, 8th Edition. New York: Houghton Mifflin, 1971.

Connor, W. E., D. B. Stone, and R. E. Hodges, "The Interrelated Effects of Dietary Cholesterol and Fat upon Human Serum Lipid Levels. *Journal of Clinical Investigation* 43:1691–1696, 1964.

Creagan E. T., C. G. Moertel, J. R. O'Fallon, *et al.* "Failure of High-dose Vitamin C (Ascorbic Acid) Therapy to Benefit Patients with Advanced Cancer: A Controlled Trial." *New England Journal of Medicine* 301:687–690, 1979.

Dahl, L. K. "Salt and hypertension." *American Journal of Clinical Nutrition* 25:231–244, 1972.

Davidson, Stanley, *et al. Human Nutrition and Dietetics*, 7th Edition. New York: Churchill, 1979.

Davis, T. R. A., S. N. Gershoff, and D. F. Gamble, "Reveiw of Studies of Vitamin and Mineral Nutrition in the United States (1950–1968). *Journal of Nutrition Education* (supplement 1):41–57, 1969.

Dayton, S., M. L. Pearce, S. Hashimoto, *et al.* "A Controlled Clinical Trial of a Diet High in Unsaturated Fat in Preventing Complications of Atherosclerosis." *Circulation* 39, 40:Supplement 2:II-1–II-63, 1969.

Dykes, M. H. M., and P. Meier, "Ascorbic Acid and the Common Cold." *JAMA* 231:1073–1079, 1975.

Food Additives, Hearings Before the Select Committee on Nutrition and Human needs of the United States, Senate, 92nd Congress, 2nd Session. Washington, D.C.: U.S. Government Printing Office, 1973.

Friend, B. "Nutrients in United States Food Supply." *American Journal of Clinical Nutrition* 20:907–914, 1967.

Hartung, G. H., J. P. Foreyt, R. E. Mitchell, *et al.* "Relationship of Diet and HDL Cholesterol in Sedentary and Active Middle-aged Men." *Circulation* 57 & 58: Supplement 2:II–204, abstract, 1978.

Irwin, M. I., and D. M. Hegsted, "A Conspectus of Research on Protein Requirements of Man." *Journal of Nutrition* 101:385–430, 1971.

Goodhart, Robert S., and Maurice E. Shils (editors). *Modern Nutrition in Health and Disease*, 6th Edition. Philadelphia: Lea and Febiger, 1973.

Hegsted, D. M., Jr. (editor). "Americans Love Hogwash." *Nutrition Reviews* 32(Supplement No. 1):1–70, 1974.

Kannel, W. B., W. P. Castelli, and T. Gordon, "Cholesterol in the Prediction of Atherosclerotic Disease." *New England Journal of Medicine* 90:85–91, 1979.

Karlowski, T. E., *et al.* "Ascorbic Acid for the Common Cold: A Prophylactic and Therapeutic Trial." *JAMA* 231:1038–1042, 1975.

Kelsay, J. L. "A Compendium of Nutritional Status Studies and Dietary Evaluation Studies Conducted in the United States, 1957–1967." *Journal of Nutrition* 99II Supplement 1:119–166, 1969.

Kermode, G. O. "Food Additives." *Scientific American* 226(3):15–21, 1972.

Keys, A. "Sucrose in the Diet and Coronary Heart Disease." *Atherosclerosis* 14:193–202, 1971.

Levy, Joseph V., and Paul Bachy-Rita. *Vitamins: Their Use and Abuse.* New York: Liveright, 1976.

Levy, Robert I., *et al. Nutrition, Lipids, and Coronary Heart Disease: A Global View.* New York: Raven Press, 1979.

Little, J. A., B. L. Birchwood, and D. A. Simmons, "Inter-relationship Between the Kinds of Dietary Carbohydrate and Fat in Hyperlipoproteinemic Patients." *Atherosclerosis* 11:173–201, 1970.

Mayer, Jean. *A Diet For Living.* New York: McKay, 1975.

Maynard, L. A. "Effect of Fertilizers on the Nutritional Value of Foods." *JAMA* 161:1478–1480, 1956.

Miettinen, M., O. Turpeinen, M. J. Karvonen, *et al.* "Effect of Cholesterol-lowering Diet on Mortality from Coronary Heart Disease and Other Causes: A Twelve-year Clinical Trial in Men and Women. *Lancet* 2:835–838, 1972.

National Research Council. Committee on Food Protection. *Toxicants Occurring Naturally in Foods*, 2nd Edition. Washington, D.C.: National Academy of Sciences, 1973.

—————. *The Use of Chemicals in Food Production, Processing, Storage and Distribution.* Washington, D.C.: National Academy of Sciences, 1973.

Nestel, P. J., K. F. Carroll, and N. Havenstein, "Plasma-triglyceride Response to Carbohydrates, Fats, and Caloric Intake." *Metabolism* 19:1–18, 1970.

Packard, Vernal S. *Processed Foods and the Consumer: Additives, Labeling, Standards, and Nutrition.* Minneapolis: University of Minnesota Press, 1975.

Patti, Charles. *The Food Book: What You Eat from A–Z.* New York: Fleet Press, 1973.

Payne, Alma, and Dorothy Callahan. *The Fat and Sodium Control Cookbook*, 4th revised Edition. Boston: Little, Brown, 1976.

Peck, Leilani B., *et al. Focus on Food.* New York: McGraw-Hill, 1974.

Schroeder, H. A. "Losses of Vitamins and Trace Minerals Resulting from Processing and Preservation of Foods. *American Journal of Clinical Nutrition* 24:562–573, 1971.

Select Committee on Nutrition and Human Needs, United States Senate. *Dietary Goals for the United States*, Stock No. 052-070-03913-2/Catalog No. Y 4. N95:D63/3, 1977.

—————. *Dietary Goals for the United States.* Second edition. Stock No. 052-070-04376-8, 1977. Washington, D.C.: U.S. Government Printing Office, 1977.

—————. *Diet Related to Killer Diseases*, Vol. II, Part 1, "Diet and Cardiovascular Disease." Stock No. 052-070-03987-6.

—————. *Diet Related to Killer Diseases*, Vol. II, Part 2, "Obesity." Stock No. 052-070-04275-3.

Smith, R. L. "The Vitamin Healers." *The Reporter* 18–25, December 16, 1965.

Stare, Frederick, and Margaret McWilliams. *Living Nutrition*, 2nd Edition. New York: Wiley & Sons, 1977.

Stern, M. P., J. W. Farquhar, N. MacCoby, *et al.* "Results of a Two-year Health Education Campaign on Dietary Behavior: The Stanford Three-Community Study." *Circulation* 54/5:826–833, 1976.

Todhunter, E. N. "Food Habits, Food Faddism and Nutrition." *World Review of Nutrition and Dietetics* 16:287–317, 1973.

U.S. Congressional House Committee on Interstate and Foreign Commerce. Subcommittee on Public Health and Environment. *Vitamin, Mineral and Diet Supplements.* Washington, D.C.: U.S. Government Printing Office, 1973.

U.S. National Institutes of Health. *Arteriosclerosis, a Report by the National Heart and Lung Institute Task Force on Arteriosclerosis.* Vol. 1, June 1971, DHEW Pub. No. (NIH) 72–137.

Whelan, Elizabeth, and Frederick J. Stare. *Panic in the Pantry.* New York: Atheneum, 1975.

White, Philip L. (editor). *Nutrition Misinformation and Food Faddism.* New York: Nutrition Foundation, Inc., 1974.

Yudkin, John. *Sweet and Dangerous.* New York: Bantam Books, 1972.

WATCHING YOUR WEIGHT

American Medical Association Council on Foods and Nutrition. "A Critique of Low-carbohydrate Ketogenic Weight Reduction Regimens. *Nutrition Reviews* 32 (supplement): 15–22, 1974.

Arees, E. A., and J. Mayer. "Anatomical Connections Between Medial and Lateral Regions of the Hypothalamus Concerned with Food Intake." *Science* 157:1574–1575, 1967.

Asher, W. L., and R. E. Dietz. "Effectiveness and Weight Reduction Involving 'Diet Pills'." *Current Therapeutic Research* 14:510–514, 1972.

Benziger, Barbara. *Controlling Your Weight.* New York: Franklin Watts, 1973.

Bloom, W. L., and M. F. Eidex. "Inactivity as a Major Factor in Adult Obesity." *Metabolism* 16:679–684, 1967.

Bray, G. A., R. E. Berry, J. R. Benfield, *et al.* "Intestinal Bypass Operation as a Treatment for Obesity." *Annals of Internal Medicine* 85:97–109, 1976.

Brozek, J. "Body Composition." *Science* 134:920–930, 1961.

Bullen, B. A., *et al.* "Physical Activity of Obese and Nonobese Adolescent Girls Appraised by Motion Picture Sampling. *American Journal of Clinical Nutrition* 14:211–223, 1964.

Burkitt, D. P., A. R. P. Walker, and N. S. Painter. "Dietary Fiber and Disease." *JAMA*, 229:1068–1074, 1974.

Chirico, A., and A. J. Stunkard. "Physical Activity and Human Obesity." *New England Journal of Medicine* 263:935–940, 1960.

Cohn, C. "Feeding Frequency and Body Composition." *Annals of the New York Academy of Sciences* 110:395–409, 1963.

Debry, G. "Study of the Effect of Dividing the Daily Caloric Intake into Seven Meals on Weight Loss in Obese Subjects." *Nutritio et Dieta* 10:288–296, 1968.

Decke, E. "Effects of Taste on the Eating Behavior of Obese and Normal Persons" In: Schacter, Stanley, *Emotion, Obesity and Crime.* New York: Academic Press, 1971.

de Vries, H. A., and D. E. Gray. "After-effects of Exercise upon Resting Metabolic Rate." *Research Quarterly* 34:314–316, 1963.

Dorris, R. J., and A. J. Stunkard. "Physical Activity: Performance and Attitudes of a Group of Obese Women." *American Journal of Medical Science* 233:622–628, 1957.

Ferguson, James M. *Habits, Not Diets.* Palo Alto, California: Bull Publishing Company, Inc., 1976.

Foreyt, John Paul, Sander Martins and Ben J. Williams. *Behavioral Approaches to Dietary Management.* New York: Brunner/Mazel, 1976.

Gilder, H., G. N. Cornell, W. R. Grafe, *et al.* "Components of Weight Loss in Obese Patients Subjected to Prolonged Starvation." *Journal of Applied Physiology* 23:304–310, 1967.

Goldblatt, P. B. "Social Factors in Obesity." *JAMA* 192:1039–1044, 1965.

Harrison, M. T., and R. M. Harden. "The Long-term Value of Fasting in the Treatment of Obesity. *Lancet* 2:1340–1342, 1966.

Hashim, S. A., and T. B. Van Itallie. "Studies in Normal and Obese Subjects with a Monitored Food Dispensing Device. *Annals of the New York Academy of Science* 131:654–661, 1965.

Hirsch, J. "Cell Lipid Content and Cell Number in Obese and Non-obese Human Adipose Tissue." *Journal of Clinical Investigation* 45:1023, 1966.

Howard, L., A. Dobs, R. Chodos, *et al.* "A Comparison of Administering Protein Alone and Protein Plus Glucose on Nitrogen Balance." *American Journal of Clinical Nutrition* 31:226–229, 1978.

Kiell, Norman (editor). *The Psychology of Obesity: Dynamics and Treatment.* Springfield, Illinois: Charles C. Thomas, 1973.

Mahoney, M. J., N. G. M. Moura, and T. C. Wade. "Relative Efficiency of Self-reward, Self-punishment, and Self-monitoring Techniques for Weight Loss. *Journal of Consulting and Clinical Psychology* 40:404–407, 1973.

Mann, G. V. "The Influence of Obesity on Health." *New England Journal of Medicine* 291:178–185, 226–232, 1974.

Marliss, E. B., F. T. Murray, and A. F. Nakhooda. "The Metabolic Response to Hypocaloric Protein Diets in Obese Man." *Journal of Clinical Investigation* 62:468–479, 1978.

Mayer, Jean. *Overweight: Causes, Costs, Control.* Englewood Cliffs, New Jersey: Prentice-Hall, 1968.

National Center for Health Statistics. "Weight by Height and Age of Adults 18–74 Years: United States, 1971–74." Washington, D.C.: U.S. Department of Health, Education, and Welfare, 30 November 1977:1–11.

Nisbett, R. E. "Determinants of Food Intake in Obesity." *Science* 159:1254–1255, 1968.

Oscal, L. B. and B. T. Williams. "Effect of Exercise on Overweight Middle-aged Males." *Journal of the American Geriatrics Society* 16:794–797, 1968.

Rickman, F., N. Mitchell, J. Dingman, *et al.* "Changes in Serum Cholesterol During the Stillman Diet." *JAMA* 228:54–58, 1974.

Schachter, Stanley. "Effects of Fear, Food Deprivation and Obesity in Eating." *Journal of Personal and Social Psychology* 10:91–97, 1968.

—————. "Obesity and Eating." *Science* 161:751–756, 1968.

Schachter, Stanley, and Judith Rodin. *Obese Humans and Rats.* Potomac, Maryland: Lawrence Erlbaum, 1974

Stunkard, A. J. "New Therapy for the Eating Disorders: Behavior Modification of Obesity and Anorexia Nervosa." In: *Treating the Obese.* W. L. Asher (editor). New York: Medcom Press, 1973.

Stunkard, A. J., and V. Burt. "Obesity and the Body Image, II." *American Journal of Psychiatry.* 123:1443–1447, 1967.

Stunkard, A. J., and C. Koch. "The Interpretation of Gastric Motility, I. Apparent Bias in the Reports of Hunger by Obese Persons." *Archives of General Psychiatry* 11:74–82, 1964.

Williams, Ben J., Sander Martin, and John P. Foreyt. *Obesity: Behavioral Approaches to Dietary Management.* New York: Brunner/Mazel, 1976.

Yang, M. U., and T. B. Van Itallie. "Composition of Weight Lost During Short-term Weight reduction: Metabolic Responses of Obese Subjects to Starvation and

Low-caloric Ketogenic and Nonketogenic Diets." *Journal of Clinical Investigation* 58:722–730, 1976.

Young, R. L., R. J. Fuchs, and M. J. Woltjen. "Chorionic Gonadotrophin in Weight Control; A Double-blind Crossover Study." *JAMA* 236:2495–2497, 1976.

Zuti, W. B., and L. A. Golding. "Comparing Diet and Exercise as Weight Reduction Tools." *Physician and Sports Medicine* 4:49–53, 1976.

STRESS

Appley, Mortimer H., and R. Trumbull (editors). *Psychological Stress*. New York: Meredith, 1967.

Barsky, A. J., III. "Patients Who Amplify Bodily Sensations." *Annals of Internal Medicine* 91:63–70, 1979.

Benson, Herbert. *The Relaxation Response*. New York: William Morrow, 1975.

Betz, B. J., and C. B. Thomas. "Individual Temperament as a Predictor of Health or Premature Disease. *Johns Hopkins Medical Journal* 144:81–89, 1979.

Bourne, Peter G. *The Psychology and Physiology of Stress*. New York: Academic Press, 1969.

Buckley, J. P. "Physiological Effects of Environmental Stimuli." *Journal of Pharmaceutical Science* 61:1175–1188. 1972.

Coelho, George W. (editor). *Coping and Adaptation*. New York: Basic Books, 1974.

Dohrenwend, Barbara S., and Bruce P. Dohrenwend. *Stressful Life Events: Their Nature and Effects*. New York: Wiley, 1974.

Dunbar, Helen Flanders. *Psychosomatic Diagnosis*. New York: Harper, 1958.

Eliot, Robert S. (editor). *Stress and the Heart*. New York: Futura, 1974.

Eliot R. S., F. C. Clayton, G. M. Pieper, and G. L. Todd. "Influence of Environmental Stress on the Pathogenesis of Sudden Cardiac Death. *Federal Proceedings* 36:1719–1724, 1977.

Garfield, Charles A. *Stress and Survival*. St. Louis: Mosby, 1979,

Goodwin, Rowland. *Stress at Work*. London: Chester House, 1976.

Gowler, Dan (editor). *Managerial Stress*. New York: Wiley, 1975.

Henry, J. P., and D. L. Ely. "Biological Correlates of Psychosomatic Illness." In: *Biological Foundations of Psychiatry*. S. Gabay and R. G. Grenell (editors). New York: Raven Press, 1976.

Hill, O. "The Psychological Management of Psychosomatic Diseases." *British Journal of Psychiatry* 131:113–126, 1977.

Hinkle, L. E., Jr., W. N. Christenson, F. D. Kane, *et al.* "An Investigation of the Relation Between Life Experience, Personality Characteristics, and General Susceptibility to Illness." *Psychosomatic Medicine* 20:278–295, 1958.

Horowitz, Mardi. *Stress Response Syndromes*. New York: Aronson, 1976.

Jenkins, C. D. "Recent Evidence Supporting Psychological and Social Risk Factors for Coronary Disease." *New England Journal of Medicine* 294:987–994, 1033–1038, 1976.

Jones, M. C. "Personality Correlates and Antecedents of Drinking Patterns in Adult Males." *Journal of Consulting and Clinical Psychology* 32:2–12, 1968.

—————. "Personality Correlates and Antecedents of Drinking Patterns in Women. *Journal of Consulting and Clinical Psychology* 36:61–69, 1971.

Klerman, G. L., and J. E. Izen. "The Effects of Bereavement and Grief on Physical Health and General Well-being." *Advances in Psychosomatic Medicine* 6:63–104, 1977.

Langer, Thomas S., and Stanley T. Michael. *Life Stress and Mental Health: The Mid-Town Manhattan Study*. London: Collier-Macmillan, 1963.

Lazarus, Richard S. *Psychological Stress and the Coping Process*. New York: McGraw-Hill, 1966.

Levi, Lennart (editor). *Emotions, Their Parameters and Measurement*. New York: Raven Press, 1975.

——————. *Stress and Distress in Response to Psychosocial Stimuli.* New York: Pergamon Press, 1972.

——————. *Society, Stress and Disease.* New York: Oxford University Press, 1971.

Levine, Sol, and N. A. Scotch (editors). *Social Stress.* Chicago: Aldine, 1970.

Moos, Rudolf H. *Human Adaptation: Coping with Life Crises.* Lexington, Massachusetts: Heath, 1976.

Mason, J. W. "A Re-evaluation of the Concept of "Non-specificity" in Stress Theory." *Journal of Psychiatric Research* 8:323–333, 1971.

——————. "A Historical View of the Stress Field: Part 2. *Journal of Human Stress* 1:22–36, 1975.

Mechanic, D. "Some Problems in the Measurement of Stress and Social Readjustment." *Journal of Human Stress* 1:43–48, 1975.

Minter, R. E., and C. P. Kimball, "Life Events and Illness Onset: A Review." *Psychosomatics* 19:334–339, 1978.

Rabkin, J. G. and E. L. Struening, "Life Events, Stress, and Illness." *Science* 194:1013–1020, 1976.

Rahe, R. H., and J. A. Ransom. "Life Change and Illness Studies: Past History and Future Directions." *Journal of Human Stress* 4:3–15, 1978.

Rowland, K. F., and B. Sokol. "Review of Research Examining the Coronary Prone Behavior Pattern." *Journal of Human Stress* 3:26–33, 1977.

Thomas, C. G. "Precursors of Premature Disease and Death: The Predictive Potential of Habits and Family Attitudes." *Annals of Internal Medicine* 85:653–658, 1976.

Thorne, M. C., A. L. Wing, and R. S. Paffenbarger, Jr. "Chronic Disease in Former College Students, VII. Early Precursors of nonfatal coronary heart disease." *American Journal of Epidemiology* 87:520–529, 1968.

Vaillant, G. "Natural History of Male Psychologic Health: Effects of Mental Health on Physical Health." *New England Journal of Medicine* 301:1249–1254, 1979.

"Vital and Health Statistics—Selected Symptoms of Psychological Distress." Series 11, No. 37, U.S. Department of HEW, PHS.

Walker, W. J. "Stress and Type A Personality—a Second Look." *Forum on Medicine* 3:272–275, 1980.

Wolf, Stewart, and Helen Goodell. *Stress and Disease.* Springfield, Illinois: Charles C. Thomas, 1968.

EXERCISE

American College of Sports Medicine. *Guidelines for Graded Exercise Testing and Prescription.* Philadelphia: Lea and Febiger, 1975.

Amsterdam, E. A., J. H. Wilmore and A. N. DeMario. *Exercise in Cardiovascular Health and Disease.* New York: York Medical Books, 1977.

Astrand, Per-Olof. *Health and Fitness.* Stockholm: Swedish Information Service, 1972.

Atomi, Y., and M. Miyashita. "Effects of Moderate Recreational Activities on the Aerobic Work Capacity of Middle-aged Women." *Journal of Sports, Medicine and Physical Fitness* 16(4):261–266, 1976.

Balke, B. "Prescribing physical activity." In: *Sports Medicine.* L. Larson (editor). New York: Academic Press, 1974.

Bloor, C. M., and A. S. Leon. "Interaction of Age and Exercise on the Heart and Blood Supply. *Laboratory Investigation* 22:160–165, 1970.

Cooper, Kenneth. *The Aerobics Way: New Data on the World's Most Popular Exercise Program.* New York: M. Evans, 1977.

Cooper, K. H., M. L. Pollock, R. P. Martin, *et al.* "Physical Fitness Levels vs. Selected Coronary Risk Factors: A Cross-sectional Study. *JAMA* 236:166–169, 1976.

Cureton, T. K. *The Physiological Effects of Exercise Programs on Adults.* Springfield, Illinois: Thomas Company, 1969.

de Vries, H. A., and G. M. Adams. "Electromyographic Comparison of Single Doses of Exercise and Meprobamate as to Effects on Muscular Relaxation." *American Journal of Physical Medicine* 51:130–141, 1972.

Fox, S. M., J. P. Naughton, and P. A. Gorman. "Physical Activity and Cardiovascular Health, III. The Exercise Prescription; Frequency and Type of Activity." *Modern Concepts of Cardiovascular Disease* 41:25–30, 1972.

Golding, Lawrence A., and Ronald R. Bos. *Scientific Foundations of Physical Fitness Programs*, 2nd Edition. Minneapolis, Minnesota: Burgess, 1970.

Grimby, G., and B. Saltin, "Physiological Analysis of Physically Well-trained Middle-aged and Old Athletes." *Acta Medica Scandinavia* 179:513–526, 1966.

Horne, William M. "Effects of a Physical Activity Program on Middle-aged, Sedentary Corporation Executives." *American Industrial Hygiene Association Journal* 36(3):241–245, 1975.

International Committee for the Standardization of Physical Fitness Tests. *Fitness, Health and Work Capacity: International Standards for Assessment* Leonard H. Larson (editor). New York: Macmillan, 1974.

Joseph, J. "Effects of Calisthenics, Jogging and Swimming on Middle-aged Men." *Journal of Sports, Medicine and Physical Fitness* 14:14–20, 1974.

Kannel, W. B., T. Gordon, P. Sorlie, and P. M. McNamara. "Physical Activity and Coronary Vulnerability: The Framingham Study. *Cardiology Digest* 6:28–40, 1971.

Koch, J., and S. Petrillo. "What You'd Better Know Before Joining a Health Club." *Today's Health* 50:17–19, 67–68, 1972.

Lopez, S., R. Vial, L. Balart, and G. Arroyave. "Effect of Exercise and Physical Fitness on Serum Lipids and Lipoproteins. *Atherosclerosis* 20:1–9, 1974.

Myers, Clayton R. *The Official YMCA Physical Fitness Handbook*. New York: Popular Library Publications, 1975.

National Center for Health Statistics. *Exercise and Participation in Sports Among Persons 20 Years of Age and Over: United States, 1975.* Washington, D.C.: U.S. Department of Health, Education and Welfare, 15 March 1978: 1–11.

Paffenbarger, R. S., Jr., and W. E. Hale. "Work Activity and Coronary Heart Mortality. *New England Journal of Medicine* 292:545–550, 1975.

————— and R. T. Hyde. "Exercise as Protection Against Heart Attack. *New England Journal of Medicine* 302:1026–1027, 1980.

Pollock, M. L., *et al.* "Physiologic Responses of Men 49 to 65 Years of Age to Endurance Training." *Journal of the American Geriatric Association*, 24(3):97—104, 197.

Pollock, Michael L., Jack H. Wilmore, Samuel M. Fox, (editors). *Health and Fitness Through Physical Activity.* Somerset, New Jersey: John Wiley & Sons, 1978.

Rose, G. "Physical Activity." In: *Atherosclerosis: Proceedings of the Second International Symposium (Chicago, November 2–5, 1969),* R. J. Jones (editor). New York: Springer-Verlag, 1970.

Sanne, H. M., and L. Wilhelmsen. "Physical Activity as Prevention and Therapy in Coronary Heart Disease." *Scandinavian Journal of Rehabilitative Medicine* 3:47–56, 1971.

Skinner, J. S. *Exercise, Aging and Longevity*, Eighth International Congress of Gerontology, Proceedings, Washington, D.C., 1969.

Wilmore, J. "Individual Exercise Prescription." *American Journal of Cardiology* 33:757–759, 1974.

Young, R. J., and A. H. Ismail. "Relationships Between Anthropometric, Physiological, Biochemical, and Personality Variables Before and After a Four-Month Conditioning Program for Middle-aged Men." *Journal of Sports Medicine and Physical Fitness* 16(4):267–276, 1976.

ARTHRITIS

Akeson, W. H. "The Connective Tissue Response to Immobility: An Accelerated Aging Response?" *Experimental Gerontology* 3:289–301, 1968.

Bollet, A. J. "An Essay on the Biology of Osteoarthritis." *Arthritis and Rheumatism* 12:152–158, 1969.

Fries, James F. *Arthritis. A Comprehensive Guide*. Reading, Massachusetts: Addison-Wesley, 1979.

Goodman, Louis S., and Alfred Gilman (editors). *The Pharmacological Basis of Therapeutics*, 5th Edition. New York: Macmillan, 1975.

Howell, D. S., *et al*. "A Comprehensive Regimen for Osteoarthritis." *Medical Clinics of North America* 55:457, 1971.

Kellgren, J. H., and I. S. Lawrence. "Osteo-arthrosis and Disk Degeneration in an Urban Population." *Annals of Rheumatic Diseases* 17:388–397, 1958.

Kellgren, J. H. "Genetic Factors in Generalized Osteo-arthrosis." *Annals of Rheumatic Diseases* 22:237–255, 1963.

Lawrence, J. S. "Generalized Osteoarthrosis in a Population Sample. *American Journal of Epidemiology* 90:381–389, 1969.

Lowman, E. W. "Osteoarthritis." *Journal of the American Medical Association* 157:487–488, 1955.

Mannik, M., and B. C. Gilliland. "Degenerative Joint Disease," In: *Harrison's Principles of Internal Medicine*, 8th Edition. George W. Thorn *et al*. (editors). New York: McGraw-Hill, 1977.

Moskowitz, R. W. "Osteoarthritis: A New Look at an Old Disease. *Geriatrics* 28:121–125, 1973.

MENOPAUSE

Adlin, E. V. "Postmenopausal Estrogen Therapy." *Annals of Internal Medicine* 91:488–489, 1979.

Boston Collaborative Drug Surveillance Program. "Estrogen and Gall Bladder Disease, Venous Thromboembolism, and Breast Tumors in Relation to Postmenopausal Estrogen Therapy." *New England Journal of Medicine* 290:51–52, 1974.

Campbell, S. *The Endometrium and the Menopause, Female and Male Climacteric*. P. A. Van Keep, D. M. Seer, and R. B. Greenblatt (editors). Lancaster, England: MTP Press, 1979.

Cutler, B. S., A. P. Forbes, F. M. Ingersoll, and R. E. Scully. "Endometrial Carcinoma After Stilbestrol Therapy in Gonadal Dysgenesis." *New England Journal of Medicine* 287:628–631, 1972.

Feinstein, A. R. and R. I. Horwitz. "A Critique of the Statistical Evidence Associating Estrogens with Endometrial Cancer." *Cancer Research* 38:4001–4005, 1978.

Gallagher, J. C., B. L. Riggs, A. Hamstra, *et al*. "Effect of Estrogen Therapy on Calcium Absorption and Vitamin D Metabolism in Postmenopausal Osteoporosis." *Clinical Research* 26:415A, 1978.

Gambrell, R. D., Jr., F. M. Massey, J. A. Castaneda, *et al*. "Reduced Incidence of Endometrial Cancer Among Postmenopausal Women Treated with Progestogens." *Journal of the American Geriatrics Society* 27:389–394, 1979.

Greenblatt, R. B. "Estrogen Use and Endometrial Cancer." *New England Journal of Medicine* 300:921–922, 1979.

Hess, E., R. Roth, and A. Kaminski. "Is There a Male Climacteric?" *Geriatrics* 10:170–173, 1955.

Hoover, R. "Menopausal Estrogens and Breast Cancer." *New England Journal of Medicine* 295:401–405, 1976.

Hoover, R., J. F. Fraumeni, R. Everson, and M. H. Myers. "Cancer of the Uterine Corpus After Hormonal Treatment for Breast Cancer." *Lancet* 1:885–887, 1976.

Horwitz, R. I., and A. R. Feinstein. "Alternative Analytic Methods for Case-control Studies of Estrogens and Endometrial Cancer. *New England Journal of Medicine* 299:1089–1094, 1978.

Hutchison, G. B. "Case-control Studies of Estrogens and Endometrial Cancer." *New England Journal of Medicine* 300:497, 1979.

MacDonald, P. C., and P. K. Siiteri. "The Relationship Between the Extraglandular Production of Estrone and the Occurrence of Endometrial Neoplasia. *Gynecological Oncology* 2:259–263, 1974.

McCarroll, A. M., D. A. D. Montgomery, J. M. G. Harley, *et al.* "Endometrial Cancer After Cyclical Oestrogen-Progestogen Therapy for Turner's Syndrome. *British Journal of Obstetrics and Gynaecology* 82:421–423, 1975.

McDonald, T. W., G. D. Malkasian, and T. A. Gaffey. "Endometrial Cancer Associated with Feminizing Ovarian Tumor and Polycystic Ovarian Disease." *Obstetrics and Gynecology* 49:654–658, 1977.

Nachtigall, L. E., *et al.* "Estrogen Replacement Therapy, I: A 10-year Prospective Study in the Relationship to Osteoporosis. *Obstetrics and Gynecology* 53:277–287, 1979.

——————, *et al.* "Estrogen Replacement Therapy, II. A Prospective Study in the Relationship to Carcinoma and Cardiovascular and Metabolic Problems." *Obstetrics and Gynecology* 54:74–79, 1979.

Neugarten, B. L., V. Wood, R. J. Kraines, and B. Loomis. "Women's Attitudes Toward the Menopause," In: B. L. Neugarten (editor). *Middle Age and Aging: A Reader in Social Psychology.* Chicago: University of Chicago Press, pp. 195–200, 1968.

Quigley, M. M., and C. B. Hammond. "Estrogen-Replacement Therapy—Help or Hazard? *New England Journal of Medicine* 301:646–648, 1979.

Rakoff, A. E., and K. Nowrozi. *The Female Climacteric, Geriatric Endocrinology (Aging.* Vol. 5. R. B. Greenblatt, editor). New York: Raven Press, 1978.

Rauramo, L. "Estrogen Replacement Therapy and Endometrial Carcinoma." *Frontiers of Hormone Research* 5:117–125, 1977.

Rigg, L. A., H. Hermann, and S. S. C. Yen. "Absorption of Estrogens from Vaginal Creams." *New England Journal of Medicine* 298:195–197, 1978.

Tikkanen, M. J., T. Kuusi, E. Vartiainen, *et al.* "Treatment of Postmenopausal Hypercholesterolaemia with Estradiol." *Acta Obstetrica Gynecologica Scandinavia* (Supplement)88:83–88, 1979.

Weiss, N. S., Szekeley, and D. R. Austin. "Increasing Incidence of Endometrial Cancer in the United States." *New England Journal of Medicine* 294:1259–1262, 1976.

SKIN AND HAIR CARE

Baker, T. J. "The Aging Face. *Clinics in Plastic Surgery* 5(1):1–2, 1978.

Brennan, H. G., *et al.* "Correcting the Aging Platysma." *Archives of Otolaryngology* 104(3):137–139, 1978.

Castañares, S. "Complications in Blepharoplasty." *Clinics in Plastic Surgery* 5:139–165, 1978.

Connell, B. F. "Eyebrow, Face and Neck Lifts for Males. *Clinics in Plastic Surgery* 5:15–28, 1978.

Fitzpatrick, Thomas B., Klaus Wolf Eisen, Irwin M. Freedburg, and K. Frank Austen. *Dermatology in General Medicine: Textbook and Atlas.* New York: McGraw-Hill, 1979.

Fox, Sidney A. *Ophthalmic Plastic Surgery,* 5th Edition. New York: Grune & Stratton, 1976.

Gordon, H. L. "Rhytidectomy." *Clinics in Plastic Surgery* 5:97–107, 1978.

Grahame, R. "A Method for Measuring Human Skin Elasticity *in Vivo. Clinical Science* 39:223–238, 1970.

Guibor, P., and B. Smith (editors). *Contemporary Oculoplastic Surgery.* New York: Stratton, 1974.

Johnson, S. D. U. "Skin Changes of the Sunset Years." *Cutis* 18:351–356, 1976.

Jones, C. E., *et al.* "Cosmetic Surgery of the Face: Philosophical Considerations." *New York State Journal of Medicine* 77:2292–2293, 1977.

Lever, Walter F. *Histopathology of the Skin.* 5th Edition. Philadelphia: Lippincott, 1975.

Lynch, P. J. "Sunlight and Aging of the Skin." *Cutis* 18:451–453, 1976.

Mahoney, M. G. "Electrolysis." *Cutis* 18:213–214, 1976.

McGregor, Ian A. *Fundamental Techniques of Plastic Surgery*, 5th Edition. Baltimore: Williams & Wilkins, 1972.

Mosienko, P., and T. J. Baker. "Chemical Peel." *Clinics in Plastic Surgery* 5:79–96, 1978.

Rees, T. D., and S. J. Aston. "Complications of Rhytidectomy." *Clinics in Plastic Surgery* 5:109–119, 1978.

Sayre, R. M., E. Marlowe, P. P. Agin, *et al.* "Performance of Six Sunscreen Formulations on Human Skin." *Archives of Dermatology* 115:46–49, 1979.

Shelley, Walter B. *Consultations in Dermatology.* Philadelphia: W. B. Saunders, 1974.

Smith, J. G., Jr., and G. R. Finlayson. "Dermal Connective Tissue Alterations with Age and Chronic Sun Damage." *Journal of the Society of Cosmetic Chemistry* 16:527–535, 1965.

Spira, M. "Blepharoplasty." *Clinics in Plastic Surgery* 5:121–137, 1978.

Spoor, J. "Cosmetic Dermatology." *Cutis* 18:753, 758–759, 1976.

Spoor, H. J. "Wrinkles." *Cutis* 17:236–241, 1976.

Stough, D. B., III. "The Esthetics of Hair Transplantation." *Cutis* 18:286–288, 1976.

Sunscreen Drug Products for Over-the-counter Human Use. *Federal Register* 43:38206–38269, (August 25), 1978.

Thomson, J. A. "Cosmetic Surgery: The Psychiatric Perspective." *Psychosomatics* 19:7–15, 1978.

THE MIND

Adams, C. W. "The Age at Which Scientists Do Their Best Work." *Isis*, 36:166–169, 1945–1946.

Atkinson, R. C., and R. M. Shiffrin. "The Control of Short-term Memory." *Scientific American* 225:82–90, 1971.

Bayley, N., and M. H. Oden. "Maintenance of Intellectual Ability in Gifted Adults." *Journal of Gerontology* 10: 91–107, 1955.

Bayley, N. "Learning in Adulthood: The Role of Intelligence." In: H. J. Klausmeier and C. W. Harris (editors). *Analyses of Concept Learning.* New York: Academic Press, 1966.

Berkowitz, B. and R. F. Green. "Changes in Intellect with Age, I. Longitudinal Study of Wechsler-Bellevue Scores. *Journal of Genetic Psychology* 103:3–21, 1963.

Birren, J. E. "Age and Decision Strategies." A. T. Welford and J. E. Birren (editors). *Interdisciplinary Topics in Gerontology* 4:23–36, 1969.

——————., and D. F. Morrison. "Analysis of the WAIS Subtests in Relation to Age and Education." *Journal of Gerontology* 16:363–369, 1961.

——————:, J. Botwinick, and A. Weiss, *et al.* "Interrelations of Mental and Perceptual Tests Given to Healthy Elderly Men." In: J. E. Birren *et al.* (editors). *Human Aging: A Biological and Behavioral Study.* Washington, D.C.: U.S. Government Printing Office, 1963.

Botwinick, Jack. *Aging and Behavior.* New York: Springer Publishing Company, 1973.

Burns, R. B. "Age and Mental Ability: Retesting with Thirty-three Year Interval." *British Journal of Educational Psychology* 36:116, 1966.

Butcher, Harold J. *Human Intelligence: Its Nature and Assessment.* London: Methuen, 1968.

Cattell, Raymond B. *Abilities: Their Structure, Growth, and Action.* Boston: Houghton, Mifflin, 1971.

Craik, F. I. M. "Short-term Memory and the Aging Process." In: G. A. Talland. *Human Aging and Behavior.* New York: Academic Press, 1968.

Cunningham, W. R., V. Clayton, and W. Overton. "Fluid and Crystallized Intelligence in Young Adulthood and Old Age. *Journal of Gerontology* 30:53–55, 1975.

Damon, A. "Discrepancies Between Findings of Longitudinal and Cross-sectional Studies in Adult Life: Physique and Physiology. *Human Development* 8:16–22, 1965.

Dennis, W. "Age and Achievement: A Critique." *Journal of Gerontology* 11:331–333, 1956.

——————. "Age and Productivity Among Scientists." *Science* 123:724–725, 1956.

——————. "Creative Productivity Between the Ages of 20 and 80 Years. *Journal of Gerontology* 21:1–8, 1966.

Doppelt, J. E., and W. Wallace. "Standardization of the Wechsler Adult Intelligence Scale for Older Persons." *Journal of the American Social Psychology* 51:312–330, 1955.

Eichorn, D. H. "Individual Changes in Adult Intelligence: Longitudinal Approaches. In: L. F. Jarvik *et al. Intellectual Functioning in Adults*. New York: Springer, 1973.

Elo, A. E. "Age Changes in Master Chess Performance." *Journal of Gerontology* 20:289–299, 1965.

Eysenck, Hans Jurgen. *Race, Intelligence and Education*. New York: Library Press, 1971.

Ganzler, H. "Motivation as a Factor in the Psychological Deficit of Aging." *Journal of Gerontology* 19:425–429, 1964.

Garfield, S., and L. Blek. "Age, Vocabulary Level, and Mental Impairment." *Journal of Consulting Psychology* 16:395–398, 1952.

Ghiselli, E. E. "The Relationship Between Intelligence and Age Among Superior Adults." *Journal of Genetic Psychology* 90:131–142, 1957.

Green, R. F. "Age-intelligence Relationship Between Ages Sixteen and Sixty-four: A Rising Trend." *Developmental Psychology* 1:618–627, 1969.

Hanley, T. "Neuronal fall-out" in the Ageing Brain: A Critical Review of the Quantitative Data. *Age and Ageing*. 3:133–151, 1974.

Heglin, H. J. "Problem Solving Set in Different Age Groups." *Journal of Gerontology* 11:310–317, 1956.

Horn, J. L., and R. B. Cattell. "Age Differences in Fluid and Crystallized Intelligence." *Acta Psychologica* 26:107–129, 1967.

Horn, John L. "Intelligence: Why It Grows, Why It Declines." In: J. M. Hunt (editor). *Human Intelligence*. New Brunswick, New Jersey: Transaction Books, 1972.

Hultsch, D. "Adult Age Differences in the Organization of Free Recall." *Developmental Psychology* 1:673–678, 1969.

Jarvik, L. F., C. Eisdorfer, and J. E. Blum (editors). *Intellectual Functioning in Adults: Psychological and Biological Influences*. New York: Springer, 1973.

Jensen, A. J. *Educability and Group Differences*. New York: Harper & Row, 1973.

Jensen, A. R. "How Much Can We Boost I.Q. and Scholastic Achievement?" *Harvard Educational Review* 39:1–123, 1969.

Jensen, Arthur. *Environment, Heredity and Intelligence*. Cambridge, Massachusetts: Harvard Reprint Series No. 2, 1970.

Jones, H. E. "Consistency and Change in Early Maturity." *Vita Humana* 1:43–51, 1958.

Kay, H. "Learning of a Serial Task by Different Age Groups." *Quarterly Journal of Experimental Psychology* 3:166–183, 1951.

Kibler, M. O., and L. W. Sontag. "Personality and other Correlates of I.Q. Change in Women." In: J. E. Birren (editor). *Relations of Development in Aging*. Springfield, Illinois: Charles C. Thomas, 1964.

Korchin, S. J., and W. B. Basowitz. "The Judgement of Ambiguous Stimuli as an Index of Cognitive Functioning in Aging." *Journal of Personality* 25:81–95, 1956.

Laurence, M. W. "A Developmental Look at the Usefulness of List Categorization as an Aid to Free Recall." *Canadian Journal of Psychology* 21:153–165, 1967.

Lehman, Harvey C. *Age and Achievement*. Princeton, New Jersey: Princeton University Press, 1953.

Lorge, Irving, *et al. Adult Education: Theory and Method*. Washington, D.C.: Adult Education Association of the USA, 1963.

Mandler, G. "Organization and memory." In: K. W. Spence and J. T. Spence (editors). *The Psychology of Learning and Motivation. Advances in Research and Theory*, Vol. 1. New York: Academic Press, 1967.

Manniche, E. and G. Falk. "Age and the Nobel Prize." *Behavioral Science* 2:301–307, 1957.

Miles, C. C., and W. R. Miles. "The Correlation of Intelligence Scores and Chronological Age from Early to Late Maturity." *American Journal of Psychology* 44:44–78, 1932.

Moenster, P. A. " Learning and Memory in Relation to Age." *Journal of Gerontology* 27:361–363, 1972.

Murdock, B. B., Jr. "Recent Developments in Short-term Memory." *British Journal of Psychology*. 58:421–433, 1967.

Nisbet, J. D. "Intelligence and Age: Retesting with Twenty-four Years' Interval." *British Journal of Educational Psychology* 27:190–198, 1957.

Owens, W. A., Jr. "Age and Mental Abilities: A Longitudinal Study. *Genetic Psychology Monographs* 48:3–54, 1953.

——————. "Age and Mental Abilities: A Second Adult Follow-up. *Journal of Educational Psychology* 51:311–325, 1966.

Schaie, K. W. "Age Changes and Age Differences." *Gerontologist* 7:128–132, 1967.

—————— and C. R. Strother. "A Cross-sequential Study of Age Changes in Cognitive Behavior." *Psychological Bulletin* 70:671–680, 1968.

Schonfield, D. and B. Robertson. "Memory Storage and Aging." *Canadian Journal of Psychology* 20:228–236, 1966.

Shuey, Audrey M. *The Testing of Negro Intelligence*, 2nd Edition. New York: Social Science Press, 1966.

Thurstone, Louis L. *Multiple-Factor Analysis: A Development and Expansion of the Vectors of the Mind*. Chicago: University of Chicago Press, 1947.

Tuddenham, R. D., *et al.* "Age Changes on AGCT: A Longitudinal Study of Average Adults." *Journal of Consulting Psychology* 32:659–663, 1968.

Waugh, N. C. and D. A. Norman. "Primary Memory." *Psychological Review* 72:89–104, 1965.

Wechsler, David. *The Measurement and Appraisal of Adult Intelligence*, 4th Edition. Baltimore: Williams and Wilkins, 1958.

——————. *Manual for the Wechsler Adult Intelligence Scale*. New York: Psychological Corporation, 1955.

THE PERSON

Aaronson, B. S. "Aging, Personality Change and Psychiatric Diagnosis." *Journal of Gerontology* 19:144–148, 1964.

Adler, Alfred. *Understanding Human Nature*. W. Beran Wolfe (translator). London: Allen & Unwin, 1962.

Allport, Gordon W. *Pattern and Growth in Personality*. New York: Holt, Rinehart & Winston, 1961.

Anderson, Wayne. *Gauguin's Paradise Lost*. New York: The Viking Press, 1971.

Arasteh, A. Reza. *Final Integration in the Adult Personality*. Leyden, the Netherlands: E. J. Brill, 1965.

Baltes, Paul B., and Orville G. Brim, Jr. (editors). *Life-span Development and Behavior*. New York: Academic Press, 1979.

Benedek, T. "Climacterium: A Developmental Phase." *Psychoanalysis Quarterly* 19:1–27, 1950.

——————. "Parenthood as a Developmental Phase." *Journal of the American Psychoanalytic Association* 7:389–417, 1959.

Birren, James E., and K. Warner Schaie (editors). *Handbook of the Psychology of Aging*. New York: Van Nostrand Reinhold, 1977.

Block, Jack, and Norma Haan. *Lives Through Time*. Berkeley, California: Bancroft Books, 1971.

Brim, O. G., Jr. "Theories of the Male Mid-life Crisis." *The Counseling Psychologist* 6:2–9, 1976.

Bromley, Dennis B. *The Psychology of Human Aging*, 2nd Edition. Baltimore: Penguin Books, 1974.

Buhler, Charlotte, and Fred Massarik (editors). *The Course of Human Life*. New York: Springer, 1968.

Butler, Robert N. "Psychiatry and Psychology of the Middle-aged." In: A. M. Freedman *et al.* (editors). *Comprehensive Textbook of Psychiatry, II*. Baltimore: Williams and Wilkins, 1974.

Cain, Leonard D. "Life Course and Social Structure." R. E. L. Faris (editor). *Handbook of Modern Sociology*. New York: Rand McNally, 1964.

Catrell, Fred. *Aging and the Aged*. Dubuque, Iowa: William C. Brown, 1974.

Clark, M. "The Anthropology of Aging, A New Area for Studies of Culture and Personality." *The Gerontologist* 7(1):55–64, 1967.

Clayton, V. "Erikson's Theory of Human Development as it Applies to the Aged: Wisdom as Contradictive Cognition." *Human Development* 18:119–128, 1975.

Crandall, V. C. "The Fels Study: Some Contributions to Personality Development and Achievement in Childhood and Adulthood." *Seminars in Psychiatry* 4:383–398, 1972.

Deutsch, Helene. *The Psychology of Women, A Psychoanalytic Interpretation, Vol. 2, Motherhood*. New York: Bantam Books, 1973.

Fiske, D. W. The Limits for the Conventional Science of Personality. *Journal of Personality* 42(1):1–11, 1974.

Frenkel-Brunswik, E. "Adjustments and Reorientation in the Course of the Life Span." In: B. L. Neugarten (editor). *Middle Age and Aging: A Reader in Social Psychology*. Chicago, Illinois: University of Chicago Press, 1968.

Freud, Anna. *The Ego and the Mechanisms of Defense*. New York: International Universities Press, 1946.

Freud, Sigmund. *The Standard Edition of the Complete Work of Sigmund Freud*. London: Hogarth, 1953.

Fromm, Erich. *Escape From Freedom*. New York: Farrar, Straus & Giroux, 1941.

——————. *Man For Himself*. New York: Rinehart, 1947.

——————. *The Sane Society*. New York: Rinehart, 1955.

Gennep, Arnold van. *The Rites of Passage*. Chicago: University of Chicago Press, 1960.

Gould, R. L. "The Phases of Adult Life: A Study in Developmental Psychology." *American Journal of Psychiatry* 129:33–43, 1972.

Gould, Roger. *Transformations*. New York: Simon & Schuster, 1978.

Graubard, S. R. (editor). "Adulthood." *Daedalus* 105 No. 2, 1976.

Gruen, W. "Adult Personality: An Empirical Study of Erikson's Theory of Ego Development." In: B. L. Neugarten (editor). *Personality in Middle and Late Life: Empirical Studies*. New York: Atherton Press, 1964.

Gutmann, D. L. "An Exploration of Ego Configurations in Middle and Later Life." In: B. L. Neugarten (editor). *Personality in Middle and Late Life: Empirical Studies*. New York: Atherton Press, 1964.

——————. The Cross-cultural Perspective: Notes Toward a Comparative Psychology of Aging." In: James E. Birren and K. Warner-Schaie (editors). *Handbook of the Psychology of Aging*. New York: Van Nostrand Reinhold, 1977.

Henry, W. E. "Personality Change in Middle and Old Age." In: E. Norbeck, D. Price-Williams, and W. M. McCord (editors). *The Study of Personality: An Interdisciplinary Appraisal*. New York: Holt, Rinehart and Winston, 1968.

Horney, Karen. *New Ways in Psychoanalysis*. New York: W. W. Norton, 1939.

Jaques, E. "Death and the Mid-life Crisis." *International Journal of Psychoanalysis* 46:502–514, 1965.

Jones, H. C., N. Bayley, J. W. Macfarlane, and M. P. Honzik. *The Course of Human Development*. Waltham, Massachusetts: Xerox College Publishing, 1971.

Jung, Carl G. *Collected Works*, 18 Volumes. New York: Pantheon, Bollingen Series, 1953.

Kuhlen, R. G. "Developmental Changes in Motivation During the Adult Years." In:

James E. Birren (editor). *Relations of Development and Aging*. Springfield, Illinois: Charles C. Thomas, 1964.

Levinson, D. J., *et al.* "Periods in the Adult Development of Men: Ages 18 to 45." *The Counseling Psychologist* 6:21–25, 1976.

——————. "The Mid-life Transition: A Period in Adult Psychosocial Development." *Psychiatry* 40:99–112, 1977.

——————. *The Seasons of a Man's Life*. New York: Alfred Knopf, 1978.

Lidz, Theodore. *The Person: His Development Throughout the Life Cycle*. New York: Basic Books, 1968.

Lifton, Robert. *The Life of the Self: Toward a New Psychology*. New York: Simon & Schuster, 1976.

Livson, F. B. "Patterns of Personality Development in Middle-aged Women: A Longitudinal Study." *International Journal of Aging and Human Development* 7(2):107–115, 1976.

Lowenthal, Marjorie F., Majda Thurnher, and David Chiriboga and Associates. *Four Stages of Life: A Comparative Study of Women and Men Facing Transitions*. San Francisco: Jossey-Bass, Inc. 1975.

Maas, Henry S., and Joseph Kuypers. *From Thirty to Seventy*. San Francisco: Jossey-Bass, 1974.

Maddi, Salvatore R. *Personality Theories: A Comparative Analysis*. Homewood, Illinois: The Dorsey Press, 1972.

Maslow, Abraham H. *Toward a Psychology of Being*. Princeton, New Jersey: D. Van Nostrand, 1962.

——————. *Motivation and Personality*, 2nd Edition. New York: Harper & Row, 1970.

McCandless, B. R. Symposium Discussion: Life-span Models of Psychological Aging. *Gerontologist* 13(4):511–512, 1973.

Nesselroade, John R., and Paul B. Baltes (editors). *Longitudinal Research in Human Development: Design and Analysis*. New York: Academic Press, 1979.

Neugarten, Bernice L. "A Developmental View of Adult Personality." In: J. E. Birren (editor). *Relations of Development and Aging*. Springfield, Illinois: C. C. Thomas, 1964.

——————. (editor). *Middle Age and Aging: A Reader in Social Psychology*. Chicago: University of Chicago Press, 1968.

—————— and N. Dowty. "The Middle Years." Silvano Arieti (editor). *American Handbook of Psychiatry* Vol. 1. New York: Basic Books, 1974.

Peck, R., and H. Berkowitz. "Personality and Adjustment in Middle Age." Bernice L. Neugarten (editor). *Personality in Middle and Late Life*. New York: Atherton, 1964.

Peskin, H., and N. Livson. "Pre- and Post-pubertal Personality and Adult Psychologic Functioning." *Seminars in Psychiatry* 4:343–353, 1972.

Riley, Matilda White. *Aging From Birth to Death*. Boulder, Colorado: Westview, 1979.

Roazen, Paul. *Erik H. Erikson: The Power and Limits of a Vision*. New York: Free Press, 1976.

Rosenberg, S. D., and M. P. Farrell. "Identity and Crisis in Middle-aged Men." *International Journal of Aging and Human Development* (2):153–170, 1976.

Terman, Luis, and Melita Oden. *The Gifted Group at Midlife*. Stanford: Stanford University Press, 1959.

Vaillant, G. E., and C. C. McArthur. "Natural History of Male Psychologic Health, I. The Adult Life Cycle from 18–50." *Seminars in Psychiatry* 4(4):415–427, 1972.

Vaillant, George E. *Adaptation to Life*. Boston: Little, Brown, 1977.

Van Den Daele, L. "Ego Development in Dialectic Perspective." *Human Development* 18:129–142, 1975.

White, Robert W. (editor). *The Study of Lives*. New York: Atherton Press, 1966.

Williams, Richard, and Claudine G. Wirths. *Lives Through The Years*. New York: Atherton Press, 1965.

Woodruff, D. S., and J. E. Birren. "Age Changes and Cohort Differences in Personality." *Developmental Psychology* 6(2):252–259, 1972.

SEX AND SEXUALITY

Athanasiou, R. "Questionnaire." *Psychology Today* 4:37–52, 1970.

Bancroft, J. H. J. "Evaluation of the Effects of Drugs on Sexual Behavior." *British Journal of Clinical Pharmacology* 3 (supplement):83–90, 1976.

Barbach, Lonnie G. *For Yourself: The Fulfillment of Female Sexuality*. New York: Doubleday & Company, 1975.

Bernard J. "Infidelity: Some Moral and Social Issues." *Science and Psychoanalysis* 16:99–119, 1970.

Berne, Eric. *Sex in Human Loving*. New York: Pocket Books, 1971.

Cameron, P. "Masculinity/Femininity of the Generations: As Self-reported and as Stereotypically Appraised." *International Journal of Aging and Human Development* 7(2):143–151, 1976.

Brown, W. A. "Serum Testosterone and Sexual Activity and Interest in Men." *Archives of Sexual Behavior* 7:97–103, 1978.

Cole, C. L., and G. B. Spanier. "Comarital Mate-sharing and Family Stability." *Journal of Sex Research* 10:21–31, 1974.

Fisher, Seymour. *The Female Orgasm: Psychology, Physiology, Fantasy*. New York: Basic Books, 1973.

Frank, E. "Frequency of Sexual Dysfunction in "Normal" Couples." *New England Journal of Medicine* 299:111–5, 1978.

Friedman, Richard C., Ralph M. Richart, and Raymond L. Van De Wiele (editors). *Sex Differences in Behavior*. New York: Wiley, 1974.

Hallstrom, T. "Sexuality in the Climacteric." *Clinics in Obstetrics and Gynaecology* 20:197–208, 1977.

Hunt, Morton. *Sexual Behavior in the Seventies*. Chicago: Playboy Press, 1974.

Johnson, R. E. "Some Correlates of Extramarital Coitus." *Journal of Marriage and the Family* 32:449–456, 1970.

Kaplan, Helen Singer. *The New Sex Therapy*. New York: Brunner/Mazel, 1974.

——————. *The Illustrated Manual of Sex Therapy*. New York: Quadrangle/The New York Times Book Company, 1975.

——————. *Disorders of Sexual Desire and Other New Concepts and Techniques in Sex Therapy*. New York: Brunner/Mazel, 1979.

Kent, S. "Sex after 45. Impotence: The Facts Versus the Fallacies." *Geriatrics* 30:164–171, 1975.

Money, John, and Anke A. Ehrhardt. *Man and Woman, Boy and Girl*. Baltimore: The Johns Hopkins University Press, 1972.

McCary, James L. *Human Sexuality*. New York: Van Nostrand Reinhold Company, 1973.

Rosen, A. C. "Gender Stereotypes, Ascribed Gender and Social Perception." *Perception and Motor Skills* 45:851–60, 1977.

Schiavi, R. C. "Androgens and Male Sexual Function: A Review of Human Studies." *Journal of Sex and Marital Therapy* 2:214–28, 1976.

Schmidt, G., V. Sigusch, and S. Schafer. "Responses to Reading Erotic Stories: Male-female Differences." *Archives of Sexual Behavior* 3:(2) 181–199, 1973.

Sherfey, M. J. "The Evolution and Nature of Female Sexuality in Relation to Psychoanalytic Theory." *Journal of the American Psychoanalytic Association* 14:28–128, 1966.

Sherfey, Mary Jane. *The Nature and Evolution of Female Sexuality*. New York: Random House, 1972.

Shope, David F. *Interpersonal Sexuality*. Philadelphia, W. B. Saunders, 1975.

Solnick, R. L., *et al.* "Age and Male Erectile Responsiveness." *Archives of Sex Behavior* 6:1–9, 1977.

Story, N. L. "Sexual Dysfunction Resulting from Drug Side Effects." *Journal of Sex Research* 10:132–149, 1974.

Walster, E. "Equity and Extramarital Sexuality." *Archives of Sex Behavior* 7:127–141, 1978.

Wood, F. *Sex and the New Morality.* New York: Association Press, 1968.

MARRIAGE

Adams, Bert N. *The American Family: A Sociological Interpretation.* Chicago: Markham, 1971.

Axelson, L. J. "Personal Adjustment in the Postparental Period." *Family Living* 22:(1):66–68, 1960.

Benedict, Ruth. "The Family: Its Function and Destiny." In: Ruth Nanda Anshen (editor). *The Family: Genus Americanum.* New York: Harper & Row, 1949.

Bernard, Jessie S. *The Future of Marriage.* New York: World, 1972.

Blood, Robert O., Jr., and Donald M. Wolfe. *Husbands and Wives. The Dynamics of Married Living.* New York: The Free Press, 1960.

Burgess, Ernest W., and P. Wallin. *Engagement and Marriage.* New York: Lippincott, 1953.

Burr, W. R. "Satisfaction with Various Aspects of Marriage over the Life Cycle: A Random Middle Class Sample." *Journal of Marriage and the Family* 32:29–37, 1970.

Cavan, Ruth. "The Later Years of Married Life." In: Ruth Cavan (editor). *The American Family*, 4th Edition. New York: Thomas Y. Crowell Company, 1969.

Chilman, C. S. "Families in Development at Mid-state of the Family Life Cycle." *The Family Coordinator*. October, 1968.

Cuber, John F., and Peggy B. Harroff. *Sex and the Significant Americans.* New York: Appelton-Century, 1965.

Deutscher, Irwin. "The Quality of Postparental Life." In: B. Neugarten (editor). *Middle Age and Aging.* Chicago: University of Chicago Press, 1968.

Duvall, E. M. *Family Development*, 3rd Edition. Philadelphia: Lippincott, 1967.

Fengler, A. P. "The Effects of Age and Education on Marital Ideology." *Journal of Marriage and the Family* 35:264–271, 1973.

Glasser, Paul, and Lois Glasser. *Families in Crisis.* New York: Harper & Row, 1970.

Havighurst, Robert J. *Developmental Tasks and Education.* New York: David McKay, 1972.

Kerckhoff, A. C., and F. D. Bean. "Social Status and Interpersonal Patterns Among Married Couples." *Social Forces* 49:264–271, 1970.

Lederer, William J. and Don Jackson. *The Mirages of Marriage.* New York: W. W. Norton, 1968.

Lowenthal, M. F., and D. Chiriboga. "Transition of the Empty Nest: Crisis, Challenge, or Relief?" *Archives of General Psychiatry* 26:8–14.

Lowery, B. J. "Problems of Middle Age. The Middle Years Family." *Nursing Times* 71(50):1994–6, 1975.

Mead, Margaret. *Male and Female.* New York: William Morrow, 1949.

Money, J. "Sex, Love and Commitment." *Journal of Sex and Marital Therapy* 2:273–276 6, 1976.

Mueller, B. J. "Reconciliation or Resignation: A Case Study." *Family Coordinator* 19:345–352, 1970.

Nash, Arnold S. "Ancient Past and Living Present." In: Howard Becker and Reuben Hill (editors). *Family, Marriage and Parenthood.* Boston: Heath, 1955.

Pineo, P. C. "Disenchantment in the Later Years of Marriage." *Journal of Marriage and the Family* 23:3–11, 1961.

Peterson, James. *Married Love in the Middle Years.* New York: Association Press, 1968.

Prados, M. "Marital Problems of the Middle Aged Group." *Canadian Psychiatric Association Journal* 7:97–105, 1962.

Rodman, H. (editor). *Marriage, Family and Society.* New York: Random House, 1965.

Rogers, Carl R. *Becoming Partners: Marriage and its Alternatives.* New York: Delacorte, 1972.

Rollins, B. C. and H. Feldman. "Marital Satisfaction over the Life Cycle." *Journal of Marriage and the Family* 32:20–28, 1970.

Rose, Arnold M. "Factors Associated with the Life Satisfaction of Middle Class, Middle-aged Persons." *Marriage and Family Living* 17:15–19, 1955.

Solomon, P. "Love: A Clinical Definition." *New England Journal of Medicine* 252:345–351, 1955.

Thurnher, M. "Mid-life Marriage: Sex Differences in Evaluation and Perspectives." *International Journal of Aging and Human Development* 7(2):129–135, 1976.

Zimmerman, Carle C. *Family and Civilization.* New York: Harper & Brothers, 1947.

ADOLESCENT CHILDREN

Baruch, Dorothy W. *How to Live with Your Teen-ager.* New York: McGraw-Hill, 1953.

Dodson, Fitzhugh. *How to Parent.* Los Angeles: Nash Publishing Company, 1970.

Drucker, Peter F. *The Age of Discontinuity: Guidelines for Our Changing Society.* New York: Harper & Row, 1968.

Elder, Glen. *Children of the Great Depression.* Chicago: University of Chicago Press, 1974.

Farnham, Marynia F. *The Adolescent.* New York: Collier Books, 1967.

Garber, Sheldon (editor). *Adolescence for Adults.* Chicago: Blue Cross Association, 1969.

Ginott, Haim G. *Between Parent and Teen-ager.* New York: Macmillan, 1969.

Levi, D., H. Stierlin, and R. J. Savard. "Fathers and Sons: The Interlocking Crisis of Integrity and Identity." *Psychiatry* 35:48–56, 1972.

Mead, Margaret. *Culture and Commitment: A Study of the Generation Gap.* New York: Doubleday, 1970.

AGING PARENTS

Ackerman, N. W. (editor). *Family Process.* New York: Basic Books, 1970.

Bierman, E. L., and W. R. Hazzard. "Old Age, Including Death and Dying." In: E. W. Smith (editor). *The Biologic Ages of Man From Conception Through Old Age.* Philadelphia: Saunders, 1973.

David, William. *Not Quite Ready to Retire.* New York: Collier, 1970.

Elder, G. H., Jr. "Occupational Mobility, Life Patterns and Personality." *Journal of Health and Social Behavior* 10:308–323, 1969.

Fabun, Don. *The Dynamics of Change.* Englewood Cliffs, New Jersey: Prentice-Hall, 1967.

Gravatt, A. E. "Family Relations in Middle and Old Age: A Review." *Journal of Gerontology* 8:197–201, 1953.

Harris, Louis, and Associates, Inc. *The Myth and Reality of Aging in America.* Washington, D.C.: National Council on the Aging, 1975.

Holter, Paul. *Guide to Retirement Living.* Chicago: Rand McNally, 1973.

Kerckhoff, A. C. "Family Patterns and Morale in Retirement." In: Ida Harper Simpson and John C. McKinney. *Social Aspects of Aging.* Durham, North Carolina: Duke University Press, 1966.

Kleemeier, Robert W. (editor). *Aging and Leisure.* New York: Oxford University Press, 1961.

Knopf, Olga. *Successful Aging.* New York: Viking, 1975.

Mead, Margaret. *Continuities in Cultural Evolution.* New Haven: Yale University Press, 1964.

Nassau, Jean Baron. *Choosing a Nursing Home.* New York: Funk & Wagnalls, 1975.

Neugarten, Bernice L. *Personality in Middle and Late Life.* New York: Atherton, 1964.

Otten, Jane, and Florence D. Shelley. *When Your Parents Grow Old*. New York: Funk & Wagnalls, 1976.

Percy, Charles H. *Growing Old in the Country of the Young*. New York: McGraw-Hill, 1974.

Shanas, Ethel. *Old People in Three Industrial Societies*. New York: Atherton, 1968.

Tournier, Paul. *Learn to grow Old*. New York: Harper & Row, 1972.

Woods, James H. *Helping Older People Enjoy Life*. New York: Harper & Brothers, 1953.

DIVORCE

Bernard, Jessie. *Remarriage: A Study of Marriage*. New York: The Dryden Press, 1956.

Bohannan, Paul (editor). *Divorce and After*. Garden City, New York: Doubleday and Company, 1970.

Burchinal, L. "Characteristics of Adolescents from Unbroken, Broken, and Reconstituted Families." *Journal of Marriage and the Family* 26:50–63, 1964.

Cantor, Donald. *Escape From Marriage*. New York: William Morrow, 1971.

Epstein, Joseph. *Divorced in America*. New York: E. P. Dutton, 1974.

Gardner, Richard A. *The Boys and Girls Book of Divorce*. New York: Bantam Books, 1971.

Gettleman, Susan, and Janet Markowitz. *The Courage to Divorce*. New York: Ballantine Books, 1974.

Glick, P. C. "First Marriages and Remarriages." *American Sociological Review* 14:726–734, 1949.

Hunt, Morton. *The World of the Formerly Married*. New York: McGraw-Hill, 1966.

Kovel, Joel. *A Complete Guide to Therapy: from Psychoanalysis to Behavior Modification*. Pantheon, 1976.

Levinger, G. "Marital Cohesiveness and Dissolution: An Integrative Review." *Journal of Marriage and the Family* 27:19–28, 1965.

Rheinstein, Max. *Marriage Stability, Divorce and the Law*. Chicago: University of Chicago Press, 1972.

Salk, Lee. *What Every Child Would Like Parents to Know About Divorce*. New York: Harper & Row, 1978.

Sheridan, Kathleen. *Living with Divorce*. Chicago: Thomas More Press, 1978.

Sheresky, Norman, and Marya Mannes. *Uncoupling: The Art of Coming Apart*. New York: The Viking Press, 1972.

Edwards, Marie, and Eleanor Hoover. *The Challenge of Being Single*. New York: New American Library, Signet Books, 1974.

U. S. Department of Health, Education and Welfare. "Marriage Statistics, 1969, and Births, Marriages, Divorces and Deaths for 1973." *Vital Statistics Report, 1969*.

WIDOW OR WIDOWER

Brim, O. G., *et al.* (editors). *The Dying Patient*. New York: Russell Sage Foundation, 1970.

Bogard, David. *Valleys and Vistas*. Grand Rapids, Michigan: Baker Book House, 1974.

Cabot, Natalie C. *You Can't Count on Dying*. Boston: Houghton Mifflin, 1961.

Caine, Lynn. *Widow*. New York: Bantam, 1975.

Consumers Union (editors). *Funerals: Consumers' Last Rights*, 1978.

Feifel, Herman (editor). *The Meaning of Death*. New York: McGraw-Hill, 1959.

Gorer, Geoffrey, *Death, Grief, and Mourning*. New York: Doubleday, 1965.

Kohn, Jane B., and Willard K. Kohn. *The Widower*. Boston: Beacon Press, 1978.

Lopata, Helena Z. *Widowhood in an American City*. Cambridge, Massachusetts: Schenkman, 1973.

Marris, Peter. *Loss and Change*. New York: Pantheon Books, 1974.

Pattison, E. Mansell *The Experience of Dying*. Englewood Cliffs, New Jersey: Prentice-Hall, 1977.

Pincus, Lily. *Death and the Family: The Importance of Mourning*. New York: Pantheon, 1974.

Schulz, R. and Alderman, D. "Clinical Research and the Stages of Dying." *Omega* 5:137–144, 1974.

LABOR AND LEISURE

Aberbanel, Karin, and Connie McClung Siegel. *Women's Work Book*. New York: Praeger, 1975.

Albee, Louis. *Over 40—Out of Work*. Englewood Cliffs, New Jersey: Prentice-Hall, Inc. 1970.

Bardwick, Judith M. (editor). *Readings on the Psychology of Women*. New York: Harper & Row, 1972.

Barfield, Richard, and James Morgan. *Early Retirement: The Decision and the Experience*. Ann Arbor, Michigan: Institute for Social Research, 1969.

Bart, P. B. "Why Women's Status Changes in Middle Age." Sociological Symposium No. 3, 1969.

Bartlett, L. E. *New Work/New Life*. New York: Harper & Row, 1976.

Bird, Caroline. *Enterprising Women*. New York: W. W. Norton, 1976.

Blauner, Robert. *Alienation and Freedom: The Factory Worker and His Industry*. Chicago: University of Chicago Press, 1964.

Cross, Wilbur. *The Weekend Education Source Book*. New York: Harper & Row, 1976.

D'Aprix, Roger M. *The Struggle for Identity: The Silent Revolution Against Corporate Conformity*. Homewood, Illinois: Dow Jones-Irwin, 1972.

D'Aprix, Roger. *In Search of a Corporate Soul*. New York: Amacom, 1976.

De Grazia, Sebastian. *Of Time, Work and Leisure*. New York: Twentieth Century Fund, 1962.

De Maria, Alfred T., Dale Tarnowieski, and Richard Gurman. *Manager Unions? An American Management Association Research Report*. New York: *American Management Association*, 1972.

Department of Health, Education, and Welfare. *Work in America*. Cambridge, Massachusetts: MIT Press, 1973.

Drucker, Peter F. *The Age of Discontinuity*. New York: Harper & Row, 1969.

Dumazedier, Joffre. *Toward A Society of Leisure*. New York: The Free Press, 1967.

Entine, Alan (editor). *Americans in Middle Years: Career Options and Educational Opportunities*. Los Angeles: Ethel Percy Andrus Gerontology Center, 1974.

Fairfield, R. P. "Changing Careers at Midstream." *The Humanist* 34:14–23, 1974.

Flexner, Eleanor. *Century of Struggle: The Woman's Rights Movement in the United States*. Cambridge: Belknap Press, 1959.

Friedmann, Georges. Translated by Wyatt Rawson. *The Anatomy of Work, Labor and Leisure, and the Implications of Automation*. New York: Free Press, 1960.

Goldberg, Herb. *The Hazards of Being Male*. New York: Nash, 1976.

Gorney, S., and C. Cox. *After Forty: How Women Can Achieve Fulfillment*. New York. Dial Press, 1973.

Heilbrun, Carolyn. *Toward a Recognition of Androgyny*. New York: Alfred A. Knopf, 1973.

Hiestand, Dale L. *Changing Careers After Thirty-five*. New York: Columbia University Press, 1971.

Hesburgh, Theodore M., *et al. Patterns for Lifelong Learning*. San Francisco: Jossey-Bass, 1973.

Huber, Richard. *The American Idea of Success*. New York: McGraw-Hill, 1971.

Jaffe, A. J. "The Middle Years." Special issue of: *Industrial Gerontology*. September, 1971.

Janeway, Elizabeth. *Man's World, Woman's Place: A Study in Social Mythology*. New York: William Morrow, 1971.

Jansen, Jo. *College by Mail*. New York: Arco, 1972.

Kaplan, Max. *Technology, Human Values and Leisure.* Nashville: Abingdon Press, 1971.

Kaye, Harvey E. *Male Survival.* New York: Grosset & Dunlap, 1974.

Kelly, J. R. "Work and Leisure: A Simplified Paradigm." *Journal of Leisure Research* 4:50–62, 1972.

Kreps, J. M. "Economics of Retirement." In: E. W. Busse and E. Pfeiffer (editors). *Behavior and Adaptation in Late Life.* Boston: Little, Brown & Co., 1969.

Krep, J. M. "Career Options after Fifty." *The Gerontologist* 2:4–8, 1971.

Levinson, Harry. *Emotional Health: The World of Work.* New York: Harper & Row, 1964.

—————. "On Being a Middle-aged Manager." *Harvard Business Review* 47(4):51–60, 1969.

Lewis, Edwin C. *Developing Women's Potential.* Ames: Iowa State University Press, 1968.

Loeser, Herta. *Women, Work and Volunteering.* Boston: Beacon Press, 1974.

Lofquist, L. H., and R. V. Dawas. *Adjustment to Work.* New York: Appleton, 1969.

Loring, Rosalind K., and Herbert A. Otto (editors). *New Life Options: The Working Woman's Resource Book.* New York: McGraw-Hill, 1976.

Martin, A. R. "Self-alienation and the Loss of Leisure." *The American Journal of Psychoanalysis* 21:157–165, 1961.

Miller, Catherine L. *How to Say Yes to Life: A Woman's Guide to Beating the Blahs.* New York: Essandess, 1971.

Monk, A. "Factors in the Preparation for Retirement by Middle-aged Adults." *Gerontologist* 11:348–351, 1971.

Neff, W. S. *Work and Human Behavior.* New York: Atherton, 1968.

Oakley, Ann. *The Housewife, Past and Present.* New York: Pantheon, 1974.

Oliver, D. B. "Career and Leisure Patterns of Middle-aged Metropolitan Out-migrants." *Gerontologist* 11:13–20, 1971.

Pieper, Josef. Translated by Alexander Dru. *Leisure, The Basics of Culture.* New York: Pantheon Books, 1964.

Pfeiffer, E., and B. C. Davis. "The Use of Leisure Time in Middle Life." *Gerontologist* 11:187–195, 1971.

Pogrebin, Letty Cottin. *How to Make It in a Man's World.* New York: Doubleday, 1970.

Rapoport, Robert N. *Mid-Career Development.* London: Tavistock, 1970.

Robbins, Paula I. *Successful Midlife Career Change.* New York: Amacom, 1979.

Rossi, A. S. (editor). *The Feminist Papers.* New York: Bantam Books, 1974.

Schaw, L. C. *The Bonds of Work: Work in Mind, Time and Tradition.* San Francisco: Jossey-Bass, 1968.

Scobey, Joan, and Lee Parr McGrath. *Creative Careers for Women.* New York: Essandess, 1968.

Shatto, Gloria M. *Employment of the Middle-Aged.* Springfield, Illinois: Charles C. Thomas, 1972.

Sheppard, Harold L. *Who are the Workers with the Blues?* Washington, D.C.: W. E. Upjohn Institute for Employment Research, 1970.

Sofer, Cyril. *Men in Mid-Career: A Study of British Managers and Technical Specialists.* Cambridge: Cambridge University Press, 1970.

Stetson, Damon. *Starting Over.* New York: Macmillan, 1971.

Thompson, Mary Lou (editor). *Voices of the New Feminism.* Boston: Beacon Press, 1970.

Thomson, Frances C. (editor). *Guide to Continuing Education in America.* New York: Quadrangle, 1972.

Watkins, B. T. "More Women Coming Back to Campus?" *Chronicle Higher Education* 9:6–9, 1974.

Wax, Judith. *Starting in the Middle.* New York: Holt, Rinehart & Winston, 1979.

Winter, Dorothy. *Help Yourself to a Job.* Boston: Beacon Press, 1977.

Wolman, Benjamin. *Victims of Success.* New York: Quadrangle/The New York Times Book Co., 1973.

Saunders, Dero A. "Executive Discontent." In: Sigmund Nosow and William H. Form (editors). *Man, Work and Society.* New York: Basic Books, 1962.

Winston, Sandra. *The Entrepreneurial Woman.* New York: Newsweek Books, 1979.

The Abindgon Bible Commentary. Nashville, Tennessee: Abingdon Press, 1929.

Adler, Alfred. *What Life Should Mean to You*. Alan Porter (editor). New York: Capricorn, 1958.

Albright, William F. *From the Stone Age to Christianity*. Revised edition. Baltimore, Maryland: Johns Hopkins Press, 1957.

Arieti, Salvano. *The Will to be Human*. New York: Quadrangle Books, 1972.

Baier, Kurt. *The Moral Point of View*. Ithaca, New York: Cornell University Press, 1958.

Barnett, Albert. *The New Testament: Its Making and Meaning*. Revised edition. Nashville, Tennessee: Abingdon Press, 1958.

Barth, Karl. *The Word of God and the Word of Man*. Translated by Douglas Horton. New York: Harper, 1957.

Binkley, Luther J. *Contemporary Ethical Theories*. New York: Philosophical Library, 1961.

Bonhoeffer, Dietrich. *Ethics*. Beth Eberhard (editor). Translated by Neville Horton Smith. New York: Macmillan, 1962.

Bowie, Walter R. *The Story of the Bible*. Nashville, Tennessee: Abingdon Press, 1934.

Browne, Lewis. *The World's Great Scriptures*. New York: Macmillan, 1946.

Buber, Martin. *I and Thou*. Translated by Walter Kaufmann. New York: Charles Scribner's Sons, 1970.

Buhler, Charlotte, and Fred Massarik (editors). *The Course of Human Life*. New York: Springer, 1968.

Bultmann, Rudolf, and Karl Jaspers. *Myth and Christianity: An Inquiry into the Possibility of Religion Without Myth*. New York: Noonday Press, 1958.

Burton, Ernest D., and Edgar J. Goodspeed. *A Harmony of the Synoptic Gospels*. New York: Charles Scribner's Sons, 1917.

Butler, Joseph. *The Analogy of Religion*. New York: Frederick Ungar, 1961.

Buttrick, George A. (editor). *The Interpreter's Dictionary of the Bible*. 4 vols. Nashville, Tennessee: Abingdon Press, 1962.

Dewey, John. *Human Nature and Conduct*. New York: Henry Holt, 1922.

Dibelius, Martin. *From Tradition to Gospel*. Translated by B. L. Woolf. New York: Charles Scribner's Sons, 1935.

Durant, Will. *The Story of Philosophy*. New York: Simon & Schuster, 1926.

Fletcher, Joseph. *Moral Responsibility*. Philadelphia: Westminster Press, 1967.

Fuller, Reginald H. *A Critical Introduction to the New Testament*. London: Gerald Duckworth, 1966.

Frankena, William K. *Ethics*. Englewood Cliffs, New Jersey: Prentice-Hall, 1963.

Fromm, Erich. *Man For Himself*. New York: Rinehart & Co., 1947.

——————. *Escape from Freedom*. New York: Farrar & Rinehart, 1951.

——————. *The Sane Society*. New York: Holt, Rinehart and Winston, 1955.

——————. *Psychoanalysis and Religion*. New Haven: Yale University Press, 1950.

Grattan, C. Hartley. *In Quest of Knowledge*. New York: Association Press, 1955.

Guignebert, Charles. *The Jewish World in the Time of Christ*. Translated by S. H. Hooke. New York: E. P. Dutton, 1939.

Guthrie, William Keith Chambers. *A History of Greek Philosophy*. Cambridge: Cambridge University Press, 1969.

Horney, Karen. *Neurosis and Human Growth*. New York: W. W. Norton, 1950.

Hill, Thomas E. *Ethics in Theory and Practice*. New York: T. Y. Crowell Company, 1956.

Harrison, Roland K. *Biblical Criticism: Historical, Literary and Textual*. Grand Rapids, Michigan: Zondervan, 1978.

Henshaw, Thomas. *New Testament Literature in the Light of Modern Scholarship*. London: George Allen and Unwin, 1952.

Hospers, John. *Human Conduct: An Introduction to the Problems of Ethics*. New York: Harcourt, Brace & World, 1961.

Jaspers, Karl. *The Great Philosophers: Socrates, Buddha, Confucius, Jesus, Plato, Augustine, Kant*. New York: Harcourt, Brace & World, 1962.

Jung, Carl G. *Collected Works*, 18 Volumes. Herbert Read, Michael Fordham, & Gerhard Adler (editors). New York: Pantheon, 1953.

The Interpreter's Bible. 12 Volumes. Nashville, Tennessee: Abingdon Press, 1951–1957.

James, William. *Pragmatism*. New York: Meridian Books, 1955.

Landis, Benson Y. *An Outline of the Bible, Book by Book*. New York: Barnes & Noble, Inc. 1963.

Lille, William. *An Introduction to Ethics*, 3d edition. New York: Barnes & Noble, 1961.

Lippmann, Walter. *A Preface to Morals*. New York: Time, Inc., 1964.

Monroe, Ruth L. *Schools of Psychoanalytic Thought*. New York: Henry Holt, 1955.

Macarthur, John R. *Biblical Literature and Its Backgrounds*. New York: Appleton-Century-Crofts, 1936.

Maslow, Abraham H. (editor) *New Knowledge in Human Values*. New York: Harper & Brothers, 1959.

—————. *Motivation and Personality*, 2nd edition. New York: Harper & Row, 1970.

—————. *The Farther Reaches of Human Nature*. New York: Viking Press, 1972.

McClelland, David C. *The Achieving Society*. Princeton: Van Nostrand, 1961.

Nielsen, Kai. "History of ethics" In: Paul Edwards, (editor). *The Encyclopedia of Philosophy*. New York: Macmillan and the Free Press, 1967.

Niebuhr, Rheinhold. *Moral Man and Immoral Society*. New York: Charles Scribner's Sons, 1932.

—————. *The Nature and Destiny of Man*. New York: Charles Scribner's Sons, 1949.

Oates, Whitney J. (editor). *Basic Writings of Saint Augustine*. New York: Random House, 1948.

Pegis, Anton C. (editor). *The Basic Writings of Saint Thomas Aquinas*. New York: Random House, 1945.

Popper, Karl R. *The Open Society and Its Enemies*, 5th edition. Princeton: Princeton University Press, 1966.

Paulsen, Friedrich. *Immanuel Kant: His Life and Doctrine*. New York: Frederick Ungar, 1963.

Robinson, John Arthur Thomas. *Christian Morals Today*. Philadelphia: Westminster, 1964.

Rogers, Carl R. *On Becoming a Person*. Boston: Houghton Mifflin, 1961.

—————. "Toward a Modern Approach to Values: The Valuing Process in the Mature Person." *Journal of Abnormal Social Psychology* 68:160–167, 1964.

Rowlingson, Donald T. *Introduction to New Testament Study*. New York: Macmillan, 1956.

Sahakian, William S. *Systems of Ethics and Value Theory*. Totowa, N.J.: Littlefield, Adams, 1968.

—————. *Ethics: An Introduction to Theories and Problems*. New York: Barnes & Noble, 1974.

Scheler, Max. *Man's Place in Nature*. Boston: Beacon Press, 1961.

Smith, Huston. *The Religions of Man*. New York: Harper, 1958.

Stevenson, Charles L. *Facts and Values: Studies in Ethical Analysis*. New Haven: Yale University Press, 1964.

Sumner, William G. *Folkways*. New York: New American Library, 1960.

Thompson, Clara. *Psychoanalysis: Evolution and Development*. New York: Hermitage, 1950.

Tillich, Paul. *The Courage To Be*. New Haven: Yale University Press, 1952.

—————. *Morality and Beyond*. New York: Harper, 1963.

—————. *The Future of Religions*. New York: Harper & Row, 1966.

Titus, Harold H., and Morris Keeton. *Ethics for Today*, 4th Edition. New York: American Book Co., 1966.

Watts, Harold H. *The Modern Reader's Guide to the Bible*. Revised edition New York: Harper & Brothers, 1959.

Wolman, Benjamin B. *Contemporary Theories and Systems in Psychology*. New York: Harper
& Row, 1960.
Werkmeister, William. *Theories of Ethics*. Lincoln, Nebraska: Johnsen, 1961.
Warnock, Geoffrey J. *Contemporary Moral Philosophy*. London: Macmillan, 1967.
Westermarck, Edward. *Ethical Relativity*. Paterson, New Jersey: Littlefield, Adams,
1960.
Wheelright, Philip. *A Critical Introduction to Ethics*, 3rd Edition. New York: Odyssey,
1959.

Index

Accommodation, Visual, 167-68
Achievement, Mental, 183-86
Acid Mantle of Skin, 150
Adams, C. W., 185
Adaptation to Dim Light, 167-68
Additives, Food, 73-75
Adler, Alfred, 190, 378
Adolescent Children, 248-73
Aerobic Exercise, 91, 114-16; Dancing, 122
Affair, Extramarital, 210-11, 248-50
Aging, 9-24, Autoimmune Theory of, 13-14; Cross-Linkage Theory of, 14-15; Radiation and, 15-17; Free Radical Theory of, 16-17; Somatic Mutation Theory of, 17-19; Random Error Theory of, 18-20, 24; Genetic Control of, 19-24; Physical and Physiological, 25; Exercise and, 116; Parents, 273-82
Alcohol, 59-61, 88-89
Alderman, David, 298-99
Alighieri, Dante, 3
Alimony, 290-92
Allport, Gordon, 202-04
Amino Acids in Protein Synthesis, 14-16; in Nutrition, 49-51
Amphetamines in Weight Control, 96
Anaerobic Exercise, 117
Antiperspirants, 152-53
Aphrodisiacs, 238
Appetite Control, Factors in, 83-86
Aquinas, Thomas, 353-55

Aristippus, 369-70
Aristotle, 375-76
Arthritis, 124-30; Medications for, 126-29
Aslan, Ana, 12
Atherosclerosis, 37-48; Regression of, 45-47
Atkins Diet, 98-100
Authoritarianism, Philosophy of, 326-70; in Religion, 340-41, 353-56, 358-60

Babylon, Scriptures of, 342-43
Bach, George, 268
Balding in Women, 132, 158; in Men, 162-64
Barth, Karl, 356-57
Basal Metabolic Rate, 91, 96-97
Bayley, Nancy, 182
deBeauvoir, Simone, 3
Behavior Modification, 85-91
Benedek, Terese, 192
Benson, Herbert, 108
Bentham, Jeremy, 371-72
Bergler, Edmund, viii
Bernard, Jessie, 248-49, 260
Berne, Eric, 224-25, 262
Biofeedback, 108
Birren, James, 171, 180, 185
Blood Pressure, 41-42
Blood, Robert, 258-59
Bogert, Louise, 61-63
Bonhoeffer, Diedrich, 356-57
Boring, Edwin, 175